The Design Patterns
Smalltalk Companion

The Software Patterns Series

John Vlissides, Consulting Editor

The Software Patterns Series (SPS) comprises pattern literature of lasting significance to software developers. Software patterns document general solutions to recurring problems in all software-related spheres, from the technology itself, to the organizations that develop and distribute it, to the people who use it. Books in the series distill experience from one or more of these areas into a form that software professionals can apply immediately. *Relevance* and *impact* are the tenets of the SPS. Relevance because each book presents patterns that solve real problems. Patterns worthy of the name are intrinsically relevant; they are borne of practitioners' experiences, not theory or speculation. Patterns have impact when they change how people work for the better. A book becomes a part of the series not just because it embraces these tenets, but because it has demonstrated that it fulfills them for its audience.

Titles in the series:

The Design Patterns Smalltalk Companion, Sherman Alpert/Kyle Brown/Bobby Woolf

Pattern Languages of Program Design 3, edited by Robert Martin/Dirk Riehle/Frank Buschmann

Please see our web site (http://www.awl.com/cseng/swpatterns) for more information on these titles.

The Design Patterns Smalltalk Companion

Sherman R. Alpert
IBM T. J. Watson Research Center

Kyle Brown
Knowledge Systems Corporation

Bobby Woolf
Knowledge Systems Corporation

ADDISON-WESLEY
An imprint of Addison Wesley Longman, Inc.

Reading, Massachusetts   Harlow, England   Menlo Park, California
Berkeley, California   Don Mills, Ontario   Sydney
Bonn   Amsterdam   Tokyo   Mexico City

Many of the designations used by manufacturers and sellers to distinguish their products are claimed as trademarks. Where those designations appear in this book and Addison-Wesley was aware of a trademark claim, the designations have been printed in initial caps or all caps.

The authors and publisher have taken care in the preparation of this book, but make no expressed or implied warranty of any kind and assume no responsibility for errors or omissions. No liability is assumed for incidental or consequential damages in connection with or arising out of the use of the information or programs contained herein.

The publisher offers discounts on this book when ordered in quantity for special sales. For more information, please contact:

Corporate & Professional Publishing Group
Addison Wesley Longman, Inc.
One Jacob Way
Reading, Massachusetts 01867

Library of Congress Cataloging-in-Publication Data

Alpert, Sherman R.
    The design patterns Smalltalk companion / Sherman R. Alpert, Kyle Brown, Bobby Woolf.
        p.   cm.
    Includes bibliographical references and index.
    ISBN 0-201-18462-1 (alk. paper)
    1. Object-oriented programming (Computer science) 2. Smalltalk (Computer program language) I. Brown, Kyle.   II. Woolf, Bobby.
III. Title.
QA76.64.A47   1998
095.13'3--dc21   97-48513
                                                                    CIP

ISBN 0-201-18462-1

Text printed on recycled and acid-free paper.
1 2 3 4 5 6 7 8 9 10 - MA - 01 00 99 98

First printing, January 1998

This book is dedicated to the memories of
Otto Brown and Helen Vlissides
who passed on during its writing

Contents

Foreword

Programmers have long had the intuition that they were doing the same thing over and over. Since the early 1970s, and perhaps before, academic and professional software engineers have tried to find a way to take advantage of this sense of déjà vu to improve software development.

The conventional approach to avoiding duplication is the obvious—don't. Write a program once and use it over and over. Reuse has its successes, but as the scope of the code to reuse grows and the community within which it is to be reused grows, the probability of the goals of reuse being achieved drops. Eventually you end up with libraries that are more trouble to reuse than just writing the whole thing over from scratch.

Objects were supposed to save us from this widely experienced but little recognized "feature" of reuse. Inheritance and polymorphism provide two excellent ways of capturing variability, of letting code be the same but different. The scope in which object reuse works well may be larger and the communities may be larger (hmmm . . ., they may not), but eventually reuse runs out of gas as a strategy for improving productivity and quality and reducing cost and risk.

Patterns take the whole experience of programming déjà vu back to the drawing board. "All programmers writing accounting systems must solve problem X, and successful solutions converge on solution Y" is the kind of experience that gives rise to libraries of reusable software.

Here's the curious experience—if you get a group of experienced object designers sitting around drinking beer and talking about their systems, you get statements like the above. "Oh, I've implemented objects like that, except mine were for exotic options trading, not missile control." There is something about programming objects that leads over and over to the same problems, and over and over to the same solutions. Of course, same doesn't mean "the same code," it means, "if you squint your eyes and tilt your head just right you can see the similarity."

The *Design Patterns* book was the first powerful public statement of this orthogonal kind of déjà vu and what to do about it. It has been wildly successful. It has changed the way the object community programs, and introduced a new and more precise language for describing design.

The book you hold in your hands is a further exploration of what is universal about the 23 patterns in *Design Patterns*. Its purpose is to tease apart what of those patterns is an artifact of a language, and what is truly universal to object programming. As such, it makes a valuable contribution to the ongoing exploration of this new way of thinking about programs. If you are interested in the conversation, or even just the results of the conversation, you will enjoy *The Design Patterns Smalltalk Companion* and learn from it.

The conversation is far from over. There are systems to describe, bars to sit in, and beer to drink. Come on in, pull up a comfy chair, and have a listen.

Kent Beck

Preface

The Design Patterns Smalltalk Companion is intended to be a companion volume to *Design Patterns: Elements of Reusable Object-Oriented Software* by Erich Gamma, Richard Helm, Ralph Johnson, and John Vlissides—the so-called Gang of Four. Their book has had an extraordinary impact on the field of object-oriented software design. Yet it has a decidedly C++ orientation. This works well for C++ developers, but it makes understanding and applying the *Design Patterns* material more difficult for others.

The Design Patterns Smalltalk Companion assumes readers are familiar with the material in *Design Patterns,* but want to understand the material better, especially from a Smalltalk development perspective. The *Smalltalk Companion* is designed to be read along with *Design Patterns.* We have tried hard not to repeat material that the Gang of Four already explained well. Rather, we clarify and add to the ideas that their book already expresses, doing so from the viewpoint of the Smalltalk developer. We reference *Design Patterns* frequently; as you read our book, we expect you will too.

The *Smalltalk Companion* also assumes you have experience with object-oriented design and programming, preferably in Smalltalk. You should already be familiar with terms like "abstract class," "polymorphism," and "inheritance" and know what it's like to develop code in a Smalltalk interactive development environment. Although we address a broad audience, this book is nonetheless not an introduction to Smalltalk programming or object-oriented design.

A Bit of History

A long time ago (it seems) in a galaxy far, far away (IBM's T. J. Watson Research Center), John Vlissides approached Sherman Alpert with the idea of writing a Smalltalk "sequel" to *Design Patterns.* At this point, *Design Patterns* was one of the hottest-selling computer science books on the market. They decided to send up a trial balloon: Sherman wrote up a few patterns and distributed them to the Gang of Four for review. Their feedback was positive: the balloon flew.

During the ensuing book contract process with Addison-Wesley, it became clear that more authors were needed to produce a polished *Smalltalk Companion* in the suggested time frame. Sherman approached Kyle Brown, a Smalltalker who had published extensively on design patterns, to see if he would like to join the effort. Kyle, in turn, made a similar offer to Bobby Woolf, his colleague at Knowledge Systems Corporation. Thus began the collaboration that has resulted in this book. At this time, *Design Patterns* is the best-selling computer science book ever. We hope you enjoy this book as much as readers apparently have the Gang of Four's.

Acknowledgments

It takes a village to raise a child. Similarly, this book has been molded and influenced by a large community of colleagues, friends, and advisers. Much of what appears here is the direct result of their help and guidance, and we have many to thank.

First, big thanks to the Gang of Four—Erich, Richard, Ralph, and John, who have acted as reviewers, advisers, supporters, and mentors from the original idea through the entire book-writing process. Special thanks to John for providing us with the original *Design Patterns* figures, for his *idraw* graphical editor for our diagrams, and for his thorough editing of our manuscript as Software Patterns series editor.

Huge thanks to the design patterns discussion group in the Computer Science Department of the University of Illinois at Urbana-Champaign (UIUC). This group, directed by Ralph Johnson, read and discussed all of our pattern sections and supplied extremely useful feedback. We could not have produced this book in its current form without their help. At various times, the following people have been part of the group: Jeff Barcalow, John Brant, Ian Chai, Annette Feng, Brian Foote, Yahya Mirza, Dragos-Anton Manolescu, Lewis Muir, Eiji Nabika, Ed Peters, Don Roberts, Joe Yoder, Kazuki Yoshida, and, of course, Ralph.

Thanks to other colleagues with whom we have discussed issues that are considered in the *Smalltalk Companion,* and who commented on earlier drafts, offered advice, or suggested Smalltalk examples of design patterns in use. Also, prior to publication we placed drafts of several of our patterns on a public FTP site and invited comments. We thank all who spent time and energy providing helpful feedback. These folks include Kent Beck, Dave Collins, Lucio Dinoto, Richard A. Harmon, Philip Hartman, Dave Isaacs, Dick Lam, Chamond Liu, Richard J. MacDonald, Jasen Minton, James O'Connor, David N. Smith, Niall Ross, Robert Schwartz, Andrey Subbotin, Debbie Utley, and David Warren. (We hope we haven't inadvertently left anyone out, but if we have, thank you too!)

We thank the members of the Knowledge Systems Corporation (KSC) reading group for their comments and suggestions: Dana Anthony, Simon Archer, Ken Auer, Stuart Broad, Ilkay Celiker, Fonda Daniels, Amy Gause, Greg Hendley, Dave Houlbrooke, Scott Krutsch, Tran Le, and Vikas Malik.

Thanks go to Larry Best of American Management Systems for graciously allowing us to include a portion of his OOPSLA'96 DesignFest problem in our case study.

We are grateful as well to Addison-Wesley's editorial and production teams, especially Marina Lang and Cate Rickard.

Sherman adds: Special thanks to the IBM Corporation and my manager, Peter Fairweather, for allowing me time and use of computational resources during the writing of the *Smalltalk Companion*. My ardent appreciation goes to John Vlissides for his support and encouragement. Thanks to the Smalltalkers with whom I've had the pleasure to collaborate at the T. J. Watson Research Center over the years. I've learned a great deal from you all: Rachel Bellamy, Dave Collins, Eric Gold, Mark Laff, Bob Mack, Petar Makara, John Richards, Mary Beth Rosson, Janice Singer, Kevin Singley, David N. Smith, and Christine Sweeney. Thanks also to Dick Lam who was a fount of C++ information. And most important, my gratitude to my family, Amy and Jake, for putting up with me and supporting me while I hid away to write.

Kyle adds: I'd like to thank my wife, Ann, for putting up with my writing habit during an especially difficult time in our lives. You mean the world to me, dear, and I can't tell you how much I appreciate your support.

Yorktown Heights, New York   *S.R.A.*

Cury, North Carolina   *K.B., B.W.*

December 1997

Chapter 1

Introduction

Welcome to *The Design Patterns Smalltalk Companion,* a companion volume to *Design Patterns: Elements of Reusable Object-Oriented Software* by Erich Gamma, Richard Helm, Ralph Johnson, and John Vlissides (Gamma, 1995). While the earlier book was not the first publication on design patterns, it has fostered a minor revolution in the software engineering world. Designers are now speaking in the language of design patterns, and we have seen a proliferation of workshops, publications, and World Wide Web sites concerning design patterns. Design patterns are now a dominant theme in object-oriented programming research and development, and a new design patterns community has emerged.

Design Patterns describes 23 design patterns for applications implemented in an object-oriented programming language. Of course, these 23 patterns do not capture *all* the design knowledge an object-oriented designer will ever need. Nonetheless, the patterns from the "Gang of Four" (Gamma et al.) are a well-founded starting point. They are a design-level analog to the base class libraries found in Smalltalk development environments. They do not solve all problems but provide a foundation for learning about design patterns in general and finding specific useful architectures that can be incorporated into the solutions for a wide variety of real-world design problems. They capture an expert level of design knowledge and provide the foundation required for building elegant, maintainable, extensible object-oriented programs.

In the *Smalltalk Companion,* we do not add to this "base library" of patterns; rather, we present them for the Smalltalk designer and programmer, at times interpreting and expanding on the patterns where this special perspective demands it. Our goal is not to replace *Design Patterns*; you should read the *Smalltalk Companion* with *Design Patterns*, not instead of it. We have tried not to repeat information that is already well documented by the Gang of Four book. Instead, we refer to it frequently; you should too.

1.1   Why Design Patterns?

Learning an object-oriented language after programming in another paradigm, such as the traditional procedural style, is difficult. Learning to program and compose applications in Smalltalk requires a complex set of new skills and new ways of thinking about problems (e.g., Rosson & Carroll, 1990; Singley, Carroll, & Alpert, 1991). Climbing the "Smalltalk Mountain" learning curve is certainly nontrivial. Once you have reached that plateau where you feel comfortable building simple Smalltalk applications, there is still a significant distance to the expert peak.

Smalltalk experts know many things that novices do not, at various abstraction levels and across a wide spectrum of programming and design knowledge and skills:

- The low-level details of the syntax and semantics of the Smalltalk language

- What is available in the form of classes, methods, and functionality in the existing base class libraries

- How to use the specific tools of the Smalltalk interactive development environment to find and reuse existing functionality for new problems, as well as understanding programs from both static and runtime perspectives

- How to define and implement behavior in new classes and where these classes ought to reside in the existing class hierarchy

- Which classes work well together as frameworks

- Recurring patterns of object configurations and interactions and the sorts of problems for which these cooperating objects provide (at least partial) solutions

This is by no means an exhaustive list, and even novices understand and use much of this knowledge. But some items, especially the last—recurring patterns of software design, or design patterns—are the province of design experts.

A **design pattern** is a reusable implementation model or architecture that can be applied to solve a particular recurring class of problem. The pattern sometimes describes how methods in a single class or subhierarchy of classes work together; more often, it shows how multiple classes and their instances collaborate. It turns out that particular architectures reappear in different applications and systems to the extent that a generic pattern template emerges, one that experts reapply and customize to new application- and domain-specific problems. Hence, experts know how to apply design patterns to new problems to implement elegant and extensible solutions.

In general, designers—in numerous domains, not just software—apply their experience with past problems and solutions to new, similar problems. As Duego and Benson (1996) point out, expert designers apply what is known in cognitive psychology and artificial intelligence as **case-based reasoning,** remembering past cases and applying what they learned there. This is the sort of reasoning that chess masters, doctors, lawyers, and architects employ to solve new problems. Now, design patterns allow software designers to learn from and apply the experience of other designers as well. As in other domains, a literature of proven patterns has emerged. As a result, we can "stand on the shoulders of giants" to get us closer to the expert peak. As John Vlissides (1997) asserts, design patterns "capture expertise and make it accessible to non-experts" (p. 32).

Design patterns also provide a succinct vocabulary with which to describe new designs and retrospectively explain existing ones. Patterns let us understand a design at a high level before drilling down to focus on details. They allow us to envision entire configurations of objects and classes at a large grain size and communicate these ideas to other designers by name. We can say, "Implement the database access object as a Singleton," rather than, "Let's make sure the database access class has just one instance. The class should include a class variable to keep track of the single instance. The class should make the instance globally available but control access to it. The class should control when the instance is created and . . ." Which would you prefer?

1.2   Why a Smalltalk Companion?

Christopher Alexander and his colleagues have written extensively on the use of design patterns for living and working spaces—homes, buildings, communal areas, towns. Their work is considered the inspiration for the notion of software design patterns. In *The Timeless Way of Building* (1979), Alexander asserts, "Sometimes there are versions of the same pattern, slightly different, in different cultures" (p. 276). C++ and Smalltalk are different languages, different environments, different cultures— although the same basic pattern may be viable in both languages, each culture may give rise to different versions.

The Gang of Four's *Design Patterns* presents design issues and solutions from a C++ perspective. It illustrates patterns for the most part with C++ code and considers issues germane to a C++ implementation. Those issues are important for C++ developers, but they also make the patterns more difficult to understand and apply for developers using other languages.

This book is designed to be a companion to *Design Patterns*, but one written from the Smalltalk perspective. One way to think of the *Smalltalk Companion*, then, is as a variation on a theme. We provide the same patterns as in the Gang of Four book but view them through Smalltalk glasses. (In fact, when we were trying out names for the *Smalltalk Companion*, someone suggested "DesignPatterns asSmalltalkCompanion." However, we decided only hard-core Smalltalkers would get it.)

But the *Smalltalk Companion* goes beyond merely replicating the text of *Design Patterns* and plugging in Smalltalk examples wherever C++ appeared. We discuss and elaborate the original patterns from the Smalltalk viewpoint. As a result, there are numerous situations where we felt the need for additional analysis, clarification, or even minor disagreement with the original patterns. Thus, many of our discussions should apply to other object-oriented languages as well.

Of course, we provide plenty of sample code in Smalltalk. Our examples are, for the most part, not simply Smalltalk versions of the *Design Patterns* examples. We often felt an alternative would be more useful than a mere translation of the C++ example.

Here in a nutshell are our goals for the *Smalltalk Companion* as a supplement to *Design Patterns*:

- Discussion of issues specific to Smalltalk implementations of the Gang of Four's design patterns

- Much more Smalltalk sample code

- More Smalltalk known uses, especially from the major Smalltalk environments' class libraries

- Exploring variations the patterns can embody in Smalltalk and in general

- Many new examples, from application domains (insurance, telecommunications, etc.) and systems development (windowing systems, compilers, etc.)

1.3   C++ != Smalltalk (or, Smalltalk ~= C++)

Smalltalk and C++ are not just different programming languages; there are fundamental differences in designing for and programming in the two languages. Designers accustomed to working in one or the other language may view design problems and their solutions in different ways.

Let's take a closer look at this assertion that working in different languages will affect the way developers think about problem solutions. At the highest level, if we look into the domain of psycholinguistics, which deals with natural languages, we quickly learn that language and thought are closely linked and influence each other. Benjamin Whorf (1956) conjectured that the language one speaks influences the way one views the world or, indeed, how one thinks. There are those who have postulated, and it is easy to imagine, that this **Whorfian hypothesis** might hold true for programming languages: the different syntax and control structures of different languages may affect the manner in which problems are solved in those languages (see, for example, Curtis, 1985, especially sec. VI).

Conversely, it seems likely that thought and worldview influence language. In fact, a number of psychological studies have shown evidence that this is indeed the case (see, e.g., Anderson, 1985). Thus it may be that object-oriented languages "evolved" because, as Goldberg and Kay (1977) assert, they allow designers to build more closely a model describing their perception of the real world. As some have proposed, object-oriented design may be more "natural" than designing for a procedural language because it provides a better match for how people naturally model the problem domain (Rosson & Alpert, 1990; Cox, 1984).

Supporting both views, Soloway, Bonar, and Ehrlich (1983) demonstrated that programming languages are easier to use when they provide a better cognitive fit to the way people naturally think about designing programming solutions. Conversely, they also found that programming languages change one's preferred design strategies and that more experience with the constructs of a particular language alters design preferences.

The upshot is that the language one implements in—C++, Smalltalk—will certainly affect the way one thinks about and designs systems and applications. Smalltalkers and C++ developers don't just program in different languages; they *speak* a different language. For example, to a Smalltalk programmer, the term *class object* means a bonafide Smalltalk object that represents a class, whereas to C++ developers, *class object* refers to an instance of a user-defined class (that is, not a built-in C-language data type). Although there is certainly a great deal of conceptual overlap in the two languages and environments, they nonetheless involve many divergent ideas, bring different issues to the fore (issues that are important in C++ simply do not exist, or are insignificant, in Smalltalk, and vice versa), and ultimately lead to different ways of thinking about program design.

Conversely, we need to take the target language into account when designing: "Failing to consider the language at design time can leave issues open . . . such designs can lead to very poor programs" (Smith, 1996a). It may be a mistake to design without consideration of the constraints the target language imposes and opportunities it allows. In the case of Smalltalk, this is true not only of the language per se but the class libraries and their built-in frameworks as well. For example, consider the Model-View-Controller framework in VisualWorks, the Model-Pane framework in Visual Smalltalk, and the Motif-style interaction framework in IBM Smalltalk—each forces certain design decisions before even beginning the design of an actual interactive application.

Pursuing these ideas further, let's take a brief look at some specific ways in which Smalltalk and C++ differ—in particular, ways that may affect design. Our intention is to support our assertion that the two languages possess a number of fundamental differences, and as a result developers cannot help but think about problems and design solutions, and implement design patterns, in different ways (we are *not* trying to establish that one language or the other is superior; we apologize in advance if this comparison offends the sensibilities of any fans of either language). Along the way, we mention some patterns that will be affected by the presence or absence of specific features.

Pure Versus Hybrid Object Orientation

Smalltalk is a "pure" object-oriented language. In Smalltalk, all computation—other than at the most primitive level (and at a level not relevant to normal programming activity)—occurs only as the result of messages sent to objects. Everything is an object, including primitive data types such as numbers, characters, and strings. C++, on the other hand, is a hybrid language, with object-oriented features added to the procedural C language base. Being able to use non-object-oriented features of the language fosters a different mind-set in designers and programmers. For example, in C++, we can have global functions that are not attached to any class, whereas in Smalltalk we are forced to reflect on who is really responsible for each piece of functionality. The hybrid approach allows one to write programs that take advantage of the benefits of both the object-oriented and procedural paradigms and makes interfacing to legacy C code much easier. On the other hand, a uniform rather than hybrid approach may be more comprehensible (Rosson & Alpert, 1990).

Classes as Objects

Everything-as-object means that classes are first-class runtime objects in Smalltalk. They are thereby capable of sending and receiving messages and generally participating in any computation. This is not the case in C++. In Smalltalk, instance creation is one of the tasks fulfilled by class objects, whereas in C++ it is built into the language itself. Thus, the distinction between Creational and Behavioral is less clear-cut in Smalltalk: in its most basic form, instance creation is just a specialization of behavior, while in C++ they are truly distinct categories. We'll see that having a class as a full-fledged object figures into the Smalltalk version of a number of patterns (Abstract Factory, Singleton, Factory Method, and others).

Mature, Comprehensive Class Libraries

One of the benefits of the major Smalltalk environments is their large set of base classes, which have been refined and debugged over the course of years. As a result of extensive use, even the low-level abstract data types included in these libraries have been enhanced over time to possess wide-ranging capabilities. Such broad functionality eliminates certain design considerations and even the requirements for some design pattern implementations. For instance, we need not design and implement internal Iterators in Smalltalk because the base Collection classes provide their own iteration methods. Other patterns, such as Composite, will also benefit from reuse of functionality in the extensive base class library.

Also, continuing the everything-as-object theme, abstract data types like numbers, strings, and Collections are implemented as user-modifiable classes in the base class libraries, not as black box data types intrinsic to the language per se. This means we can enhance the functionality of such objects by defining our own methods within these classes. If we require a new type of Iterator, for example, we can write a new method in Collection rather than having to define a new Iterator class.

Strong Versus Weak Typing

C++ is a strongly typed language; all variables are declared to the compiler to be of a particular type or class. Smalltalk employs a broader form of dynamic (or late) binding. Variables are not declared to be of any particular class, and it is not until runtime—

when objects are actually instantiated and referenced by variables—that a variable becomes associated with a specific type (class).

In both languages, any single variable may point to instances of different classes at different points in time. But in Smalltalk, they may be instances of any class in the entire hierarchy, whereas in C++ they may be instances of only a particular base class or its derived subclasses. The same is true for objects within collections. In C++, all objects in a list must be of a particular type or class (or its subclasses), whereas in Smalltalk, a `Collection`, in general, may contain heterogeneous instances of any class. This will figure into many patterns. For example, in Smalltalk, Iterators are more powerful since they are inherently polymorphic; we need not define different types of Iterators for lists with different types of elements. Strong versus weak typing plays similar roles in Composite, Command, and Adapter. In the last, for example, a C++ Adapter must declare the type of its Adaptee and thus may only adapt objects of that declared class or its derived subclasses; in Smalltalk, the Adaptee may be of any class whose interface includes the messages sent by the Adapter to the Adaptee.

Weak typing offers increased flexibility, but there are a number of advantages to strong typing. For example, the lack of strong typing means the lack of type safety. Further, declaring variables to be of a specific class allows for more comprehensive static analyses of programs and compile-time optimizations.

Blocks

A block is an object that contains a chunk of Smalltalk code that is not executed until the block receives a message to do so. That is, evaluation of the block of code does not occur when it is encountered sequentially in a method, as language statements normally are, but is deferred until we explicitly send the block the `value` message (or variations thereof). Since blocks are objects, we can create them in code and pass them around to other objects; hence blocks let us hand off pieces of code to be evaluated by some other object, perhaps only if some situation or condition occurs. This turns out to be extremely useful in general, and we will see it used in patterns such as Iterator. Blocks also effectively allow us to attach idiosyncratic code to individual instances of a class (as opposed to methods, which apply behavior to all instances of a class). We will see this applied to pluggable adapters in the Adapter pattern. The block construct even allows us to define our own control structures within the language (Ungar & Smith, 1987), rather than being limited by the compiler to a fixed set of conditional and looping constructs. Most languages, including C++, have no analogous construct that makes an arbitrary piece of code a first-class object that can react to messages.

Reflection and Metalevel Capabilities

Smalltalk allows us to write code to obtain information about the Smalltalk environment itself. Classes and methods exist in the base class library that let programs find out about the relationships among classes in the class hierarchy, the methods in the currently executing process, or the messages understood by instances of a specific class. Such capabilities are key components in the Smalltalk programmer's tool kit. They allowed the reflective tools of the development environment itself—class and method browsers, the debugger—to be built in Smalltalk. Since their code is included in the class libraries, we can further enhance and refine these tools to suit new needs or integrate them into new tools for program understanding (e.g., Carroll et al., 1990). Again, it's a mind-set issue. Smalltalkers feel comfortable using Smalltalk's reflective capabilities to build and integrate new programming tools into the Smalltalk environment.

For example, using the metalevel construct `doesNotUnderstand:`, we can capture all messages intended for an object in order to "decorate" that object with enhanced functionality or to have one object act as a Proxy for another located in a database on disk or on another machine and decide whether and when to forward captured messages to such external objects. We can also store a message selector in symbolic form and at any time invoke that message in an object using the built-in `perform:` message (and its variations). This is similar to C++'s ability to invoke a function using a function pointer, the difference being that the Smalltalk version allows us to use a symbolic representation of a message's signature. We'll see `perform:` used in the Smalltalk implementations of patterns such as Adapter, Observer, and Command, and the fact that we can use a symbolic version of a selector will play a role in Interpreter.

Inheritance Semantics

There are quite a few differences in the way inheritance works in the two languages; we mention two disparities here. First, C++ supports multiple inheritance, while Smalltalk allows classes to have only a single immediate superclass. Multiple inheritance offers an immediate solution for some problems (e.g., the class adapter version of the Adapter pattern in *Design Patterns*). In Smalltalk we are forced to devise alternative solutions to such problems. On the other hand, multiple inheritance introduces added complexity to a programming language; programmers must know how name collisions are handled and what convention is in place to deal with repeated inheritance (e.g., inheriting from two classes that both inherit from the same superclass). Indeed, multiple inheritance has deliberately been left out of modern Smalltalk environments because of the trade-off between complexity and utility: The belief is that multiple inheritance is not useful enough as to outweigh the added complexity it brings (particularly for program comprehension).

Second, in C++, dynamic binding of a function (declared in a superclass and overridden in one or more subclasses) works only if the function is declared **virtual** in the superclass. As Rumbaugh et al. (1991) point out, this can be an impediment to extensibility and incremental reuse (reusing portions of a superclass's behavior via inheritance while overriding other methods for specialization). The only reason the class's original programmer would declare a method virtual would be if he or she *anticipated* the possibility of that operation being overridden by a yet-to-be-defined subclass— and this decision must be made for every function defined in the class (Rumbaugh et al., 1991).

Interactive Development Environment

Smalltalk development—in the major Smalltalk products—always takes place in the context of an interactive development environment. There are a number of implications of this, including facilitating experimentation and testing and the availability of tools for program understanding and finding reusable classes and methods. With respect to design, we avoid one design decision altogether because the environment provides for incremental compilation of individual methods as they are saved: Smalltalk programmers need not recompile or possess the source for an entire class in order to modify or add methods in that class. Hence, we eliminate one concern regarding where new functionality ought to reside. For example, one of the *Design Patterns* motivations for the Visitor pattern is that C++ programmers may be reluctant to add new functionality to an existing class because they can thereby avoid recompilation of that entire class, which is time-consuming at best or impossible lacking the source code; hence, it makes sense to locate this functionality in a new class that operates on instances of the preexisting class. By eliminating this extraneous concern, incremental compilation allows for more responsibility-driven design, placing code where it functionally or logically belongs.

Abstract Classes, Private Methods

C++ includes language-based features that provide for explicit—and enforced—implementation of desirable features for which Smalltalk provides no such support. For example, unlike C++, Smalltalk does not provide compile-time mechanisms for declaring and enforcing the privacy of a method. Programmers may document a method as private (e.g., with comments), but there is no built-in mechanism to prevent an external object from actually invoking that method. Similarly, Smalltalk includes no mechanism for preventing the instantiation of a class intended to be abstract. We'll see this play a role in patterns like Singleton, which require a more complex solution in Smalltalk because we need a runtime substitute for the C++ privacy mechanism.

There are many other differences between the two languages and advantages and disadvantages to both. Overall, C++ is designed for efficiency and to help prevent programmer errors (Rumbaugh et al., 1991), and Smalltalk is intended to be more flexible. Again, we do not wish to imply either language is in some sense "better" than the other. Rather, the ultimate point is this: **they're different,** and therefore Smalltalk programmers and C++ programmers are likely to instantiate design patterns differently. Hence our goal in this book is to offer the Smalltalkers' view of the 23 patterns in *Design Patterns*.

1.4   Our Pattern Discussions

The patterns that the Gang of Four and we discuss possess a particular level of abstraction. In general, patterns may occur at many different levels of granularity and abstraction in object-oriented applications, ranging from the micro to macro. Conventions for such low-level concerns as how to name methods and variables, how to implement lazy initialization, and how to format code would be considered micropatterns (many of the patterns in Kent Beck's *Smalltalk Best Practice Patterns* [1997b] reside in this category). At the other end of the continuum are macropatterns such as Visual-Works's overarching architecture for interactive applications, the Model-View-Controller framework. Buschmann et al. (1996) assert that, overall, patterns range from *idioms* to *design patterns* to *architectural patterns*. Our design patterns focus on the center ground. They describe the structure and implementation of useful microarchitectures for portions of well-designed and well-programmed applications.

As in *Design Patterns,* our pattern essays are organized into three chapters covering Creational patterns, Structural patterns, and Behavioral patterns. Creational patterns involve the process of instantiating objects. Structural patterns deal with composing objects into more complex structures to effectively enhance the functionality of the structures' components. Behavioral patterns concern the functional behavior of systems, how objects can communicate, cooperate, and distribute responsibilities to accomplish goals.

We also classify patterns according to their *scope,* specifying in each pattern's heading whether it applies primarily to classes or instances. Class patterns focus on static relationships among classes established through inheritance. Object patterns involve dynamic runtime relationships among instances. For example, the Template Method pattern is classified as Class Behavioral because its implementation is effected via inheritance and the overriding of methods. The superclass defines a broad method that invokes one or more secondary methods, and subclasses may override any or all of those subordinate methods; hence the components of the pattern are all static and class-based. Strategy is categorized as Object Behavioral because, even though inheritance is involved in the definition of Strategy classes, the pattern's *primary* features involve the interaction among objects.

Despite the same overall organization, our pattern essays do not fully duplicate the format of the Gang of Four patterns. We're not writing new patterns per se; the Gang of Four has already written them. We are instead presenting the Smalltalk versions of these patterns. Thus, we don't necessarily need every pattern subsection used in the Gang of Four patterns. Each of our patterns adheres to a malleable template of sections, as follows:

- A brief **Intent** section, usually the exact text from *Design Patterns*, although occasionally slightly reworded.

- The pattern's **Structure** diagram. Often this varies from the *Design Patterns* diagram. We've modified many structure diagrams for greater clarity, to include Smalltalk-required objects such as class objects, or to reflect a Smalltalk version of the pattern that differs from the C++ implementation. Even when our diagrams are structurally identical, they reflect Smalltalk syntax and semantics rather than those of C++.

- The **Discussion** section in which we consider issues such as the pattern's motivation, how the Smalltalk version differs from the C++ rendering, advantages and drawbacks of the pattern, and general issues to consider when applying the pattern. This section is in a general narrative style like Christopher Alexander's patterns (Alexander et al., 1977).

- Optional **Collaborations** and **Applicability** sections. At times, these issues are considered in the the Discussion narrative.

- **Implementation,** which considers issues in implementing the pattern in Smalltalk and/or in general.

- The **Sample Code** section provides the Smalltalk code for an example making use of the pattern. Occasionally, when the content or flow warrants, Implementation and Sample Code are considered interleaved in a single section.

- **Known Smalltalk Uses.** Since this is the *Smalltalk Companion,* we felt it appropriate to present only Smalltalk applications and Smalltalk library classes that make use of the design patterns.

- **Related Patterns.** This section is optional. If what *Design Patterns* had to say suffices, we are silent in this section.

1.5   Which Smalltalk Dialects?

There are now a host of Smalltalk development environments. In the very recent past, it seems as if a new one is being announced every time we look at Smalltalk-related sites on the World Wide Web. Of course there are (were) the "Big Three:" ParcPlace, Digitalk, and IBM. ParcPlace formerly marketed its Smalltalk-80 derivative under the name Objectworks, but more recently the product is called VisualWorks. They also sell a World Wide Web–enabled server version of Smalltalk named VisualWave. The Digitalk environments were formerly called Smalltalk/V but now sell under the name Visual Smalltalk. Many of the older Smalltalk/V environments are still available. In fact, Smalltalk/V Win16 (the 16-bit Windows version) is currently available for free, combined with the WindowBuilder Pro/V UI builder from Objectshare, as Smalltalk Express. IBM Smalltalk is bundled with the visual programming application builder, VisualAge, although you can purchase or install the Smalltalk development environment without this front-end visual programming environment.

ParcPlace and Digitalk have merged to become ParcPlace-Digitalk and had announced plans to merge their two Smalltalk dialects. However, as of this writing, ParcPlace-Digitalk has announced it will no longer do product development on Visual Smalltalk, although it will continue to support existing versions. This is unfortunate as there are still lots of folks designing for and programming in Visual Smalltalk.

There are numerous smaller players as well, including newcomers Dolphin Smalltalk, Smalltalk MT, and Squeak, as well as Cincom ObjectStudio (formerly Enfin), Gemstone (Smalltalk bundled with an object-oriented database system), SmalltalkAgents, Smalltalk/X, GNU Smalltalk, and probably others we've missed. There exists at least one version of Smalltalk for every major platform: PCs (including DOS, OS/2, 16- and 32-bit Windows operating systems), Macs, UNIX machines, IBM AS/400s, even IBM mainframes.

In this book, we focus on the Smalltalk dialects that have been around the longest and are thus likely to have the most users. These are also the Smalltalk dialects we have the most experience using. Although we refer occasionally to other environments, we primarily consider VisualWorks and Visual Smalltalk and, to a lesser extent, IBM Smalltalk. We've drawn many of our examples of patterns in use from the base class libraries of these environments. When we cite code from these environments or offer our own code examples and there are differences among the various Smalltalk dialects with regard to that code, we are explicit about which dialect we're speaking.

Nonetheless, keep in mind that Smalltalk is Smalltalk. Despite the discrepancies among the various dialects, they are more alike than different, and the majority of our code examples will work in any Smalltalk dialect, either as is or with relatively minor adaptations.

1.6   Smalltalk Code Examples

Our goal in presenting code is to portray one or more ways a particular pattern can be implemented in Smalltalk. As with any code, you, the reader, may look at an example and say, "Hey, I could've implemented that by doing such-and-such instead." There are always a variety of ways to code a particular design solution; we'll never cover them all. Instead, our goal is to demonstrate one or more ways in which a pattern may be implemented in actual code. It's then up to you to go off and use the things you learn in your own applications; when you do so, you may find variations of our implementations that suit your own style and aesthetics.

Speaking of our Smalltalk examples also raises the issue of how we have formatted code in the *Smalltalk Companion*. Code formatting is a difficult subject: "between them, any two computer scientists will have at least three different opinions on how to indent code" (Wilson, 1997, p. 122). There are numerous reasonable ways to format a particular piece of code, but formatting is a "religious" issue: "No other topic generates more heat and less light than code formatting" (Beck, 1997, p. 171). As far as we're concerned, the overriding issues are that code ought to be formatted so as to be easily read and understood by another programmer, and the format should help convey the semantics of the code. We mention this because you will see slight formatting differences in the code of the three coauthors. Nonetheless, overall our examples follow conventional Smalltalk style as you will find in the formatting guidelines offered by Beck and Skublics, Klimas and Thomas (1996).

1.7   Conventions Used in This Book

With regard to conventions, they are simple and few. When we include a piece of code, a class name, or a method name in the midst of a prose paragraph, it will look `like this`. When we provide sample code offset from the prose, it appears as follows:

```
Class>>method: parameter
    "This is a sample instance method."
    ^self == parameter
```

The method names in code samples use the convention employed by many Smalltalk debuggers:

```
ClassName>>methodName
```

That is, the method name appears to the right of the ">>" and the class in which the method resides appears on the left of ">>". So a class method would look like this:

```
Class class>>method
    "This is a sample class method."
    ^self basicNew initialize
```

We refer to specific pages in *Design Patterns* quite often. Also, each pattern heading references the page on which the original pattern appeared. References to pages in *Design Patterns* appear as "DP *nn*," where *nn* is the page number—for example, "This corresponds to the C++ code shown on page DP 84."

Finally, most of our diagrams follow the same conventions as in the Gang of Four book. For example, we include OMT-style Class and Object Diagrams (Rumbaugh et al., 1991) as well as Interaction Diagrams à la Jacobson et al. (1992). A good source for information on these notations is Appendix B of *Design Patterns*, but here we provide annotated samples of these notations to illuminate their syntax and semantics.

Our Class Diagrams incorporate a subset of the full OMT notation, while enhancing the notation with pseudocode or actual Smalltalk code for important methods. A particular class is portrayed in a Class Diagram as shown below. The instance variables and method names are optional; we often leave them out for clarity.

ClassName
method1 method2
instanceVariableA instanceVariableB

The basic form of our OMT-style Class Diagrams is as follows:

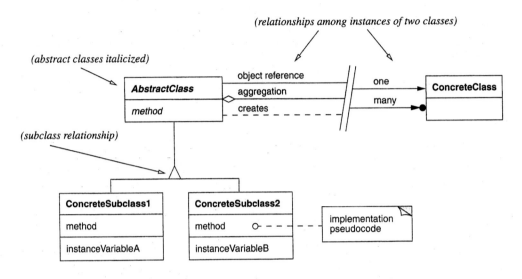

Here's another illustrative Class Diagram example:

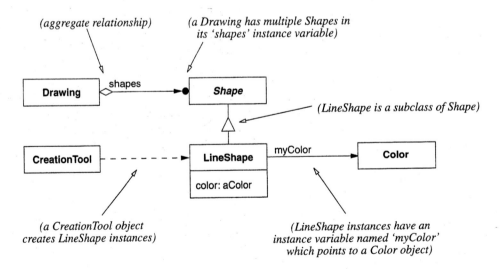

Interaction Diagrams portray the dynamic runtime interaction among objects:

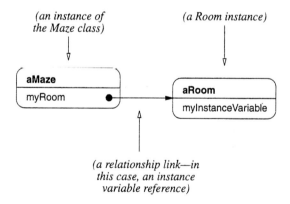

An Object Diagram shows (a portion of) the structure of instances and how two or more are related (typically by an instance variable reference). An Object Diagram does not portray dynamic information such as message sends:

We use other diagramming notations whenever appropriate. For example, it was particularly useful in the State pattern discussion to portray the example application in terms of a state transition diagram, which shows the various states an object or system can be in, along with connecting links labeled with the events or messages that can force transitions between states. All of our notations are either self-explanatory or are described in the accompanying text.

We hope you enjoy and learn from the *Smalltalk Companion.* Although you may think all of its contents are going to be new to you, you will find yourself saying, "Oh, yeah, I've used this pattern before." On the other hand, there's much here to master, even for experienced Smalltalkers. If you do learn something new, we will have been successful.

Chapter 2

Aha!

Before launching into our descriptions of specific design patterns, we present a case study of sorts, involving multiple patterns. In the *Design Patterns* preface, the Gang of Four speak about moving from a "Huh?" to an "Aha!" experience with regard to understanding design patterns. We present here a little drama portraying such a transition. It consists of three vignettes: three days in the life of two Smalltalk programmers who work for MegaCorp Insurance Company. We are listening in on conversations between Don (an object newbie, but an experienced business analyst) and Jane (an object and patterns expert). Don comes to Jane with his design problems, and they solve them together. Although the characters are fictitious, the designs are real and have all been part of actual systems written in Smalltalk. Our goal is to demonstrate how, by careful analysis, design patterns can help derive solutions to real-world problems.

2.1   Scene One: States of Confusion

Our story begins with a tired-looking Don approaching Jane's cubicle, where Jane sits quietly typing at her keyboard.

DON: Hey, Jane, could you help me with this problem? I've been looking at this requirements document for days now, and I can't seem to get my mind around it.

JANE: That's all right. I don't mind at all. What's the problem?

DON: It's this claims-processing workflow system I've been asked to design. I just can't see how the objects will work together. I think I've found the basic objects in the system, but I don't understand how to make sense from their behaviors.

JANE: Can you show me what you've done?

DON: Here, let me show you the section of the requirements document I've got the problem with:[1]

1. *Data Entry.* This consists of various systems that receive health claims from a variety of different sources. All are logged by assigning a unique identifier. Paper claims and supporting documents are scanned. Scanned paper claims and faxes are processed via OCR (optical character recognition) to capture the data associated with each form field.

2. *Validation.* The scanned and entered forms are validated to ensure that the fields are consistent and completely filled in. Incomplete or improperly filled-in forms are rejected by the system and are sent back to the claimant for resubmittal.

3. *Provider/Plan Match.* An automated process attempts to match the plan (the contract under which the claim is being paid) and the health care provider (e.g., the doctor) identified on the claim with the providers with which the overall claim processing organization has a contract. If there is no exact match, the program identifies the most likely matches based on soundex technology (an algorithm for finding similar-sounding words). The system displays prospective matches to knowledge workers in order of the likelihood of the match, who then identify the correct provider.

4. *Automatic Adjudication.* The system determines whether a claim can be paid and how much to pay if and only if there are no inconsistencies between key data items associated with the claim. If there are inconsistencies, the system "pends" the claim for processing by the appropriate claims adjudicator.

5. *Adjudication of Pended Claims.* The adjudicator can access the system for a claim history or a representation of the original claim. The adjudicator either approves the claim for payment, specifying the proper amount to pay, or generates correspondence denying the claim.

I've identified that there's a "Claim" that the rest of the system revolves around. What's got me stymied is that the Claim seems to be different things to different people! It seems that working on a Claim means something different to everyone I talk to. Every time I think I've identified its responsibilities, something new crops up. Not only that, but simple responsibilities for a Claim like "Open an editor on yourself" or "Save yourself" seem to take on several different meanings, depending on where in the workflow you are.

---

[1] These requirements are based on the problem posed by Larry Best for the OOPSLA'96 DesignFest.

JANE: Hmmm. I remember reading something like this. Let me find it. *[Rustles around through the papers on her desk]* Oh, here it is. There's an article in this issue of *Object Magazine* about using the State pattern in order management systems.[2]

DON: Haven't you been listening? This is a claims processing system, not an order management system.

JANE: I know, but the interesting thing was how the author applied the State pattern to a workflow problem. *[Leafs through the magazine]* Okay, here's the article. *[Scans it]* Hmmm . . . I see . . . Have you drawn a state transition diagram of the states that a Claim can be in?

DON: *[Taken aback]* A state transition diagram? No, I hadn't thought about that. Why would you do that?

JANE: It's like this. The workflow actions are transitions between States. Each Claim has a set of states it can be in, depending on what happened to it last. For instance, what's the first item in your workflow?

DON: Data Entry.

JANE   Tell me what's next.

DON: Validation.

JANE: So do all Claims make it through Validation?

DON: No. Some of them are rejected in the Validation stage. The ones that make it through then have to be Matched to their provider and plan.

JANE: So you could draw a diagram like this? *[Jane picks up a pen and paper and draws the following diagram.]*

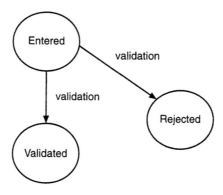

DON: *[Guardedly]* Yeah, I guess so. Where are you going with this?

---

[2]Brown (1996).

JANE: Just follow through with me. So what's the next step in the workflow?

[The two of them work through all of the steps of the workflow, finally arriving at the following diagram.]

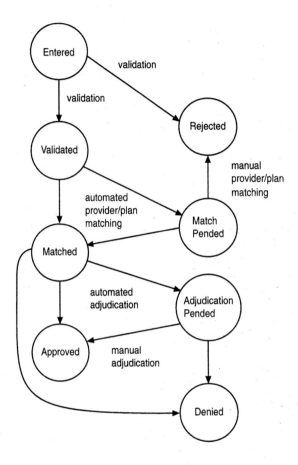

DON: Great. We've got a state transition diagram. How does this help me figure out how my Claim works?

JANE: Well, the article shows that you can apply the State design pattern to design your workflow objects. Each of the States that we had in the previous diagram would become classes. The Claim would hold on to a single instance of one of these State classes at a time. Your design might look like this: *[Turning to a new sheet of paper, Jane draws the OMT diagram on the facing page.]*

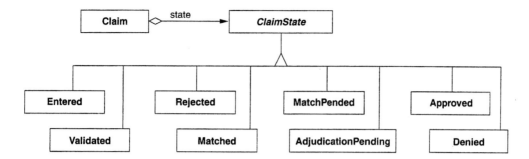

DON: Again, how does this help me?

JANE: *[Grinning]* I'm getting there! Now, you told me that one of the problems that you had was that "edit" seemed to change its meaning depending on where in the workflow a claim was, right?

DON: *[Gratified that the conversation has finally turned back to his problem]* Right. For instance, a data entry person sees this UI *[shows a picture of an interface]*. On the other hand, if the system doesn't find a match for provider and plan, they see this screen *[shows a second picture]*. And the adjudicators who have to adjust the claims manually see this screen. *[He shows a third picture.]* My problem is, how do I know which of these screens to show?

JANE: Well, what you do is delegate the code for "edit" down to the specific State that the Claim holds. For instance, look at this *[she points to Entered state on the class diagram]*. If the Claim is in this state, then it returns the first screen you just showed me. If the claim is in the MatchPended state, it returns this second screen. And if it's in the AdjudicationPending state it returns the last screen. To find out what screen to display, the Claim asks its State for a screen, and it then tells that UI to open.

DON: *[Softly]* Hey, that's much simpler than what I was thinking about. I expected to have to have a lot of conditional code that would check who had operated on the Claim last and then display the screen based on that. This really makes it easier.

JANE: That's the power of design patterns.

DON: You mentioned that term earlier. What does it mean?

JANE: Design patterns are recurring solution approaches for design problems you see over and over. There's also a book with the same name. It's built around 23 patterns, each representing an object-based solution to a specific class of problems.

DON: *[A bit incredulous]* So does this book have all of the answers to all of my problems?

JANE: No, of course not. It just presents a few of the most common problems and their solutions. The solution we just talked about is called the State pattern. You see, each pattern starts off with a sentence saying what the pattern is intended to be used for. The State pattern's intent begins, "Allow an object to alter its behavior when its internal state changes." Doesn't that sound like what your Claim needed to do?

DON: Now that you've phrased it that way, yeah, it does. But I never would have been able to guess that earlier. How did you know that was the pattern you needed to use?

JANE: Well, it was lucky that I had read that article. But as you get more comfortable with the patterns in *Design Patterns,* you start to see more easily how they can be applied to new problems. You want to borrow my copy?

DON: Not now. I've got to start writing up this new design. Maybe later. Thanks for the help!

2.2   Scene Two: Rules Were Not Meant to Be Broken

[A few days later, Don again asks Jane for help with a tough design problem.]

DON: Jane, do you have a few minutes?

JANE: Sure. What's up?

DON: Well, I've got another design problem, and I was wondering if you could help me.

JANE: I'd be glad to.

DON: I'm trying to figure out some aspects of how the adjudication process will work. You know, that's how claims are either approved and paid out, or denied.

JANE: Yeah, I remember your describing that to me.

DON: Here's my problem. It comes down to the way claims are reimbursed. There are all these different rules that the requirements describe. I'm not sure how to represent them.

JANE: Why don't you show me the requirements document? *[Don hands her the document and they read the following paragraph.]*

> A policy consists of a list of covered items, with a payment rule associated with each item. There are several different types of payment rules:
>
> - For a particular item, do not reimburse the procedure at all (i.e., reject it).
>
> - For a particular item, pay a flat dollar amount (e.g., pay $25 for procedure 123.4).
>
> - For a particular item, pay a percentage of the charge for the item (e.g., pay 50 percent of the hospital charge for procedure 234.5).

In addition, there are two more types of payment rules:

- Stop-loss rules govern the maximum amount payable for a line item (e.g., pay 70 percent of the charge or $500, whichever is lesser).

- Query-based rules are based on the attributes of the claimant (e.g., if the claimant is female, pay $200 for this procedure; else pay $150).

DON: Somehow I've got to match these procedure codes up with these different rules. But each of these rules is determined by the user! It would be nice if I could just code these into the Policy, but the problem is that I don't know ahead of time which rules the user will want.

JANE: It sounds to me as if each of these "rules" is a reimbursement Strategy.

DON: That's an interesting way to phrase it. What do you mean by that?

JANE: Strategy is another pattern. Here, let me read you its intent *[reaches for her copy of* Design Patterns *and reads the following sentence from the inside front cover]*: "Define a family of algorithms, encapsulate each one, and make them interchangeable. Strategy lets the algorithm vary independently from clients that use it."

DON: Well, the reimbursement doesn't sound like much of an algorithm to me. But I'm game. Show me how this Strategy thing would work.

JANE: Let's see if we can't make each of these rules into a strategy object. The basic idea is that each rule calculates a total for a line item. Right?

DON: Right.

JANE: So each of our objects should understand a message called reimbursementFor: aLineItem. We'd have a class for each rule. What was the first rule you described?

DON: It's the one that says, "Don't reimburse this procedure."

JANE: That's a sort of special case. The implementation for reimbursementFor: for this one would be easy: it always returns zero.

DON: What about this second one—the one that pays a flat dollar amount?

JANE: That one would just have an instance variable that holds on to the amount that is reimbursed. The reimbursementFor: method would return the value of that instance variable.

DON: I'm starting to get this now. So the next one that says "pay a certain percentage of the line item cost" would store the percentage, and the method reimbursementFor: would return the result of multiplying that percentage times the cost of the line item. Right?

JANE: You've got it. The three classes would be in a hierarchy like this:

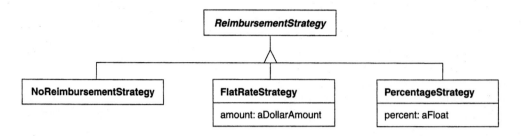

JANE: The `Claim` would need to look up what rule applies for a particular procedure code and then apply the rule for that procedure.

DON: Not bad! That solves part of the problem for us. What about this next one? The stop-loss rule doesn't act like the two previous ones. It seems more like you have to run one of the other rules first and then make a decision about which amount to reimburse based on the result of the first rule.

JANE: I think you've got something there. Let me see *[reaches for* Design Patterns *and begins thumbing pages].* There's a pattern in here that says something about how you could modify an object's behavior at runtime to add new behavior. Ah, here it is! It's the Decorator pattern *[opens the book and shows Don the diagram on page 177].* Do you see from this diagram how this Decorator contains an instance of another object but implements the same interface as the object it contains? I'll bet we could do something similar for this problem.

DON: You've lost me again. Which object is containing what other object?

JANE: Let me be more specific. Let's say that we have another rule, called a `StopLossStrategy`, that contains some other Strategy inside it. It implements the method `reimbursementFor:` by first forwarding that message on to the Strategy it contains and then checking to see if the result of that exceeds its stop-loss amount.

DON: *[Hesitates]* I think I see where you're leading. So you're telling me that it would look something like this? *[He takes Jane's drawing and adds a new class (see facing page).]*

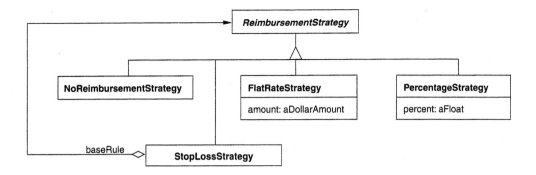

JANE: That looks right to me.

DON: Hey, this design patterns stuff is really powerful! Now we've combined more than one pattern in a single design. From the way you described them earlier, I thought they stood on their own.

JANE: Not always. Design patterns can be used alone, but more often than not, you see several of them in a design. There are certain patterns that are commonly used in conjunction with other patterns. *Design Patterns* lists these in a section named "Related Patterns" at the end of each pattern.

DON: It's nice to know the authors thought of that. But how do you know which of these patterns to apply? It seems as if you just seem to pull them out of thin air.

JANE: Not really. I'll admit it's not a scientific process by any means. When I was at the last PLoP (Patterns Languages of Programs) conference, I overheard someone ask one of the patterns experts how they went about deciding what patterns to use. He said it consisted of "thinking about half-forgotten bits of papers I've read, scanning the inside front cover of *Design Patterns,* and sometimes just guessing." I think the real key is to read the patterns and try to apply them enough that they become second nature.

DON: I see. Sounds like I need to actually read some of these patterns.

JANE: I think you'd learn a lot if you did. So are you ready to borrow my copy? *[She holds out the book to Don.]*

DON: Sure. *[He takes the book.]* I need to get back to documenting this design. By the way, do you have any ideas about the query-based rules?

JANE: Well, we can use the Interpreter pattern for handling runtime queries. The pattern is on page 243 in *Design Patterns* if you want to look it up.

DON: Great! I'll read about it. *[He waves the book as he dashes out of Jane's cubicle.]* Thanks!

2.3   Scene Three: Database Schemes and Dreams

A few weeks later, Don runs into Jane in the hallways of MegaCorp.

DON: Jane! I wanted to thank you for pointing me toward the Interpreter pattern. I was able to build a `QueryStrategy` as another subclass of `Abstract-ReimbursementStrategy`. I built a parser and hierarchy of parse nodes like the pattern said, and used that to decide whether a particular rule applied. It ended up being really straightforward once I understood the pattern.

JANE: Terrific. I'm glad it worked out for you.

DON: Not only that, but I'm starting to find other patterns in the system. It turns out that we were using some of the patterns in *Design Patterns* without even knowing it. For instance, our `Policy` class had several different boilerplate versions that came preconfigured for the guys in the field to work from. When they wanted to make a new `Policy`, they'd just pick an existing boilerplate version and have the system make a copy of it. It turns out that was the Prototype pattern. Once we read the pattern, we recognized it right away. In fact, we liked the "Prototype Manager" idea in the pattern so much that we adopted it for our design.

JANE: That doesn't surprise me. The design patterns listed are supposed to be some of the most common and accepted solutions to these problems. It makes sense they'd be rediscovered time and time again.

DON: Another interesting thing is that now that I've found the patterns in our code and explained them to everyone, we're all starting to use the name of the patterns as a verbal shorthand. We keep saying, "Oh, that class is just a Decorator" or "Wouldn't you want to use a Template Method here?"

JANE: That's one of the most valuable parts of the whole design patterns idea: providing a common vocabulary that designers can converse with. Now that we all have the same set of terms to work from, it gets a lot easier to talk about design.

DON: I agree. It's really changed the way my team works. So what are you working on these days?

JANE: Actually, I'm documenting the relational database access framework that we've been working on for the past several months. I'm planning on using the design patterns we employed in its design as part of the documentation of the system that I'm writing.

DON: Show me what you mean!

JANE: Okay. Take a look at my whiteboard. *[They walk together to Jane's cubicle, where she waves her hand at the diagram on her whiteboard (see facing page).]* Let's start over here. *[Points to the class named `ForeignKeyProxy`]* This class—

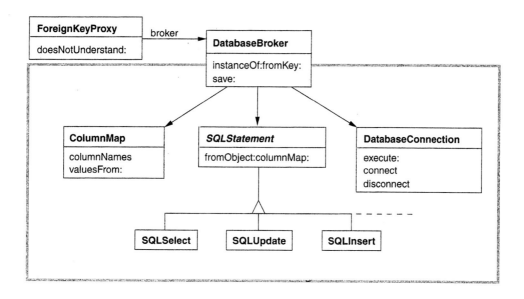

DON: *[Interrupts Jane in midsentence]* I can tell from the class name. That's a Proxy. So it stands in for some other object until that object gets loaded. Right?

JANE: You're really getting the hang of this, aren't you? You're right. This object holds onto a Foreign key into a database table. When it's needed, it works with the DatabaseBroker to instantiate the actual object from that table and then it replaces itself with that object.

DON: Well, that one is obvious from the class name. What other patterns are in this design?

JANE: We've got a DatabaseBroker class that acts as a Facade for this whole subsystem. That means that the clients of that class don't need to see the details of the subsystem; they just work through the public interface of this class. Now, the class DatabaseConnection is a Singleton. That means—

DON: That only one instance of that class will ever be in the system at once. What about the rest of these classes? Aren't there patterns there too?

JANE: *[With a lopsided grin]* No, there aren't. It's easy to get carried away with design patterns. Sometimes you start seeing them everywhere, even where they're not. They won't solve all your problems; they'll just help you find solutions to some of the more common ones. By the way, isn't your team about to start documenting their user interface classes?

DON: Yeah, they are. Oh, do you mean we should look for patterns in those classes too? But those were mostly just built with the VisualWorks GUI builder. We added some classes of our own, but mostly we just used what was provided by the tools.

JANE: But patterns are a great way to describe how existing tools and applications work. For instance, the VisualWorks `ApplicationModel` classes act like Mediators between the different Views on the window. And the way Visual-Works handles the updating between Views and Models—that's an implementation of the Observer pattern.

DON: You know, it might help to describe some aspects of our system like that. From what we've talked about, it seems that patterns are good if you're building a new design, talking about design options with other designers, or you're trying to document an existing design. Right?

JANE: I couldn't have put it better myself. By the way, when can I have my copy of *Design Patterns* back?

DON: *[Smiling]* When I'm done with it.

Chapter 3

Creational Patterns

Abstract Factory (31) Provide an interface for creating families of related or dependent objects. Let clients create products in any family of products in an abstract fashion, without having to specify their concrete classes.

Builder (47) Separate the construction of a complex object from its internal representation so that the same construction process in a client can be used to create different representations.

Factory Method (63) Define an interface for creating an object, but let subclasses decide which class to instantiate. Factory Method lets a class defer instantiation to subclasses.

Prototype (77) Specify the kinds of objects to create using a prototypical instance, and create new objects by copying this prototype.

Singleton (91) Ensure a class has only one instance, and provide a global point of access to it.

ABSTRACT FACTORY (DP 87)   Object Creational

Intent

Provide an interface for creating families of related or dependent objects. Let clients create products in any family of products in an abstract fashion, without having to specify their concrete classes.

Structure

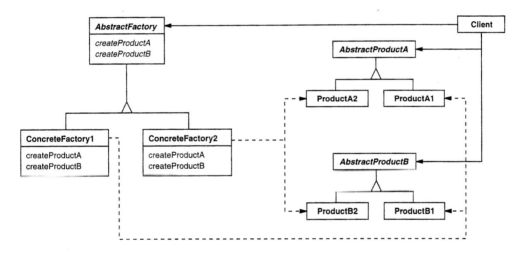

Discussion

Ironically, at times the context under which a pattern applies may be as complex as the pattern solution. This is the case in Abstract Factory. The pattern is really quite simple; the problem context contains many parts. Let's first take a look at the situation under which the Abstract Factory pattern is applicable.[1]

To begin with, we have an application that needs to build a product bit by bit from component subparts. It may be constructing an automobile, which contains a body, engine, transmission, and passenger compartment. Second, the application wants components in a single product to be from the same parts *family*, that is, parts that belong together: a Ford car should have a Ford engine and a Ford transmission. These are parts in the Ford family. Third, we have multiple parts families: Ford parts, Toyota parts, Porsche parts, and so forth. The corresponding classes are spread out throughout the class hierarchy, each in its appropriate

---

[1]We suggest you read the Builder (47) pattern essay after Abstract Factory; the two patterns are closely related and share several issues.

subhierarchy: engines in the `CarEngine` subhierarchy, bodies in the `CarBody` hierarchy, and so on. Hence, we need a way for the application to (1) easily retrieve individual car components from a single parts family while disallowing cross-family errors (we don't want a Toyota engine to go in a Ford car), and (2) use the same parts retrieval code for all parts families. We can accomplish both desiderata with the Abstract Factory pattern.

We have the following car and car parts classes:

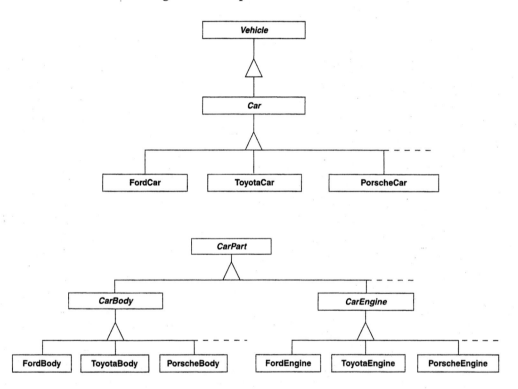

`Vehicle` and `CarPart` are subclasses of `Object`. Of course, this class structure is a gross oversimplification on many levels. Car companies, such as Ford, have several different models of cars, bodies, engines, even engine types (e.g., gasoline-powered or diesel engines). Thus a real-world model would have many more levels of abstraction than what we've shown here. However, keeping things simple and manageable suits our pattern illustration purpose.

We begin the pattern implementation by defining an abstract factory class, `Car-PartFactory`. This is the class that "provides an interface for creating families of related or dependent objects without specifying their concrete classes" (see the Intent section). It defines the abstract **Product**-creation methods, such as `make-Car`, `makeEngine`, and `makeBody`. Then, we define concrete factory subclasses, one per Product family. Each subclass redefines the Product creation methods to

create and return the appropriate parts. So we add a new subhierarchy under
`Object`:

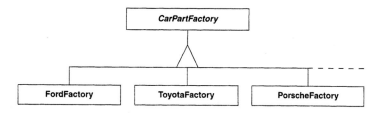

To implement the part creation methods, we start with the abstract factory class,

```
CarPartFactory>>makeCar
    self subclassResponsibility

CarPartFactory>>makeEngine
    self subclassResponsibility

CarPartFactory>>makeBody
    self subclassResponsibility
```

and add the concrete subclasses that override these methods:

```
FordFactory>>makeCar
    ^FordCar new

FordFactory>>makeEngine
    ^FordEngine new

FordFactory>>makeBody
    ^FordBody new


ToyotaFactory>>makeCar
    ^ToyotaCar new

ToyotaFactory>>makeEngine
    ^ToyotaEngine new

ToyotaFactory>>makeBody
    ^ToyotaBody new
```

Overall, our factories look like this:

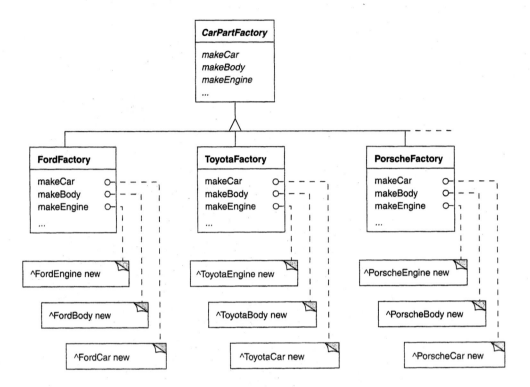

With Abstract Factory, it's up to the factory's client to put the pieces together. The factory ensures that the parts are from a single parts family, but the factory only returns the parts; it does not assemble them into a final product. That's the client's job.[2] (We'll see later that this is a major difference between the Abstract Factory and Builder (47) patterns.)

Let's assume a `CarAssembler` object is the factory client, and it has an instance variable named `factory` that references a `CarPartFactory` object:

```
CarAssembler>>assembleCar
    | car |
    "Create the top-level part, the car object which
    starts out having no subcomponents, and add an
    engine, body, etc."
```

---

[2]This is true even when the factory's parts are themselves complex composed parts. For example, a factory may return a preassembled part such as a composite pane incorporating several subcomponent widgets. Nonetheless, to the factory client, this is a single part that may be incorporated into a more complex product, like a window.

```
car := factory makeCar.³
car
    addEngine: factory makeEngine;
    addBody: factory makeBody;
    ...
^car
```

If `factory` were an instance of `FordFactory`, the engine that gets added to the car would be a `FordEngine`; if it were a `ToyotaFactory`, a `ToyotaEngine` would be created by `factory makeEngine` and would then be added to the car in progress.

There's still one piece of the puzzle missing. How does the `CarAssembler` (the factory client) obtain an instance of a specific `CarPartFactory` subclass? It might instantiate a particular subclass itself, based on the consumer's choice, or it may be handed a factory instance by an external object. In both cases, however, the code to create the car and its component subparts remains the same. That is, since all `CarPartFactory` classes implement the identical messaging protocol polymorphically, the factory's client does not care what type of factory it is talking to. It just sends the generic messages offered by the factory protocol.

Because of the power of polymorphism, the client implements one version of code, rather than a bunch of conditionals, and can still produce any type of car. As a comparison, without the Abstract Factory pattern, the car creation code could have looked something like this:

```
CarAssembler>>assembleCar
    "Without Abstract Factory."
    | car |
    car := (consumerChoice == #Ford
            ifTrue: [FordCar new]
            ifFalse: [consumerChoice == #Toyota
                ifTrue: [ToyotaCar new]
                ifFalse: [consumerChoice == #Porsche
                        ifTrue: [PorscheCar new]
                        ifFalse: [...]).
    car addEngine:
            (consumerChoice == #Ford
                ifTrue: [FordEngine new]
                ifFalse: [...]).
    ...
    ^car
```

---

³At first blush, it may seem confusing to start the car assembly process by saying `factory makeCar`, creating a new `Car`, which is the ultimate product of the assembly task. In fact, this is the conventional way of building a complex object. In Visual Smalltalk, for instance, when we start to construct a `Menu`, we say `Menu new`. What we have at this point is a mere shell of a menu; it doesn't function as a menu until we add subcomponent `MenuItems`. Similarly, `factory makeCar` returns an empty shell of a `Car` to which we must add components like an engine and body.

Here, the `CarAssembler` decides itself what sort of car to build and what its subparts ought to be, and it performs the actual part instantiation. The Abstract Factory solution lets us abstract all of these behaviors out of the `CarAssembler` object and into a separate one, the factory. After configuring the `CarAssembler` with a specific car factory, the `CarAssembler` simply calls on this factory to create the car and its subparts.

The Abstract Factory approach results in a more modular, more easily extensible design. To add new types of cars to the system, we need only add a new subclass of `CarPartFactory` and code to instantiate it, rather than having to revisit `CarAssembler>>buildCar` to add new parts in multiple locations within a complex set of conditional statements.

There are two abstractions in effect here. First, all `CarPartFactorys` implement the same message interface. That lets the factory client send the same part creation messages without caring exactly what type of `CarPartFactory` it's sending them to. Second, the ConcreteProducts (the car parts classes) implement the same interface, defined in the abstract superclasses of each part subhierarchy. So, for example, all `Cars` know how to respond to the `addEngine:` and `addBody:` messages. `CarBody` objects all implement the `color:` and `color` messages. All `CarEngines` similarly offer a common messaging interface. The same is true for other parts.

To round out this discussion, let's assume that the factory client is handed its factory object by an outsider, as in *Design Patterns*. This implies the `CarAssembler` never knows exactly what sort of `CarPartFactory` it is using. This can be accomplished by either (1) defining the factory client, the `CarAssembler`, to have an instance variable that references its factory object, or (2) just passing the factory object as an argument to the client's car creation method. In the first case, we would define the `CarAssembler` class and the relevant methods as follows:

```
Object subclass: #CarAssembler
    instanceVariableNames: 'factory'
    classVariableNames: ''
    poolDictionaries: ''

CarAssembler>>factory: aCarPartFactory
    "Setter method"
    factory := aCarPartFactory

CarAssembler class>>using: aCarPartFactory
    "Instance creation method"
    ^self new factory: aCarPartFactory
```

The outside object, the client of the `CarAssembler`, would create and initialize its `CarAssembler` with the appropriate factory instance. Let's say the Car-Assembler's client is an interactive 3D automobile visualization application. The user can select the car of choice at the user interface; in response, the application renders a three-dimensional graphical image of the car on the screen. The user can see what the car looks like and navigate in three-dimensional space to "tour" (get closer, internal views of) the interior, the engine, or anything else of interest. Let's say the car to build is based on the user's selection of a button on the screen—that is, the user can click on a *Ford, Toyota,* or *Porsche* button to make his or her car choice. In response, the user interface code might do something like this:

```
CarAssemblerUI>>fordButtonClicked
    "The user clicked the 'Ford' button."
    | assembler car |
    assembler := CarAssembler using: FordFactory new.
    car := assembler assembleCar.
    "Now, draw the assembled car on the screen:"
    ...
```

For solution variation number 2, the `CarAssembler` does not have an instance variable referencing its factory object. Instead the factory is simply passed in when its client wants a car assembled. This changes the `assembleCar` method to take a single argument:

```
CarAssembler>>assembleCarUsing: aCarPartFactory
    | car |
    car := aCarPartFactory makeCar.
    car
        addEngine: aCarPartFactory makeEngine;
        addBody: aCarPartFactory makeBody;
        ...
    ^car
```

Implementation and Sample Code

We have presented the essential ingredients of the Abstract Factory pattern— enough for you to use it in your own applications. In this section, we discuss a number of variations on the Abstract Factory theme—in particular, various ways of implementing the factory object. Some of these variations are considered in *Design Patterns;* in addition we've added some Smalltalk-specific varieties. We'll point out some upsides and downsides of individual implementations, but we're not advocating one solution over another; rather, we're simply demonstrating that this, like all other patterns, may be implemented in a variety of ways. The choice often depends on additional constraints imposed by the specific application and interactions with other objects therein, or personal preferences and aesthetics. As Christopher Alexander and his colleagues assert, a pattern provides the fundamental ideas and concepts for the solution of a particular problem, but you can realize it "in your own way, by adapting it to your preferences, and the local conditions" (Alexander et al., 1977, p. xiii).

A Vanilla Implementation for Car Factories

In our example application, CarPartFactory defines the interface for all car factories. Alternative factories are defined as subclasses of CarPartFactory, and each of these overrides the appropriate part creation methods. In the most straightforward, vanilla implementation, each of these methods hard-codes the class to instantiate and return, as in:

```
FordFactory>>makeEngine
    ^FordEngine new

PorscheFactory>>makeEngine
    ^PorscheEngine new
```

This approach localizes the code for each part. Of course, localizing methods means localizing later changes. Let's say Toyota begins to buy its engines from Ford (stranger things have happened in the auto industry!). The new type of engine implies changing only the ToyotaFactory>>makeEngine method to return a FordEngine instance; all client code remains unchanged.

A Constant Method Solution

The previous implementation is the most straightforward, but in it we hard-coded the classes to instantiate in each method for each part in every factory class. This requires a makeEngine, makeBody, and so on method in CarPart-Factory and every one of its concrete subclasses. We can alternatively apply one of the Constant Method variations of the Factory Method (63) pattern. Here we'll define each part creation method just once and have each factory class merely "name" the parts classes to instantiate using Constant Methods (Beck, 1997) that simply return a class object.

We start by redefining the part creation methods in the abstract superclass as factory methods:

```
CarPartFactory>>makeCar
    ^self carClass new

CarPartFactory>>makeEngine
    ^self engineClass new

CarPartFactory>>makeBody
    ^self bodyClass new
```

Then we define the Constant Methods in each factory class:

```
FordFactory>>carClass
    ^FordCar

FordFactory>>engineClass
    ^FordEngine
```

```
FordFactory>>bodyClass
    ^FordBody

PorscheFactory>>carClass
    ^PorscheCar

PorscheFactory>>engineClass
    ^PorscheEngine

PorscheFactory>>bodyClass
    ^PorscheBody
```

We've modularized the code such that when a new car factory class is defined, it need only name its corresponding parts classes. Still, in the car assembly example, the difference between this and the vanilla implementation is not dramatic.

A Part Catalog Solution

In the preceding implementations, each part of a car requires its own method in the factory classes (e.g., makeBody, makeEngine). This can lead to a profusion of methods in the factory. If we ever add new types of parts to cars—say, a new type of deluxe CD audio system—we would have to add a new makeDeluxeCD-AudioSystem method in CarPartFactory and all of its subclasses, and in doing so we will have enlarged the interface that factory clients must know about.

Design Patterns describes a way around this problem (DP 90 and following) that takes advantage of the fact that classes are first-class objects in Smalltalk. The implementation has CarPartFactory storing the classes of the car parts in a "part catalog" and having a single parameterized part creation method rather than one per part.

This approach involves adding a partCatalog instance variable to the CarPartFactory class and initializing it as a Dictionary whose keys are part types (as Symbols) and whose corresponding values are the appropriate classes. The partCatalog in the FordFactory class would look like this:

Key	Value
#car	\<the FordCar class object>
#engine	\<the FordEngine class object>
#body	\<the FordBody class object>
. . .	. . .

Here are the new CarPartFactory class definition and methods that make this approach possible:

```
Object subclass: #CarPartFactory
    instanceVariableNames: 'partCatalog'
    classVariableNames: ''
    poolDictionaries: ''

CarPartFactory class>>new
    ^self basicNew initialize

CarPartFactory>>initialize
    partCatalog := Dictionary new
```

Subclasses would override the `initialize` method to build their own version of the part catalog:

```
FordFactory>>initialize
    super initialize.
    partCatalog
        at: #car put: FordCar;
        at: #body put: FordBody;
        at: #engine put: FordEngine;
        ...
    ^self

PorscheFactory>>initialize
    super initialize.
    partCatalog
        at: #car put: PorscheCar;
        at: #body put: PorscheBody;
        at: #engine put: PorscheEngine;
        ...
    ^self
```

We now define a single method, in the abstract superclass, for part creation. It takes the part type as an argument:

```
CarPartFactory>>make: partType
    "Create a new part based on partType."
    | partClass |
    partClass := partCatalog at: partType ifAbsent: [^nil].
    ^partClass new
```

Now car factory clients (such as `CarAssemblers`) can create all parts using this single message. Part creation code now looks like this:

```
anAutoFactory make: #engine.
anAutoFactory make: #body.
```

rather than this:

```
anAutoFactory makeEngine.
anAutoFactory makeBody.
```

With this part catalog approach, concrete classes in the `CarPartFactory` hierarchy need only define a single method for initializing their unique part catalogs. All other part creation behavior is defined in the abstract `CarPartFactory` class.

Another Implementation of Different Part Catalogs

Given the "part catalog" approach, there is another way of implementing the different factories. Here again we use subclassing to provide for alternative factories, thus still requiring clients to choose among `FordFactory`, `ToyotaFactory`, and `PorscheFactory`. But since the part catalog ought to be the same for all instances of each factory class, we can define `partCatalog` as a class instance variable, code a class method in each of the factory classes to initialize the class variable appropriately, and invoke that initialization method just once for each class.

We redefine the abstract class as follows:

```
Object subclass: #CarPartFactory
   instanceVariableNames: ''
   classVariableNames: ''
   poolDictionaries: ''

CarPartFactory class
   instanceVariableNames: 'partCatalog'

CarPartFactory class>>make: partType
   "We moved this method; it's a class method now."
   | partClass |
   partClass := partCatalog at: partType ifAbsent: [^nil].
   ^partClass new
```

We now have an class instance variable for each concrete `CarPartFactory` subclass. Unlike class variables whose contents are shared among all subclasses, each subclass gets its own private version of that class instance variable. So when we initialize `FordFactory`'s `partCatalog`, we don't affect `ToyotaFactory`'s `partCatalog`. We can initialize each class's catalog as follows:

```
CarPartFactory class>>new
   partCatalog isNil ifTrue: [self initialize].
   ^self basicNew

CarPartFactory class>>initialize
   "Initialize the part catalog. This is now a class method."
   partCatalog := Dictionary new
```

```
FordFactory class>>initialize
   "Initialize the *local* part catalog."
   super initialize.
   partCatalog
      at: #car put: FordCar;
      at: #body put: FordBody;
      at: #engine put: FordEngine;
      ...
```

All we have left is to redefine our single part creation instance method to use the class instance variable rather than an instance variable. It simply invokes the class method with the same signature:

```
CarPartFactory>>make: partType
   "Create a new part based on partType."
   ^self class make: partType
```

Nonetheless, as pointed out on page DP 90, this approach requires a new concrete factory subclass for each product family (one for Fords, one for Toyotas, etc.). Although we've narrowed the messaging interface to a single method, factory clients still must choose among several factory classes to instantiate. That, to a small extent, may reduce its flexibility: Although it is certainly a simple task to add new subclasses as new product families arise, we can build a more compact single-class implementation.

A Single Factory Class

The single-class solution is to implement only one factory class and to initialize each *instance's* part catalog (we're back to having partCatalog as an instance variable) with the appropriate part classes to instantiate. In other words, CarPartFactory will have no subclasses; clients will always instantiate CarPartFactory itself.

In this approach, we implement simple class methods in CarPartFactory, each with a meaningful factory creation name. Each of these methods performs the necessary initialization for different types of factories. They look like this:

```
CarPartFactory class>>fordFactory
   "Create and return a new Ford factory."
   | catalog |
   catalog := Dictionary new.
   catalog
      at: #car put: FordCar;
      at: #engine put: FordEngine;
      ...
   ^self new partCatalog: catalog
```

```
CarPartFactory class>>porscheFactory
   "Create and return a new Porsche factory."
   | catalog |
   catalog := Dictionary new.
   catalog
      at: #car put: PorscheCar;
      at: #engine put: PorscheEngine;
      ...
   ^self new partCatalog: catalog
```

When a `CarPartFactory` client wants to create a Ford factory, the message-send looks like:

```
carFactory := CarPartFactory fordFactory.
```

Parts are created exactly as before:

```
carFactory make: #engine.
```

A Sneaky Single-Class Implementation

We can implement another single-class factory using an approach that benefits from the facts that (1) we've defined all of our classes following a consistent naming convention, and (2) Smalltalk is reflective. All parts class names are prefixed with the car manufacturer name and all end in a part name suffix: `FordEngine`, `ToyotaEngine`, `PorscheEngine`; `FordCar`, `ToyotaCar`, `PorscheCar`. We can take advantage of this as follows:

```
CarPartFactory>>makeCar: manufacturersName
   "manufacturersName is a Symbol, such as
   #Ford, #Toyota, or #Porsche."
   | carClass |
   carClass := Smalltalk
                  at: (manufacturersName, #Car) asSymbol
                  ifAbsent: [^nil].
   ^carClass new

CarPartFactory>>makeEngine: manufacturersName
   | engineClass |
   engineClass := Smalltalk
                  at: (manufacturersName, #Engine) asSymbol
                  ifAbsent: [^nil].
   ^engineClass new
```

We can do this because all global variables are referenced by an entry in the `Smalltalk` dictionary, and classes are referenced by a global of the same name as the class. Thus, the expression `Smalltalk at: #FordEngine` retrieves the `FordEngine` class object.

With this approach, car factories will always be instances of `CarPartFactory`. Car-part creation now takes the following form (where `carCompany` is a `Symbol` obtained from the user):

```
carFactory := CarPartFactory new.
car := carFactory makeCar: carCompany.
car
    addEngine: (carFactory makeEngine: carCompany);
    ...
```

There is a downside to this approach, however. The code is harder to understand from either a static inspection or a dynamic runtime trace because it references and sends messages to classes whose identity is constructed on the fly. For example, if we were to use tools of the Smalltalk development environment to find all methods that reference, say, the `FordCar` class, the `makeCar:` method would not be included in the resultant method list. Even though `makeCar:` implicitly references all of the car classes, it does not specify them explicitly in the code.

Known Smalltalk Uses

UILookPolicy

In VisualWorks, a `UIBuilder` has the responsibility (among other things) of constructing a window based on a set of widget specifications. For each widget, the `UIBuilder` calls on its associated `UILookPolicy` object to perform the actual widget instance creation. Different subclasses of `UILookPolicy` polymorphically implement these creation messages in order to instantiate different widgets according to the currently selected look and feel (Windows, OS/2, Motif, Macintosh, or default Smalltalk look). But the `UIBuilder` has no knowledge of what type of look policy object it is dealing with. That is, it doesn't know or care whether it is linked to an instance of `Win3LookPolicy`, `CUALookPolicy`, or any other policy object; it merely sends the generic widget creation messages defined in the abstract `UILookPolicy` protocol. Thus, the look policy object acts as an Abstract Factory for widgets.

Using Constant Methods

We have already shown how Abstract Factory can be implemented using Constant Methods. An example is presented again by `UILookPolicy` (we mention this example in the Factory Method pattern as well). For example, here's the method in `UILookPolicy` that creates slider widgets:

```
slider: spec into: builder
    ...
    component := self sliderClass model: model.
    ...
```

The `model:` message instantiates the class returned by `sliderClass. UILook-Policy` defines the default version of `sliderClass`, and some of its concrete subclasses override it in order to create sliders with a different look:

```
UILookPolicy>>sliderClass
    ^SliderView

MacLookPolicy>>sliderClass
    ^MacSliderView

Win3LookPolicy>>sliderClass
    ^Win3SliderView
```

Related Patterns

Builder

Abstract Factory is closely related to Builder (47). The primary difference is in terms of who is in charge of the overall product assembly. In Abstract Factory, the factory returns parts that are guaranteed to work or go together. But it is the factory client who assembles them into a single final product. Every message sent to the factory results in a new part or subcomponent of the overall final product—that is, each part creation method in the factory returns a component part—and the factory's client adds each of these parts to its evolving product. On the other hand, a Builder has its own internal state for maintaining the product while it is being assembled. The Builder is told, "Add component A," "Add component B," and it is the Builder that adds these subcomponents to its encapsulated Product. For each "Add component X" message-send, the Builder returns nothing. When the Builder's client has finished adding subparts, the client tells the Builder, "Give me the final product." Only then does the Builder returns the ultimate product.

Factory Method

We have demonstrated that a factory object may invoke a Constant Method variation of the Factory Method (63) pattern to decide which classes to instantiate. Additionally, Factory Method is actually a competitor to Abstract Factory, but the two patterns are in some sense the structural inverse of the other. In the textbook vanilla implementation of Abstract Factory, we define multiple concrete factory classes in order to account for multiple parts families—one class per family. Then we can have a single application object instantiate parts from any family using the same code. The application simply instantiates the factory class associated with the desired parts family (if you want Ford parts, you instantiate `Ford-Factory`). Notice in the Structure diagram that a single client points to a factory object from a subhierarchy of factory classes.

If we use a Factory Method approach, we can avoid defining an entire hierarchy of factory classes. But we would need a hierarchy of application classes instead. We would need an abstract application class that defines the bulk of the behavior for all concrete subclasses but leaves the definition of the factory methods to the subclasses. Each subclass would override the factory methods accordingly: a Ford application class would have its factory methods return Ford parts, a Toyota-related application class would have factory methods that create and return Toyota parts objects, and so forth.

BUILDER (DP 97)   Object Creational

Intent

Separate the construction of a complex object from its internal representation so that the same construction process can create different representations.

Structure

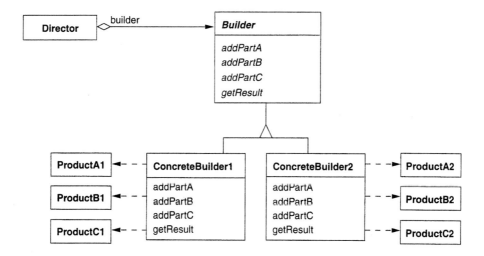

Discussion

We suggest you read the Abstract Factory pattern (31) before continuing here because there are several mutual issues with regard to the problem context—the situation under which the two patterns may apply—and the pattern solutions.

Suppose an application needs to build complex objects based on user selections or specifications from other objects. Say it's a car assembly application much like that described in Abstract Factory. The application must be able to build different products, specifically Ford, Toyota, or Porsche cars.[4] We *could* set a flag in the application to specify the type of product to create. Each time we need to create a component (say, an engine) of the overall product, we would perform a conditional based on that flag *(see next page):*

---

[4]For illustrative purposes, we'll use an oversimplification. Of course, there are more than three automakers, several different models produced by each manufacturer, etc.

```
AnApplication>>createEngine
   "Without Builder"
   manufacturer == #Ford
      ifTrue: [^FordEngine new].
   manufacturer == #Toyota
      ifTrue: [^ToyotaEngine new].
   ^PorscheEngine new
```

We would need the same sort of logic for every car and car component. We would also have to give this object the know-how to assemble the subcomponent parts (engines, bodies, transmissions) into a coherent final product (a car). That's a lot of behavior for a single class. And it's not very extensible. Just because we have three known car brands now is no guarantee that users or the application domain won't require some other component types in the future (e.g., a new car line, Saturn, is introduced to the market). We need a design that lets us extend the application's functionality—that is, add new component types—without modifying the main application itself.

The Builder pattern offers a solution. It makes a separate Builder object responsible for creating and assembling components on the application's behalf. The application can use a Ford Builder to put Fords together, a Toyota Builder to assemble Toyotas, or a Porsche Builder to assemble Porsches.

Builder separates a thing being built and details of how it gets constructed from a client of that thing. The thing being built is called the **Product;** in our example, this is the overall car. The client is called the **Director** because it's in control of the overall construction process. The Director knows what generic subcomponents go in the Product (in our example, an engine, a car body, etc.) but not which component classes to instantiate for different types of Products (e.g., if a Ford is being constructed and an engine is required, we ought to instantiate the FordEngine class). Further, the Director does not know how to put the Product together, so it enlists the help of an external helper, a Builder object. The Builder provides a message interface for both adding subcomponent parts and retrieving the ultimate Product.

We need several different types of Builders (a Ford, a Toyota, and a Porsche Builder), and the application will select the one to use at runtime depending on user preference or programmatic circumstances. To make this possible, we will define multiple Builder classes and have them all respond polymorphically to the same set of building messages. Hence the code in the Director won't care what sort of Builder it's talking to, so long as it adheres to the established Builder protocol. Thus, by plugging different Builders together with a Director, the same Director can construct very different Products without having to change the Director object.

The Builder pattern greatly simplifies the implementation of the Director class since the Director has no direct knowledge of the Product's internal representations encapsulated within the Builder or of how to put the Product together. Additionally, it's easy to change a Builder's behavior or add new types of Builders to an application because the Builders have been separated out into separate classes that typically reside in a single subhierarchy. Hence, we know where to go to make these modifications, and enhancements to the available Builders require no modification to the Director itself.

Collaborations

The following interaction diagram portrays the Builder pattern's collaborations. It differs somewhat from the *Design Patterns* collaboration diagram on page DP 99, which has both a Director object and a client to that Director, the latter presumably an object central to the application. We don't believe it's necessary to have both; there's no real reason for an intervening Director sitting between the application and the Builder. Once again, you may choose to implement the pattern that way, but it's really a matter of personal aesthetics. Should the application itself be in charge of the building process or delegate this task to a separate Director? Our version of the pattern lets the application assume the Director role.

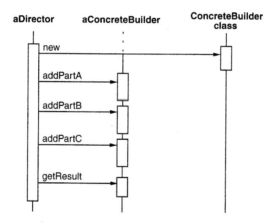

Our diagram is also different because in Smalltalk we need to account for the runtime messages sent to class objects for instance creation. Once a Builder class is selected and instantiated, the Director repeatedly asks the Builder object to build new parts (messages addPartA, addPartB, and addPartC). In response, the Builder adds parts to its developing Product. When a subcomponent part is added, the Builder does not respond with—that is, return—anything of interest (of course, since all methods return something, the receiver object—the Builder— is returned by default). When the building process is complete, the Director asks the Builder for the resultant Product by sending getResult.

Implementation

Adding Parts

The Builder has some form of internal state: as subcomponent specifications are received, the Builder adds new parts to its encapsulated Product. Actually, the Builder has the choice of instantiating subcomponents each time the Director says, "Add part so-and-so," or of merely saving the "so-and-so" specification and building the final Product in its entirety when the get Result message is received. In either case, nonetheless, some data are encapsulated within the Builder until the final Product is retrieved by a client.

There are at least three variations on the "add part" theme.

1. The interaction diagram shows that the Director merely tells the Builder to add specific types of parts to its Product—for example, add a component of type A, add a part of type B, add a four-cylinder engine, add a two-door coupe body. The Builder just instantiates the appropriate class and adds the new part to its evolving Product.

2. The Director may hand "raw material" to its Builder and tell the Builder to perform some transformation on that raw part and add the result to the Product. *Design Patterns* offers the example of converting the information in a file from one format (e.g., Rich Text Format) to another (e.g., TeX). There, an "Add part" request might imply, "Here's an RTF font-change token; convert it to a TeX font-change specification, and then add it to your Product." Thus the Builder must be implemented with more know-how than simply instantiating the appropriate class.

3. The Director can give an abstract specification of a component to the Builder, leaving it to the Builder to interpret the specification, construct an object based on it, and add that object to its Product. This is essentially what is done in VisualWorks's `UIBuilder`: the VisualWorks `UIPainter`, which lets users lay out the widgets of a user interface (UI) window, generates an abstract specification based on the layout. This includes specifications for all of the window's widgets: their type, location, size, content (e.g., the text to appear in a label), etc. These specifications are saved in a method of the application class associated with the UI window. At application start-up, these "window specs" are passed to a `UIBuilder`, which creates each widget and adds it to the overall window.

Multiple Families of Products

We typically have multiple parts families but want a Builder to create parts from a single family. In our example, we want cars and their subparts instantiated from the Ford, Toyota, or Porsche family. In Abstract Factory, we discussed how the code in a factory object may choose among product families. The implementation issues are the same for Builder. We can define multiple Builder classes, each of which hard-codes the component classes to instantiate; we can use part catalogs; we can apply the Factory Method pattern; we can even define a single Builder class with different methods that create parts from different Product families. We've shown how to implement all of these options in Abstract Factory, but let's look in more detail at the Factory Method solution for Builder and follow that with an alternative solution not considered previously.

Using Factory Method (63).   Different Builders add the same component with the identical message; for example, to add a two-door sedan body, we send add2DoorSedanBody to the Builder. This method looks the same in all the Builder classes except for the actual class that gets instantiated:

```
CarBuilder>>add2DoorSedanBody
    "Do nothing. Subclasses will override."

FordBuilder>>add2DoorSedanBody
    self car
        addBody: Ford2DoorSedanBody new

ToyotaBuilder>>add2DoorSedanBody
    self car
        addBody: Toyota2DoorSedanBody new

PorscheBuilder>>add2DoorSedanBody
    self car
        addBody: Porsche2DoorSedanBody new
```

Alternatively, we can avoid the duplication of code and implement a factory method in each concrete Builder class, as follows:

```
CarBuilder>>add2DoorSedanBody
    "Define this once for all subclasses. Subclasses will
    override the 'create2DoorSedanBody' factory method."
    self car
        addBody: self create2DoorSedanBody

CarBuilder>>create2DoorSedanBody
    "Factory method; This should only be implemented
    by my concrete subclasses."
    self implementedBySubclass        "Visual Smalltalk"
    "self subclassResponsibility"     "VisualWorks, IBM, others"

FordBuilder>>create2DoorSedanBody
    "Factory method; Return an instance of the Ford
    2-door-sedan body class."
    ^Ford2DoorSedanBody new

ToyotaBuilder>>create2DoorSedanBody
    "Return an instance of the Toyota 2-door-sedan
    body class."
    ^Toyota2DoorSedanBody new
```

```
PorscheBuilder>>create2DoorSedanBody
    "Return a Porsche 2-door-sedan body object."
    ^Porsche2DoorSedanBody new
```

Using Abstract Factory (31).   There is another alternative method for selecting among Product families. Let's look at an existing example of this approach from VisualWorks.

A UIBuilder is asked to build the widgets of a window. Since VisualWorks supports the interface look and feel of multiple operating systems, there are multiple families of widgets: a Motif family (classes like MotifRadioButton), an OS/2 CUA family (CUARadioButton), and so on. The UIBuilder must create widgets from the currently selected look-and-feel family. For example, if the user selected the OS/2 CUA look, the UIBuilder must instantiate CUARadio-Button when a radio button is being created.

We could solve this problem as we have already described: define several Builder classes and instantiate the one we want. Here we might define UIBuilder as an abstract class, with concrete subclasses such as MotifUIBuilder, CUAUI-Builder, and MacUIBuilder. Instead, VisualWorks applies the Abstract Factory pattern as a secondary helper pattern.

A UIBuilder is configured with a UILookPolicy object to which it delegates its widget creation tasks; that is, the Builder asks its look policy to instantiate each of the widgets in the window. Different concrete subclasses of the abstract UILookPolicy class implement the same widget creation messages but construct widgets according to a particular look and feel: MacLookPolicy creates radio buttons, which appear as they do on a Macintosh screen, and MotifLook-Policy instances create Motif-like buttons. Depending on the desired look and feel, one of these subclasses is instantiated as the UIBuilder's look policy object. The UIBuilder has no knowledge of what sort of look is being constructed or what sort of look policy object it is talking to; it merely sends the widget creation messages defined in the abstract UILookPolicy protocol.

So the UILookPolicy object acts as a factory for the UIBuilder, and the UIBuilder/UILookPolicy framework is an instance of the Abstract Factory pattern. There is a single Builder class, UIBuilder, but it can create Products from multiple Product (widget) families.

Sample Code

Now let's look at an example that expands on our car assembly application. Suppose we have an application that allows a user to walk into a generic car sales showroom, step up to a computer in a kiosk, and assemble an order for a car. This application might alternatively be deployed on the Web as a virtual car sales showroom. Imagine that this showroom does not sell cars made by a particular company; rather, the customer can select *any* brand of car. She may also choose the options she desires. Imagine a typical user scenario wherein the user selects a Honda automobile and options such as the two-door sedan body type, four-cylinder engine, automatic transmission, air-conditioning, luxury audio package, and deluxe paint trim, and then selects a menu item that says *Order*.

We'd like this application to have a common user interface for all cars and options, and we'd like to assemble a virtual car based on the user's selections. That is, as in the Abstract Factory example, the application will render a three-dimensional, navigable image of the car on the screen, allowing the customer to view and "tour" the car. Before actually ordering the car, she can change the car's configuration and view it again. Finally, the application generates an order for the car as the user described it.

Assume Product classes similar to those used in Abstract Factory, except there will be more of them. Since we're allowing for the selection of options, we'll have classes like the following rather than just a `FordEngine` class:

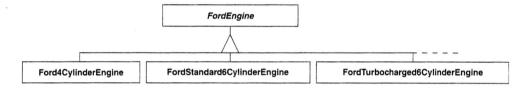

We'll have similar subhierarchies under `ToyotaEngine`, `PorscheEngine`, `FordBody`, `ToyotaBody`, `PorscheBody`, and likewise for all other components.

With regard to the Builder portion of this application, we start by defining a `CarBuilder` hierarchy:

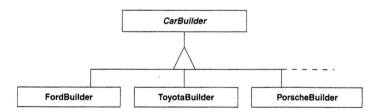

```
Object subclass: #CarBuilder
    instanceVariableNames: 'car'
    classVariableNames: ''
    poolDictionaries: ''

CarBuilder class>>new
    ^self basicNew initialize

CarBuilder>>car
    "getter method"
    ^car

CarBuilder>>car: aCar
    "setter method"
    car := aCar
```

```
CarBuilder subclass: #FordBuilder
    instanceVariableNames: ''
    classVariableNames: ''
    poolDictionaries: ''

CarBuilder subclass: #ToyotaBuilder
    ...

CarBuilder subclass: #PorscheBuilder
    ...
```

The `car` instance variable in `CarBuilder` references the Builder's Product. When a Builder is first instantiated, `car` is initialized to an instance of the appropriate `Car` subclass (an empty shell; a Car with no subcomponents yet):

```
FordBuilder>>initialize
    self car: FordCar new

ToyotaBuilder>>initialize
    self car: ToyotaCar new

PorscheBuilder>>initialize
    self car: PorscheCar new
```

As the Builder receives requests to add components, it adds them to `car`. Let's define the "add a subcomponent" messages: we define these messages in the abstract superclass to do nothing, overriding them as necessary in concrete Builder subclasses:

```
CarBuilder>>add4CylinderEngine
    "Do nothing. Subclasses will override."

FordBuilder>>add4CylinderEngine
    self car addEngine: Ford4CylinderEngine new

ToyotaBuilder>>add4CylinderEngine
    self car addEngine: Toyota4CylinderEngine new

PorscheBuilder>>add4CylinderEngine
    self car addEngine: Porsche4CylinderEngine new


CarBuilder>>addStandard6CylinderEngine
    "Do nothing. Subclasses will override."

FordBuilder>>addStandard6CylinderEngine
    self car addEngine: FordStandard6CylinderEngine new

ToyotaBuilder>>addStandard6CylinderEngine
    self car addEngine: ToyotaStandard6CylinderEngine new

PorscheBuilder>>addStandard6CylinderEngine
    self car addEngine: PorscheStandard6CylinderEngine new
```

We're assuming here that Cars know how to add subcomponents to themselves with messages like addEngine:, addBody:, and so on. Although not implemented in our example code, these methods might also signal an error if a client attempts to add more than one engine, body, transmission, or some other part.

Now let's talk about the user interface of the sample application. Users will be able to select a car manufacturer from a menu and then choose the engine type, body type, and other features from corresponding menus. When the user wants to view what has been built so far, he selects *Draw* from the *Action* menu. In response, the application renders the car in the graphics pane (below the menu bar). When the user wants to order the car, he selects *Order* from the same menu. The user interface might look like the following (where additional pull-down menus would be added for *Audio System, Trim,* and other subcomponents):

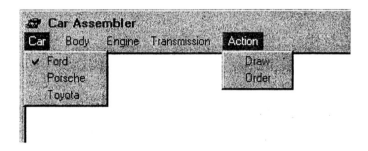

Let's say the user interface is implemented by a CarAssemblerUI object. The CarAssemblerUI is configured with a CarBuilder instance, and the CarAssemblerUI tells this Builder to create and add car components based on the user's selections. Here's some of the code that implements this application in Visual Smalltalk. First, we define the user interface application as a subclass of ViewManager:

```
ViewManager subclass: #CarAssemblerUI
    instanceVariableNames: 'builder'
    classVariableNames: ''
    poolDictionaries: ''
```

The window will include the menus mentioned earlier, along with a single graphics pane in which the car will be drawn. One question to ask now is, How will the CarAssemblerUI instantiate the appropriate Builder class based on the user's choice of car manufacturer? Let's look at the method that builds the *Car* menu, from which the user makes this choice. The method capitalizes on one of Smalltalk's reflective capabilities: determining all subclasses of a class. The menu is constructed with a menu item for each concrete CarBuilder subclass. Each menu item's label is obtained by sending the manufacturer message to the corresponding class. The action associated with each item is a message that invokes the `CarAssemblerUI>>userChoseBuilder:` method, passing the corresponding Builder class object as its argument:

```
CarAssemblerUI>>carMenu
  "Build the car-manufacturers menu."
  | menu |
  menu := Menu new
          title: 'Car';
          owner: self.
  CarBuilder subclasses do: [:aClass |
    menu
      appendItem: aClass manufacturer  "the label"
      action: (Message                 "the action"
              receiver: self
              selector: #userChoseBuilder:
              arguments: (Array with: aClass)) ].
  ^menu
```

When the user selects a manufacturer from the *Car* menu, `userChoseBuilder:` creates the appropriate Builder by instantiating the class passed as the message argument. Subsequently, this Builder is used for creating and assembling all of the car's subcomponent parts:

```
CarAssemblerUI>>userChoseBuilder: builderClass
  builder := builderClass new.
  ...
```

For this to work, we need to define the `manufacturer` method in each of the `CarBuilder` classes:

```
CarBuilder class>>manufacturer
  self implementedBySubclass

FordBuilder class>>manufacturer
  ^'Ford'

ToyotaBuilder class>>manufacturer
  ^'Toyota'

PorscheBuilder class>>manufacturer
  ^'Porsche'
```

Now we need the menus for car subcomponents. We're making the simplifying assumption that all `Cars` may be constructed with the same generic parts; for example, all may include either a four-cylinder, standard six-cylinder, or turbocharged six-cylinder engine. Of course, different Builders instantiate different classes for each engine type. In the case of four-cylinder engines, the application must instantiate `Ford4CylinderEngine`, `Toyota4CylinderEngine`, or `Porsche4CylinderEngine`.

Here's the code that specifies the methods to invoke for the *Engine* menu's entries:

```
CarAssemblerUI>>engineMenu
   ^Menu new
      title: 'Engine';
      owner: self;
      appendItem: '4-Cylinder'
            selector: #engineIs4Cylinder;
      appendItem: '6-Cylinder Standard'
            selector: #engineIsStandard6Cylinder;
      appendItem: '6-Cylinder Turbocharged'
            selector: #engineIsTurbocharged6Cylinder;
      yourself
```

So when the user selects *4-Cylinder* from the *Engine* pull-down menu, the Car-AssemblerUI>>engineIs4Cylinder method is invoked. That method simply sends a generic add4CylinderEngine message to its Builder:

```
CarAssemblerUI>>engineIs4Cylinder
   "The user has selected the '4-cylinder' menu item
    from the 'Engine' pulldown menu. Tell my Builder."
   self builder add4CylinderEngine
```

Each Builder class implements add4CylinderEngine to instantiate the appropriate class depending on its parts family (these methods were defined earlier). The methods for other components are implemented in a similar fashion:

```
CarAssemblerUI>>engineIsStandard6Cylinder
   "The user has selected the 'Standard 6-cylinder'
    menu item from the 'Engine' pulldown menu."
   self builder addStandard6CylinderEngine

CarAssemblerUI>>engineIsTurbocharged6Cylinder
   "The user has selected the 'Turbocharged 6-cylinder'
    menu item from the 'Engine' pulldown menu."
   self builder addTurbocharged6CylinderEngine
```

When the user clicks on the *Order* or *Draw* menu items from the *Action* menu, the application must retrieve the Builder's Product (the assembled car) before passing it to an object that draws, or constructs an order based on, the assembled car.

Let's look at the method invoked when the user selects *Order*:

```
CarAssemblerUI>>orderCar
   "The user has selected the 'Order' menu item, signaling
    all car/components selections have been made."
```

```
| completeCar |
"Get the assembled car from my Builder:"
completeCar := builder assembledCar.
completeCar isNil ifTrue: [^MessageBox message:
  'You haven''t finished assembling a complete car yet!'].
...
"Assemble and print an invoice for the assembled car:"
CarInvoiceMaker new printInvoiceFor: completeCar
```

CarBuilder>>assembledCar is the Builder's "get result" method. It verifies that the car has all essential subcomponents, such as an engine and body, and then returns the completed car:

```
CarBuilder>>assembledCar
    "Return my final Product after verifying there's
    a completed Product to return."
    car isNil ifTrue: [^nil].
    car engine isNil ifTrue: [^nil].
    ...
    ^car
```

Structurally, our application looks like the following diagram.

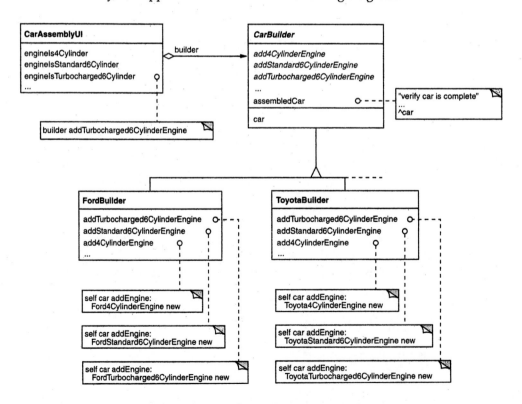

Notice the difference between this and the similar Abstract Factory diagram. In Abstract Factory, the factory can be asked to create an individual component, and it returns the appropriate object. If the factory client wants, it may add each of these parts to a larger product, but the factory itself has no knowledge of this.

A Builder can also be asked to create an individual component, but for each such request, the Builder returns nothing of interest; instead, the newly created component is added to the Product encapsulated within the Builder. Later, when all the subcomponents have been added, the Builder can be asked for its ultimate Product.

Known Smalltalk Uses

Design Patterns mentions three known uses of the Builder pattern in VisualWorks (DP 105). We'll describe one of these, `ClassBuilder`, in detail along with additional examples.

ClassBuilder

In VisualWorks, `ClassBuilder` instances are called on to create new classes or modify existing ones. For example, a typical class creation message looks like this:

```
ASuperclass subclass: #ASubclass
    instanceVariableNames: 'var1 var2'
    classVariableNames: 'ClassVar1'
    poolDictionaries: ''
    category: 'Companion Examples'
```

Here's the implementation of this message directly from the VisualWorks image:

```
Class>>subclass: t instanceVariableNames: f classVariableNames: d
    poolDictionaries: s category: cat
    "This is the standard initialization message for
    creating a new class as a subclass of an existing
    class (the receiver)."

^self classBuilder
    superclass: self;
    environment: self environment;
    className: t;
    instVarString: f;
    classVarString: d;
    poolString: s;
    category: cat;
    beFixed;
    reviseSystem
```

The first message (`self classBuilder`) creates an instance of `ClassBuilder` using a factory method. As shown on the following page, the `Behavior>>classBuilder` method looks like this (class `Class` inherits from `Behavior`):

```
Behavior>>classBuilder
   ^ClassBuilder new
```

Subsequently, this ClassBuilder instance is sent a bunch of messages to set various subcomponent attributes of the class being created or modified. For example, the class's superclass is set, and the class's name is assigned. Finally, in reviseSystem the ClassBuilder either constructs a new class object (if the class does not already exist) or modifies the existing class. This is the "get result" Builder message.

MenuBuilder

MenuBuilder in VisualWorks implements methods to add individual menu parts (menu items, separator lines, submenus). The *information* about each part is appended to the MenuBuilder's internal representation of its Product, but nothing is actually built until the final "get result" message is received. When all the parts have been added, the Director asks the MenuBuilder for the finished Product by sending the menu message. In response, the MenuBuilder constructs and returns a Menu object.

UIBuilder

A UIBuilder in VisualWorks constructs user interface windows and their subcomponent widgets. Specifications for individual interface widgets can be supplied to a UIBuilder with the add: message. When all the widget specifications are added, the UIBuilder can be asked to open the resultant Product, a window. A large set of examples can be found in the UIBuilder class in the VisualWorks image (see the class methods in the *examples* category).

Related Patterns

Strategy

Builder is similar to the Strategy (339) pattern; in fact, it can be said that Builder is a specialization of Strategy. The difference between the two is their intended use. Builder is used to construct new objects, bit by bit, on behalf of a client; different types of Builder objects implement the same generic building protocol but may actually instantiate different classes. Strategy is used to provide an abstract interface to an *algorithm*; that is, a strategy object is a reification of an algorithm as an object; different strategy objects provide alternative implementations of the same generic service.

Abstract Factory

We have already seen that the Builder and Abstract Factory (31) creational patterns are closely related. Both are used in situations where we want to instantiate Products from one of several Product families. The difference is that an Abstract Factory is called on to instantiate and return all component parts (each time it is invoked, the factory returns a Product), and its client *may* assemble them into a more complex object. A Builder is called on in a piecemeal fashion to add components to an ultimate Product, and the Product is encapsulated within the Builder object. The Builder, rather than its client, is the Product assembler now. When the client has added all the component parts it requires, it asks the Builder for its final Product.

FACTORY METHOD (DP 107) · Class Creational

Intent

Define an interface for creating an object, but let subclasses decide which class to instantiate. Factory Method lets a class defer instantiation to subclasses.

Structure

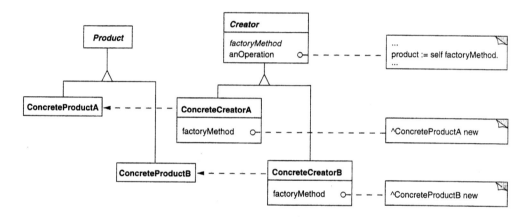

Discussion

Factory Method is straightforward enough, and yet demonstrates the beauty of object-oriented programming. It capitalizes on polymorphism, dynamic binding, and information hiding to deliver an elegant solution to an otherwise potentially messy problem. It also facilitates the creation of frameworks and concrete instantiations thereof.

A framework defines a set of subhierarchies and how instances of these classes work together to produce the core of a specific class of application (e.g., a document editor) or a particular type of reusable service, function, or application component (e.g., a user interface framework). The abstract classes at the root of each participating hierarchy branch define the generic operations implemented by the framework, thereby delineating how the objects in the framework behave and interact. Actual instantiations of the framework consist of instances of the concrete subclasses of these root classes.

In a typical framework, objects from one hierarchy—let's call its base class `Principal`—are associated with instances from a second hierarchy—call its topmost class `Associate`. Often different classes in the `Principal` tree need to collaborate with different subclasses of `Associate`. For example, instances of

`Principal2`, a subclass of `Principal`, might have to be paired with instances of `Associate2`, and `Principal3` objects must collaborate with `Associate3` instances. Factory Method facilitates this class architecture by letting each class in the `Principal` hierarchy specify its collaborating class and by locating this decision in a method whose only task is to instantiate the desired class.

The latter design decision simplifies the overall code by having the instantiation task cleanly separated into its own method. It also potentially avoids the replication of lots of code. We may have an arbitrarily complex method in `Principal` that at some point creates its corresponding `Associate` object; with Factory Method we abstract out of that a separate method simply for the `Associate` object instantiation. Without Factory Method—if we hard-code the name of the class to be instantiated inline—we'd have methods in the abstract class that look like this:

```
Principal>>start
   "Without Factory Method."
   ...
   "Associate is an abstract class. Subclasses must
    override this method and change the following line!"
   associate := Associate new.
   associate message1.
   ...
```

Now each `Principal` subclass would have to copy and implement the entire `start` method, if only to override the one line that instantiates the associate object. For example, in `Principal2`, whose instances must be paired with instances of `Associate2`, we would be forced to reimplement `start` like this:

```
Principal2>>start
   "This method is copied from Principal>>start except
    here instantiate Associate2 for my associate object."
   ...
   associate := Associate2 new.
   associate message1.
   ...
```

Factory Method provides a better, more easily extensible solution. We can leave constant those parts of the `start` method that are the same for all classes in the `Principal` hierarchy and abstract out the piece that varies by subclass. That piece is just the code that instantiates the appropriate `Associate` class; it gets moved into a separate method, a **factory method.** Now, `start` looks like this:

```
Principal>>start
   "With Factory Method."
   ...
   associate := self createAssociate.
   associate message1.
   ...
```

The responsibility for creating the associate object has been transferred from the main method to the independent `createAssociate` factory method. As a result, each subclass may simply override `createAssociate` without having to redefine the `start` method. `Principal` and each of its subclasses define their own versions of `createAssociate` to instantiate whichever `Associate` class they require:

```
Principal>>createAssociate
    self subclassResponsibility

Principal2>>createAssociate
    ^Associate2 new

Principal3>>createAssociate
    ^Associate3 new
```

Another benefit is that if we ever need to change the `Associate` class for a particular `Principal` class, the change occurs in a single location. In fact, the `Principal` class may have multiple methods that reference an `Associate` subclass. When these methods hard-code the class name, changing that name involves tracking down those references in every method. In contrast, when using a factory method, we need only change that single method. Even when there is only one `Principal` method that references `Associate`, our job is still simplified because we don't have to dig through code looking for this reference; it is much easier to find the single factory method to fix.[5]

Implementation Using Template Method

Factory Method is always implemented using the Template Method (355) pattern. In the Template Method section, we explain how that pattern involves a broad message that is implemented in terms of several narrower messages in the same receiver. The broader template method is defined in a superclass, and the narrower primitive methods are implemented in that class or its subclasses. The template method invokes primitive methods by sending messages to `self`. In the context of the Factory Method pattern, the factory method is a primitive method. In our example, `start` is the template method, and `createAssociate` is a primitive.

The Document Processing Framework

We'll look at Factory Method's application in a couple of frameworks: the example described in *Design Patterns* and then the granddaddy of Smalltalk frameworks, Model-View-Controller (MVC).

---

[5]This is not as unusual a situation as it may seem. For example, many applications in Smalltalk/V used the `TextPane` class for text widgets. In more recent versions of this environment, such as Visual Smalltalk, the ParcPlace-Digitalk folks implemented a new `TextPaneControl` class that uses the platform's native text widget. As a result, many existing applications had to be modified to instantiate `TextPaneControl` rather than `TextPane`. If they had instantiated their text panes with a factory method rather than inline, this would have been a simple task.

A framework for simple document processing applications appears in *Design Patterns* on page DP 107. We'll provide an example derived from that framework. The abstract classes `Editor` (called `Application` in *Design Patterns*) and `Document` capture the key abstractions and interactions between editors and documents. Their concrete subclasses can be instantiated to create different sorts of editors, such as drawing or text editors.

There are specific, desired mappings between `Editor` subclasses and `Document` subclasses. A drawing editor in this framework provides access to drawing documents, and a text editor offers editing of text files. For the former application, `DrawingEditor` is defined as a subclass of `Editor` and `DrawingDocument` as a subclass of `Document`. For text editing, we have the `TextEditor` and `TextDocument` subclasses.

The framework's definition includes a single factory method in `Editor`, which should be defined as follows:

```
Editor>>createDocument
    "Factory method to instantiate my associated
     Document class. Subclasses must override."
    self subclassResponsibility
```

Each concrete `Editor` subclass overrides the document-creation factory method to instantiate different `Document` subclasses. Thus, we have generic knowledge of how the hierarchies interact in the abstract classes but push application-specific knowledge down to the concrete subclasses. A welcome side effect is that the code in the subclasses can be minimized. In this example, as in many other frameworks, much of the subclasses' behavior is inherited while they polymorphically override document-creation behavior.

Here is the structure diagram for our document processing framework, including sample code that implements the Factory Method pattern:

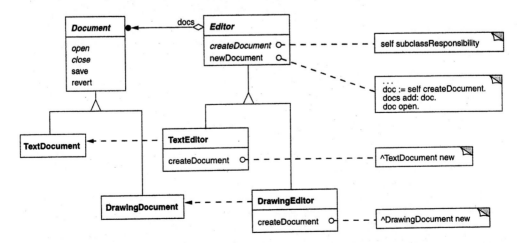

When you want to create a new text editor application, you instantiate `Text-Editor`. When the `TextEditor` needs to create a document, the `newDocument` method—which it inherits from `Editor`—is invoked. That method includes the statement

```
doc := self createDocument.
```

`createDocument` is the factory method overridden by concrete subclasses of `Editor`. So the local `TextEditor>>createDocument` ends up getting invoked, and it creates a new `TextDocument`. Similarly, when a `DrawingEditor`'s `createDocument` method executes, it creates a new `DrawingDocument`. Factory Method thus enforces the desired application-specific relationships—`TextEditor`→`TextDocument` and `DrawingEditor`→`DrawingDocument`—by a generalized mechanism.

Factory Method in Model-View-Controller

As we've seen, Factory Method is useful in situations where there are two hierarchies related to each other. A classic example is provided by the Smalltalk-80 MVC framework where each view (a window or screen widget) has a controller that handles user interaction with the view (via mouse or keyboard). Different types of views require different types of controllers. For example, a `TextView` requires a `TextController`, while a `BitView` needs a `BitEditor` controller. Here is a small portion of the two hierarchies showing their associations (indentation represents relative position in the subhierarchies; some intervening abstract classes are not shown):

View Class	Corresponding Controller Class
View	Controller
ComposedTextView	ParagraphEditor
TextEditorView	TextEditorController
InputFieldView	InputBoxController
TextView	TextController
DebuggerTextView	DebuggerController
ListView	ListController
ChangeListView	ChangeListController
SelectionInListView	SelectionInListController
BitView	BitEditor
ColorBitView	BitEditor (inherited)
BooleanWidgetView	WidgetController
ActionButton	WidgetController (inherited)

There are obviously many classes involved, and new ones may need to be added. Hence, we need an easy and extensible way to associate a particular Controller class with a particular View class.

The designers of VisualWorks had a choice of ways to approach this problem. They could have introduced a registry of class associations. In Smalltalk, this would be implemented with a Dictionary whose keys are View classes and whose values are the associated Controller classes. One problem with this solution concerns maintenance. Suppose a new View subclass must be defined for a new type of widget, and this View requires a new type of Controller. After defining the required classes, we must remember to update the registry. We'd also need a registry entry for every View subclass—even those that wish to use the same controller type as their superclass.

Instead, VisualWorks applies the Factory Method pattern. After a View is instantiated, its controller is created as follows. The first time a client asks for the View's controller with the getController message, lazy initialization handles its creation (this code is directly from the VisualWorks image):

```
View>>getController
    "Answer the receiver's current controller. If the
    receiver's controller is nil (the default case), an
    initialized instance of the receiver's default
    controller is installed and returned."

    controller == nil
        ifTrue: [self setController: self defaultController].
    ^controller
```

In setController:, the view's controller instance variable is set to the result of the expression self defaultController. defaultController is a factory method. Its implementation in the root view class looks like this:

```
View>>defaultController
    ^self defaultControllerClass new
```

In the vanilla Factory Method pattern, described above, defaultController would be the stand-alone factory method; it would both specify and instantiate the appropriate class. For example, this could have been the implementation strategy for View and its subclasses:

```
View>>defaultController
    ^Controller new

TextView>>defaultController
    ^TextController new
```

In a slight modification of the pattern, however, VisualWorks incurs an extra level of indirection. Here defaultController is defined once in the root View class, and it instantiates the class retrieved by sending a second message, `defaultControllerClass`. The latter method simply returns the class to be instantiated. Now subclasses override only the `defaultControllerClass` method to merely name their associated `Controller` class.

The default implementation of `defaultControllerClass` looks like this:

```
View>>defaultControllerClass
    "Answer the class of the default controller for
    the receiver."
    "Subclasses should redefine defaultControllerClass if
    the class of the default controller is not Controller."
    ^Controller
```

The method is overridden by those `View` subclasses that require a different type of controller—for example:

```
TextView>>defaultControllerClass
    ^TextController

BitView>>defaultControllerClass
    ^BitEditor
```

A class that wishes to use the same type of controller as its superclass simply inherits `defaultControllerClass` as is.

Note that the first method in this solution, the "get default instance" factory method (`defaultController`), is also a template method, defined once in class `View` and inherited by all subclasses that may override the embedded "get the class of the default instance" primitive method (`defaultControllerClass`). This method in essence simply returns a constant, a class object—thus, naturally enough, it is what Beck (1997) calls a **Constant Method.** So this variation of the Factory Method pattern invokes the Template Method and Constant Method patterns to separate the class specification from the actual instance instantiation.[6]

Implementation

Three Basic Flavors

We've seen the factory method implemented in three basic ways in Smalltalk environments:

1. As in *Design Patterns*, the factory method specifies and instantiates the collaborator class.

---

[6]We've shown how a variation of the Factory Method pattern is used in the Model-View-Controller framework. If you want to know more about MVC in general, details can be found in a large number of books and articles, including Collins (1995), Hopkins and Horan (1995), Howard (1995), Krasner and Pope (1988), Lewis et al. (1995), Lewis (1995), and Liu (1996).

```
Application>>mainMethod
    ...
    collaborator := self defaultCollaborator.
    ...

Application>>defaultCollaborator
    ^Collaborator new
```

2. As in the VisualWorks `View-Controller` example, the factory method may be split into two methods: a "get default instance" factory method and a "get default class" Constant Method.

```
Application>>mainMethod
    ...
    collaborator := self defaultCollaborator.
    ...

Application>>defaultCollaborator
    "This is the factory method; the instance is
    created here, but based on the class retrieved
    from a secondary Constant Method"
    ^self defaultCollaboratorClass new

Application>>defaultCollaboratorClass
    "This is the Constant Method. It specifies the
    class to instantiate to work with 'Application'
    instances"
    ^Collaborator
```

This is one of those solutions that relies on Smalltalk's classes being runtime objects. Since classes are capable of responding to messages, `default-CollaboratorClass` can just return a class object and leave it to `defaultCollaborator` to send it the `new` message. We could not have implemented the pattern this way in C++ because it has no class objects; there, the factory method must return the new instance rather than merely "naming" the class to instantiate.

3. In a third slight variation, the instantiation occurs in the main method, and an auxiliary Constant Method just returns the class to instantiate (as in variation 2):

```
Application>>mainMethod
    ...
    collaborator := self defaultCollaboratorClass new.
    ...

Application>>defaultCollaboratorClass
    "Constant Method; return the collaborator class"
    ^Collaborator
```

This third version can scarcely be called a Factory Method example; we have no separate method for creating the collaborator object. Instead, only the class to instantiate is abstracted out of the main method, but its instantiation occurs *in* that main method. The reason we're including it in this discussion is that this approach has been used extensively in Smalltalk; in addition, it shares the basic intent of Factory Method: "Define an interface for creating an object, but let subclasses decide which class to instantiate."

In fact, overall, the Constant Method flavors—versions 2 and 3—are overwhelmingly how the intent of Factory Method is achieved in the base Smalltalk classes. Interestingly, version 3 is the most often used variety in Visual Smalltalk, whereas version 2 is more common in VisualWorks.

A Solution Using Class Instance Variables

This variation on the basic pattern uses a class instance variable to determine which collaborator class to instantiate and lets us define a single factory method for all the classes in a subhierarchy. Let's apply it to the Editor example. We begin by adding the following to the Editor class definition:

```
Editor class instanceVariableNames: 'documentClass'
```

We define the factory method that all classes in the subhierarchy will use to create documents:

```
Editor>>createDocument
    ^self class documentClass new
```

Next we define the documentClass class method, which returns the class to instantiate. Again, this will be defined only once in the superclass:

```
Editor class>>documentClass
    "Return my class instance variable that specifies
     the document class to instantiate for my instances."
    ^documentClass
```

Now each subclass in the Editor hierarchy initializes its documentClass variable to the document class it wants to use:

```
DrawingEditor class>>initialize
    documentClass := DrawingDocument

TextEditor class>>initialize
    documentClass := TextDocument
```

So we need to define a single method—initialize—in each subclass. The rest of the Factory Method implementation is inherited from Editor. Also, by not hard-coding the class to be instantiated in a method, we can change that class on the fly by changing a class's `documentClass` variable.

Sample Code

Let's return to the example from the Builder (47) pattern. We have an abstract `CarBuilder` class with subclasses like `FordBuilder`, `ToyotaBuilder`, and `PorscheBuilder`. Each class responds to the same building protocol, but different builder classes instantiate different parts classes. For example, when a client wants to install a four-cylinder engine in a car, it sends `add4CylinderEngine` to its Builder. Different builders implement `add4CylinderEngine` differently: a `FordBuilder` creates an instance of `Ford4CylinderEngine`, but a `Toyota-Builder` instantiates `Toyota4CylinderEngine`.

One implementation question is, How does each Builder specify the class to instantiate in its `add4CylinderEngine` method? The question applies in general to all car parts. In the Builder pattern, we showed each Builder hard-coding the class names. Factory Method offers an alternative approach.

Here's what the `add4CylinderEngine` method looked like in the Builder pattern:

```
CarBuilder>>add4CylinderEngine
    "Do nothing.  Subclasses will override."


FordBuilder>>add4CylinderEngine
    self car addEngine: Ford4CylinderEngine new


ToyotaBuilder>>add4CylinderEngine
    self car addEngine: Toyota4CylinderEngine new
```

Instead, we can implement this method in the concrete builder classes using Factory Method:

```
FordBuilder>>add4CylinderEngine
    "Add a 4-cylinder engine; it is created by
    invoking a factory method."
    self car addEngine: self fourCylinderEngine[7]


ToyotaBuilder>>add4CylinderEngine
    self car addEngine: self fourCylinderEngine
```

To complete the implementation, we need to implement the builder-specific factory methods:

---

[7]Note that we've changed the naming convention slightly. We couldn't name the Constant Method `4CylinderEngine` because method names may not begin with a numeral.

```
FordBuilder>>fourCylinderEngine
    "The Ford 4-cylinder engine factory method."
    ^Ford4CylinderEngine new

ToyotaBuilder>>fourCylinderEngine
    ^Toyota4CylinderEngine new
```

We now have an obvious opportunity for refactoring. The add4Cylinder-Engine method is the same in all CarBuilder subclasses, so we can define this method once in the abstract superclass and eliminate it entirely from every subclass. The method in CarBuilder looks just like what we defined above, but now it appears in a single place:

```
CarBuilder>>add4CylinderEngine
    self car addEngine: self fourCylinderEngine
```

By invoking the Factory Method pattern, we actually wind up with a cleaner and more easily maintainable implementation. If we ever want to change add-4CylinderEngine's behavior, we only need to change a single location rather than multiple subclasses.

Known Smalltalk Uses

Factory Method is one of the more widely used patterns in Smalltalk. We've shown the MVC example; here we mention several others. All of these use one of the Constant Method variations of the pattern.

Visual Smalltalk Window Policies

In Visual Smalltalk, each TopPane (representing an application window) is associated with an instance of one of the subclasses of WindowPolicy. Window-Policy objects help construct an application window's menu bar. Different subclasses add different pull-down menus to the menu bar. For example, StandardWindowPolicy objects add the *File* and *Edit* menus, SmalltalkWindow-Policys add to that a *Smalltalk* pull down, and NoMenusWindowPolicy is self-explanatory. When a TopPane begins building its menu bar, it first calls on its window policy object to add its menus (other application-specific pull-down menus are added later). A TopPane may be explicitly configured with a WindowPolicy instance by its client, but if it is not (the typical case), it asks its owner application for a window policy class and instantiates it as follows:

```
owner windowPolicyClass new
```

ViewManager defines a default windowPolicyClass method that returns StandardWindowPolicy. ViewManager subclasses override this method if they need to use different policy objects.

Some ViewManager subclasses override windowPolicyClass with a method that decides at run time which policy class to use, depending on the current context. For example, Browser>>windowPolicyClass returns one class if the currently executing image is the Smalltalk development environment and another if not.

VisualWorks Look Policies

Another example of Factory Method occurs in UILookPolicy in VisualWorks. When a look policy object is asked to create, say, a radio button, the button's look depends on the policy object's class. For example, a Win3LookPolicy instance creates radio buttons with a Windows 3.x look, while a MotifLookPolicy object creates diamond-shaped Motif-style radio buttons.

Here's the method in the abstract UILookPolicy class that creates radio buttons:

```
UILookPolicy>>radioButton: spec into: builder
    ...
    component := self radioButtonClass model: model.
    ...
```

radioButtonClass returns a class object, and the model: method instantiates that class. Each class in the UILookPolicy hierarchy defines its own version of radioButtonClass:

```
UILookPolicy>>radioButtonClass
    ^DefaultLookRadioButtonView

Win3LookPolicy>>radioButtonClass
    ^Win3RadioButtonView

MotifLookPolicy>>radioButtonClass
    ^MotifRadioButtonView
```

WindowBuilder Resource Managers

In the WindowBuilder package from ObjectShare, you get more than just a visual user interface builder; the package also includes several "managers" for system resources, such as fonts and bitmaps. Each manager requires a different type of editor window to let users manage these resources. For example, a WBFontManager requires a WBFontManagerWindow, a WBBitmapManager needs a WBBitmapManagerWindow, and a WBNLSManager uses a WBNLSManagerWindow.

When a client wants to open a window to permit users to administer a particular resource, it sends the edit message to the appropriate manager. This method is defined in class WBPoolManager, the superclass of all manager classes:

```
WBPoolManager>>edit
    self editorClass new openOn: self.
```

Each manager class specifies its associated editor window class in its `editor-Class` method—for example:

```
WBFontManager>>editorClass
    ^WBFontManagerWindow

WBBitmapManager>>editorClass
    ^WBBitmapManagerWindow
```

topPaneClass

One responsibility of `ViewManager` objects in Visual Smalltalk is to construct an application's windows and panes. Each window has a top-most pane. For most application windows, it's an instance of `TopPane`; for dialog boxes, it's a `DialogTopPane`.

When the `ViewManager` begins the window-creation process, it determines which top pane class to create with this code:

```
self topPaneClass new
```

`WindowDialog` defines `topPaneClass` as a Constant Method:

```
WindowDialog>>topPaneClass
    ^DialogTopPane
```

For other subclasses of `ViewManager`, the following method determines which class to instantiate:

```
ViewManager>>topPaneClass
    Smalltalk includesKey: #MDISystem)
        ifFalse: [^TopPane].
    Smalltalk isRunTime ifFalse: [
        (Smalltalk at: #MDISystem) isActive
            ifTrue:[^Smalltalk at: #MDIChild] ].
    ^TopPane
```

Again, at times a factory method may decide which class to instantiate at runtime rather than being immutably hard-coded.

Factory Method for *External* Classes

In modern operating environments, we sometimes need to specify the name of a non-Smalltalk, or external, class from within Smalltalk. For example, we may need class names known to an object request handler (e.g., OLE Automation) or may need to pass "class" names of native widgets as arguments to operating system API functions.

As an example, consider how Visual Smalltalk interacts with Windows95 to create buttons, scroll bars, and other widgets in the user interface. When a `SubPane` subclass is instantiated and opened, Visual Smalltalk must tell Windows95 what kind of native widget to create. Opening an instance of the Smalltalk `Entry-Field` class requires a native widget whose Windows95 class is named "Edit"; a Smalltalk `ToolBar` pane corresponds to the Windows "ToolbarWindow32" class; and so on. `SubPane>>buildWindow:`, which is inherited by all subclasses, includes the following message:

```
self
    create: self windowClass
    title: self initialText
    style: ...
```

The method invoked by this message calls a Windows95 function that creates the native screen widget whose Windows class is specified by `self windowClass`. Concrete subclasses of `SubPane` implement their own versions of `window-Class` to return their corresponding Windows95 widget class name, as in:

```
EntryField>>windowClass
    ^'Edit'
```

This is an example of the Factory Method pattern, but for a class name external to Smalltalk.

Related Patterns

Template Method and Constant Method

We have already seen that Factory Method uses the Template Method (355) pattern and often what Beck (1997) calls the Constant Method pattern.

Builder and Abstract Factory

Factory Method can be used in the implementation of Builder (47) and Abstract Factory (31). We illustrated the Builder case in the Sample Code section. Often we can use Factory Method instead of Abstract Factory—the two patterns may compete as solutions to the same problem of abstracting object creation out of a primary application method.

PROTOTYPE (DP 117) Object Creational

Intent

Specify the kinds of objects to create using a prototypical instance and create new objects by copying this prototype.

Structure

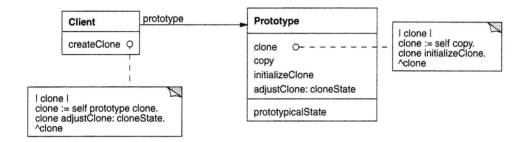

Design Patterns shows Prototype implementing its `clone` operation to simply return a copy. This diagram shows more detail: the Prototype or the Client may wish to adjust the copy before using it—that is, we may want the new instance's state to be derived from, but slightly different from, the Clone's.

This diagram shows how a client clones a Prototype:

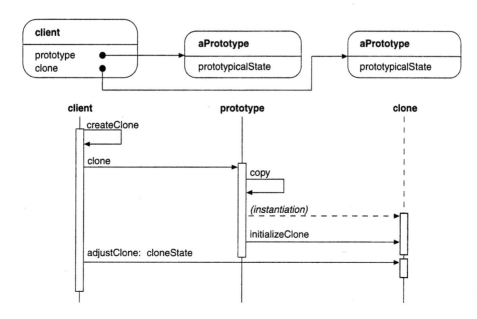

Discussion

The essence of the Prototype pattern is this: keep a prototypical instance of a class available, and when you need an instance of that class whose state is based on the prototype's state, clone the prototypical instance instead of sending new to the class. Hence the key ingredient of the pattern is a class with a preestablished prototypical instance that can create new instances of the class by cloning itself. In the cloning process, the class is not responsible for instance creation; the prototypical instance is. Each prototypical instance—called a **Prototype**—can potentially customize its cloning process, thus creating new instances—called **Clones**—whose initial state is more customized than it would be if the class itself had created the instances. The Clones can then also act as Prototypes and clone themselves.

Music Editor

The Motivation in *Design Patterns* illustrates why the pattern is helpful. A music editor has a GraphicTool that creates new graphics and adds them to the document it is editing. GraphicTool knows nothing about the notes, rests, and staves that the user will add to a score, and yet it can instantiate an open-ended number of these Graphic objects. GraphicTool does it by taking advantage of a property common to all Graphic objects: their ability to copy themselves. When the user adds an element to the score, the tool copies a prototypical graphic for that element—without really knowing what kind of graphic it is— and adds the copy to the document. GraphicTool can instantiate any Graphic subclass like this, including subclasses defined long after GraphicTool.

This example does not really hold true in Smalltalk. A Smalltalk GraphicTool would just need to know the instance creation protocol for a Graphic, such as Graphic class>>new. To add a graphic to the document, the editor would simply tell the tool what subclass of Graphic to instantiate. GraphicTool would take that class, create an instance of it, and add it to the document. That's impossible to do directly in C++ because there is no way for a variable to specify a class. But it's simple in Smalltalk.

Prototype in Smalltalk

Design Patterns notes that Prototype is a lot less useful in languages with metaclasses like Smalltalk and Objective-C because the metaclass already acts like a prototype (see item 4, "Reduced Subclassing," DP 120). The metaclass[8] lets each class customize its instance creation process. For example, the message for creating a Point is not Point class>>new but Point class>>x:y: (a Constructor Method; Beck, 1997). Thus almost any class side acts like a Prototype.

There are three reasons to use the Prototype pattern in Smalltalk:

---

[8] And the class methods it enables, a.k.a. the "class side."

1. The initial state of an object is known only as it differs from an existing object. We'll examine this more closely in the section on boilerplates.

2. The initial state is determined at runtime and cannot be determined at compile time. This usually occurs because the user defines the object's state at runtime. In this case, the user configures the prototype, and the system duplicates it to produce other ones. An example can be seen in the section on ThingLab in Known Smalltalk Uses.

3. Initializing an object is prohibitively expensive; copying an existing instance is preferable. This can happen when the state of an object is the result of many time-consuming calculations or the state must be obtained from an external data source.

Authors of language comparisons often overlook Smalltalk's metaclass model. Nevertheless, it is one of the powerful features that makes programming in Smalltalk a pleasure. Smalltalk is unique among the most popular object-oriented languages in that its classes are first-class objects that can be both extended with additional behavior and passed around as any other object. As *Design Patterns* notes in several cases, this feature changes the implementation of many of the Creational design patterns in Smalltalk, such as Abstract Factory, Factory Method, and, of course, Prototype.

Copy versus Clone

Design Patterns shows `clone` implemented as `copy`, but we show `clone` as involving more than `copy`. Why?

In Smalltalk, the `clone` method might be implemented simply to use the `copy` message defined in `Object`. The purpose of `copy` is to create an exact duplicate of the original object. But when a Prototype clones itself, the Clone's state is often similar to but not exactly the same as the Prototype's state. There are two points at which to adjust the Clone's state:

1. *During cloning:* The Prototype uses `initializeClone` to do the adjustment, probably ignoring the Prototype's state.

2. *After cloning:* The Client uses Prototype methods such as `adjustClone:` to specify Clone state explicitly.

The difference between `initializeClone` and `adjustClone:` is that the Client has no control over what `initializeClone` does, but it can control whether it uses `adjustClone:` and what parameters it passes in. Thus `copy` makes a Clone that is an exact duplicate of the Prototype. `copy` with `initializeClone` lets the Prototype adjust the Clone's state. `copy` with `adjustClone:` lets the Client adjust the Clone's state.

Boilerplate Objects

Sometimes a user does not want to specify the full configuration of a complex object but just how it differs from a standard one. Let's say you are designing a system that defines insurance policies. Instead of building a new policy from scratch, an insurance agent will start from a standard policy and derive a customized one from it. The standard policy is called a **template** or **boilerplate**. This kind of editing occurs in any business whose documents differ only slightly from each other.

When we are modeling these kinds of processes in an object-oriented language like Smalltalk, there are two basic strategies for deriving the customized document from the boilerplate:

1. *Prototype:* Copy the original document and edit the copy.

2. *Decorator:* Store only the differences between the original document and the new document.

We compare both approaches in the Sample Code section.

Understanding copy

To understand how to use the Prototype pattern in Smalltalk, you must first understand how the copy method works. All three major Smalltalk implementations—VisualWorks, Visual Smalltalk, and IBM Smalltalk—define the same copying method:

- Object>>copy—This method returns another instance "just like the receiver" (Goldberg & Robson, 1989, p. 97).

In all three dialects, copy is defined in terms of:

- Object>>shallowCopy—This method returns a copy of the receiver with the instance variables of the copy pointing to the same objects as the instance variables of the receiver.

Visual Smalltalk and IBM Smalltalk have an additional method:

- Object>>deepCopy—Return a copy of the receiver with the instance variables of the copy pointing to copies of the instance variables of the receiver. deepCopy goes one level further than copy does.

Instead of deepCopy, VisualWorks adds postCopy into copy's implementation:

```
Object>>copy
    ^self shallowCopy postCopy
```

- Object>>postCopy—This method extends copy to make the copy go arbitrarily deep. Each class can extend postCopy to go as deep as necessary. In this way, copy is implemented as a Template Method (355) in VisualWorks.

Shallow Copy versus Deep Copy

Let's illustrate the differences between a **shallow copy** and a **deep copy** with an example. Suppose you build three OrderedCollections with the following code:

```
| original shallow deep |
original := OrderedCollection new.
original
    add: 'abc';
    add: 'def'.
shallow := original shallowCopy.
deep := original deepCopy
```

If we inspect the resulting objects built by this code, we see three apparently identical OrderedCollections containing the strings 'abc' and 'def'. However, the objects held in those collections have different identities. This code shows that the structure of the shallow copy is different from the deep copy:

```
(original at: 1) == (shallow at: 1)          "Returns true"
(original at: 1) == (deep at: 1)             "Returns false"
```

This is because shallowCopy copies only the receiver of the message, not its instance variables, while deepCopy copies both. In either case, the object returned is a new object that is not identical to the receiver. However, this is not true of the object's instance variables. The following diagram shows the difference:[9]

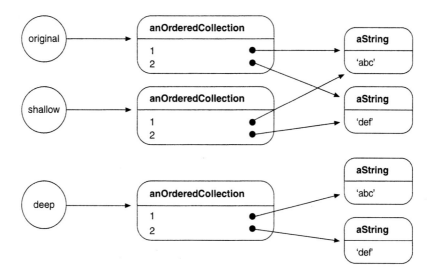

---

[9] From Goldberg and Robson (1989), p. 98.

Copying Domain Objects

For most purposes, shallowCopy is all you'll need, especially if an object contains only simple objects like Strings or Integers. You usually replace these objects in the copy rather than modify them. However, the following classes illustrate the limitations of shallowCopy:

```
Object subclass: #Person
   instanceVariableNames: 'name address dateOfBirth'
   classVariableNames: ''
   poolDictionaries: ''

Object subclass: #Address
   instanceVariableNames: 'street city state zipCode'
   classVariableNames: ''
   poolDictionaries: ''
```

Assume that an instance of Person contains an instance of Address in its address instance variable. Sending shallowCopy to a Person creates an instance that points at the same name, address, and dateOfBirth as the original. If we replace the name and dateOfBirth objects in the copy, the original is unaffected. If, however, you try changing the Address, you have not only changed the address in the copy but in the original as well.

This is the problem that motivated the deepCopy message. If you send deepCopy to the same instance of Person, you would get back a Person object containing an entirely new Address as well. You'd also have a new version of every other instance variable—in this case, new String and Date instances for name and dateOfBirth, respectively.

But deepCopy—as implemented by the vendors—is not enough. Suppose your Person class contained another instance variable, dependents, which contained an OrderedCollection of Persons. In that case, a deepCopy would return a new Person containing a new OrderedCollection in its dependents variable—an OrderedCollection of the same Person instances as the original. People have tried to get around this limitation of deepCopy by including new methods like deepDeepCopy, but those soon fail as well.

LaLonde and Pugh (1994b) present a general solution to the deep copy problem that works in most instances. It introduces a new method, veryDeepCopy, that resolves the circular reference problem of the original Smalltalk-80 implementation of deepCopy. Their approach works in all dialects.

Another alternative to deepCopy uses the binary object storage facilities that each Smalltalk offers. Visual Smalltalk includes an add-on called ObjectFiler that records an object onto a disk file. VisualWorks includes a nearly identical facility, named BOSS (Binary Objects Streaming Service), and IBM Smalltalk offers an add-on called ENVY/Swapper. Each of these correctly handles circular references and can be used in place of a deepCopy. You simply write an object out to a stream and then read it back to get a completely independent copy of the object.

Implementation

The Implementation issues raised in *Design Patterns* apply in Smalltalk:

1. *Using a prototype manager.* A class might not have a fixed number of prototypes. When the class does not know how many prototypes it will have, it must be prepared to manage any number of them. For example, the `Policy` class in the Sample Code section below should be able to handle `Policy` prototypes introduced at runtime.

   Design Patterns introduces a separate **prototype manager** object for managing these prototypes. As with other patterns in which an object manages instances of a class, that object in Smalltalk is often the class itself. That means the `Policy` class itself can manage instances of `Policy`. This technique is discussed in more detail in Flyweight (189) and Singleton (91).

2. *Implementing the clone operation. Design Patterns* explains that in Smalltalk, the `clone` message is often just `copy`. However, as the Smalltalk Structure diagram shows, the cloning process can involve more than that; it can also include `initializeClone` to adjust the Clone's state after the simple copy. The Client could just send `copy` to clone the prototype, but if the class is really a Prototype class, it should implement `clone` and make its own decisions about how `clone` is implemented. That lets clients use `clone` when they want to clone the prototype and `copy` when they simply want to duplicate it.

3. *Initializing clones. Design Patterns* suggests using some sort of `initialize` method so that programmers can customize the cloning process. That advice isn't quite accurate for Smalltalk. By convention, the `initialize` message is a special one that should be used only as part of instance creation. Moreover, the client will need to provide parameters, so the method ought to be called something like `initializeWithData:` (not a very good method name). This is the purpose of `adjustClone:` and methods like it. They allow the client to customize the cloning process after the Prototype has actually cloned itself.

Sample Code

Consider again our insurance example. The class of primary interest is the Policy, which represents a contractual agreement between the members of an organization and the insurance company. Insurance agents start from one of three basic templates: one for individuals, one for small organizations (fewer than 100 members), and one for large organizations. These differ primarily in what is covered under the plan.

The insurance agent will choose one of these template policies and modify it in various ways. First, he will fill in the missing information, such as covered organization name and plan administrator name. Then he will begin the real business of writing the policy for this organization. In our problem domain, this amounts to redefining medical procedures that are covered under the plan. In this way, he will be defining a new Policy that is based on an existing Policy, but that is a unique object in its own right.

To implement an insurance policy prototype in VisualWorks, we begin with a simple policy definition with just a few instance variables.

Policy
policyNumber
coverageStartDate
lengthOfCoverage

```
Object subclass: #Policy
    instanceVariableNames:
        'policyNumber coverageStartDate lengthOfCoverage'
    classVariableNames: ''
    poolDictionaries: ''
    category: 'Insurance'
```

The key to implementing Prototype is an appropriately deep copy method. Each of the objects that our `Policy` contains are simple, shallow objects. To obtain a new policy from a boilerplate Policy, the client sends the following message:

```
Policy>>derivedPolicy
    "Return a new Policy derived from this Policy."
    ^self copy
```

In this simple example, we do not need to define a `postCopy` method. Because it's okay to replace each of the simple objects in the `Policy` rather than change them, `copy` is sufficient.

Now let's make our example a bit more complicated. A Policy must know the organization it covers so that the insurance company can match the policy number on the claim against the organization's. The insurer can also check that the person who submitted the claim is covered under this policy.

Now our classes look like this:

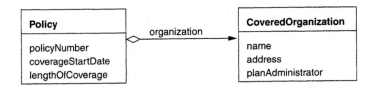

```
Object subclass: #Policy
    instanceVariableNames: 'policyNumber coverageStartDate
        lengthOfCoverage organization'
    . . .
```

```
Object subclass: #CoveredOrganization
    instanceVariableNames: 'name address planAdministrator'
    classVariableNames: ''
    poolDictionaries: ''
    category: 'Insurance'
```

The added complexity brings with it a need to change how a `Policy` gets copied. We can do it by overriding VisualWorks's `postCopy` method, as described earlier:

```
Policy>>postCopy
    "Make an independent copy of this Policy's attributes"
    super postCopy.
    organization := organization copy
```

This version of `postCopy` shows how you would clone an object containing another object that will be modified rather than replaced. You must give the new container a copy of the original's object.

This approach works well for simple objects, but it doesn't handle collections and other nested objects, which require a more sophisticated implementation. For example, health insurance policies contain a mapping from covered medical procedures to the manner in which a claim is reimbursed. In our application, the mapping is represented by a `Dictionary` that maps procedure codes (standard numeric codes that represent a medical procedure) to an instance of a `ProcedureRule`, which specifies how that procedure will be reimbursed. (The procedure code 123.4 might correspond to an appendectomy, for example.) A particular policy might say that an appendectomy will be reimbursed at 80 percent of the cost charged by the hospital. Each of our `Policy` objects will contain a `Dictionary` of code-to-rule mappings.

Now our `Policy` class looks like this:

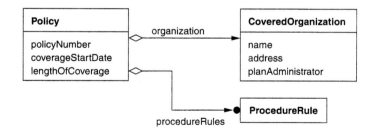

```
Object subclass: #Policy
    instanceVariableNames: 'policyNumber coverageStartDate
        lengthOfCoverage organization procedureRules'
    ...
```

This prompts more changes to the `postCopy` method. First, we must create a new `Dictionary` to hold the procedure rules. Then we `copy` each rule before placing it into the `Dictionary`:

```
Policy>>postCopy
    "Make an independent copy of this Policy's attributes"
    | newDictionary |
    newDictionary := Dictionary new.
    procedureRules keysAndValuesDo:
        [:key :value | newDictionary at: key put: value copy].
    procedureRules := newDictionary.
    organization:= organization copy
```

This approach has the advantage that it's usually easy to implement once you understand the different aspects of copying. However, it has a few drawbacks as well. In particular, the increasing complexity is its Achilles' heel. As a design evolves, this method is likely to require repeated modification. Missing a modification can result in unpredictable and subtle failures that can be difficult to detect. Moreover, it may consume excessive space. `postCopy` copies instance variables of the original object that may not be needed in the new object. More important, this approach provides no explicit history of changes. There is no easy way to trace what is different between the original and the copy without a variable-by-variable comparison. Since many applications need this kind of history, this approach may not be the most appropriate in all cases.

Implementation Using Decorator

In general, use the Prototype approach for boilerplate objects whenever the classes that represent the template are simple and not nested very deeply. In more complex cases, you should consider using a Decorator (161) approach. The idea is to create a class that records the differences (or deltas) between the original object and the copy.

Decorator describes how to create a decorator object that encapsulates another object, effectively augmenting its state or behavior, or both. In our case, we want to add the ability to record changes to the original object. Consider the following design:

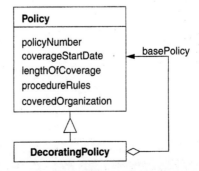

Decorator introduces a new subclass of `Policy`, `DecoratingPolicy`, that adds a new `basePolicy` instance variable that points to the boilerplate policy. All policies derived from a boilerplate would be instances of `DecoratingPolicy` rather than `Policy`.

To understand how this would work, look at the implementation of `ruleAt:`, a key method in both `Policy` and `DecoratingPolicy`. Here's how `ruleAt:` is implemented in the original `Policy` class:

```
Policy>>ruleAt: aProcedureCode
    ^self procedureRules
        at: aProcedureCode
        ifAbsent: [self defaultRule]
```

Here, `ruleAt:` returns the rule keyed by `aProcedureCode` or returns a default rule if there is no rule at that key. The `setRuleFor:rule:` method is similarly simple:

```
Policy>>setRuleFor: aProcedureCode rule: aProcedureRule
    self procedureRules
        at: aProcedureCode
        put: aProcedureRule
```

Now compare the implementation of `ruleAt:` in the `DecoratingPolicy` class:

```
DecoratingPolicy>>ruleAt: aProcedureCode
    ^self
        at: aProcedureCode
        ifAbsent: [self basePolicy ruleAt: aProcedureCode]
```

Notice that `DecoratingPolicy` looks first in its own dictionary for the rule stored at a procedure code. If it finds a matching rule, it returns it. If it doesn't find one, the search continues to the `basePolicy`. The `DecoratingPolicy` doesn't override the `setRuleFor:rule:` method because the inherited implementation is correct.

Let's look at another example, the method `lengthOfCoverage`:

```
Policy>>lengthOfCoverage
    "Return the length of time, in years, this Policy
    is in effect."
    ^lengthOfCoverage
```

The Decorator implements the method slightly differently:

```
DecoratingPolicy>>lengthOfCoverage
    "If the value has not yet been set, return the
    base policy's value."
    ^lengthOfCoverage isNil
        ifTrue: [self basePolicy lengthOfCoverage]
        ifFalse: [lengthOfCoverage]
```

The Decorator implements many getter methods like this, returning the value in the boilerplate if the value in the new policy is not set.

To obtain a new policy from a boilerplate policy, the client sends the following message:

```
Policy>>derivedPolicy
    "Return a new Policy derived from this one."
    ^DecoratingPolicy new basePolicy: self
```

This implementation has several advantages. First, no copying is necessary, reducing storage costs. Second, the decorator itself constitutes a history of what has changed from the template policy. A side effect of this design is that changes to the base policy apply to all derived policies.

There are also a few drawbacks to this implementation. It requires some complicated coding in the Decorator subclass which might not be easy to maintain. This approach is probably best for more complex objects or when the base changes.

Known Smalltalk Uses

VisualWorks TextAttributes

The VisualWorks text display classes contain a straightforward and easily understood use of the Prototype pattern. Instances of the class TextAttributes maintain information that affects the display of a piece of text, including CharacterAttributes for font mapping, a line grid, baseline, alignment, tab stops, and indents. Often a user will want to modify a TextAttributes to change one or the other of these instance variables, but he or she will need to start from one of the system-provided baseline TextAttributes instances.

For this reason, the TextAttributes method styleNamed: uses the copy method to manufacture a new instance derived from a reference instance:

```
TextAttributes class>>styleNamed: aSymbol
    "Answer the style named aSymbol from the text style dictionary."
    ^(TextStyles at: aSymbol) copy
```

VisualWorks Database Framework

The VisualWorks database classes contain an unusual use of Prototype. The database framework translates rows of data read from a relational database query into objects. The value of the bindOutput instance variable in ExternalDatabaseSession determines the class of the result returned by the query. The variable's value is an empty instance of the target class. The session uses this instance as a prototype and copies it for each new row of data.

ThingLab

In the two previous uses of the Prototype pattern, classes knew they had prototypes. That is, we knew while writing the code precisely which class to instantiate for our prototypical instances. Since we had this knowledge, we could have substituted a competing pattern, such as Factory Method.

Perhaps a more compelling use of the Prototype pattern occurs when we want to create prototypical objects during program execution and save them for later use. A classic example occurs in ThingLab (Borning, 1981, 1986), a constraint-oriented graphical editor. ThingLab lets a user construct graphical objects and apply geometric constraints to them. Once the user defines a new graphical object (or "part," or "thing"), it may be used to build other parts. In ThingLab, when a new thing is created, the system programmatically defines a new class and saves the thing in that class as its prototypical instance. When a user wants to reuse a thing, the `prototype` message is sent to the associated class to retrieve a clone. The Prototype pattern lets the user (not a programmer) define arbitrarily complex objects at runtime.

Related Patterns

We've already seen an example of using the Decorator (161) pattern as an alternative to Prototype. Here, we'll mention another related design pattern, which happens not to be a Gang of Four pattern.

Prototype can be used along with or instead of Type Object (Johnson & Woolf, 1998). The two patterns are alternative solutions to the problem of instantiating objects that aren't known at compile time. Type Object can create new "classes" at runtime without compilation, while Prototype employs a prototypical object that can clone itself. Both patterns let the user describe a new object at runtime and then create objects based on that description. In Prototype's case, the "description" is nothing more than the prototype object itself; Type Object's description is a set of other objects that have been built at runtime to describe the structure of the objects that will be created.

The two patterns can work together to handle initialization chores. A class normally customizes its instances' initialization by implementing `initialize`. With Type Object, different types of objects are instances of the same class, so they cannot customize `initialize` by type. However, each type can have its own prototypical instance whose state is set independently of the other prototypes. Then when a type object wishes to create an instance that is initialized for its type, it clones its prototypical instance to create a new instance with a custom initial state.

SINGLETON (DP 127)   Object Creational

Intent

Ensure a class has only one instance, and provide a global point of access to it.

Structure

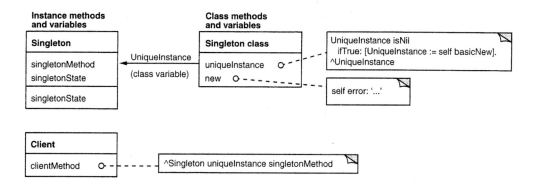

This diagram portrays the ideal Singleton implementation, ensuring a unique instance and providing secure and singular access to that instance. In this example, the class also happens to be named `Singleton`. The diagram portrays the structure and protocol of the `Singleton` class (the class variables and class methods) as well as that of `Singleton` instances.

Since there's only one instance of the `Singleton` class, client objects and the `Singleton` class both reference the same object:

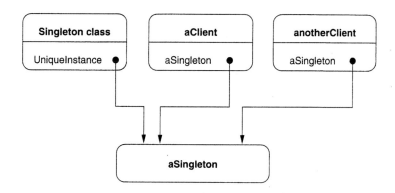

Discussion

Sometimes it's necessary or desirable to have only one instance of a particular class exist at any given time. For example, we want only a single manager for all of the windows in the Smalltalk environment. Singleton lets you ensure this. The pattern makes a class responsible for keeping track of its sole instance, providing the only access to that instance, and preventing the creation of multiple instances.

If we look at the major Smalltalk development environments, we find many Singleton or Singleton-like implementations in common use. Some of these strictly meet all of the preceding criteria, yet, surprisingly, many do not. The overriding characteristic of these implementations is that they all provide for a single active instance of a class at any point in time. However, not all of them incorporate code explicitly preventing the creation of multiple instances of that same class, nor do all implementations provide for secure access controlled by the Singleton class itself.

In many of these cases, access to a Singleton instance is provided through a global variable. In Visual Smalltalk, for example, the sole instance of `Notification Manager` is stored in the `Notifier` global variable. So methods all over the class hierarchy hard-code the `Notifier` global when they wish to access the system's window manager, as in this code, which participates in Visual Smalltalk's image start-up process:

```
SessionModel>>startupWindowSystem
    "Private - perform OS window system startup."
    | oldWindows |
    ...
    Notifier initializeWindowHandles.
    ...
    oldWindows := Notifier windows.
    Notifier initialize.
    ...
    ^oldWindows
```

How dangerous are Singletons stored in global variables? In the case of a class like Visual Smalltalk's `OperatingSystemInformation`—whose single instance is stored in the global `OperatingSystem`—it doesn't much matter; as the class name implies, instances of the class exist merely for informational purposes. One instance is as able to report information (such as the current OS version number) as another. However, in the case of `NotificationManager`, creating a new instance and having the global `Notifier` reference it would be disastrous. A `NotificationManager` maintains a list of all open windows and funnels operating system messages to the appropriate window. A new instance initializes its list of windows to an empty list. Thus, creating a new `Notification Manager` and installing it in `Notifier` would result in all existing windows becoming inaccessible since `Notifier` would no longer point to them.

Routing all accesses to a Singleton through a single class method is preferable to a global because the method provides a single point of access. The only way to get to the Singleton instance is by sending a message to the class. In this method, the class takes responsibility for the Singleton instance—when it's created, how it's initialized, when it's released for garbage collection—as well as preventing the creation of multiple instances. A global variable can't do any of this.

Despite these drawbacks, many Singletons accessible only through global variables exist in the various Smalltalk environments and have served users for years. *Design Patterns* states that Singletons accessed through global variables are not really examples of the Singleton pattern (DP 127). One might argue that these other examples *are* Singletons and they're just not implemented optimally. After all, they meet the Singleton criteria specified in the Intent section. For our continuing purposes of drawing on existing examples from various Smalltalk images, we'll assume their intent is indeed to be Singletons, but they're implemented in a less-than-optimal fashion.

Singleton Variations

We've observed three main variations of the Singleton pattern in the major Smalltalk development environments—**persistent, transient,** and **single-active-instance.** Descriptions of each follow:

1. *Persistent Singleton.* There exists only one instance of a particular class, and its identity never changes. For example, the unique instance of `NotificationManager` is created once, lives on throughout Smalltalk image start-ups and shutdowns, and is always the single instance used by clients.

2. *Transient Singleton.* Only one instance of the class exists at any time, but that instance may change. For example, a `SessionModel` in Visual Smalltalk maintains information about the state of the current Smalltalk session and handles image start-up and shutdown tasks. A new singleton instance is created at image start-up and is used throughout that Smalltalk session.

3. *Single-Active-Instance Singleton.* In this variation, a single instance is active or enabled at any point in time, but other dormant instances may also exist. For example, the VisualWorks development environment supports the notion of programming projects. A project keeps track of code changes made while the project is active; when a programmer opens a project and makes modifications to classes and methods, the project records all these changes. Each project is represented by an instance of `Project`. There may be several existing projects in the programming environment, but only one is active at any time. The `Project` instance associated with the current programming project is accessible from the `Project` class.

   This example begs the question: is this a Singleton? At the least, it requires a broader interpretation of the pattern. Like a canonical Singleton, there's a single instance of a class available to clients at any point in time, and the class provides access to that one instance. It's just that there are other non-available instances lying around as well. We'll include it here, but it does demand a liberal reading of the pattern's Intent.

Reserved Words

Smalltalk also provides three special-case Singleton-like reserved literals built into the language itself: nil, true, and false. Although we don't access these objects by sending messages to their classes, they meet the Intent of the Singleton pattern: their classes—UndefinedObject, True, and False—each have only one instance and all prevent creation of additional instances.

Implementation

Singleton's implementation issues concern the two criteria specified in the Intent section: ensure a class has only one instance, and provide a global point of access to it.

Ensuring a Unique Instance

Singleton classes are responsible for making sure only one instance exists. The secure way to do this is to instrument the new and new: messages to prevent clients from creating new instances. Specifically, since Smalltalk does not provide a way to make these messages private, these methods must return errors rather than instantiating the class.

Surprisingly, many of the examples of Singletons in the major Smalltalk environments reflect an unsafe implementation by not including such precautionary measures against the creation of additional instances. It is merely assumed that users will adhere to convention and will not instantiate these classes. The safer approach is implemented on page DP 130 and is shown slightly modified below:

```
Object subclass: #Singular
    instanceVariableNames: ''
    classVariableNames: 'UniqueInstance'
    poolDictionaries: ''

Singular class>>new
    "Override the inherited 'new' to assure there
    is never more more than one instance of me."
    self error: 'Class ', self name,
                ' cannot create new instances'
```

Existing Singleton examples adopt the same sort of preventive approach. In Visual Smalltalk, for instance, UndefinedObject overrides new as follows:

```
UndefinedObject class>>new
    "Create a new instance of the receiver. Disallowed
    for this class because there is only a single
    instance, nil."
    ^self invalidMessage
```

The `invalidMessage` method results in a walkback. The `new:` class method is implemented the same way. Attempts to create a new `UndefinedObject` are therefore blocked. In VisualWorks, the error produced by `new` is explicit about `nil`'s Singletonness:

```
UndefinedObject class>>new
    self error: 'You may not create any more undefined objects--
use nil'
```

Notice that Smalltalk requires a runtime solution to prevent the creation of multiple instances. The instance creation methods (such as `new`) for a Singleton class should really be private so that clients can't create instances of the class. This is easy in C++ but impossible in Smalltalk. The C++ examples in *Design Patterns* (DP 129, 131, 132) demonstrate how a constructor (the function for creating instances) can be defined as *protected*, thereby preventing clients from calling the function and creating new instances.

This is a real advantage of C++ over Smalltalk, which has no way to deny access to methods. Smalltalk programmers often use comments to label methods "private," or they collect such methods in a "Private" category in class browsers that support method categories. In some newer Smalltalk systems, there is even environmental support for declaring a method private. For example, browsers in IBM Smalltalk include a "public/private" toggle button to differentiate public and private methods from a browsing standpoint. However, Smalltalk possesses no language-based mechanism for enforcing that privacy—clients are not prevented from invoking these ostensibly private methods.

The upshot is that Smalltalk requires a runtime solution to ensure a single instance. Again, this solution typically involves simply overriding `new`, although for classes whose instances contain indexed instance variables, we have to override `new:` as well. (Smith, 1996b, offers a runtime solution to the generic private method problem that involves verifying that the message sender is `self`.)

Providing Access

We've seen that some Singleton implementations provide access via a global variable. The more secure approach is to put the Singleton's class object in charge and route all access through it. For the class we just defined, that access might look like this:

```
Singular class>>current
    "Return the Singleton instance for this class;
     if it hasn't been created yet, do so now."
    UniqueInstance isNil
       ifTrue: [UniqueInstance := self basicNew].
    ^UniqueInstance
```

All clients wishing access to the sole instance of Singular must use the class method current. Our earlier implementation of new does nothing but prevent the creation of multiple instances, making current the only way to create and access the single instance. Here, current uses lazy initialization to set up the class variable, UniqueInstance, thereby ensuring we incur instantiation costs only if and when a client requests the unique instance. When a client wishes to send a message to the Singleton instance, it codes:

```
Singular current someMessage.
```

Accessing a Singleton Via new?

An alternative way to access the Singleton might be to define new to simply return the Singleton instance rather than causing an error. In the following implementation of this approach, we do so by invoking the preferred access method, current:

```
Singular class>>new
    ^self current
```

However, this can be quite confusing. The conventional semantics of new are that it instantiates and returns an instance that didn't exist before. Having it return an existing instance instead is misleading. The following code illustrates the potential pitfall:

```
| roadRunner wileECoyote |
roadRunner := SingleToon new.
wileECoyote := SingleToon new.
roadRunner position: 100@200.
wileECoyote position: 200@300.
```

It's not clear to the reader (or, perhaps, the writer) of this code that roadRunner and wileECoyote reference the same object: the Singleton instance of Single-Toon. The last line modifies the object referenced by roadRunner, something perhaps not intended by the programmer.

Singletons in a Single Subhierarchy

There are also situations in which we have a logical grouping of classes—typically a branch of the class hierarchy—and wish to have one Singleton instance for the entire group rather than one per class. *Design Patterns* explores this notion in the context of a single maze factory for the entire system rather than one per maze factory class. The example on page DP 133 creates a new instance of Maze-Factory or one of its subclasses, depending on a string in an environment variable. The object thus created is installed in the MazeFactory class as the sole maze factory.

Perhaps surprisingly, the implementation of this Singleton scenario is quite similar to the code we have already shown. We can define the top-most class in the subhierarchy with a `UniqueInstance` class variable and have it reference the single Singleton for the subhierarchy. This works because all classes in the subhierarchy share that class variable's value. Thus, if we install the Singleton maze factory in `MazeFactory`'s class variable, all subclasses will reference that same object.

Suppose as an alternative scenario that we have a hierarchy branch and want *each* class in it to have a unique Singleton instance. We cannot simply inherit the `UniqueInstance` class variable and reuse it in each subclass; we need a separate variable for each subclass. Of course, we can define each subclass with its own class variable and code a separate access method in each. This is not particularly clever or elegant. Instead we can define a single class instance variable in the top-most superclass along with a single access method in that class and have all subclasses inherit this implementation. Each subclass will get its own copy of the variable, letting each have its own Singleton instance. The single accessor method will return the class instance variable belonging to the message's receiver.

The code that implements this approach follows:

```
Object subclass: #Single
    instanceVariableNames: ''
    classVariableNames: ''
    poolDictionaries: ''

Single class instanceVariableNames: 'uniqueInstance'

Single class>>current
    uniqueInstance isNil
        ifTrue: [uniqueInstance := self basicNew].
    ^uniqueInstance
```

Each `Single` subclass is automatically a Singleton class, inheriting the Singleton behavior defined in the superclass.

Notice that `current` instantiates the class using `self basicNew` rather than the more conventional `self new`. We cannot invoke the new method because, as in our earlier code, new signals an error. The typical alternative, `super new`, poses problems here because subclasses of `Single` that inherit `current` would wind up invoking `Single class>>new`, and we'd have precisely the same problem.

Naming the Access Method

A Singleton class provides access to its sole instance through an accessor method, but what should that method be called? Programmers often name this method `default` or `current`—for example, `SourceManager current` in Visual Smalltalk and `Screen default` in VisualWorks.

The name `current` sometimes means that there are multiple instances of the class: one active and the others dormant. This would be appropriate when the class is a single-active-instance Singleton. But you can't rely on that—many transient Singleton classes in Visual Smalltalk use the `current` message, as we have done in our preceding code.

The name `default` can be misleading as well. Some classes use it to provide a truly default value, not a Singleton instance. In VisualWorks, for example, `Time default` retrieves a `Time` object containing the current time of day; the same is true for `Date current`. Neither of these is a Singleton. The difficulty here is that natural language is ambiguous: words like *default* can be interpreted in different ways. As Fowler (1997) asserts, naming is one of the more difficult problems in object-oriented analysis, and "no name is perfect" (p. 9).

Design Patterns recommends simply naming this method `instance`; Buschmann et al. (1996) suggest `getInstance`. Perhaps we ought to use a name providing more information about the object being retrieved, such as `defaultNotifier` or `currentSourceManager`. These would be applications of what Beck (1997) calls Intention Revealing Selectors. However, many would argue that an expression like `SourceManager currentSourceManager` is redundant, and the established Smalltalk conventions (`SourceManager current` or `Screen default`) are more appropriate.

The best advice is to use common sense in choosing names, always stepping back to reflect on your code, remembering that someone else will have to read and understand it.

Class Methods Only?

When a class should have just one instance, a Smalltalk programmer might be tempted to implement all of its behavior as class methods. Since class objects are fully capable of sending and receiving messages, a class can be designed to have no instances and no instance methods and can implement the entire Singleton protocol on the class side (that is, as class methods). In fact, Visual Smalltalk's `OLESessionManager` and `OLERegistryInterface` classes implement their behavior in this manner, as did the `Compiler` class in older versions of Smalltalk/V (including Smalltalk Express).

There are two reasons to avoid implementing objects completely on the class side—one theoretical and one practical. The theoretical reason is that it extends metaclass protocol in an unnatural fashion. "Ordinary objects are used to model the real world. Metaobjects describe these ordinary objects" (Rivard, 1996). Classes are supposed to be metaobjects—part of the Smalltalk environment rather than domain objects. Their primary roles include instance creation, instance accessing (as in Singleton), and sharing resources common to all instances of the class. These roles are implemented in class methods. Separating class methods from instance methods separates the creation and management of instances from the specification of their behavior. Having domain- or application-specific behavior implemented by class methods muddies this separation. That sort of behavior belongs on the instance side.

The practical reason for avoiding class side implementation regards extensibility: the design will be difficult to maintain and extend if the system later requires more than one instance of this object. Once a system has lots of code dealing with an object through class messages, switching to a nonSingleton design means finding and modifying all that code. That change is much easier if the Singleton's behavior is already implemented by instance methods.

Sample Code

Suppose a company has a system that uses a home-brewed database. Specifically, it stores and retrieves data from a single flat disk file using custom file-access routines rather than using a commercial relational or object-oriented database product. Commercial databases handle file and record locks for the application, but since our application is reading and writing a flat disk file, it must provide its own locking mechanism. We'll show the implementation of a very simple file-level lockout.

Imagine the company has a multithreaded application where one thread might be writing a record to the file while another issues a read request. The database access object will control file-level locking using an instance variable that indicates whether a write operation is in progress. Read operations will wait until the current write is complete. Now here's the problem that calls for using the Singleton pattern: since the database accessor uses an instance variable for locking, we want to have a single accessor object so it can effectively prevent reading from the file until a pending write is finished. (Of course, this is only a portion of the requirements for a real database manager. For instance, we would need a more sophisticated record-level locking mechanism to prevent conflicting reads and writes. Our more important goal is simply to demonstrate an application that makes use of the Singleton pattern.)

Here are the three key definitions implementing `DatabaseAccessor` as a Singleton:

```
Object subclass: #DatabaseAccessor
   instanceVariableNames: 'lock'
   classVariableNames: 'Instance'
   poolDictionaries: ''

DatabaseAccessor class>>singleton
   Instance isNil
      ifTrue: [Instance := self basicNew initialize].
   ^Instance

DatabaseAccessor class>>new
   ^self error: 'DatabaseAccessor has only one instance. ',
       'To retrieve it, send "DatabaseAccessor singleton".'
```

Next we define the `DatabaseAccessor` instance behavior:

```
DatabaseAccessor>>initialize
    lock := false.
    "Open the file"
    ...


DatabaseAccessor>>write: aDatabaseRecord
    "Set the lock and fork the 'real' write method."
    lock := true.
    [self writePrim: aDatabaseRecord] fork

DatabaseAccessor>>writePrim: aDatabaseRecord
    "Write the record in aDatabaseRecord to the file."
    ...
    "Now that the write is complete, unlock:"
    lock := false.

DatabaseAccessor>>read: aKey
    "Return the DatabaseRecord keyed by aKey."
    | record |
    "Don't read while a write is in progress."
    [lock] whileTrue: [Processor yield].
    "Now, read the record:"
    record := DatabaseRecord new.
    ...
    ^record
```

When the client application wants to read a record, it codes:

DatabaseAccessor singleton read: aKey

Similarly, when writing records, a client sends a `write:` message to the Singleton database access object retrieved by sending `DatabaseAccessor default`.

Known Smalltalk Uses

The discussion has already considered a number of known uses of Singleton in the base Smalltalk libraries. Here we enumerate examples within several Singleton implementation categories.

Persistent Singletons

There are several Persistent Singleton examples in the Visual Smalltalk image. We've already spoken about the `Notifier` instance of `NotificationMan-ager`. `Clipboard`, a global referencing the Singleton `ClipboardManager`, gives clients access to the operating system's clipboard resource. The global `Pro-cessor` is the Singleton instance of `ProcessScheduler`; it manages `Process` objects and multi-processing tasks. IBM Smalltalk has precisely the same arrangement as the latter example; the global `Processor` references the Singleton `ProcessScheduler`.

Transient Singletons

The Singleton instance of `SourceFileManager` in VisualWorks keeps track of the code files (the source and changes files). Visual Smalltalk has a similar class named `SourceManager`, accessed with `SourceManager current`.

The Singleton `SessionModel` in Visual Smalltalk keeps track of information about the current Smalltalk session. It is accessed through the class using the message `SessionModel current`.

VisualWorks implements a `Screen` class whose single instance represents the display currently in use (`Screen default`). This class is defined as a Singleton because VisualWorks does not support multiple monitors. Visual Smalltalk also has a class called `Screen`, whose sole instance is stored in the global variable `Display`.

Single-Active-Instance Singletons

VisualWorks can manage as many `Projects` as the developer wants, but there is only a single active project at a time (`Project current`). The current project dictates the current change set (`ChangeSet current`) and the current set of visible windows (maintained in the global `ScheduledControllers`, an instance of `ControlManager`). All of these classes can have multiple instances, but only one instance is "live" at any time.

Singleton per Class in a Subhierarchy

`DynamicLinkLibrary` in Visual Smalltalk is an abstract class implementing communication between Smalltalk and code in an external dynamic link library (DLL). A specific DLL file is accessed through its own concrete subclass. The abstract class defines a class instance variable (`current`) for storing a Singleton instance for each subclass, along with a corresponding accessor method of the same name. So sending `current` to any subclass (e.g., `GDIDLL current`) retrieves that class's Singleton instance.

Chapter 4

Structural Patterns

Adapter (105) Convert the interface of a class into another interface clients expect. Adapter lets classes work together that couldn't otherwise because of incompatible interfaces.

Bridge (121) Decouple an abstraction from its implementation so that the two can vary independently.

Composite (137) Compose objects into tree structures to represent part-whole hierarchies. Composite lets clients treat individual objects and compositions of objects uniformly.

Decorator (161) Attach additional responsibilities and behavior to an object dynamically. Decorators provide a flexible alternative to subclassing for extending functionality.

Facade (179) Provide a unified interface to a set of interfaces in a subsystem. Facade defines a higher-level interface that makes the subsystem easier to use.

Flyweight (189) Use sharing to support large numbers of fine-grained objects efficiently.

Proxy (213) Provide a surrogate or placeholder for another object to control access to it.

ADAPTER (DP 139) Object Structural

Intent

Convert the interface of a class into another interface clients expect. Adapter lets classes work together that couldn't otherwise because of incompatible interfaces.

Structure

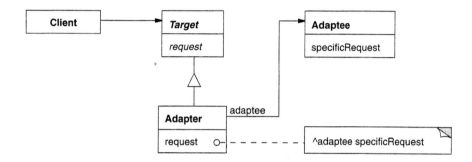

Discussion

An Adapter is used to make a nonconformist object conform to an interface known to a client.[1] The client knows only how to communicate with its collaborating objects (**Targets**) using a particular protocol. We also have an existing class that does not adhere to the Target interface and want to reuse its functionality. We want an instance of this class, call it *T*, to act as a Target too, so we need an Adapter between the Client and *T* to translate Target messages into messages that *T* understands. We call *T* the **Adaptee** in this scenario. When the client wants to send a message to *T*, it sends it instead to *T*'s Adapter, which forwards a semantically equivalent message to *T*.

Class Adapter

In Smalltalk, we cannot implement the class version of the Adapter pattern described in *Design Patterns*. There, multiple inheritance is invoked to create a new class whose behavior is the amalgam of two superclasses. Since Smalltalk does not support multiple inheritance, this brand of Adapter is not available to us.

---

[1]Both *Adapter* and *Adaptor* are acceptable spellings. We use the former here to conform with *Design Patterns*. However, especially when discussing VisualWorks Adapters, you'll also see the Adaptor spelling.

A C++/Smalltalk Difference

Looking at the code on page DP 147, we see that a C++ Adapter must declare the type of its Adaptee. That being the case, it may adapt only objects of that declared class or its derived subclasses. In Smalltalk, without strong typing, the Adaptee may be of any class as long as that class implements the messages sent by the Adapter to the Adaptee.

Implementation

Here, we'll consider the implementation of several Adapter variations.

Tailored Adapter

Let's begin with an Adapter tailored to a particular adaptation scenario. In the example from *Design Patterns* (DP 139), a DrawingEditor maintains a collection of graphical objects, instances of classes in the Shape hierarchy. The Drawing-Editor uses messages from the Shape protocol to communicate with these drawing objects. For text, however, we wish to make use of the functionality already available in the existing TextView class. We want the DrawingEditor to be able to interact with TextViews just as it does with Shape objects, but TextView does not conform to the Shape protocol. So we define the TextShape Adapter class as a subclass of Shape. A TextShape has an instance variable that references a TextView object and implements the messages in the Shape proto-col; each of these messages simply forwards a different message to the encapsu-lated TextView. We then plug a TextShape between the DrawingEditor and the TextView.

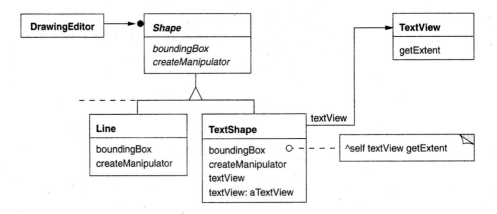

TextShape, rather than implementing Shape functionality directly, merely acts as a translator, converting Shape messages into ones understood by the Text-View Adaptee: when the DrawingEditor sends a message adhering to the Shape protocol to a TextShape, the TextShape forwards a different but semantically equivalent message to its TextView instance.

Here the interfaces of both the Adapter and the Adaptee are *known* when the Adapter is defined; thus we can tailor an Adapter to this specific case, translating specific `Shape` messages to specific `TextView` messages. We call this a **Tailored Adapter**.

Here is the interaction diagram for a `TextShape` Adapter showing one of the messages it translates for its Adaptee:

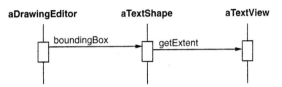

Message-Forwarding Pluggable Adapter

In the Tailored Adapter, we were able to write custom methods for message translation because we knew the protocols of both Adapter and Adaptee at design time. The Adapter class is coded for a unique translation situation, and each of the Adapter's methods hard-codes the specific message(s) to forward to the Adaptee.

A second sort of Adapter scenario occurs when the interface of the Adaptee is not known at design time. We cannot simply translate messages from one interface to another because the Adaptee's interface is unknown a priori. In such a case, we can use a Pluggable Adapter to convert and forward messages in a generic fashion. Like a Tailored Adapter, a Pluggable Adapter serves as a translator between a Client and an Adaptee. Here, however, we need not define a new Adapter class for each specific case. Let's consider a motivating example of the use of Pluggable Adapters.

In the Model-View-Controller (MVC) paradigm for interactive applications, view objects (representing widgets on the screen) are connected to the underlying application model so that changes in the model will be reflected in the user interface, and changes made by users at the interface will result in changes to the underlying model data. View objects are implemented so they can be used in any interactive application. Hence they use a general protocol to communicate with their models; in particular, the getter message sent to models is `value` and the generic setter message is `value:`. For instance, this is how a VisualWorks `TextEditorView` obtains its contents:

```
TextEditorView>>getContents
    | t |
    t := model value.
    ^t == nil
       ifTrue: [Text new]
       ifFalse: [t]
```

Application model objects, on the other hand, typically have multiple aspects rather than a single value. Even if they represent a single aspect, model objects use domain-specific accessor messages with more meaningful names than value and value:. The problem, then, is how do we hook up a view and its model if the view sends messages like value that the model doesn't understand? The solution is that we can tell a Pluggable Adapter what message to translate value into—that is, what messages to forward to its Adaptee when the value message is received. We do the same for value:.

Let's look at a concrete example. Suppose we have an employee maintenance application. The application model includes an attribute (here, simply an instance variable) representing an employee's social security number, and the application's user interface includes an input box view that displays the social security number of an employee. The model's methods for accessing and setting the social security number are named socialSecurity and socialSecurity:. The input box must display the current social security number but knows only how to ask for its model's value. Thus we have to convert the value message to socialSecurity. We can use a Pluggable Adapter object for this purpose. Here's an interaction diagram for our example:

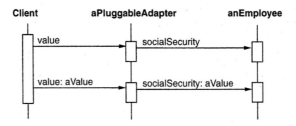

This diagram is a simplification; it portrays conceptually how a Pluggable Adapter works. However, the messages sent to the Adaptee are actually implemented using perform:, which permits the symbolic representation of messages and indirect messaging. A Pluggable Adapter can store a message selector as a Symbol and at any time tell its Adaptee to *perform* that selector as if it were an ordinary message-send. For example, the direct message anObject socialSecurity is equivalent to anObject perform: selector when selector references the Symbol #socialSecurity. This is the key to implementing the message-forwarding form of a Pluggable Adapter, or **Message-Based Pluggable Adapter**. The Adapter's client informs the Pluggable Adapter of the message selectors corresponding to value and value:, and the Adapter stores these selectors internally. In our example, this means the client tells the Adapter to associate the Symbol #socialSecurity with value, and #socialSecurity: with value:. When either message is received, the Adapter forwards the associated message selector to its Adaptee using perform:. We'll see exactly how this works in the Sample Code section.

Parameterized Adapter

A Message-Based Pluggable Adapter sends a single message to its Adaptee when one of its generic messages (value or value:) is received from the client. There are other ways of invoking behavior in the Adaptee when client messages are received. We'll consider one here: blocks.

We can have an Adapter for which a Client can supply entire blocks of code to perform when each generic Adapter message is received, rather than supplying a message selector. The block can be used for any purpose involving the Adaptee but will typically be for accessing a particular aspect of the Adaptee. We can name the Adapter class ParameterizedAdapter. It will have one instance variable for storing a get block, used for retrieving a value based on the Adaptee, and another for the set block, for setting some facet of the Adaptee.

```
Object subclass: #ParameterizedAdapter
    instanceVariableNames: 'adaptee getBlock setBlock'
    classVariableNames: ''
    poolDictionaries: ''

ParameterizedAdapter class>>on: anObject
    ^self new adaptee: anObject
```

Assuming setter messages for all of the instance variables, a client can create a ParameterizedAdapter and supply its blocks as follows:

```
adapter := ParameterizedAdapter on: myGraphicalObject.
adapter
    getBlock: [:graphic | graphic boundingBox leftTop x];
    setBlock: [:graphic :newValue |
                graphic boundingBox leftTop x: newValue].
```

When the value message is received by the Adapter, the following method is invoked to retrieve the value as specified by the get block:

```
ParameterizedAdapter>>value
    ^getBlock value: adaptee
```

For our example, adapter value returns the *x*-coordinate of the left-top corner of the Adaptee's bounding box.

The value-setting block is used as follows. The first argument of the block is bound to the Adaptee and the second to the new value being set by a client:

```
ParameterizedAdapter>>value: anObject
    setBlock value: adaptee value: anObject
```

So the client could say adapter value: 10 to change the origin of the Adaptee's bounding box.

Design Patterns refers to this type of Adapter as a **Parameterized Adapter** (DP 145); it's really just another kind of Pluggable Adapter—we're just telling the Adapter to perform a block rather than forward a single message selector each time value or value: is received. We can simply call it a **Block-Based Pluggable Adapter**. In fact, in VisualWorks the class that implements what we've called a Message-Based Pluggable Adapter is AspectAdaptor, and what *Design Patterns* calls a Parameterized Adapter is implemented by the PluggableAdaptor class. (See Known Smalltalk Uses.)

Alternative Solutions

Tailored Adapters in Smalltalk?   If we know the specific mappings of Client-initiated messages to Adaptee methods at design time, as in the Tailored Adapter case, why not just code these translation methods directly in the Adaptee class and avoid using an Adapter altogether? Returning to our Shape example, if we know boundingBox must be translated to getExtent, we can simply code this translation directly in the TextView class. Then we can let the DrawingEditor send messages directly to TextView instances without an intervening Adapter object.

In C++, we might not want to adopt this approach because adding a method to a class means having to recompile the entire class, and this may not be possible at all if we don't have the source code for the class. In Smalltalk, with incremental compilation of individual methods, this is a nonissue. So we can simply code:

```
TextView>>boundingBox
    "Translate the message and delegate to me"
    ^self getExtent
```

The upshot is that you will be hard-pressed to find in Smalltalk an object whose only job is that of a Tailored Adapter.

Tailored Adapter Subclasses.   We may not want to bloat a generically usable class, such as a user interface widget class, with application-specific translation messages every time it is used by a new application. We still have another alternative. Rather than define a new Adapter class in the Shape hierarchy, we can implement a subclass of TextView with the same sort of translation methods:

```
TextView subclass: #TextViewShape
    . . .
```

We let TextViewShape inherit all of the TextView methods and simply add the translating methods in the subclass. These methods look like the previous code:

```
TextViewShape>>boundingBox
    "Translate the message and delegate to me"
    ^self getExtent
```

From the perspectives of program understanding and maintenance, it may be slightly more confusing to load up a single class with a bunch of domain- or application-specific messages. On the other hand, it may be more difficult to understand the code with extra, intervening Adapter objects. However, the `TextShape` class defined earlier resides in the `Shape` hierarchy and implements the abstract `Shape` protocol; this is a more cogent and coherent design than having a class in a discontiguous branch of the class hierarchy implement the same protocol. Also, if the protocol ever changes, modifications will occur in a single hierarchy branch rather than in several distinct locations, thus facilitating change and extensibility.

Adapter Role.   There are numerous types of Pluggable Adapters in the base VisualWorks image because the use of Adapters is a deep part of the VisualWorks user interface framework. But other Smalltalk environments have very different user interface frameworks. In some of these dialects, it would be difficult to find an object whose *only* job is that of Adapter.

In Visual Smalltalk, for instance, the panes in a window assume the *role* of Pluggable Adapter in addition to their widget behaviors. All panes—`TopPane` and its subclasses or `SubPane` subclasses—are capable of handling multiple user interaction events. Each pane can be told what messages to send and to whom when each event occurs. Without this pluggable mechanism, panes would be capable only of sending a generic message for each event. Hence they act as Adapters in that they can be configured to send a particular message understood by the application when a generic user action occurs.

For example, we can set things up so a pane forwards a message to another object (typically the application object) when the pane needs its contents filled. This is roughly equivalent to the situation when a VisualWorks widget sends the `value` message to its model (which may actually be an Adapter on some aspect of an application model) so the widget's contents or state can be set. Similarly, a pane can be told to send a specific message to another object when the pane changes, for example, by the user's making a selection. This is like a VisualWorks widget sending the `value:` message to inform the application (possibly via an Adapter) of a new value for one of its aspects.

When an application, often a `ViewManager` subclass, constructs a window, it sets up the event-message associations for each pane. For example, here's a portion of the window-building code from the `MethodBrowser` class:

```
MethodBrowser>>createView
    | pane |
    ...
    self addSubpane:
        ((pane := ListPane new)
            when: #needsContents send: #methodList:
                to: self with: pane;
```

```
when: #needsMenu send: #listMenu:
      to: self with: pane;
when: #clicked: send: #method:
      to: self with: pane;
...)
```

When the `ListPane` needs its contents (its list), it will forward the `method-List:` message to the `MethodBrowser` and pass itself as the message's argument. When a user clicks on an entry in that list, the `method:` message is sent, again with the `ListPane` as the argument so the `MethodBrowser` can ask the pane for its current selection. In this way, the pane itself adapts generic events to application-specific messages. (Visual Smalltalk's event machinery is also discussed in detail in Command (245) and Observer [see SASE in Visual Smalltalk, p. 314].)

IBM Smalltalk adopts a similar approach in allowing widgets to adapt events to application-specific messages and thus fulfill an Adapter role in addition to their interactive widget behaviors. Application objects can register to be informed when user actions occur by using the *callback* and *event handler* mechanisms (IBM Smalltalk differentiates user actions into two levels of abstraction: low-level mouse and key press operations—handled by the event handler machinery—and higher-level actions like closing a window or a complete button-down/button-up action on a button widget—handled by callbacks). Both mechanisms let the application specify a message to be sent for each widget event. (More details of IBM Smalltalk's callback and event handler mechanisms can be found in our Observer pattern in the section SASE in IBM Smalltalk, p. 317, and in Smith, 1995, and Shafer & Herndon, 1995.)

Even in VisualWorks, with its multiple Adapter classes, certain views can fill an Adapter role. Some `View` classes are implemented to be pluggable, such that the application model can specify the aspect which the view "observes," as well as application-specific messages for certain events. For example, the `TextView` class comment states: "TextView is a 'pluggable' view. . . . The chief mechanism is a set of selectors, which can be thought of as an adaptor to convert the generic TextView operations into model-specific operations." `TextView`s can be created with the following message:

```
newTextView := TextView
            on: self
            aspect: partMsg
            change: acceptMsg
            menu: menuMsg
            initialSelection: selection
```

For example, the `partMsg` argument might have the value `#text`, a message the application implements to supply its text aspect. When the `TextView` needs its contents, it obtains them from its model using the following application-supplied message:

```
TextView>>getContents
   | text |
   partMsg == nil ifTrue: [^Text new].
   text := model perform: partMsg.
   text == nil ifTrue: [^Text new].
   ^ text
```

Sample Code

We've already shown most of the code to implement a Parameterized Adapter (or Block-Based Pluggable Adapter). Here we'll show how to implement the Tailored and Message-Based Pluggable Adapters.

Tailored Adapter

For readers interested in seeing the Smalltalk implementation of the basic Adapter from *Design Patterns*, we start with the sample code for a Tailored Adapter. The following code implements the TextShape Adapter. The TextShape class resides in the Shape hierarchy and thus implements the Shape abstract interface. The class defines an instance variable that will reference the TextView Adaptee:

```
Shape subclass: #TextShape
   instanceVariableNames: 'textView'
   classVariableNames: ''
   poolDictionaries: ''

TextShape class>>new
   "Return a new instance of me pointing
    to an instance of TextView."
   ^self basicNew textView: TextView new
```

Next we define simple getter and setter methods . . .

```
TextShape>>textView
   "Return my Adaptee"
   ^textView

TextShape>>textView: aTextView
   "Set my Adaptee"
   textView := aTextView
```

. . . and the actual translation methods, such as:

```
TextShape>>boundingBox
   "Translate and delegate this to my TextView object."
   ^self textView getExtent
```

As mentioned in *Design Patterns* (DP 147), Adapters may also forward messages to their Adaptees without translation. This occurs when a portion of the

Adaptee's protocol coincides with that of the Adapter. Specifically, a message may be directly forwarded when it has the identical selector name and semantics in both Adapter and Adaptee. This is simply delegation; the Adapter delegates responsibility for answering to the Adaptee. An example is the following isEmpty implementation:

```
TextShape>>isEmpty
    ^self textView isEmpty
```

Nonetheless, the Adapter must translate at least some portion of the Target protocol; otherwise, we don't need an Adapter.

Message-Based Pluggable Adapter

A message-forwarding Pluggable Adapter typically implements a single generic getter-setter message pair such as value and value:. The Client must tell the Adapter how each of these should be translated; that is, the Client supplies the message selectors to be forwarded to the Adaptee in place of value and value:. These translations are represented symbolically: the Client specifies the selectors as Symbols, and the Adapter stores them in this format. This will become clear as we look at the code.

We begin with the Adapter's class definition and getter-setter methods for the Adaptee:

```
Object subclass: #MessageAdapter
    instanceVariableNames: 'adaptee getSelector setSelector'
    classVariableNames: ''
    poolDictionaries: ''

MessageAdapter class>>on: anAdaptee
    "Instance creation"
    ^self new adaptee: anAdaptee

MessageAdapter>>adaptee: anObject
    adaptee := anObject

MessageAdapter>>adaptee
    ^adaptee
```

Next come the methods Clients use to tell the Adapter how to translate messages:

```
MessageAdapter>>getSelector: aSymbol
    "Setup my getter message translation.
     aSymbol is the selector to send to my Adaptee
     when I receive the #value message"
    getSelector:= aSymbol
```

```
MessageAdapter>>setSelector: aSymbol
   "Setup my setter message translation.
    aSymbol is the selector to send to my Adaptee
    when I receive the #value: message"
   setSelector:= aSymbol

MessageAdapter>>onAspect: aspectSymbol
   "A handy method to set both setter and getter
    messages in one shot; assumes both have the same name,
    differing only by the ':' suffix for the setter."
   self
      getSelector: aspectSymbol;
      setSelector: (aspectSymbol, ':') asSymbol
```

When the Adapter receives the generic getter (`value`) or setter (`value:`) message, it responds by sending the corresponding translated message to the Adaptee:

```
MessageAdapter>>value
   "Return the aspect of my Adaptee specified by
    my getSelector"
   ^adaptee perform: getSelector

MessageAdapter>>value: anObject
   "Set the aspect of my Adaptee specified by
    my setSelector"
   ^adaptee perform: setSelector with: anObject
```

A `MessageAdapter` is instantiated and initialized by code such as the following:

```
adapter := MessageAdapter on: myApplicationModel.
adapter
   getSelector: #socialSecurity;
   setSelector: #socialSecurity:.
```

Alternatively, to be more succinct, we could replace the latter three lines of code with:

```
adapter onAspect: #socialSecurity.
```

Known Smalltalk Uses

AspectAdaptor

What we've implemented as a Message-Based Pluggable Adapter—the `MessageAdapter` class—is much the same as the VisualWorks `AspectAdaptor` class. An `AspectAdaptor` can be sent the `accessWith:` `getSymbol` `assignWith:` `putSymbol` message to set its getter and setter message selectors.

Path-Based Adapter

AspectAdaptor's superclass, ProtocolAdaptor, also implements a variation on the Adapter theme. We may be interested in a particular aspect of the Adaptee that cannot be retrieved (or set) by a single getter (or setter) message. Suppose the Adaptee is a graphical object, as in the ParameterizedAdapter example. As in that example, we want the Adapter to retrieve a specific aspect of the Adaptee—in particular, the *x*-coordinate of the origin of the graphic's bounding box—when the value message is received. Rather than associating a single selector or a block with the value message, ProtocolAdaptor's concrete subclasses allow Clients to specify a *list* of selectors to send to the Adaptee, as in this AspectAdaptor example:

```
adaptor := AspectAdaptor new.
adaptor
    subject: myGraphicalObject;
    accessPath: #(boundingBox origin x).
```

The argument to the subject: message becomes the Adaptee. When the AspectAdaptor receives the value message, it successively sends each message in its access path array to retrieve a specific aspect of the Adaptee. We can label this a **Path-Based Adapter**. In this case, the Adaptee is a graphical object. First the boundingBox message is sent to it, returning a Rectangle; then the origin message is sent to the Rectangle returning a Point; and finally x is sent to the Point, retrieving its *x*-coordinate. So if the graphic's bounding box is a Rectangle whose top left corner is 1@2, the following statement returns 1:

```
adaptor value
```

Interestingly, AspectAdaptor lets you mix and match approaches: you may specify only the getter and setter messages, only an access path, or both. Thus the following code is equivalent to the preceding:

```
adaptor := AspectAdaptor new.
adaptor
    subject: myGraphicalObject;
    accessPath: #(boundingBox origin);
    accessWith: #x assignWith: #x:.

adaptor value    "returns 1"
```

This example also allows us to set the *x*-coordinate of the top left corner of the bounding box. The following statement changes the origin to 10@2:

```
adaptor value: 10.

adaptor value    "now returns 10"
```

The same sort of path-based adaptation has been used in two constraint-based graphical editors to provide access to specific aspects of graphical objects in a general way. We need this in a constraint-based editor, for example, to constrain a line to be horizontal. Here, a constraint object must access the y-coordinates of the line's end points. For this, we could use two Path-Based Adapters; in both, the line object would be the Adaptee, and we would need respective access paths `#(endPoint1 y)` and `#(endPoint2 y)`. To handle this situation, ThingLab (Borning, 1981) implemented a Path-Based Adapter mechanism so, as in a `ProtocolAdaptor`, the generic method to retrieve a graphical object's value could retrieve a specific aspect thereof (actually, with an empty access path, the entire graphical object would be retrieved); the same basic technique was adapted for use in Grace (Alpert, 1993). In both cases, the Path-Based Adapter was implemented in environments lacking an existing `ProtocolAdaptor`–like class. In both, the code that uses the access path array to retrieve a particular aspect of the subject (Adaptee) looks essentially like this:

```
^accessPath
    inject: subject
    into: [:obj :msg | obj perform: msg]
```

PluggableAdaptor

VisualWorks also includes a class named `PluggableAdaptor`. Here, rather than supplying the symbolic names of accessor selectors, clients specify blocks of code to be executed when the `value` or `value:` messages are received.

It is interesting to note the difference. With the selector approach, the ultimate behavior is implemented in the Adaptee; the Adapter merely knows which message to send to invoke that behavior. In contrast, supplying the adaptive behavior via blocks means the code that gets executed resides in (an instance variable of) the Adapter, making it in a real sense independent of the Adaptee's definition. Blocks provide more flexibility; the downside is that the code is more difficult to understand.

VisualWorks User Interface Framework

Every interactive application constructed with the VisualWorks `UIPainter` uses the `UIBuilder` framework at runtime to build the user interface windows and widgets. Every application that uses this framework uses Adapters between the user interface widgets and the underlying application model.

More Examples from the VisualWorks Image

There are many more Adapter variations in the VisualWorks base class library, all implemented by the classes in the `ValueModel` hierarchy (however, see the following section). Woolf (1995b) provides an in-depth discussion of `ValueModels`; see also the sections on VisualWorks adapters in Lewis (1995) and Howard (1995).

Looks Like a Duck, But Does It Quack Like One?

`ValueModel` also includes subclasses that appear to be Adapters—they're in the `ValueModel` hierarchy and they implement the `value` and `value:` messages—but they're not truly Adapters according to the Gang of Four criteria. In a true Adapter, the Adaptee is a persistent subcomponent for the life of the Adapter, and when the Adapter receives a message, it forwards a second (often different) message to its Adaptee. On the other hand, instances of `ValueHolder`, a `Value-Model` subclass, simply wrap another object. When one of these wrapper objects is sent the `value` message, it simply returns the wrapped object; it does not send a message to it. More important, when a "true" Adapter receives the `value:` message, a secondary message is forwarded to the Adaptee. That message *may* modify the Adaptee, but the encapsulated Adaptee object remains the same object. When a `ValueHolder` wrapper receives the `value:` message, it *replaces* its embedded object; it's now a different object. The Visual Smalltalk `Shared-Value` class behaves in this same fashion.

Although these implementations are not truly Gang of Four Adapters, they are still adaptation *things* that developers have found quite useful in particular application contexts. The point is, at times we can implement something akin to a pattern—something that's not quite a true example of the pattern definition—and it can still be useful. Like Adapters, `ValueHolders` and `SharedValues` are beneficial in adaptation situations when we want to wrap an object and have the wrapper respond to the generic `value` message; it does so in a different fashion from a Gang of Four Adapter, but it nonetheless does so in a way useful for widgets and other objects that know only to send the `value` message to retrieve an object's value. Wrappers (`SharedValues` or `ValueHolders`) can also be used to simulate true call-by-reference semantics, which is disallowed in Smalltalk. (In Smalltalk, a method can send messages to an argument but cannot assign a new object to the argument using the assignment operator (`:=`); when an argument is a wrapper, however, the method can send the `value:` message to the argument—replacing the wrapped object—and the sender can subsequently retrieve the new object by sending `value` to the wrapper.) The ultimate point is that in addition to applying patterns exactly as is, we can often mold or adapt (no pun intended) the canonical definition of a pattern to slightly different application contexts.

Related Patterns

Observer

Often an Adapter participates in the Observer (305) pattern. Certain Adapters can be told to trigger a message-send to a specific object or a set of dependent objects when a change occurs. In VisualWorks, for example, Adapters reside in the `ValueModel` hierarchy, and `ValueModel` implements the `onChange-Send:to:` message. This is used to notify a specific object when the Adapter is told to change:

```
adapter onChangeSend: #changeOccurred to: self
```

When `adapter` receives the `value:` message, it will send the `change-Occurred` message in addition to its normal Adaptee value-setting behavior.

Command

An Adapter can be used as a `Command` object in the Command (245) pattern. In fact, the two objects fulfill similar roles; they sit between a client and an Adaptee, translating messages sent by the former to others forwarded to the latter. A Command simply has a specialized role in which the client is a user interface widget or control (e.g., a button or a menu item), and the message sent to the Adaptee is the action to perform in response to activating the control (e.g., pushing a button, selecting a menu item).

Bridge and Facade

An Adapter changes the interface of the Adaptee, at least from the Client's perspective. Other patterns are also used to present a different messaging interface to a Client. In the Bridge (121) pattern, the Abstraction object defines an abstraction of its Implementation object's interface. The goal is to hide implementation details behind the Abstraction interface. The Abstraction object effectively translates messages and forwards them to the Implementation object, where the real work is performed. Bridge has a different intent and applicability from Adapter, however. Adapter is applicable when we have objects that only know how to communicate with their collaborators using a certain protocol but need to collaborate with objects that don't understand this protocol. Bridge "is meant to separate an interface from its implementation so that they can be varied easily and independently" (DP 149). It is not meant to adapt an existing object to an incompatible protocol.

A Facade (179) provides an abstract interface to an entire subsystem of objects, whereas an Adapter adapts a single object to its Client. Although their implementations and applicability are quite different, the two patterns are similar in spirit, that is, providing an alternative interface for Clients.

Decorator

A Decorator (161) also sits between a Client and another object (the Component), receiving Client messages and forwarding some or all to the Component. A Decorator, though, completely adheres to the interface of its Component and is used to enhance its functionality. Unlike an Adapter, it does not adapt the interface of the Component it decorates.

BRIDGE (DP 151)   Object Structural

Intent

Decouple an abstraction from its implementation so that the two can vary independently.

Structure

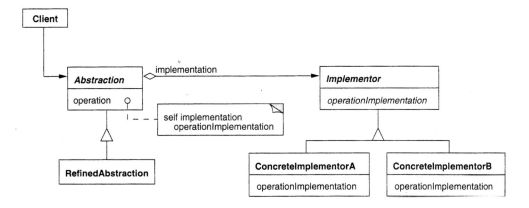

Discussion

Everyone talks about the importance of separating interface from implementation. It's one of the main topics in the *Design Patterns* introduction (DP 11–18). At the object level, this means declaring an interface as a **type,** and then implementing it as a **class.** When a single type can be implemented several different ways, several classes implement that single type. Yet for any particular object, its class binds together its interface and its implementation.

The Bridge pattern splits apart an interface and its implementation into two separate, collaborating objects. Together, these two objects act as one logical object, with a combined interface and implementation. The two objects are instances of two separate classes: an Abstraction and an Implementor. The Abstraction represents the type—the interface that the logical object will show to clients. However, the Abstraction does not implement its interface; it delegates it to its implementation (*Design Patterns* calls this relationship "imp"). The Implementor actually implements the interface that the Abstraction provides.

The **Abstraction** and **Implementor** classes are usually hierarchies. Various **RefinedAbstractions** represent subtypes of the more general Abstraction type. Various ConcreteImplementors represent alternative approaches to implementing the Implementor. A key feature of the Bridge pattern is that any Abstraction works with any Implementor. Thus the relationship between the two hierarchies—the interface they will use to collaborate together—is defined in the two classes at the top of the hierarchies. Subclasses should not change or extend this interface because that would ruin the ability of any class from one hierarchy to work with any class from the other hierarchy. Thus, all of the classes in the Implementor hierarchy need to have the same interface so that they will all work with any of the Abstraction classes. If the Implementors delegate back to the Abstractions, all of the Abstraction classes need to provide a single, privileged interface for the Implementors to use. However, since the Abstraction subclasses represent subtypes, their public interfaces can extend the basic one declared by the top Abstraction class.

Why Bridge?

Why split an object into separate interface and implementation pieces? For the same reason you ever split one logical object into two or more separate classes: so that the parts can vary independently. Each hierarchy represents a property that can vary independently of the other. In Bridge, the two properties being separated are interface and implementation. Trying to implement two orthogonal (independent) properties in one hierarchy invariably leads to code duplication.

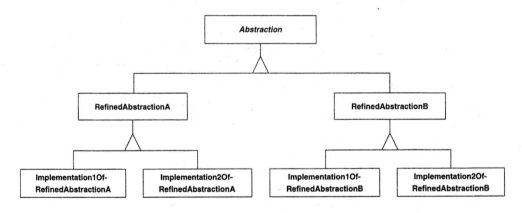

For a more concrete example, see the diagram of a single Window class hierarchy in *Design Patterns* (DP 151).

Inevitably, the code in `Implementation1OfRefinedAbstractionA` is going to be very similar to the code in `Implementation1OfRefinedAbstractionB`. The real difference between these two classes is what they inherit. Ideally, "Implementation 1" should be coded in just one place that both `RefinedAbstractionA` and `RefinedAbstractionB` can reuse.

This problem of needing a flexible alternative to subclassing is the main motivation of Decorator (161). That pattern separates a generic Component class into two subhierarchies: various ConcreteComponents that can be decorated and various Decorators that can decorate. The limitation of this Decorator approach is that the difference between a decorated component and an undecorated one should be transparent to the client, so Decorator and ConcreteComponent must share the same Component interface and neither can extend that interface. In Bridge, these alternate ways of implementing a single interface are extracted into a completely separate hierarchy that can have a completely different interface from the first hierarchy. While the Implementors must all have the same interface, the Abstraction subclasses can extend the Abstraction interface.

IBM Smalltalk Collections

Early versions of IBM Smalltalk contain a model example of Bridge, documented by LaLonde and Pugh (1995). These versions implement a collection in two parts: an interface that describes how it works and an implementation that makes it work as efficiently as possible. For example, the diagram below shows the classes that implement Set. If a set is small, its elements are stored in a linear list, EsLinearSet. If the set is large, it stores its elements in a EsLinearHashSet, a hash table. This arrangement makes look-up as fast as possible in either case. If a small set with a EsLinearSet grows, the Set will switch its implementation to a EsLinearHashSet when it has enough elements:

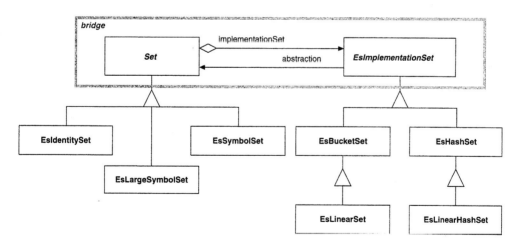

This is an example of Bridge. The Set hierarchy is the Abstraction, and the Implementor is the EsImplementationSet hierarchy. An EsImplementationSet implements its Set. The Set does not contain the elements; it uses its EsImplementationSet to do that. The EsImplementationSet is hidden from the client; it knows only about the Set.

The original IBM Collection hierarchy manifests other examples of Bridge. OrderedCollection and SortedCollection are subclasses of Additive-SequenceableCollection, which in turn uses subclasses of EsOrdered-CollectionImplementor and EsSortedCollectionImplementor to implement their abstractions. Similarly, `Dictionary` uses the appropriate `EsImplementationSet` to store its associations.

The `Collection` hierarchy stopped using Bridge as of IBM Smalltalk 3.0. Apparently the efficiency gains were not worth the increase in complexity. A developer can still choose from a `Set`, `EsIdentitySet`, `EsSymbolSet`, and `EsLargeSymbolSet`, but these collections now store their elements in a uniform way. The first three classes are for small collections and use an `Array` for storage, whereas an `EsLargeSymbolSet` uses an `Array` of `EsSymbolSets`.

A Window Hierarchy

The Motivation in *Design Patterns* provides a classic example of Bridge. It describes implementing a window in two parts. One part represents the kind of window: regular, iconic, or transient. The other part represents the window system (look and feel) that creates the window: X-Windows, Presentation Manager, and so forth. Any type of window will work with any window system because of the common interface defined in their superclasses, `Window` and `Window-Implementation` (which *Design Patterns* calls "WindowImp"). As this diagram shows, this common interface is the Bridge in the Bridge pattern:

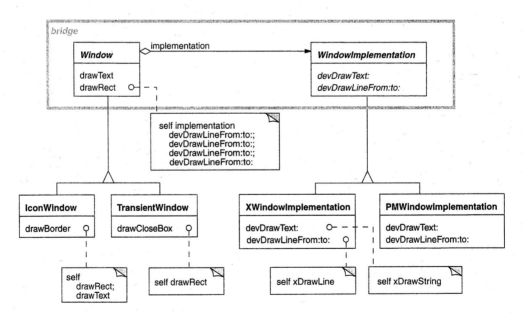

This separation of widget from window system would seem perfect for Visual-Works since it can emulate several look-and-feel standards; however, it doesn't need Bridge to do so. Each widget is actually a hierarchy instead of just a class. The superclass defines the widget's interface, and subclasses implement the interface for different look-and-feels. For example, `CheckButtonView`—the checkbox class—has subclasses such as `Win3CheckButtonView`, `MacCheck-`

`ButtonView,` and `MotifCheckButtonView`. This is a hierarchy of specialized subclasses, not a Bridge. IBM Smalltalk is similarly portable across platforms and capable of using several different native widget sets, but it does not implement this as a Bridge.

Widget-to-Implementation Bridge

Although VisualWorks 2.5 does not use Bridge to implement widgets that can emulate any look-and-feel, a proposed version of VisualWorks attempts to use Bridge to implement its widgets. Yelland describes a proposed architecture for VisualWorks that uses native platform widgets instead of emulated ones while maintaining platform portability (Yelland, 1996; for discussion of Yelland's paper, see Flyweight (189)).

A hierarchy of widget classes define the widgets' interface to the rest of the Smalltalk system (e.g., `RadioButtonWidget` and `ListWidget`, subclasses of `Widget`). It also contains a hierarchy of widget implementations for each platform supported (`Win32RadioButtonBridge`, `Win32ListBridge`, and so forth in the `Win32Bridge` hierarchy). Thus all the VisualWorks widget classes inherit from a common superclass, while all of the Bridge classes for a particular platform inherit behavior common to all widgets on that platform.

This instance diagram shows how a radio button would be configured on a Windows machine as opposed to a Macintosh:

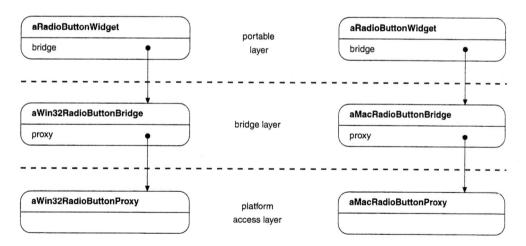

The division of platform-neutral and platform-specific widgets also allows the Smalltalk image to save itself in a platform-neutral form. The save process does not preserve the platform-specific objects. When the image is run again and it reactivates the platform-neutral widgets, they create the platform-specific widgets appropriate for the current platform.

Yelland calls this separation of widgets into `Widget` and `WidgetBridge` hierarchies an example of the Bridge pattern, but it actually seems to be an example of Adapter (105) that adapts a `Widget` to a `WidgetProxy`. Proxies for different platforms have different interfaces, yet a `Widget` class expects all implementations to have the same interface, so each `WidgetProxy` class has a corresponding `WidgetBridge` class that adapts it to the standard interface that the `Widget` class expects.

The framework also includes an Abstract Factory (31), `WidgetPolicy`, to map the `Widgets` to their `WidgetBridges`. A true example of the Bridge pattern does not use an Abstract Factory to find its Implementor classes.

This framework separates the interface (the `Widgets`) from their implementations (the `WidgetProxys`), so it does contain the spirit of the Bridge pattern. But by inserting a "Bridge" object (a `WidgetBridge`) between the interface and implementation objects, the framework is not implemented according to the Bridge pattern.

Hypothetical Example

So how could you use Bridge in Smalltalk? Suppose a system required trees with several different kinds of nodes. Some nodes in the tree can be edited; others cannot. Since this is a tree, some nodes are Composites (137), and others are Leaves. The problem is how to implement a hierarchy that supports all four combinations: editable versus noneditable, composites versus leaves. The answer is to use two hierarchies: one for the editable property and the other for the composite hierarchy. The editable classes provide an interface for the node that is implemented by the classes in the composite hierarchy. As the following diagram shows, this is a perfectly good example of Bridge:

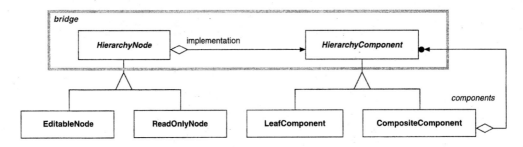

This design was considered for an application we worked on but was ultimately rejected because it proved to be more complex than the application required.

A Seldom-Used Pattern

There are few examples of Bridge in Smalltalk. It's a potentially useful pattern, yet it's not used much. *Design Patterns* mentions several examples from other languages, but none from Smalltalk (DP 160). The best example in Smalltalk is the way collections were implemented in early versions of IBM Smalltalk, but that design has been taken out of later versions. Other languages use Bridge to implement collections—*Design Patterns* cites libg++ for C++—but Smalltalk does not find Bridge necessary. Platform-portable Smalltalk dialects might use it to implement their various GUI look-and-feels the way *Design Patterns* Motivation suggests, but they don't. The proposed VisualWorks architecture for native widgets calls part of its design Bridge, but the implementation is actually Adapter (105) aided by Abstract Factory (31). NeXT's AppKit uses Bridge to implement device-independent graphical images, but Smalltalk image classes (such as the Image hierarchy in VisualWorks) achieve platform independence without using Bridge. Handle/body is similar to Bridge, but it's so specialized that it's a C++ idiom, not a language-neutral pattern.

Collaborating Hierarchies

Although examples of Bridge in Smalltalk are rare, the principles behind the pattern are highly applicable through a broader pattern we'll call Collaborating Hierarchies. When an object has more than one property that can be specialized through subclassing and these properties are orthogonal to each other, collaborating hierarchies separate each property into its own hierarchy whose subclassing can vary independently of the others. The relationship and interface between the hierarchies is defined in the classes at the top of the hierarchies so that any subclass in one hierarchy can work with any subclass in another. Client objects can collaborate with any of the hierarchies. Typically, one client will collaborate with one hierarchy while another will collaborate with the other.

This sounds a lot like Bridge, and Bridge is a specialization of Collaborating Hierarchies. In Bridge, the two properties that need to vary independently are always interface (Abstraction) and implementation (Implementor). The client always collaborates with the Abstraction and only the Abstraction, such that the Implementor is hidden from the client. The Implementor classes do not have a public interface for clients, only a privileged interface for the Abstraction.

Examples of Collaborating Hierarchies

Collaborating hierarchies are the source of object pairs that work together. View-Controller in VisualWorks is a good example. A View needs a Controller, and vice versa. The diagram on the next page shows these relationships for text widgets:

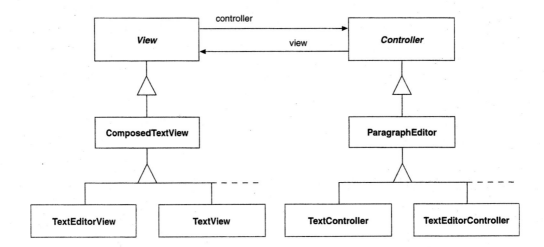

To create a `View-Controller` pair, a client creates an instance each from the `View` and `Controller` hierarchies and puts them together. Many class combinations won't produce very useful behavior, but many work well. The two hierarchies can be extended independently to create new combinations from both existing and new classes.

A more flexible but less pure example of collaborating hierarchies is `ValueModels` and value-based subviews in VisualWorks. Each value-based subview (e.g., a widget such as a checkbox or input field) expects a `ValueModel` for its model. Any `ValueModel` will do as long as its value is of the correct type. Since any value-based subview class can use any `ValueModel` subclass, numerous combinations are possible. Although there is a single `ValueModel` hierarchy, however, there is no "`ValueBasedSubview`" hierarchy; the value-based subview classes are scattered throughout the `View` hierarchy (Woolf, 1995a).

These are examples of collaborating hierarchies, but they are not examples of Bridge. Few collaborating hierarchies consist of interface and implementation hierarchies. `View-Controller` is a separation of responsibilities. Although both hierarchies can be said to be an interface for the other, neither is really an implementation of the other. Furthermore, neither contains the other. Clients can access either one and collaborate with it independently of the other. `View` and `Controller` are mutual Strategies (339), not a Bridge. The same is true of `ValueModels` and value-based subviews.

Another example of collaborating hierarchies is the relationship between `Geometric` and `GeometricWrapper` in VisualWorks. `GeometricWrapper` is part of the visual decorator hierarchy, but it doesn't decorate a `Geometric`; it adapts one. (For a diagram of these classes, see the Sample Code section.)

The `Geometric` hierarchy implements common two-dimensional shapes from geometry like `Circle`, `Rectangle`, and `LineSegment`. They are not implemented as visuals, but they can be displayed visually using a `GeometricWrap-`

per. A GeometricWrapper wraps a Geometric to give it a visual interface and properties like line thickness. StrokingWrapper draws the outline of the Geometric, and FillingWrapper draws a closed Geometric filled in.

GeometricWrapper is implemented as a subclass of Wrapper, which is the root of the hierarchy of visual decorators. Thus GeometricWrapper would seem to be a Decorator (161). However, since Geometrics are not visuals but GeometricWrappers are, GeometricWrapper isn't really a Decorator, so it shouldn't be implemented in the Wrapper hierarchy at all. Since a GeometricWrapper converts a Geometric's mathematical interface into a visual's interface, it is actually an Adapter (105) and should be implemented in the leaf visual hierarchy.

But is GeometricWrapper simply an Adapter? Both Geometric and GeometricWrapper are hierarchies. The first represents different shapes; the latter provides different ways of drawing them. Any closed shape can be drawn filled or stroked. Thus you can choose a shape from one hierarchy and a way to draw it from another hierarchy, put them together, and you've got a geometric visual. Combinations of open shapes with filling wrappers won't work, but any other combination will. These are Collaborating Hierarchies where one of the hierarchies is a hierarchy of Adapters.

Another example is the relationship between Window and WindowDisplayPolicy in VisualWorks. It is an example of Collaborating Hierarchies where one of the hierarchies is a Strategy (339) hierarchy for the other.

Most Windows delegate their display behavior to a separate WindowDisplayPolicy that actually performs the redisplay. (The exception, TransientWindow, duplicates the code in WindowDisplayPolicy instead of delegating to it.) WindowDisplayPolicy's subclass, DoubleBufferedWindowDisplayPolicy, also redisplays its window, but uses double-buffered graphics that consume more memory but reduce flicker. Thus the display policy classes are Strategy (339) objects that determine exactly how a window will redisplay itself.

But more than just Strategy, these are Collaborating Hierarchies. Both ScheduledWindow and WindowDisplayPolicy are hierarchies, albeit small ones, and any window works with any display policy.

Implementation

In addition to the implementation issues raised in *Design Patterns*, here are two more to consider that apply to both Bridge and Collaborating Hierarchies:

1. *Abstraction and Implementor hierarchies. Design Patterns* specifies that Bridge be implemented in two hierarchies. This is necessary in C++ because of its static typing. In Smalltalk, classes of the same type do not have to be implemented in the same hierarchy. In most patterns, implementing classes of the same type in the same hierarchy is desirable even if not required. In Bridge or Collaborating Hierarchies, the two sets of classes should be implemented

in two hierarchies, and the relationship between the top abstract classes should be made explicit; otherwise, the pattern will be virtually impossible to recognize, much less use and maintain.

2. *Strong coupling.* LaLonde and Pugh (1995) raise the issue of whether the Abstraction and Implementor should be strongly coupled; that is, should the Implementor have a reference back to its Abstraction in addition to the Abstraction's reference to the Implementor? This allows the Implementor to tell the Abstraction to replace it with another Implementor. For example, the Set Bridge in IBM Smalltalk is strongly coupled.

Sample Code

With so few true examples of Bridge that have actually been implemented in Smalltalk, it's difficult to show code examples. Instead, let's look at the code for VisualWorks's Geometric/GeometricWrapper Collaborating Hierarchies. Here's the structure of this framework:

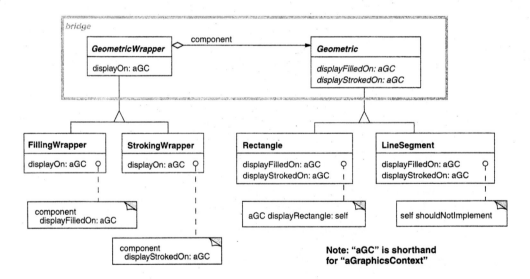

The Geometric hierarchy models abstractions from geometry with subclasses like Rectangle, Circle, LineSegment, and Polyline. Let's consider Rectangle and LineSegment as representative:

```
Object subclass: #Geometric
    instanceVariableNames: ''
    classVariableNames: '...'
    poolDictionaries: ''

Geometric subclass: #Rectangle
    instanceVariableNames: 'origin corner'
    classVariableNames: ''
    poolDictionaries: ''
```

```
Geometric subclass: #LineSegment
    instanceVariableNames: 'start end'
    classVariableNames: ''
    poolDictionaries: ''
```

A basic feature of a `Geometric` is that it can tell whether it intersects a rectangular area. It can intersect in two ways: its outline can intersect the area, or its region (filled in area) can intersect it. (Just because the outlines don't intersect doesn't mean the regions cannot. If a closed geometric contains the test rectangle, its outline does not intersect, but its region does.) Only a closed geometric knows its region, so `Geometric` implements `canBeFilled` to determine if a geometric is closed:

```
Geometric>>canBeFilled
    "Is this geometric closed?"
    ^false

Rectangle>>canBeFilled
    ^true
```

`LineSegment` does not implement `canBeFilled` because it inherits `Geometric`'s implementation of `false`. (This is an example of a concrete operation; see Template Method (355).)

Geometrics are useful shapes, but as mathematical abstractions, they don't actually look like anything. They're not visuals any more than numbers or points are, so geometrics are not implemented in the `VisualComponent` hierarchy. Still, there are times when you want to display them visually in a window as shapes. The problem is how to display objects that are not visuals as though they are.

This is why VisualWorks also implements the `GeometricWrapper` hierarchy. `Geometrics` are not visuals, but `GeometricWrappers` are, and they know how to interface with a `Geometric` to determine how to draw its shape. (For a discussion of how visual trees work, see Composite (137). For a discussion of the role of `Wrapper` visuals, see Decorator (161).)

There are two ways to display a geometric: as an outline or as a region (only closed geometrics have regions). Hence, there are two kinds of `GeometricWrappers`: `FillingWrapper`, which displays a region, and `StrokingWrapper`, which displays an outline. The `Geometric` is actually stored as the wrapper's `component`:

```
VisualPart subclass: #Wrapper
    instanceVariableNames: 'component'
    classVariableNames: ''
    poolDictionaries: ''

Wrapper subclass: #GeometricWrapper
    instanceVariableNames: ''
    classVariableNames: ''
    poolDictionaries: ''
```

```
GeometricWrapper subclass: #FillingWrapper
    instanceVariableNames: ''
    classVariableNames: ''
    poolDictionaries: ''

GeometricWrapper subclass: #StrokingWrapper
    instanceVariableNames: 'lineWidth'
    classVariableNames: ''
    poolDictionaries: ''
```

All visuals implement the message displayOn: to display themselves, and
GeometricWrapper is no exception. (See Chain of Responsibility (225) for a
discussion of Object-Oriented Recursion and how a message like displayOn:
recurses through the visual tree.) A Wrapper displays itself by displaying its
component, and so a GeometricWrapper displays itself by displaying its
Geometric. However, a GeometricWrapper doesn't know whether to display
its Geometric's outline or its region. Therefore, its implementation of displayOn: *should be* deferred to its subclasses. (This is an abstract method in Template Method (355).) On the other hand, subclasses do know whether to display
an outline or a region, so they tell the Geometric what to do.

```
GeometricWrapper>>displayOn: aGraphicsContext
    "Display this object on aGraphicsContext."
    self subclassResponsibility

FillingWrapper>>displayOn: aGraphicsContext
    component displayFilledOn: aGraphicsContext

StrokingWrapper>>displayOn: aGraphicsContext
    lineWidth == nil
        ifFalse: [aGraphicsContext lineWidth: lineWidth].
    component displayStrokedOn: aGraphicsContext
```

Each Geometric is responsible for drawing itself either filled (its region) or
stroked (its outline). Rectangle can do both, but since LineSegment is not
closed, it can only draw itself stroked. A shape uses a GraphicsContext to
draw itself:

```
Geometric>>displayFilledOn: aGraphicsContext
    "Use aGraphicsContext to draw this shape's region."
    self subclassResponsibility

Geometric>>displayStrokedOn: aGraphicsContext
    "Use aGraphicsContext to draw this shape's outline."
    self subclassResponsibility

Rectangle>>displayFilledOn: aGraphicsContext
    aGraphicsContext displayRectangle: self

Rectangle>>displayStrokedOn: aGraphicsContext
    aGraphicsContext displayRectangularBorder: self
```

```
LineSegment>>displayFilledOn: aGraphicsContext
    self shouldNotImplement

LineSegment>>displayStrokedOn: aGraphicsContext
    aGraphicsContext displayLineFrom: start to: end
```

Any `GeometricWrapper` can be used to display any closed `Geometric`. Even open `Geometrics` work with outlining wrappers. The `GeometricWrapper` provides the visual abstraction of a shape drawn as its region or outline, and the `Geometric` implements the shape's appearance in terms of the messages needed to draw it. The `GeometricWrapper` hides the `Geometric` from the rest of the system.

For an example of how to display geometrics in a window, look at the example method, `Geometric class>>twoSquares`:

```
Geometric class>>twoSquares
    | g1 g2 |
    . . .
    g1 := (0 @ 0 extent: 100 @ 100) asFiller.
    g2 := (100 @ 100 extent: 100 @ 100) asStroker.
    . . .
```

The code creates a `Rectangle` and sends `asFiller` to it. The `Rectangle` creates a `FillingWrapper` on itself and returns the wrapper (`asFiller` would fail if the `Geometric` were not closed). Similarly, g2 gets a `StrokingWrapper` on another `Rectangle`. These two wrappers are added to the window so that it displays them.

Known Smalltalk Uses

Bridge is very rare in Smalltalk; there is not much need to split an object into separate interface and implementation hierarchies. The complexity this adds usually outweighs the benefits.

Collaborating Hierarchies is very common in Smalltalk. A single logical object is often split into two or more hierarchies where each hierarchy allows a single property to vary independently of the others through subclassing. Each hierarchy can represent any property necessary, not just interface or implementation.

Bridge

Several of the `Collection` subhierarchies in early versions of IBM Smalltalk are implemented with one Bridge each.

The `Button` class in VisualWorks has been mentioned as a potential example of Bridge, but it is not. `Button` is a member of the `Wrapper` hierarchy that contains a `LabeledButtonView`—a hierarchy of platform-specific button implementations for checkbox, push, and radio buttons. This seems like Bridge because the Button acts like an abstraction and the `LabeledButtonView` acts like an implementation. However, `Button` is not a hierarchy like the Abstraction is. `Button` is simply a Decorator (161) that stores platform-neutral information (e.g., what kind of button it is and what its label is).

Similarly, SpecWrapper in VisualWorks is also described as a Bridge, but it is not. A member of the Wrapper hierarchy, it binds the abstract description of a widget with the object that implements it. To switch to a different look-and-feel, SpecWrapper throws out the widget and uses the spec and the new look-and-feel setting to generate a new widget. This is another example of Decorator (161), though a fairly unusual one.

Collaborating Hierarchies

The GeometricWrapper and Geometric hierarchies in VisualWorks are Collaborating Hierarchies where the wrappers are a hierarchy of Adapters (105). The same is true of the Window and WindowDisplayPolicy hierarchies, where the policies are a hierarchy of Strategies (339).

Yelland (1996) describes a proposed version of VisualWorks that uses Bridge to split a widget into a platform-neutral interface object and a platform-specific implementation object that adapts a Proxy (213). However, this is really two sets of Collaborating Hierarchies, not Bridge. The first set is Widget/Widget-Bridge, and the second set is WidgetBridge/WidgetProxy. The first hierarchy is a Strategy hierarchy where each widget is a strategy for how to display its value. The second hierarchy is a set of Adapters, and the third hierarchy is a set of Proxies that wrap the native widgets themselves.

The View-Controller pair of hierarchies in VisualWorks is a pair of Collaborating Hierarchies—two Strategy hierarchies. Similarly, as described earlier, the ValueModel and value-based subview pairings in VisualWorks are also Collaborating Hierarchies; the subviews are Strategies, and the ValueModels are Adapters.

Related Patterns

Bridge versus Decorator

Bridge and Decorator (161) attack the same problem: subclassing gone berserk. When you have to implement the same subclass of two different classes, you've got a problem. Decorator solves it by extracting the subclass's extra behavior into a separate class whose instances can be wrapped around the base classes' instances to add the extra behavior. It requires that all of the classes have the same interface. It also enables multiple decorators to be nested inside one another, on top of a single concrete component.

Bridge extracts all of the implementation details out of the original classes and moves them into a separate Implementor hierarchy. Then it reimplements the original hierarchy to make it a set of Abstractions that represent subtypes and delegate their implementation to the Implementors. Abstraction subclasses can have extended interfaces, but they cannot be nested like Decorators. However, the Bridge pattern can be applied repeatedly so that the Implementor hierarchy for one example might turn out to be the Abstraction hierarchy for a second example.

Bridge and Proxy

LaLonde and Pugh (1995) mention that a Proxy (213) can be implemented in Smalltalk as a Bridge, with `Proxy` being the Abstraction and `Object` being the Implementor.

Collaborating Hierarchies

The namesake class of most Structural and Behavioral patterns can be implemented in a hierarchy, and that hierarchy is often part of a pair of Collaborating Hierarchies. For example, a `GeometricWrapper` is an Adapter (105) for its `Geometric`, and `WindowDisplayPolicy` is a Strategy (339) for its `Window`.

COMPOSITE (DP 163)   Object Structural

Intent

Compose objects into tree structures to represent part-whole hierarchies. Composite lets clients treat individual objects and compositions of objects uniformly.

Structure

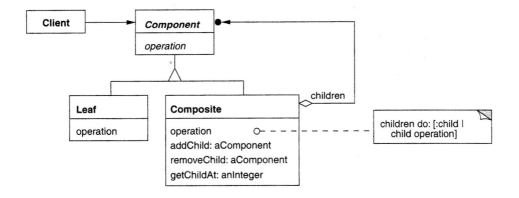

A typical Composite object structure might look like this:

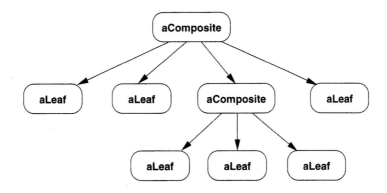

Discussion

The key to the Composite pattern is two classes: one that represents simple (or **Leaf**) objects and one that represents a group of objects. The group object, or **Composite**, acts like a Leaf by delegating its behavior to the objects in the group.

Both classes support the same core interface, allowing clients to collaborate with them interchangeably. The Composite itself takes advantage of the common interface because its group members can include both Leaf objects and Composites. A Composite can contain other Composites and so on until the final Composites contain nothing but Leaves. The result is a tree of Composite and Leaf objects.

The tree is one of the most common and powerful data structures in procedural programming (Sedgewick, 1988, Chap. 4), and its importance applies to object programming as well. Any hierarchical, compositional relationship lends itself to being modeled as a tree: all of the various departments and offices within a government, the systems within a multiprocessor, the sales territories of a multinational corporation. The question is: In what ways do the levels in the hierarchy behave the same? What makes every branch of the tree look like the whole tree and in fact look like its own branches? The issue is not what makes the levels and branches different, but what makes them the same because behavior that is the same is reusable.

Tree Structure

There are three ways to structure a tree, as shown below: top down, bottom up, and doubly linked. The nodes and their relationships to each other are the same in all three structures. However, their structures are different because of the direction of their pointers. In a top-down tree, each branch points to all of its children, so a client can ask a branch for its children, but a node doesn't know its parent. In a bottom-up tree, each node points to its parent, but a branch doesn't know its children. In a doubly linked tree, each node knows both its parent and its children. The direction of the pointers determines the direction of messages through the tree: down, up, or both. (See Chain of Responsibility (225).)

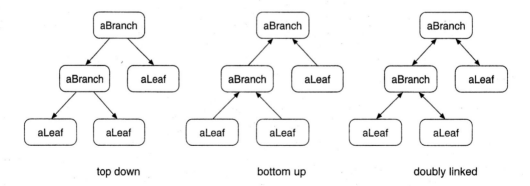

The Composite pattern defines a top-down tree, and messages travel down the tree.

Window Trees

Perhaps the best-known but seemingly unlikely example of a tree structure is a window in a windowing system. A window may look like a simple rectangular area, but Smalltalk stores it internally as a tree. The tree has three types of nodes: window, subview, and widget. The instance diagram below shows the object structure of a simple window:

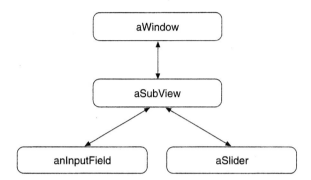

The window itself is the tree's root, with the window's subviews and their subviews comprising the branch nodes, culminating in widgets that are leaf nodes. Each node in the tree refers to its parent node as its **container** and to its child nodes as its **components.** The structure is a tree, not a graph, because each node has exactly one parent (except for the root, which by definition has no parent).

The three different kinds of nodes are easy to recognize by looking at how many components each one has. The window node has just one component. The widgets are leaf nodes because they have no components. The subview node is a branch node because it has multiple components. Subviews are the Composite in the Composite pattern.

The Composite and Leaf classes support the core interface defined by their common Component superclass. Thus a client of a node in a tree does not have to distinguish between branch nodes and leaf nodes.

Now let's look at the main classes in the VisualComponent hierarchy in VisualWorks. The Component class is VisualComponent, CompositePart is the Composite class, and the Leaf classes are DependentPart and SimpleComponent. Wrapper is an interesting one; it's actually the Decorator class in the Decorator (161) pattern, but as shown on the next page, in Composite it is another Leaf class.

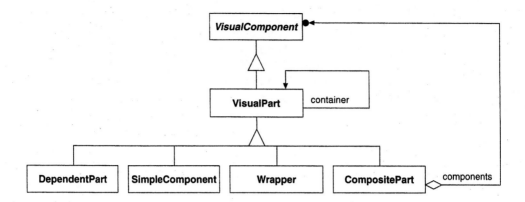

These VisualComponent classes are the participants in the Composite and Decorator patterns:

Pattern	Participant	VisualWorks Class
Composite and Decorator	Component	VisualComponent
Composite and Decorator	Leaf/ConcreteComponent	VisualPart subclasses
Composite	Composite	CompositePart
Decorator	Decorator	Wrapper

Other dialects implement similar visual classes that incorporate the Composite pattern:

Pattern	Participant	Visual Smalltalk Class
Composite and Decorator	Component	SubPane
Composite and Decorator	Leaf/ConcreteComponent	SubPane subclasses
Composite	Composite	GroupPane
Decorator	Decorator	none

Pattern	Participant	IBM Smalltalk Class
Composite and Decorator	Component	CwBasicWidget
Composite and Decorator	Leaf/ConcreteComponent	CwPrimitive subclasses
Composite	Composite	CwComposite
Decorator	Decorator	none

A Composite and a Leaf have the same core interface that allows them to work polymorphically. For example, any visual in VisualWorks knows its preferred bounds. A leaf visual knows how big it wants to be. A composite visual computes its bounds from those of its components; it determines their preferred bounds and merges them into a single rectangle. Another example is the way all visuals know how to draw themselves. A leaf visual just draws itself. Most composite visuals just draw themselves by telling their components to draw themselves.

Hence, any branch of a visual tree, from a single node to the entire tree, can be treated as a single visual and told how to behave. How the behavior is produced is a function of the branch's structure, but that is hidden from the client.

Visual Smalltalk and IBM Smalltalk implement graphical windows in a similar manner. Their classes are also listed in the table above. The composite visual classes are GroupPane in Visual Smalltalk and CwComposite in IBM Smalltalk. Both visual hierarchies are examples of the Composite pattern.

Nested Composites

A key advantage of the Composite pattern is not just that a Composite can be used to group together Leaves but also that it can be used to group together other Composites as well. In other words, a Composite can contain other Composites, which in turn can contain other Composites, until finally all of the branches terminate in Leaves. This forms a recursive structure such that the tree can have as many levels as necessary and the difference between an entire tree and a branch of a tree is indistinguishable. The object diagram in the Structure section (p. 137) illustrates this well.

Not all examples of the Composite pattern support this type of unlimited nesting. If the pattern is interpreted strictly, an example is not really an example unless it supports unlimited nesting. However, one of the main principles of the pattern is the ability to treat an object and a collection of those objects uniformly, and any example with this feature can be better understood in terms of the pattern even if the example doesn't employ all of the pattern's features.

Limited Types of Children

In general, a Composite can contain both Composite and Leaf nodes. However, some domains restrict this. For example, a computer can be modeled as a composite of circuit boards that contain chips *(see following page)*:

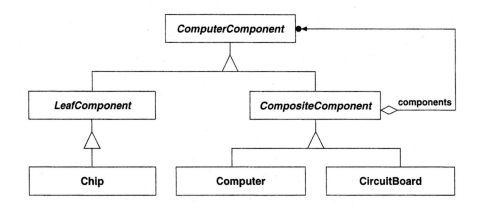

`Chip` is a Leaf class, and `Computer` and `CircuitBoard` are Composite classes. The topmost Composite class can contain any Components, but its subclasses must be more restrictive.

Unrestricted application of the Composite pattern would allow computers to contain other computers, circuit boards to contain computers, and a computer could contain both circuit boards and chips that are not part of any circuit board (which makes you wonder what those chips are mounted on).

To prevent invalid configurations that the Composite pattern would otherwise allow, the implementations of `Computer` and `CircuitBoard` must contain code to prevent them. These classes must ensure that a `Computer` contains `CircuitBoards` and no `Chips` or other `Computers`, and that a `CircuitBoard` contains `Chips` and not other `CircuitBoards` or `Computers`.

Thus the Composite pattern is so general as to allow any tree structure, even those that may not make sense from a domain perspective. If the domain constrains valid trees, those constraints must be coded in the Composite class and its subclasses.

Is the Composite pattern really necessary for this sort of example? If one main advantage of the pattern is that it allows children to be nested arbitrarily but the domain does not, why use the pattern? Since the computers we're modeling constrain how the components can be nested, the constraints can be shown more accurately like this:

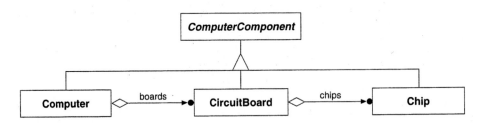

Which model is better? The advantage of using the Composite pattern is that the composite nature of `Computer` and `CircuitBoard` can be defined and implemented once, in `CompositeComponent`. Without the pattern, much of the code implemented in `Computer` to handle its `boards` must also be implemented in `CircuitBoard` to handle its `chips`. If new requirements introduced another composite part, say `InputOutputDevice`, that class would have to duplicate the composite behavior yet again. On the other hand, as long as each Composite class is duplicating the code, the code can more easily handle the constraints; for example, the instance variables can be called `boards` and `chips` instead of the more generic `components`.

The judgment call is this: How much do you want `Computer` and `Circuit-Board` to behave alike? Are they completely different objects, or are they both just collections of smaller computer parts? Either way, it's a tree structure of three levels. Since the levels are alike, use the Composite pattern to capture the design similarities, allow client objects to treat each kind of node similarly, and avoid code duplication.

Limited Number of Children

In general, a Composite can have any number of children. A composite node usually doesn't care how many children it has. Most domains allow this and even expect it. For example, a composite visual doesn't care how many component visuals it contains. A computer usually doesn't limit how many circuit boards it can contain, nor is there a limit on the number of chips a circuit board can contain. A Composite's implementation supports this by using a `Collection` for its children.

Some domains, however, limit the number of child nodes a branch can have. For example, a binary tree node cannot have an unlimited number of child nodes— just two at most. To model a single-celled organism that reproduces by splitting in two, you would track an organism, its pair of children, their children pairs, and so on. Thus, each organism is limited to two children, not an unlimited number of children.

The Composite pattern allows branches with a fixed number of children as well as an unlimited number. *Design Patterns* shows how the unlimited case is implemented using a `children` variable that is a `Collection`. To support a limited number of children, implement a separate variable for each potential child. For example, if the Composite can have only two children, it should implement two variables, like `leftChild` and `rightChild` or `mother` and `father`. The Composite would also handle the case where one or more of the children are unspecified.

The Composite operations are implemented differently in a Composite with a limited number of children. In the unlimited case, the children are stored in a `Collection`; a method iterates over them using a message like `do:` (see Iterator (273)). With a limited number of children, the Composite operation sends messages to each child explicitly. If the operation has results, the Composite operation gathers those results and merges them. For example, the typical code for an operation in a Composite with an unlimited number of children would be:

```
Composite>>operation
    self children do: [ :child | child operation]
```

Here's the same operation in a Composite with exactly three children:

```
Composite>>operation
    "Assumes none of the children is nil."
    self firstChild operation.
    self secondChild operation.
    self thirdChild operation
```

Abstract Leaf and Composite Classes

Examples of the pattern often have numerous concrete Leaf classes that share a lot of common implementation. For example, it is common for a tree node to be able to return a list of its children. A Composite returns its components; a Leaf, no matter what kind, always returns an empty collection.

The problem is where to implement this common behavior. Implementing the behavior in Component means that it will be inherited not only by all of the Leaf classes but by the Composite classes as well. However, moving it down into the Leaf classes means that the same code will need to be duplicated several times over.

The better solution is a common Leaf superclass of all concrete Leaf classes. This superclass, usually abstract, implements code that is common to all of the concrete Leaf classes but not appropriate for the Composite classes. Similarly, a common Composite superclass is helpful for implementing code that should be inherited only by concrete Composite classes, such as the components instance variable.

Implementing Composite and Leaf as abstract classes modifies the Structure diagram to look like this:

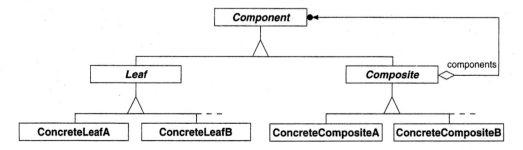

Composite Is a Subclass

One potentially confusing aspect of the Composite pattern for novice designers is that the Composite class is a subclass of the Component class. This may seem counterintuitive because a Composite instance is a parent of the Components it contains. Consider the Structure object diagram at the beginning of this section, which shows a typical tree structure with Composites that contain Components. Each Composite is the parent of its Components. This parent-child relationship among instances may suggest a similar relationship among the classes that implement the instances—that is, that the Component class should be a subclass of the Composite class. But it is the Component class that defines the interface that the Composite class must fulfill, not vice versa. So the Component class is the superclass of the Composite class. Don't confuse class inheritance with part-whole relationships among instances.

No Component Superclass

Sometimes in Smalltalk, a Composite class and its Leaf class aren't even in the same hierarchy. Instead, the Composite class is often part of the Collection hierarchy. An example implemented this way has the intent of using the Composite pattern but badly missed the design and implementation. Because such an example lacks the common Component superclass, there is no clear definition of the interface that both classes are supposed to support. This wouldn't even be possible in C++ because of the compiler's strong typing. It could be done in Java using a common interface that both classes implement, but the two classes would probably duplicate code that would be better implemented in a common abstract superclass. This technique works in Smalltalk because of the language's dynamic typing, but it is an unnecessary abuse of that flexibility. Avoid this technique when implementing the Composite pattern in your own code.

A `FontDescriptionBundle` in VisualWorks is one example of Composite implemented across two separate hierarchies. As the name suggests, a `FontDescriptionBundle` is a collection of `FontDescriptions`. A `FontDescription` represents a platform-independent description of a font that will be bound to a font on the runtime platform. `FontDescription` is a Proxy (213). `FontDescriptionBundle` lets clients search a platform for multiple `FontDescriptions` at once.

`FontDescriptionBundle` is clearly a composite `FontDescription` because it bundles together multiple `FontDescriptions` and the two classes implement the same interface. For example, `FontDescription>>findMatchOn:allowance:` searches the platform's fonts for a suitable match. `FontDescriptionBundle` implements the same message to look for a suitable match for any of its fonts. The operation is less likely to fail with a `FontDescriptionBundle` because it will accept a font that matches any of the bundle's descriptions. On the other hand, this is a weak example of Composite because these trees are only two levels deep.

Because the two classes have a common interface and purpose, we would expect them to live in the same class hierarchy, but they do not. `FontDescription` is a subclass of `Object`, but `FontDescriptionBundle` is a subclass of `Ordered-Collection`. The classes' lack of a common superclass makes it difficult to add new behavior to both classes polymorphically. A developer who implements a new message in `FontDescription` must remember to implement it in `Font-DescriptionBundle` as well—which lives in a totally separate hierarchy. Making these classes behave polymorphically would be simpler and less error prone if they had a common superclass for the developer to extend.

Component's Core Interface

Design Patterns suggests that the Component class should have both generic operations and ones that are Composite specific. This is reflected in the Structure diagram, which shows that Component (not Composite) should declare messages like `Add()`, `Remove()`, and `GetChild()`. Implementation points 3 through 5 (DP 167–169) discuss this as a trade-off between safety and transparency.

Design Patterns, heavily weighted toward C++, favors transparency so that the type checking in C++ isn't too burdensome. If Component did not declare the Composite-specific messages, clients couldn't treat Composites and Components uniformly. First, a client would have to cast the Component into a Composite before it could send Composite-specific messages. Smalltalk does not have these typing constraints, so it favors safety over transparency. Since only Composite can implement these messages in a useful way, they are not added to Component, and thus Leaf does not implement them.

The transparency that *Design Patterns* favors is problematic. The question is: If Component is going to declare these Composite messages, how should Leaf implement them? It could implement them to do nothing and return `nil`, or to fail and return errors. Safety says that a class should not understand messages that it cannot implement meaningfully. Transparency says that all Component subclasses should implement the same interface so that they can be used interchangeably.

Smalltalk resolves this dilemma by employing a concept called a core interface. A **core interface** is one that does not declare enough behavior to implement all of an object's responsibilities but is sufficient to support key collaborations. For example, the `Collection` classes `Set`, `OrderedCollection`, and `Sorted-Collection` all share two protocols that the proposed ANSI Smalltalk standard calls "extensible" and "contractible" (X3J20, 1996). That means they understand messages like `add:` and `remove:`. This core interface is important because it allows these classes to be used interchangeably, whereas `Array` could not be used in their place. However, the classes' full interfaces are not the same. `OrderedCollection` understands `at:put:`, but `Set` and `SortedCollec-tion` do not. `SortedCollection` implements `sortBlock:` to set that attribute, an operation `OrderedCollection` and `Set` do not support. But these

`Collection` classes work similarly enough that a client using their core add/remove interface needn't know the collection's class or its full interface.

Core interfaces let you play fast and loose with an object's protocol in a way that's much more difficult to achieve in strongly typed languages. In C++ or Java, a class's interface must be declared up front, and the compiler ensures that an object implements all messages sent to it. All messages that any subclass understands must be part of the interface, which means that all subclasses must implement those messages. Smalltalk is dynamically typed, so the compiler does not verify that an object understands the messages it is sent. The core interface only needs to include messages that all subclasses understand. However, at runtime, if the object does not understand the message, a message-not-understood error occurs.

One key of the Composite pattern is to treat Composite and Leaf objects interchangeably as Components. To do that in a strongly typed language, the Component must declare any message that any subclass will implement. Thus it declares messages like `addChild:`, `removeChild:`, and `getChildAt:`, and then it forces Leaf to try to implement them. In a dynamically typed language like Smalltalk, the superclass (Component) need only declare the messages that all subclasses will implement. The trade-off is that clients who wish to treat Composites and Leaves interchangeably must use only the core interface they share. There's no escaping that clients that wish to add or remove components must know whether the receiver is a Composite, since Leaves don't handle add and remove well no matter how they're implemented. But as long as code is not adding or removing components, it should be able to treat Composites and Leaves interchangeably.

Thus the structure diagram of the Composite pattern in Smalltalk is somewhat different from the one shown in *Design Patterns.* The Component in *Design Patterns* implements Composite messages like `Add()`, `Remove()`, and `GetChild()`. When implementing the pattern in Smalltalk, the Component usually does not define these messages because they are not appropriate for all subclasses. In Smalltalk, Component defines only messages that are appropriate for *all* subclasses, such as `operation`. These are the only messages that the client can use transparently. To use the Composite messages, the client must first determine that it is collaborating with a Composite, not just any Component.

Implementing the Core Interface

To implement the core interface for the Composite pattern, first implement the interface itself in the Component class with Template Methods (355). This implementation will define the interface's messages in terms of a small number of kernel messages. The Component should use as few kernel messages as possible because both the Composite and Leaf classes will have to implement all of them.

Second, defer implementation of the kernel message in the Component class. The class should defer implementation of these messages to subclasses by implementing them as `subclassResponsibility` or `implementedBySubclass`.

Third, implement the kernel messages in the Composite and Leaf subclasses. In the Leaf class, the message simply performs its behavior. In the Composite class, the message forwards the message to each of its children and merges their behavior.

Fourth, avoid extending the core interface in any subclasses of Composite or Leaf. These subclasses can have extended interfaces, but because they are not part of Component's interface, client objects will not be able to use this extended protocol polymorphically. Thus to use the extended interface, the client will first have to determine the type of the receiver. This goes against the spirit of the Composite pattern.

This fourth step is especially difficult. It means that all subclasses essentially need to have the same interface as the Component class. Thus, the Component class must declare not only the interface it needs but also an interface extensive enough to satisfy all subclasses as well. In practice, the messages that subclasses add are instance creation messages. When a client is creating an instance, it knows the instance's specific class and uses its extended interface instead of Component's.

In the Composite class, for example, the addChild: message is an extension, but it is used as part of instance creation when the client knows that it just created a Composite. Similarly, a client checks to see if a node has a child it wants to remove, so it knows that the node must be a Composite before sending the removeChild: message. If the node weren't a Composite, it couldn't contain the child in the first place.

Field Format Description Trees

Another rather unusual example of the Composite pattern occurs in a framework for reading record-oriented flat files. Each record is composed of fields, where each field is a simple type such as a string or a number. Each file record corresponds to a record construct defined in a procedural language. In an object-oriented language, the record construct corresponds to a class, and each set of record data in the file corresponds to an instance of the class.

A framework for reading record-oriented flat files requires at least two classes, Field and Record, where Record is a collection of Fields. These two classes will work much better if they're implemented using the Composite pattern, because it lets them implement a message like readFromStream: polymorphically. Field implements it to read the next field from the file stream, and Record implements it to read each of its fields from the stream, plus it reads its record delimiter if it has one. A client can use the same message to read a single field or a complete record without regard to which one it's actually reading.

The Composite pattern allows the framework to start nesting file structures. Although it doesn't make much sense to nest one record inside another, it does make sense for a common series of fields to be nested inside another common series of fields. This is essentially a subrecord nested in a record. For example, the fields for a Customer might contain the fields for his Address. This corresponds to a domain object like `Address` being nested as a single object inside another domain object like `Customer`. Thus a `Record` is really just a `CompositeField` with an optional record delimiter. The true Composite class is `Composite-Field`, which acts like a single field but actually contains multiple `Fields`. This allows nested objects to be stored in the Record as nested fields. This diagram shows the classes in this example:

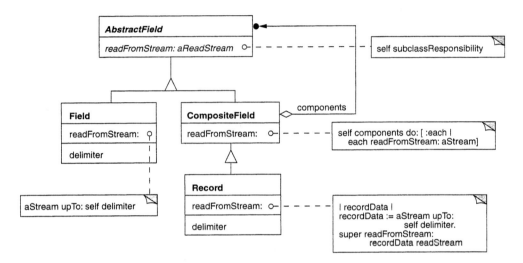

`Field` is a simple `AbstractField`, so it just reads itself from the `Stream`. (This example doesn't show what happens with the data once they are read.) `CompositeField` contains a series of fields, so it reads itself from the Stream by reading each of them. `Record` takes this one step further: It reads only as far as the next record delimiter to get the data for the record; then it reads its fields from those data.

Missed Opportunities

Occasionally you find a class that would be easier to use if it had been implemented using the Composite pattern. If a client has to distinguish between an object and a collection of them, its code will be awkward and case driven. The client's implementation can be simplified by applying the Composite pattern to the classes it collaborates with. Then the client will be able to treat an object and a collection of objects the same way.

For example, `SelectionInList` in VisualWorks tracks both a list of objects and the one that is currently selected. It is implemented using two `ValueModels`: one that holds the collection, and another that holds the selection's index in the collection. `SelectionInList` is often used alongside `ValueModels`, but they cannot be used interchangeably because they have different interfaces.

SelectionInList and ValueModel should be interchangeable so that chains of ValueModels can easily contain SelectionInLists as well. To make the classes interchangeable, they must have the same polymorphic interface. SelectionInList should have the same interface as ValueModel, where its value is its selection. Then any widget could use a ValueModel without regard to whether it was a SelectionInList.

Thus some pattern should be applied to SelectionInList and ValueModel to make them polymorphic. Because SelectionInList is composed of two ValueModels and because it should behave like a ValueModel, applying the Composite pattern will cause the proper transformation. It will move SelectionInList into the ValueModel hierarchy and implement its ValueModel interface by delegating to its component ValueModels and merging their behaviors together.

Once SelectionInList is part of the ValueModel hierarchy, it will have to implement standard ValueModel messages like value. Here's an example of how that would be implemented:

```
SelectionInList>>value
    | list selectionIndex |
    list := self listHolder value.
    selectionIndex := self selectionIndexHolder value.
    ^selectionIndex = 0
       ifTrue: [nil]
       ifFalse: [list at: selectionIndex]
```

Notice how SelectionInList, a Composite, implements value by delegating the message to each of its component ValueModels and merging their results together (in this case using at:). This is classic Composite behavior.

Implementation

In addition to the implementation issues discussed in *Design Patterns* (DP 166–170), there are several more issues to consider when implementing a Composite:

1. *Use a Component superclass.* A Composite class should be implemented in the same hierarchy as its Leaf class with a common Component superclass, not in two separate hierarchies. It's important to have the common Component superclass that defines the Composite and Leaf's common interface. The earlier discussion of FontDescriptionBundle shows the problems of not implementing both the Composite and Leaf in the same hierarchy.

2. *Consider implementing abstract Composite and Leaf subclasses.* This will divide the Component hierarchy into two distinct subhierarchies: classes that are composed of Components (Composites) and classes that cannot be decomposed (Leaves).

3. *Only Composite delegates to children.* It is tempting for classes in the Composite hierarchy to manipulate the components directly, but that is better left to the Composite superclass. The hierarchy's code will be more reusable and

flexible if the Composite class does little more than delegate to its components, and the subclasses extend this protocol to add behavior before and after the delegation. For details on implementing hierarchies this way, see Template Method (355).

4. *Composites can be nested.* Not only can a Composite contain Leaves, it can also contain other Composites. Programmers often forget this and implement the Composite to assume that its children are leaves. The first time a client inserts a Composite into another Composite as a child, the top Composite fails because of an oversight in its implementation. For an example, see the implementation of `CompositeAsset>>containsSecurity:` in the Sample Code section.

5. *Composite sets the parent back-pointer.* Trees are often doubly linked so that a branch node points to its children and each child points back to its parent. In such a structure, you want to set both pointers simultaneously so that you don't set one and forget to set the other. The best place to do this is in `Composite>>addChild:`. Not only does the method add the Component as a child of the Composite, but it also sets the Component's parent to be the Composite. No other code should set the Component's parent. Similarly, `Composite>>removeChild:` should break the links in both directions.

6. *Can the Composite contain any type of child?* This is a domain-specific issue, not an implementation issue. If the design constrains the types of objects within Composite objects, the Composites' implementations must enforce these constraints through validation code. For example, an implementor of `addChild:` may need to verify the child's type before adding it.

7. *Is the Composite's number of children limited?* If so, use a separate named variable to store each child. Otherwise, use a single `Collection` variable that can store an unlimited number of children. If the limit is large and the children do not have distinct roles within the Composite, use the `Collection` variable and enforce the limit in the `addChild:` method. Implement the Composite operations to either iterate through the `Collection` or consider each of the named variables in turn.

8. *There are four ways for the Composite to forward its operation messages to its component:*

   - *Simple forward:* Send the message to all of the children and merge the results without performing any other behavior.

   - *Selective forward:* Conditionally forward the message to only some of the children, and merge the results.

   - *Extended forward:* Perform extra behavior before or along with forwarding the message to some or all of the children, and merge the results.

   - *Override:* Perform behavior instead of forwarding the message to the children; the behavior may do nothing.

Sample Code

Let's look at a typical example from the financial domain. An Account is composed of its Securities, and a client's Portfolio is composed of its Accounts. A Security can be a Stock, a Bond, or some other type of asset.

A client will often want to know the value of his Portfolio, which is determined by summing the value of all his Securities in all his Accounts. A client might also want to know if he owns a particular Security. That is determined by searching for that Security in all of the Accounts in his Portfolio.

The basic object model for this domain would look like this:

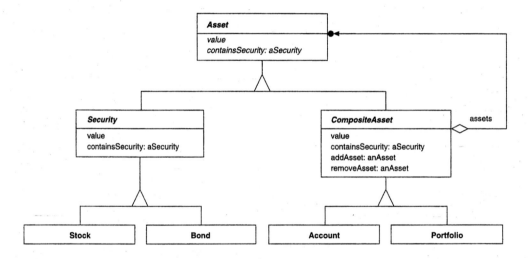

To implement this object model, first we'll implement `Asset` as the Component class. `Asset` declares two messages, `value` and `containsSecurity:`, that its subclasses should implement:

```
Object subclass: #Asset
    instanceVariableNames: ''
    classVariableNames: ''
    poolDictionaries: ''

Asset>>value
    "Return the value of this Asset."
    ^self subclassResponsibility

Asset>>containsSecurity: aSecurity
    "Answer whether this Asset contains aSecurity."
    ^self subclassResponsibility
```

Next we'll implement `Security`. It will need an instance variable to store its value. Since it can also implement `value` and `containsSecurity:`, it does so:

```
Asset subclass: #Security
    instanceVariableNames: 'value'
    classVariableNames: ''
    poolDictionaries: ''

Security>>value
    "See superimplementor."
    ^value

Security>>containsSecurity: aSecurity
    "See superimplementor."
    "For a Leaf, we'll say it includes aSecurity
    if it is aSecurity."
    ^self = aSecurity
```

Now we'll implement the Composite class, `CompositeAsset`. It needs an instance variable, `assets`, to store its children and a method to access this variable. It also implements `value` and `containsSecurity:` as Composite operations:

```
Asset subclass: #CompositeAsset
    instanceVariableNames: 'assets'
    classVariableNames: ''
    poolDictionaries: ''

CompositeAsset>>assets
    "Return the list of assets."
    ^assets

CompositeAsset>>value
    "See superimplementor."
    "Return the sum of the assets."
    ^self assets
        inject: 0
        into: [ :sum :asset | sum + asset value]

CompositeAsset>>containsSecurity: aSecurity
    "See superimplementor."
    "See if one of the assets is aSecurity."
    ^self assets includes: aSecurity
```

Look closely at the implementation of `containsSecurity:`. It assumes that `assets` is a `Collection` of `Security`s. That will usually be true when the Composite is an `Account` but not when it's a `Portfolio`. Hence, this implementation will always return `false` for a `Portfolio`, but this bug will not be obvious or easy to find. Remember that a Composite does not just contain Leaves; it can also contain other Composites. So `containsSecurity:` must be implemented as though the assets may be other Composites:

```
CompositeAsset>>containsSecurity: aSecurity
    "See superimplementor."
    "See if one of the assets is aSecurity."
```

```
self assets
   detect: [ :asset | asset containsSecurity: aSecurity]
   ifNone: [^false].
^true
```

This improved implementation of `containsSecurity:` is an example of Object-Oriented Recursion (see Chain of Responsibility (225)), as is the implementation of `value`. Notice that implementors in Composite should use object-oriented recursion; the problem with the original implementation of `containsSecurity:` is that it used `includes:` and so did not use object-oriented recursion.

Known Smalltalk Uses

Collection

`Collection` is the most general example of the Composite pattern in Smalltalk and also the least useful. It implements the pattern with the Component class (`Object`), the Composite class (`Collection`), and numerous Leaf classes (all other subclasses of `Object`). An element in a `Collection` can be another `Collection`, so the structure supports unlimited nesting.

`Object` defines operations that `Collection` reimplements as Composite operations. For example, `Object` defines `printString` to display the receiver's class. `Collection` reimplements it to display not only the `Collection`'s class but also the `printStrings` of the elements in the `Collection`. However, `Object` does not have a very customized interface, so neither does `Collection`. This is the least domain-specific example of the Composite pattern.

Visuals

The major Smalltalk dialects use the Composite pattern to implement their windowing systems. Visuals can be nested recursively, so they're a fairly strict example of the pattern.

Field Format Descriptions

The File Reader (Woolf, 1997) reads record-oriented flat files by reading each record one field at a time. The ability of a group of fields to act like a single field is an example of the Composite pattern. The Composite pattern in the File Reader is implemented with three classes, `FieldFormatDescription` (Component), and two subclasses, `LeafFieldFormat` (Leaf) and `CompositeFieldFormat` (Composite). The Composites support unlimited nesting.

Media Elements

The Composite pattern is used in EFX, a digital video editing and special effects environment (Alpert et al., 1995), to represent aggregate and primitive media elements uniformly. EFX's user interface incorporates a horizontal time line for specifying the content of a video composition. The user adds rectangular bars that represent media elements: video clips, audio segments, and special effects. Their position and width along the time line determine when they play and for how long. The editor provides multiple tracks that enable multiple media to co-occur in time.

At any time, multiple media elements in any number of tracks can be selected and grouped. The result is a single group element containing the other elements, portrayed visually as a grouped media element in a single track. Such aggregate elements understand the same core protocol as individual media elements. All know how to draw themselves in the time line, all provide trimming methods to increase or decrease their time span, all implement accessor messages for their start time and duration, and so on. The group element also supports nesting so that primitive and group elements may be aggregated into larger group elements. This nesting ability supports the strict definition of Composite.

Sentence Structures

ParCE, a natural language parser (Alpert & Rosson, 1992), represents sentence constituents as objects. It parses a sentence into a parse tree. In the tree, nonterminal constituent objects (Composites) represent the sentence, noun phrases, prepositional phrases, and so on. The Composites ultimately contain the appropriate terminal constituent objects (Leaves representing nouns, verbs, determiners, etc.). All of these constituent objects—the individual words, the phrases, and the sentences—respond to the same message protocol for parsing, printing, and accessing. Longer sentences are represented by deeper nested trees, the strict definition of the pattern.

Brokerage Accounts

Frameworks that model the financial domain often implement a Composite class such as `Account` to represent brokerage accounts. Classes like `Asset` and `Security` define the Component and Leaf classes. `Account` defines a Composite asset that is composed of other `Assets`. Other Composite assets might be a customer's `Portfolio`, a broker's `BrokerAccountsUnderManagement`, and a branch's `BranchAccountsUnderManagement`. (See the Sample Code section for details.) Since each `Asset` subclass can only contain assets of another specific `Asset` subclass, nesting is limited to a specific number of levels, so `Assets` are a broader interpretation of the Composite pattern.

SignalCollection

`SignalCollection` is a Composite class in the `Collection` hierarchy in VisualWorks. It does not contain a collection of `Signals`; it *is* a collection of `Signals`.

VisualWorks implements exception handling with two separate classes, `Signal` and `Exception`. `Signal` describes the types of errors that can occur; `Exception` describes a specific error. An Exception refers to its Signal to know what kind of error occurred. This is an example of the Type Object pattern (Johnson & Woolf, 1988).

To trap an Exception, the developer specifies the Signal whose Exceptions should be trapped. Signals form a hierarchy, so a Signal will trap any Exceptions for itself or any of its child Signals. However, to trap multiple Signals from different parts of the hierarchy, the programmer has to specify each Signal individually and tell the whole list to trap Exceptions. He does this by creating a SignalCollection that contains the list of Signal roots and telling it to trap Exceptions just as if it were a single Signal.

Because Signal and SignalCollection have the same interface for trapping Exceptions and because SignalCollection works by delegating its behavior to its Signals, these two classes are an example of the Composite pattern. As with any other example where the Composite class is implemented in the Collection hierarchy, this example would be better implemented if Signal and SignalCollection were implemented in the same hierarchy. Because a SignalCollection rarely contains other SignalCollections, they are not nested, so this example is a broader interpretation of the pattern.

Composite ProgramNodes

SequenceNode is a Composite class in the ProgramNode hierarchy in Visual-Works. Smalltalk compiles source code into a tree of parse nodes that are ProgramNodes. There are different ProgramNode subclasses for various programming constructs, such as LiteralNode, BlockNode, Assignment-Node, and ConditionalNode. SequenceNode represents a series of statements (i.e., lines of code) within a method or a block. Each of these statements is itself a ProgramNode, making this an example of the Composite pattern.

A more subtle example of Composite in the ProgramNode hierarchy is ConditionalNode. A ConditionalNode has three main parts: condition, trueBody, and falseBody. They form an ifTrue:ifFalse: statement like this:

```
condition ifTrue: trueBody ifFalse: falseBody
```

Each of these parts is itself a ProgramNode. ConditionalNode is an example of a Composite with a limited number of children—in this case, three child variables for its three main parts.

Other examples of Composite in the ProgramNode hierarchy are Arithmetic-LoopNode, AssignmentNode, CascadeNode, LoopNode, SimpleMessage-Node, and MessageNode. All of these classes contain multiple ProgramNodes and combine them to act like a single ProgramNode. A parse node tree can be very deep with numerous nesting possibilities, so this fits a fairly strict interpretation of the pattern.

CompositeFont

`CompositeFont` is a Composite class in the `ImplementationFont` hierarchy in VisualWorks. The hierarchy looks like this:

```
Object ()
   ImplementationFont ()
      CompositeFont (currentFont fonts ...)
      DeviceFont ()
         ...
      SyntheticFont (baseFont ...)
```

`ImplementationFont` is an Adapter (105) that adapts fonts to a standard object interface. `DeviceFont` actually adapts one of the native fonts on the platform. `SyntheticFont` is a Decorator (161) that adds effects that may not be available in the platform's fonts. `CompositeFont` combines multiple platform fonts to form characters that may not otherwise be available in a single platform font, such as international characters. It makes the combination of fonts act like one font.

This is an example of both Composite and Decorator. It has the Component class (`ImplementationFont`), the Leaf/ConcreteComponent (`DeviceFont`), Composite (`CompositeFont`), and Decorator (`SyntheticFont`). However, `CompositeFonts` are rarely nested, so it represents a broader interpretation of Composite.

FontDescriptionBundle and SPSortedLines

`FontDescriptionBundle` is a Composite class in VisualWorks. Its Leaf class is `FontDescription`. VisualWorks uses a `FontDescription` to search for a native font on the current platform that matches the description. The `FontDescription` may actually be a `FontDescriptionBundle` that describes a range of fonts.

This example is difficult to recognize as a Composite because `FontDescription` and `FontDescriptionBundle` are not implemented in the same hierarchy as the pattern recommends. Instead, `FontDescription` is a subclass of Object, and `FontDescriptionBundle` is in the `Collection` hierarchy.

`SPSortedLines` is a Composite class in VisualWorks whose Leaf class is `SPFillLine`, a line segment that has special behavior for determining if it intersects with another line segment. `SPSortedLines` is a collection of such line segments. This is another example of the Composite pattern where the Composite and Leaf classes are not implemented in the same hierarchy.

`FontDescriptionBundles` are usually not nested, nor are `SPSortedLines's`, so they are weaker examples of the pattern.

Composite Numbers

Some `Number` classes are actually implemented using other `Numbers`. They are composite numbers. Any `Number` class that is not a platform data type (e.g., integer, float, or double) is probably a composite number. These composite numbers are examples of the Composite pattern. For example, the `Fraction` class in Smalltalk is a composite number. It contains two numbers—a numerator and a denominator—and uses them to compute its value. When dividing two numbers, storing the result as a `Fraction` instead of a `Float` avoids round-off error (although it also hurts efficiency). Since a `Fraction` acts like a single `Number` but is composed of two separate `Numbers`, it is a Composite.

Another example is a fixed decimal number class, such as `FixedPoint` in VisualWorks and `Decimal` in IBM Smalltalk. A fixed decimal is like a floating-point number except that the fractional portion is stored as an integer to avoid round-off error. It is a composite number because it is composed from simpler numbers, usually `Integers`.

Composite numbers often don't nest because such a nested number tree can usually be reduced to a single composite number. For example, there is no reason to store a `Fraction` whose numerator and denominator are also `Fractions`; it can be simplified to a single fraction with `Integer` components without any loss of precision. However, aggressive use of composite numbers leads to trees that cannot be simplified, so these nested trees conform to the strict interpretation of the pattern.

Beck (1996) briefly discusses a pattern called Impostor, a more domain-specific example of a Composite number. He uses the pattern to implement `MoneySum`, an object that will add two `Money` objects with different currencies without converting them to a single currency. Rather than actually adding the `Moneys`, `MoneySum` just stores them, along with any others that might later be added to them. Later, when the sum is actually needed, such as to display the value in a certain currency, `MoneySum` performs all of the conversions at once; it converts its contents to that currency and adds them. Doing all the conversions at once is usually more efficient than doing many intermediate ones. Because `MoneySum` and `Money` have the same interface, they can be used interchangeably. Thus `MoneySum` is a Composite `Money`. An Impostor can contain other Impostors, nesting that supports strict interpretations of the pattern.

Related Patterns

Composite, Decorator, and Object-Oriented Recursion

Composite and Decorator (161) are often used together in the same hierarchy because both require limiting the interface of their Component to a core interface that a client can use with any node in the structure. Once the type's interface has been limited for one pattern, the other pattern can easily be applied to support that core interface. Boiling down an extensive Component interface into a simplified core interface is difficult, but once that is done, either Composite or Decorator can be applied easily.

A Composite communicates with its Components through Object-Oriented Recursion (see Chain of Responsibility (225)). A series of nested Composites culminating with a Leaf form a chain. When the top Composite in such a chain receives a message, it forwards the message to its children. When the message reaches a Leaf, it is ultimately handled there.

Chain of Responsibility provides more details about using these three patterns together.

Composite versus Decorator

Trees often contain both Composite nodes and Decorator (161) nodes, as well as Leaf nodes. To tell them apart, look at how many components a node has. A Leaf node obviously has no components, a Decorator node has exactly one component, and a Composite node has multiple components. If a node can have multiple components but currently has only one component or none, it is still a Composite node because it can have multiple components.

Iterator

The Composite often uses the Iterator (273) pattern to forward a message to its children.

DECORATOR (DP 175)   Object Structural

Intent

Attach additional responsibilities to an object dynamically. Decorators provide a flexible alternative to subclassing for extending functionality.

Structure

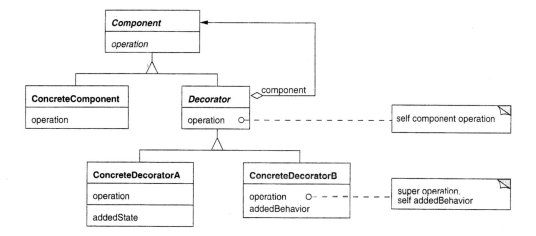

Discussion

A class implemented as a Decorator does not provide core functionality itself. Instead, Decorator instances enhance the core functionality of the objects they decorate. A Decorator and the object it decorates (its **Component**) have the same supertype—that is, they have the same core interface. Thus clients generally can't tell the difference between a Component and its Decorator.

The way to recognize a Decorator class is that it has an instance variable whose type is the same as the Decorator's; that is, both the Decorator and its component have the same Component interface. The Decorator delegates its implementation to this instance variable, but in the process it implements some of the messages to add extra behavior in addition to (or instead of) simple delegation.

The name *decorator* seems to imply that this pattern can be used only with visuals, such as wrapping scroll bars around a text view, but the pattern is actually more versatile. It can be used to add functionality to any kind of object, not just a visual.

Systems Pattern

Decorator is a common pattern but a fairly systems-oriented one, meaning that it is commonly used for implementing basic systems frameworks like windowing systems, streams, and fonts. However, it is fairly uncommon for modeling domains, so most Smalltalk applications developers do not use it often. Visual-Works uses Decorator to implement its base frameworks far more heavily than the other dialects do, so most Smalltalk examples are from VisualWorks. We will discuss one domain example, insurance caps, but first let's look at how Decorator works in general.

Wrapper Hierarchy

The `Wrapper` hierarchy in VisualWorks is a classic example of the Decorator pattern. VisualWorks implements graphical user interfaces using the Model-View-Controller (MVC) framework discussed in *Design Patterns* (DP 4–6) and in Factory Method (DP 107). In MVC, the model contains the state that can be displayed, the view displays the state, and the controller handles input that manipulates the state. The MVC framework embodies several design patterns, including Observer (305), Composite (137), and Strategy (339), as well as Decorator.

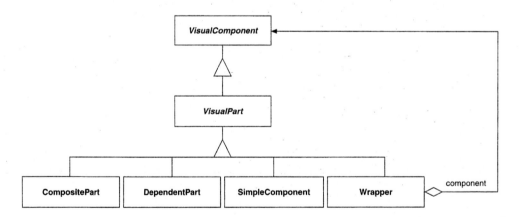

The View in the MVC triad is implemented as the `VisualComponent` hierarchy; its main classes are shown above. `VisualComponent`'s main subhierarchy is `VisualPart`. `VisualPart` has leaf subclasses such as `DependentPart` and `SimpleComponent`, composite subclasses like `CompositePart` (an example of Composite (137)), and Decorator subclasses like `Wrapper`.

`Wrapper` implements the Decorator pattern without altering any of its component's behavior; it is the subclasses of `Wrapper` that actually change the behavior of their components. `Wrapper` has an instance variable called `component` that is a `VisualComponent`. Right away you know that something unusual is going on because `Wrapper` is a subclass of `VisualComponent`, and yet its instance variable is also a `VisualComponent`. This forms a recursive structure of `Visual-`

Components (Wrappers) whose components are in turn VisualComponents. Wrapper subimplements various key messages from VisualPart and VisualComponent, but its implementation of those messages does little more than forward the same message to its component.[2] That's all Wrapper does. Thus, a visual wrapped in a Wrapper behaves no differently than it would without the wrapper.

This lack of real behavior is typical for the top class in a Decorator hierarchy. The class will do little more than define an instance variable and override key messages to forward them to the instance variable. Decorator subclasses are implemented as typical subclasses; they subimplement their superclass to change its behavior. In the case of a Decorator subclass, it takes the top class's generic decoration behavior that does nothing and changes it to add specific decoration behavior. You see this in all Decorator hierarchies, not just Wrapper.

Once Wrapper has defined the Decorator pattern, its subclasses have tremendous freedom to affect the behavior of both the view and the controller. All the subclass has to do is change the implementation of any message that Wrapper forwards to its component. For example, a BoundedWrapper sets the bounds of its visual—the screen space allotted for it. By wrapping a visual with a BoundedWrapper, the wrapper overrides the visual's bounds. When a client asks the component what its bounds are, the wrapper intercepts the message and returns its own bounds instead of its visual's as shown in the diagram below:

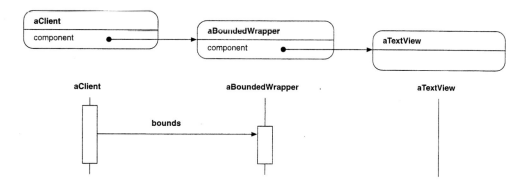

There are other common uses for Wrapper subclasses. ReversingWrapper highlights a visual by switching the foreground and background colors when drawing it. GraphicsAttributeWrapper sets the graphics attributes of its visual, such as its color and line width. PassivityWrapper can be toggled

---

[2] *Subimplement* is a synonym for *override:* implement a method that would otherwise be inherited from a superclass. A subclass can subimplement a method in two ways: it completely replaces it, ignoring the inherited implementation, or it extends the superclass's method, referencing the inherited implementation via the super pseudovariable and adding to that implementation.

between enabled and disabled mode. When enabled, it forwards messages unaffected. When it's disabled, it makes its visual look disabled by drawing it grayed out and act disabled by blocking all controller messages. Thus, simply by introducing `Wrapper` as a Decorator class, it is now possible to control all kinds of properties of a visual simply by subclassing `Wrapper`.

Nested Decorators

A single Component often has multiple Decorators nested on it. For example, to add scrolling to a visual, VisualWorks wraps a `ScrollWrapper` around it. However, it usually also wraps a `BorderedWrapper` around the `ScrollWrapper`. `BorderedWrapper` is a subclass of `BoundedWrapper` that sets a visual's bounds and draws a border to outline those bounds. Wrapping a `Bordered-Wrapper` around a `ScrollWrapper` sets the bounds of the scrollable area and displays those bounds visually.

The order of the Decorators is important. If the `ScrollWrapper` wrapped the `BorderedWrapper`, it would scroll the bounded rectangle; that would not work very well.

Abstract Leaf and Composite Classes

Examples of the pattern often have numerous concrete ConcreteComponent classes that share a lot of common implementation. For example, an operation often has a default atomic implementation that is appropriate for all Concrete-Components but not appropriate for Decorators because they must delegate the operation to their components.

The problem is where to implement this common behavior. Implementing the behavior in Component means that it will be inherited by all of the Concrete-Component classes and by the Decorator classes as well. However, moving it down into the ConcreteComponent classes means that the same code will need to be duplicated several times over.

The better solution is a common "Decoratee" superclass of all Concrete-Component classes. This superclass, usually abstract, implements code that is common to all of the ConcreteComponent classes but not appropriate for the Decorator classes.

The Structure diagram already contains an abstract Decorator class for implementing code that is common to all `ConcreteDecorators`. As shown on the facing page, adding an abstract Decoratee class modifies the diagram to look like this:

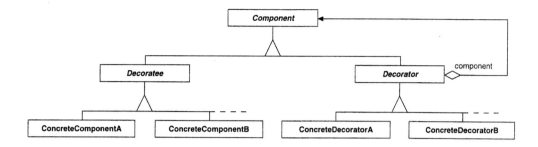

Decorator Is a Subclass of Component

One confusing aspect of the Decorator pattern is that the Decorator class is a subclass of the abstract Component class that it decorates. This is counterintuitive because a Decorator instance is a parent of the component it decorates. Consider the following diagram, which shows a typical tree structure with Decorators on the Components. Each Decorator is a parent of its Component; the Component is the Decorator's child. It then seems obvious to make the Component class a subclass of the Decorator class. Yet the Component class defines the interface that the Decorator class must fulfill, so the Component class is the superclass of the Decorator class:

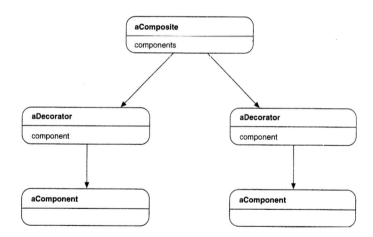

Remember the difference between the class diagram at the beginning of this pattern and the object diagram shown above. The class hierarchy is what you would see in a hierarchy browser; the object diagram is what you would see in an inspector or series of inspectors. The class diagram is static; the hierarchy will always look this way unless you recompile the class definitions. The object diagram is dynamic; the instances can be configured in many different combinations and this is just a typical example. In the class structure, Component is the superclass of Decorator. In the object structure, a Decorator is the parent of a Component.

A Single Decorator Class

A strongly typed language like C++ virtually requires that the Decorator pattern be implemented as a separate subhierarchy of the Component hierarchy. Smalltalk does not force this constraint. For example, the `ValueModel` hierarchy in VisualWorks contains three Decorator classes: `BufferedValueHolder`, `RangeAdaptor`, and `TypeConverter`. Most `ValueModel` classes are Adapters (105) where the Adaptor or (subject) can usually be any kind of `Object`. However, these three `ValueModel` classes are Decorators, not Adapters, because they expect their subjects to be other `ValueModels`. As this diagram shows, the `ValueModel` Decorator classes are completely unrelated to each other in the hierarchy, yet they still work as Decorators:

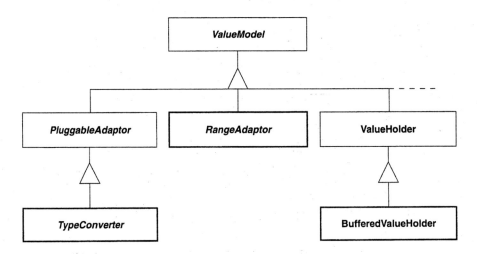

Although Smalltalk does not require it, multiple Decorator classes in the same hierarchy should have a common Decorator superclass. Otherwise, each ConcreteDecorator class must define its own Decorator behavior. None of the subclasses in the `Wrapper` hierarchy has to define its Decorator behavior because it inherits it from a common superclass, `Wrapper`. All a subclass has to do is define how it wants to decorate the visual. On the contrary, the three `ValueModel` Decorator classes duplicate behavior that would have to be implemented only once if they were subclasses of a common `ValueModelDecorator` superclass.

Another shortcoming of lacking a common Decorator class is the difficulty in recognizing that the classes follow the Decorator pattern. For example, `BufferedValueHolder` looks like a `ValueHolder` with a buffer. This actually looks like an antiexample of the Decorator pattern—that is, it uses subclassing to extend `ValueHolder` instead of a Decorator. Although `BufferedValueHolder` is implemented as a subclass of `ValueHolder`, it does not have a `ValueHolder` built into it. Instead, it expects its subject to be a `ValueModel`—any kind of `ValueModel`, including a `ValueHolder`. So a `BufferedValueHolder` can be used to add a buffer to any `ValueModel`. That would be a lot more obvious if it were called "BufferedValue**Model**" (not "BufferedValue**Holder**") and were a subclass in a Decorator branch instead of a subclass of a ConcreteComponent.

The following diagram shows a hypothetical `ValueModel` hierarchy that implements the Decorator pattern better. It introduces a `ValueModelDecorator` class to implement the Decorator pattern and makes `BufferedValueHolder`, `RangeAdaptor`, and `TypeConverter` its subclasses. Notice that `ValueModel` combines the Component and ConcreteComponent classes.

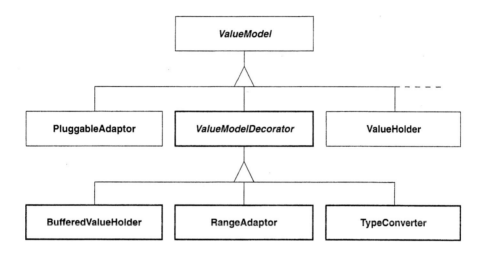

`ValueModel` Decorators provide another example of the power of nesting Decorators. If a `ValueModel` needs a buffer, you wrap it with a `Buffered-ValueModel`. If it needs its type converted, you wrap it with a `TypeConverter`. Better still, to both buffer a value and change its type, use a `Buffered-ValueHolder` and a `TypeConverter`. Order is not critical in this case, but it is still significant. If the `BufferedValueHolder` decorates the `TypeConverter`, the converted value is buffered, while the reverse buffers the unconverted value.

Decorator's Core Interface

The Component class must define the core interface that the Decorator and ConcreteComponent subclasses implement. For more information about what a core interface is and how to implement one, see Composite (137).

As with Composite, subclasses in a Decorator structure should avoid extending their Component's interface. If a Decorator subclass extends the Component's interface, the client will have to recognize that the component has this type of Decorator on it before the client can use that Decorator's extended interface.

Insurance Caps

Although Decorator is rarely used in modeling domains, here is a domain example. Decorator has been used in the insurance domain to cap the payments made to a policyholder for a claim. A health insurance policy would reimburse various medical procedures at various rates. The policy probably defines a maximum amount, known as a cap, that it will pay for a single claim. If all holders of this policy have the same cap, it can be built into the policy. But if various policyholders with the same type of policy have different caps or if the cap is very difficult to build into the policy, the cap can be implemented as a Decorator on the policy.

`Policy` will have a method like `reimbursementForClaim:` that processes the claim and computes the reimbursement amount. Because different policyholders have different caps, this method will ignore all caps based on policyholder. Thus the reimbursement amount could exceed the cap for some policyholders. To prevent this, each `Policyholder` holds not a `Policy` but a `PolicyCap`, which in turn holds the `Policy`. The `PolicyCap`'s implementation of `reimbursementForClaim:` obtains the reimbursement amount from the `Policy`, tests it against the cap, and returns whichever is less.

Here's some code for this example. First we declare the Component class, the abstract superclass defining the interface for both the ConcreteComponent and the Decorator. We'll call this Component `AbstractPolicy` and implement the most interesting message, `reimbursementForClaim:`.

```
Object subclass: #AbstractPolicy
    instanceVariableNames: ''
    classVariableNames: ''
    poolDictionaries: ''

AbstractPolicy>>reimbursementForClaim: aClaim
    "Calculate and return how much money
    the policy will pay for aClaim."
    ^self subclassResponsibility
```

Next we implement the ConcreteComponent class, `Policy`. It's the easy one to implement because it acts the way a policy does. We'll omit the details of `reimbursementForClaim:` because it can get rather complex and really has nothing to do with the Decorator pattern:

```
AbstractPolicy subclass: #Policy
    instanceVariableNames: '...'    "reimbursement variables"
    classVariableNames: ''
    poolDictionaries: ''

Policy>>reimbursementForClaim: aClaim
    "See superimplementor."
    "... code to calculate the reimbursement ..."
```

Finally, we'll implement the Decorator class, `PolicyCap`. Because it is a Decorator, it needs an instance variable to point to its Component. We'll call it `policy`. It also needs an instance variable to hold the amount of the reimbursement cap.

```
AbstractPolicy subclass: #PolicyCap
    instanceVariableNames: 'policy capAmount'
    classVariableNames: ''
    poolDictionaries: ''
```

The `PolicyCap` calculates the reimbursement amount in two steps. First, it asks its `policy` how much the reimbursement should be. Second, it returns either that amount or the cap, whichever is less.

```
PolicyCap>>reimbursementForClaim: aClaim
    "See superimplementor."
    | uncappedAmount cappedAmount |
    uncappedAmount := self policy reimbursementForClaim: aClaim.
    cappedAmount := uncappedAmount min: self capAmount.
    ^cappedAmount
```

Other insurance functions could also be implemented as Decorators. For example, `PolicyDeductible` could be another Decorator that subtracts the policyholder's deductibles and copayments from the reimbursement amount.

Stream Decorators

The Known Uses section of the Decorator pattern in *Design Patterns* discusses a `StreamDecorator` class (DP 183). `StreamDecorator` has subclasses for compressing an ASCII stream and for converting 8-bit ASCII into 7-bit ASCII.

Smalltalk developers have discovered another use for `Stream` decorators. Streams are typically used to store characters and bytes, because that's what flat files hold. Yet Smalltalk stores complex objects, not just characters and bytes. How can those objects be stored in files?

VisualWorks provides a framework called BOSS (the Binary Object Streaming Service) for storing objects in files. The `BOSSTransporter` hierarchy is a set of streamlike classes for reading and writing objects. One subclass, `BOSSReader`, implements the `next` protocol; the other, `BOSSWriter`, implements the `nextPut:` protocol. Both use an instance variable called `stream` (either a `ReadStream` or a `WriteStream`) to implement their behavior. For example, `BOSSWriter` converts each object into a `BOSSBytes`—a special `ByteArray`— and then uses the `WriteStream` to write those bytes into a file.

`BOSSTransporter` provides another example of a Decorator class that is not implemented in the same hierarchy as its Component classes. Both `Stream` and `BOSSTransporter` are subclasses of `Object`; that's all they have in common.

This would not work very well in C++ because of its strong typing; the client would have to know whether it was using a Stream or a BOSSTransporter. It could not switch between the two interchangeably because they're not in a single Component hierarchy. Java could handle this if it declared a "streaming" interface and declared both Stream and BOSSTransporter to implement it.

Just because Smalltalk can handle Decorators and Components in completely separate hierarchies doesn't mean it's a good idea to do so. Putting them in the same hierarchy ensures they will support the same interface, which lets clients use them interchangeably. When the Component and Decorator hierarchies are separate, both hierarchies must be maintained to keep their interfaces polymorphic. It is always better to avoid dual maintenance when possible.

The File Reader framework (Woolf, 1997) contains a better example of a Stream Decorator. It implements FormattedStream as a subclass of Stream. As a Stream, FormattedStream implements the usual messages like next, nextPut:, and atEnd. Its main instance variable is dataStream, an instance of Stream. FormattedStream implements nextPut: to accept an object and uses a StreamFormatDescription to convert the object into a record. It then uses the dataStream to write that record into a file. FormattedStream>> next reverses the process to read a record out of a file and convert it back into an object. Because the dataStream can be any type of Stream, the "file" can be any object that can be streamed across.

Missed Opportunities

For every use of the Decorator pattern, there seems to be an opportunity missed. The key to the Decorator pattern is that it is a flexible alternative to subclassing. Rather than adding behavior to a class by creating a subclass of it, we can add the behavior by creating a Decorator for it. Then that Decorator can be used to decorate any other class of the same type. In addition, Decorators can be nested, so rather than having to choose between a subclass or its peer, you can decorate with both.

There are numerous hierarchies that may benefit from a more flexible alternative than subclassing. For example, in the VisualWorks Stream hierarchy, ExternalReadStream has a subclass called CodeReaderStream, and ExternalWriteStream has a subclass called CodeWriterStream, as the diagram on the facing page shows.

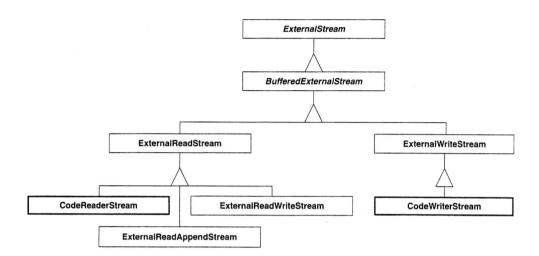

Although the `CodeReaderStream` and `CodeWriterStream` protocols are counterparts of each other, such reciprocal behavior is often encapsulated into a single class. But if there were a single `CodeStream` class, how could it be used with both `ExternalReadStreams` and `ExternalWriteStreams`? It should be implemented as a `Stream` Decorator, much like those in ET++ (DP 183).

For that matter, the separation and combinations in the `Stream` hierarchy between read-write behavior and internal-external implementation are a subclassing nightmare. First, the hierarchy splits into internal and external subhierarchies; then the subhierarchies duplicate the implementation for behaviors like read, write, append, and combinations thereof. If these behaviors were implemented as Decorators, they could be wrapped around internal and external streams in any combination desired.

Here's another example. `ApplicationModel` in VisualWorks has several abstract subclasses that add helpful behavior: `SimpleDialog` creates modal windows; `LensApplicationModel` interfaces with the Object Lens framework; third-party vendors have added their own abstract subclasses like `ValueInterface` (Abell, 1996). But what if you want a modal window that is Lens enabled? Do you subclass `SimpleDialog` or `LensApplicationModel`?

If these classes were implemented as `ApplicationModel` Decorators, you could easily use both. A regular window would be declared a subclass of `ApplicationModel`. If an instance of the window needs to be modal, wrap it with a `SimpleDialog` Decorator. If another instance needs to gather its data using the Lens, wrap it with a `LensApplicationModel` Decorator. If you need both, nest the two Decorators.

The `Collection` hierarchy is another example of inflexible subclassing that could benefit from the Decorator pattern. There are four basic ways to store a collection: as an array (`Array`, `OrderedCollection`), a linked list (`LinkedList` and `Link` in VisualWorks), a hash table (`Set`), or a (balanced binary) tree. Various

Collection classes enhance these basic storage structures: duplicate elimination (Set), sorting (SortedCollection), and dependency notification (List in VisualWorks). The problem comes when you need a collection to preserve order but eliminate duplicates. You'll probably implement OrderedSet as a subclass of OrderedCollection. But if you also need a collection that sorts and removes duplicates, you'll also need to implement SortedSet as a subclass of SortedCollection. The code in OrderedSet and SortedSet will be very similar; the main difference will be their superclasses.

A more flexible solution would divide the Collection hierarchy into Concrete-Component and Decorator branches. ConcreteComponent classes would implement array, linked list, hash table, and perhaps tree. Decorator would implement duplicate elimination, sorting, and dependency notification. Then an "ordered set" would be an array with a duplicate elimination decorator. A "sorted set" would be an array with a duplicate elimination decorator on a sorting decorator. (In fact, an OrderedCollection might become an Array that is wrapped with a "growable collection" decorator.) This solution would be much more flexible than the subclassing approach of the current Collection hierarchy, although perhaps less efficient. (See Bridge (121) for IBM's approach to implementing collections.)

Implementation

In addition to the issues mentioned in *Design Patterns*, there are several more issues to consider when you implement a Decorator:

1. *Use a Decorator superclass.* The Decorator subhierarchy does not require an abstract Decorator class at its base, but such a class is very helpful. An abstract Decorator class in the Component hierarchy makes the Decorator classes easier to implement and makes the pattern more obvious to anyone reviewing or maintaining the code. Look at the ValueModel Decorator classes scattered throughout the ValueModel hierarchy. Do those look like Decorators? The BOSSTransporter hierarchy is completely separate from the Stream hierarchy. Does it look like a Stream Decorator? The Decorator subclass of Component not only makes the pattern easier to implement, it makes the pattern easier to recognize and maintain as well.

2. *Consider a ConcreteComponent subclass.* A separate ConcreteComponent subclass of the Component class will divide the Component hierarchy into two distinct subhierarchies: Decorator for classes that can decorate and ConcreteComponent for classes that can be decorated but are not decorators themselves.

3. *Only Decorator delegates to the component.* All Decorator subclasses should defer their default behavior to the component by inheriting Decorator's delegation methods. This will separate the messages that can be enhanced from the ones that a particular Decorator subclass actually changes.

4. *Don't assume a Decorator subclass will delegate directly to a ConcreteComponent.* Since Decorators can be nested, the Decorator may be delegating to another Decorator.

5. *Three ways to forward.* A Decorator can forward its operation messages to its component in three ways:

   • *Simple forward:* Send the message to the component without performing any other behavior.

   • *Extended forward:* Perform extra behavior before and/or after forwarding the message to the component.

   • *Override:* Perform behavior instead of forwarding the message to the component; this behavior may be to do nothing.

Sample Code

The File Reader's main hierarchy, `FieldFormatDescription`, contains a textbook example of the Decorator pattern. A `FieldFormatDescription` knows how a field should be read from a file. It knows whether the field is delimited or fixed length, what the delimiter or length is, and so forth. The main things a description knows how to do are read and write the field. Its three subclasses are `LeafFieldFormat`, `CompositeFieldFormat` (an example of Composite (137)), and `FieldFormatDecorator`. This diagram shows the hierarchy:

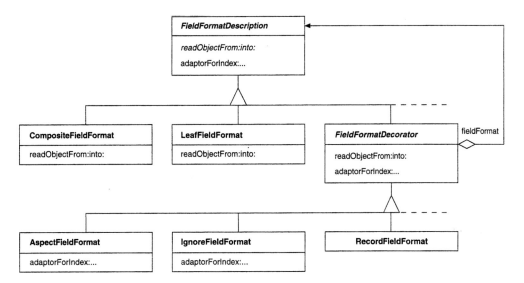

Let's look at how the pattern is implemented. The superclass, `FieldFormat-Description`, declares the core interface for the entire hierarchy. It fulfills the role of the Component class. As an abstract class, it defines basic messages like `readObjectFrom:into:` and `adaptorForIndex:andSubjectChannel:`.

```
Object subclass: #FieldFormatDescription
    instanceVariableNames: ''
    classVariableNames: ''
    poolDictionaries: ''

FieldFormatDescription>>readObjectFrom: dataStream into: aValueModel
    self subclassResponsibility

FieldFormatDescription>>adaptorForIndex: anInteger
andSubjectChannel: aValueModel
    ^(IndexedAdaptor subjectChannel: aValueModel)
        forIndex: anInteger
```

`FieldFormatDecorator` is a subclass of `FieldFormatDescription` that implements the Decorator class. It has an instance variable, `fieldFormat`, that acts as the pointer to the Decorator's component. It implements the core `Field-FormatDescription` messages by delegating them to its `fieldFormat`:

```
FieldFormatDescription subclass: #FieldFormatDecorator
    instanceVariableNames: 'fieldFormat'
    classVariableNames: ''
    poolDictionaries: ''

FieldFormatDecorator>>readObjectFrom: dataStream into: aValueModel
    fieldFormat
        readObjectFrom: dataStream
        into: aValueModel

FieldFormatDecorator>>adaptorForIndex: anInteger
andSubjectChannel: aValueModel
    ^fieldFormat
        adaptorForIndex: anInteger
        andSubjectChannel: aValueModel
```

There are many helpful behaviors that can be added to a field description in the process of reading and writing a field, and the hierarchy implements those behaviors as Decorators. `RecordFieldFormat` enhances a description (usually a `CompositeFieldFormat`) to expect a record delimiter at the end. It does this by overriding `readObjectFrom:into:` so that it reads the record into a separate stream and then reads the field(s) from it. Notice that this method does not delegate to its `fieldFormat` directly; it lets its superclass do that using `super>>readObjectFrom:into:`.

```
RecordFieldFormat>>readObjectFrom: dataStream into: aValueModel
    | recordStream |
    recordStream :=
        (dataStream upTo: recordDelimiter) readStream.
    super readObjectFrom: recordStream into: aValueModel
```

Decorators help map values from fields into the resulting Smalltalk object. By default, the result object is an `Array`, so each value is mapped by an `Indexed-Adaptor` (a kind of `ValueModel`). This default is implemented in `FieldFormatDescription>>adaptorForIndex:andSubjectChannel:` (shown on previous page). An `AspectFieldFormat` maps a field to a domain object's aspect. It overrides `adaptorForIndex:andSubjectChannel:` to return an `AspectAdaptor` instead of an `IndexedAdaptor`. An `Ignore-FieldFormat` maps a field's value to the bit bucket, so it uses a `ValueHolder`. `AspectFieldFormat` and `IgnoreFieldFormat` are implemented as decorators so that they can be used to map both leaf and composite fields.

```
AspectFieldFormat>>adaptorForIndex: anInteger
andSubjectChannel: aValueModel
   ^(AspectAdaptor subjectChannel: aValueModel)
     forAspect: aspect

IgnoreFieldFormat>>adaptorForIndex: anInteger
andSubjectChannel: aValueModel
   ^ValueHolder new
```

Thus any field or group of fields can be treated as a record. A field can also be mapped to an aspect, or it can be ignored. The decorators can be nested to, for example, group a set of fields as a record and map it to an aspect. Since it doesn't make sense to both map a field to an aspect and ignore it, code in `Aspect-FieldFormat` and `IgnoreFieldFormat` prevents both of those decorators from being applied to a single field.

Known Smalltalk Uses

Wrapper

The `Wrapper` hierarchy in VisualWorks is discussed above. `Wrapper` subclasses are Decorators that can be added to `VisualComponents`.

ValueModels

Several of the `ValueModel` classes in VisualWorks are decorators, as discussed above.

Stream Decorators

`BOSSTransporter` in VisualWorks is a `Stream` decorator. `FormattedStream` in the File Reader framework is also a `Stream` decorator. Both examples are discussed above.

FieldFormatDecorator

`FieldFormatDecorator` is a `FieldFormatDescription` decorator in the File Reader framework. It is discussed in the Sample Code section.

SyntheticFont

SyntheticFont is a decorator in the ImplementationFont hierarchy in VisualWorks. An ImplementationFont maps a Smalltalk font to one of the fonts built into the operating system. (This is an Adapter (105).) A Synthetic-Font adds properties to the font that the platform font may not support. For example, a SyntheticFont has a strikethrough setting. When strikethrough is on, the SyntheticFont draws its characters by drawing them first with the ImplementationFont and then drawing a line through them to look like this: ~~example of strikethrough~~.

Related Patterns

Decorator versus Adapter

Decorator and Adapter (105) are often confused. Both are also known as "Wrappers" because they wrap another object to change it. However, a Decorator preserves the interface of its Component; an Adapter specifically converts the interface of its Adaptee into the interface that its Client expects. A Decorator changes or adds behavior to its Component; it has no value otherwise. An Adapter can change or add behavior to its Adaptee, but its primary purpose is to convert its interface. If an Adapter has the same interface as its Adaptee, it has no value. Decorators can easily be nested because they have the same interface, but Adapters can't, nor does it make sense to in most cases.

Decorator versus Proxy

Decorator is also confused with Proxy (213). A Proxy controls access to its Subject while preserving its Subject's interface. A Proxy generally does not change its Subject's behavior except to make it available or unavailable. Various Decorator subclasses represent different behaviors that can be added. Various Proxy subclasses represent different ways of controlling access.

For example, CachedImage is a class in the PixelArray/Image hierarchy in VisualWorks that looks like a Decorator but is really a Proxy. It wraps an image by caching the Image as a Pixmap, a form that is more efficient but less flexible. The reason CachedImage is not implemented as a subclass of Image is that Image is an abstract class with numerous concrete subclasses. By implementing CachedImage as a wrapper, it can be wrapped around any Image subclass.

Yet CachedImage is not a Decorator because it does not add behavior; it simply adds efficiency. The initialization of the caching is invoked only the first time the CachedImage is used, not every time the way Decorator behavior would be. Most important, CachedImage fails the can-be-nested test: wrapping a CachedImage around another CachedImage adds no benefit. Thus Cached-Image is a Proxy that diverts use of an Image to use a more efficient Pixmap instead.

Decorator, Composite, and Object-Oriented Recursion

Decorator and Composite (137) are often used together in the same hierarchy. Both patterns require limiting the interface of their Component to a core interface that a client can use with any node in the structure. Thus, once the type's interface is limited for one pattern, the other pattern is easy to implement. Boiling down an extensive Component interface into a simplified core interface is difficult. Once that is done, either Decorator or Composite can be applied easily.

A Decorator communicates with its Component through Object-Oriented Recursion (see Chain of Responsibility (225)). A series of nested decorators culminating with a concrete component form a chain. When a message is sent to the top decorator in such a chain, each decorator decides whether to handle the message, forward it to its component, or both. If the message reaches the concrete component, it is ultimately handled there.

See Chain of Responsibility (225) for more details about using these three patterns together.

Composite versus Decorator

Trees often contain both Composite (137) and Decorator nodes, as well as ConcreteComponent nodes. How do you tell them apart? Look at how many components a node has. A ConcreteComponent node obviously has no components, a Decorator node has exactly one component, and a Composite node has multiple components. If a node can have multiple components but currently has only one component or none, it is still a Composite node because it can have multiple components.

FACADE (DP 185)   Object Structural

Intent

Provide a unified interface to a set of interfaces in a subsystem. Facade defines a higher-level interface that makes the subsystem easier to use.

Structure

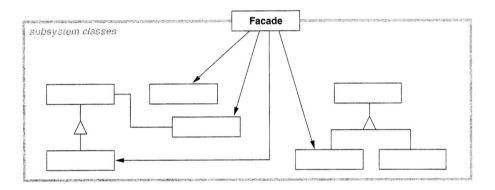

Discussion

One of the biggest advantages of object-oriented technology is that it reduces the complexity of large systems. Many of the patterns in *Design Patterns* specifically address managing complexity, and Facade is one of them. Subsystems designed for flexibility and extensibility are often hard to use "out of the box," because programmers feel they have to understand every class in the subsystem before they can use it. Facade solves the problem by providing a simplified interface that handles common case usage without worrying about complexities associated with the full generality of the subsystem.

Central to the pattern is a Facade object that presents a unified point of contact to the objects in a subsystem. The Facade provides an interface to the subsystem while hiding the underlying classes from its clients.

File System Facade

To put the pattern in perspective, let's examine a real-world example. One application we worked on used a Facade to hide a file system's implementation from the rest of the application. The application was implemented in Objectworks (ParcPlace's predecessor to VisualWorks) and used the vendor's file handling frameworks extensively. The problem was that the vendor kept refactoring those frameworks to distribute behavior better and to make the interface more intuitive. Although these improvements were helpful in many cases, they wrought havoc on our application because it had a lot of code that accessed the file system directly. Every time the vendor changed the interfaces, the code had to be migrated to the new interface—a time-consuming and error-prone task. There had to be a better way.

To solve this problem, we developed a `FileSystem` class that acted as a Facade to the vendor's file handling frameworks. We gave it a simplified interface that combined common multistep operations into a single message (an example of *procedural abstraction*—something that can be done in non-object-oriented languages and, nonetheless, another important tool in the object-oriented programmer's tool kit):

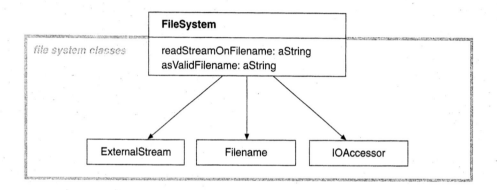

We implemented the Facade to delegate the work to the vendor frameworks as appropriate. Finally, we converted the parts of the application that needed file services to use the Facade, which made the file system look as if it was implemented in one object. Then whenever the vendor modified the file handling frameworks, we migrated only `FileSystem` to the new interface, and the rest of the application worked fine.

`FileSystem` illustrates Facade in its simplest form, where one class combines several others to make them act as one. The Facade provides a lot of behavior and seems to be doing a lot of work, but all it does is farm out most of that work to the other objects.

Note that the Facade avoids returning subsystem objects to its client. As a result, the client can be ignorant of the subsystem and its intricacies, leaving that knowledge to the Facade. A Facade is like a good office assistant: you ask him to take care of a task, and he does it without your knowing the details. Yet most Facades cannot completely hide their subsystems. For example, in `FileSystem`, `read-StreamOnFilename:` returns a readable stream, and `asValidFilename:` might return a `Filename`. Both return values are defined by the subsystem.

Because clients are unaware of the ultimate recipient of their messages, the messages often undergo a name change in the Facade interface. The "real" receiver typically becomes the message's first argument. For example, `String>>asValidFilename` requires the class and protocol for validating file names. The

`FileStream` Facade can hide these details, but it changes the message name to `asValidFilename:` with a string as the parameter. Facade reduces the complexity of understanding a subsystem, but the additional level of indirection that Facade entails comes with a price.

Facades in Distributed Object Systems

Reducing complexity is the primary motivation for using the Facade pattern. Another motivation arises in distributed object systems like GemStone or ParcPlace Distributed Smalltalk. These products essentially divide a logical image into two (or more) separate parts: one image that represents a "client" that displays information to a user and a "server" image that processes client requests for information. Often developers design systems like this without considering distribution, at least not initially. Later they realize that a design that's appropriate for objects in a local space may not be appropriate for distributed object spaces.

For example, an `ApplicationModel` in a local Smalltalk system may collaborate with many different domain objects. In a distributed system, the network overhead of remote messages may make such a design undesirable. Suppose the `ApplicationModel` queries a collection of `Employees` for information. If the `Employees` are on one machine and the `ApplicationModel` on another, the resulting network traffic may well be prohibitive. A common solution introduces a Facade that handles collaborations with the group of `Employees`. It also incorporates a Proxy for the remote Facade, with the Proxy residing in the client's memory space and the actual Facade remaining on the remote system. In this way the total number of required Proxies is reduced, and the number of network transmissions needed for each interaction is reduced as well:

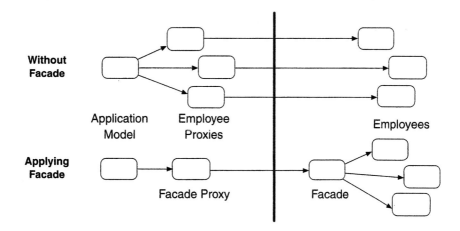

In Gemstone, the same motivation might apply to reducing the total number of objects that are "faulted" or loaded into the client image from the database. Moving the locus of execution from the client side to the server side has many benefits. In addition to reducing the total amount of network traffic, we would reduce the amount of space needed by the application on the client side as well.

Multiple Facades

Design Patterns (DP 193) states that "usually only one Facade object is required. Thus Facade objects are often Singletons." From this one might infer that a system can have only one Facade, but in fact it means that there is usually just one Facade per subsystem. If a system has multiple subsystems, the system can easily use multiple Facades simultaneously.

For example, the VisualAge for Smalltalk Communications/Transactions feature contains an example of multiple Facades working together. This feature provides a set of classes and VisualAge parts that implement an interface to different communications protocols. VisualAge lets you choose from TCP/IP, NetBIOS, APPC, MQSeries, and several other protocols. Each of these has a distinct and incompatible C API. But VisualAge provides a common interface to each through a Facade that hides the complexity of each and the differences between them.

For example, `AbtSocket` represents a TCP/IP Socket, `AbtAPPCConversation` represents an APPC Conversation, and `AbtMQQueue` represents an MQSeries queue. These classes hide a number of classes that implement these particular protocols behind their simplified facades. In VisualAge, each of these classes shares a public protocol for an abstract communication dialogue. Each class responds to the following methods:

- `connect`—Connect this part to the remote server.
- `disconnect`—Close the dialogue and disconnect from the server.
- `sendBuffer`—Send an `AbtBuffer` containing information to the server.
- `sendString`—Send this string as an `AbtBuffer` to the server.
- `receiveBuffer`—Return an `AbtBuffer` containing information received from the server.

This is only a partial list, but it's representative. The details of how these messages are handled by the particular protocols are entirely hidden behind the Facades. The interesting thing is that the Facades all share this common interface, which makes them interchangeable. (*Design Patterns* (DP 188) discusses multiple Facade subclasses in the first Implementation point.)

This makes it possible to write client software that does not depend on the peculiarities of any particular communications protocol. It might be possible, for example, to write a client for APPC and then switch over to using TCP/IP with a minimum of recoding. It is also possible to write clients that use multiple communications protocols; you could write a system that communicates by both APPC and TCP/IP simultaneously.

Common Facade Mistakes

There are a few common mistakes novice designers make when applying the Facade pattern. The first is subclassing the Facade class to add new behavior to the subsystem. Often programmers make this mistake when they don't understand the intent of the Facade pattern. The Facade should not add new behavior to the subsystem; it should merely provide centralized and simplified access to it. If the Facade does not provide enough behavior, then it may be extended or subclassed, but only when the desired behavior is already present in the subsystem. If it is not, then the subsystem, not the Facade, needs fixing. The new behavior should be added to the subsystem classes first and then to the Facade.

The second common mistake (closely related to the first) is to turn a Facade class into a Manager class (see the section on Manager classes in Mediator (287)).The Facade begins to take over the work of the subsystem by implementing more and more functionality itself. The result is likely to be a large and complex class, hard to understand and maintain.

A Facade's methods should be few and concise. If the Facade starts sprouting methods that have no analog in the subsystem, change the subsystem to fulfill those responsibilities.

ENVY/Developer Subapplications

Design Patterns (DP 188) explains that the Facade pattern saves time by reducing the compilation dependencies between classes. Since Smalltalk is not a file-based compiled language like C++, this is not an issue for Smalltalk programmers. However, there is a related problem unique to Smalltalk that the Facade pattern can help solve.

Many Smalltalk development projects use ENVY/Developer, perhaps the most popular code management system for Smalltalk. The primary unit of source code control in ENVY is a logical grouping of classes known as an *application*. As the following diagram shows, applications can contain both classes and *subapplications,* which are also logical grouping of classes within an application. A subapplication in turn can contain more subapplications and classes:

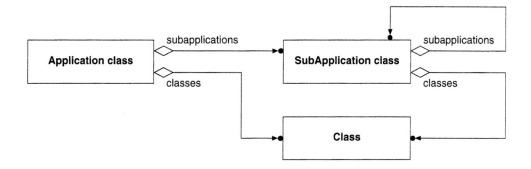

A process called *loading* brings applications into an ENVY image from an ENVY repository. A load is atomic, which means the classes and methods in an application all load completely or not at all. If an error occurs that causes the load to fail, a class will not be partially loaded, nor will classes be loaded without others they depend on. ENVY guarantees that the image will never be in an inconsistent state due to a failed class load.

When an application loads, it attempts to load each of its subapplications. Each subapplication has a Boolean expression, called a *configuration expression*, that determines when the subapplication should be loaded. ENVY loads all subapplications whose configuration expression evaluates to true.

Developers can implement Smalltalk systems that are platform- and dialect-independent using a combination of ENVY subapplications and the Facade pattern. To do it, platform-specific and dialect-specific code must be isolated, placed behind a Facade, and stored in a subapplication. That code must then be reimplemented for each alternative platform or dialect, wrapped in its own Facade and stored in its own subapplication. The Facades all have the same interface and are thus interchangeable, as are the subapplications themselves. The rest of the system interacts with the isolated code through the Facade so that it doesn't know which implementation it is using. This way, ENVY uses the configuration expressions to select and load the subapplication for the proper implementation. Meanwhile, the rest of the system remains platform- and dialect-independent.

Here's an example. Suppose you were building a graphics conversion program that converted between multiple image formats. This program would consist of many `Stream` manipulations that use methods that are identical among the dialects of Smalltalk. However, there are a few dialect-specific differences that could pose a problem if you wanted to implement the program in three dialects.

The specifics of opening a file, attaching the file to a `Stream`, and closing it are different among VisualAge, VisualWorks, and Visual Smalltalk. But the methods to manipulate the bytes in a `Stream` (`next:`, `upTo:`, `nextPut:`) are basically the same among the dialects. If you wanted to port a program from one dialect to another easily, you could isolate the dialect-specific parts behind a class named `FileHandlingFacade`. This class would understand methods like `openFile-Named:`, `closeFile`, and `fileStream`. You build three different versions of this class, one for each dialect. The code for each version of the class would be vastly different; only the public protocols of the Facade class would remain the same.

You would then construct three subapplications in ENVY, one for each dialect, for the three versions of the class. There would be different configuration expressions for each dialect—each expression checking the VM type and choosing the appropriate subapplication. Only the matching type would evaluate to true, and the corresponding subapplication would be loaded.

Implementation

Besides the implementation issues mentioned in *Design Patterns,* there are two more to consider:

1. *Messages perform complex actions.* When designing a Facade's interface, it's tempting to use it as a factory that returns the right objects to the client. But then the client has to know what type of object is being returned and how to collaborate with it to get the desired behavior. In this case, the Facade is not hiding the complexities of the subsystem very well. The client will be much simpler if it tells the Facade what it wants done and lets the Facade do all of the work.

2. *The receiver becomes the first parameter.* Messages are transformed when they're moved to a Facade because the receiver, the Facade, is no longer very significant. Thus the original receiver becomes the message's first argument. For example, as shown earlier, `String>>asValidFilename` becomes `FileSystem>>asValidFilename: aString`.

Sample Code

Many relational database frameworks employ the concept of a **database broker,** an object that handles the storage and retrieval of objects from a relational database. In many frameworks the broker is a Facade onto a supporting database subsystem.

Let's consider a simple case in which the objects to be saved can all be written into a single row of a relational database. For simplicity's sake we will look only at saving objects and not consider retrieving objects. Our framework will contain the following classes:

- `SQLStatement` is the abstract superclass of all classes that generate valid SQL strings when given a domain object and a `ColumnMap`. It has three subclasses: `SQLInsert`, `SQLUpdate`, and `SQLSelect`.

- `DatabaseConnection` represents a connection to a relational database. It can connect to the database, disconnect from it, and execute valid SQL strings.

- `ColumnMap` provides the mappings from instance variable names to table column names for a particular class of domain object.

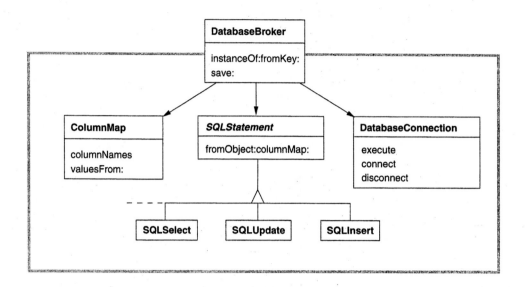

To see how this works, let's look at the method `save:` in `DatabaseBroker`. This
is the method in the Facade that brings together the objects in the subsystem. Clients of the Facade need know only that this method saves objects into the database; the details of the subsystem are irrelevant.

```
DatabaseBroker>>save: anObject
    "Save this object into the database."
    |columnMap statement|
    columnMap := anObject class columnMap.
    statement := (anObject isPersistent)
        ifTrue: [SQLUpdate new
                    fromObject: anObject
                    columnMap: columnMap]
        ifFalse: [SQLInsert new
                    fromObject: anObject
                    columnMap: columnMap].
    self databaseConnection execute: statement
```

To see some of the interactions between objects in the subsystem, we'll look at the
implementation of `SQLInsert>>fromObject:columnMap:`.

```
SQLInsert>>fromObject: object columnMap: columnMap
    "Create an insert statement from this object
    and its column map."

    | stream |
    stream := WriteStream on: String new.
    stream
        nextPutAll: 'INSERT INTO ';
        nextPutAll: columnMap tableName;
        nextPut: $(.
```

```
columnMap columnNames do:
   [:name |
   stream
      nextPutAll: name;
      nextPut: $,].
"Eliminate the last comma:"
stream position: stream position - 1.

stream nextPutAll: ') VALUES ('.
(columnMap valuesFrom: anObject) do:
   [:value |
   stream
      nextPutAll: value;
      nextPut: $,].
stream position: stream position - 1.
stream nextPut: $).
^stream contents
```

To complete the example, let's consider some of the methods of `ColumnMap`. A `ColumnMap` contains a `Dictionary` that maps the names of the columns in a database table to the names of the instance variables holding the corresponding values in the object:

```
ColumnMap>>columnNames
   "Return the column names for my mapping."
   ^columnMappings keys

ColumnMap>>valuesFrom: anObject
   "Return a collection of the values of the
   instance variables that correspond to my columns."
   ^self columnNames collect:
      [:key | anObject perform: (columnMappings at: key)]
```

This simple example[3] shows only how items would be saved; retrieving is a more complex process, but it involves the same framework objects. Still, the code for the Facade is no more complicated for retrieving than it is in saving.

An interesting side note is that the `DatabaseConnection` can be another Facade. Both VisualWorks and VisualAge provide classes with methods like `DatabaseConnection`'s. They are Facades onto subsystems that handle more complex API's like Oracle and OBDC.

Known Smalltalk Uses

It is surprising that although Smalltalk vendors provide numerous frameworks, there are few occurrences of Facade. One that *Design Patterns* describes is the

---

[3]This example is drawn from the Crossing Chasms pattern language of object-relational integration. More details of the pattern language can be found in Brown and Whitenack (1996).

class `Compiler` in VisualWorks. It acts as a facade to the parsing and compilation classes. The IBM Smalltalk class `EsCompiler` and the Visual Smalltalk class `Compiler` play similar roles in their respective dialects.

Another small-scale facade found in VisualWorks is the class `TableInterface`. A table is represented visually by three instances of `TableView`: one representing the row labels, another the column labels, and a third the rows and columns. A `TableInterface` acts as a Facade to a `TableDecorator` and a `SelectionInTable`. It hides the details of these classes, particularly their interactions, from the programmer who wants to use a table.

A `SelectionInTable` is the model for the `TableView` held in the `TableDecorator`. `TableInterface` keeps the user from having to construct this connection and maintain the Observer notifications that keep the two synchronized. It also hides the Observer connections between the `TableViews`. `TableViews` represent the row labels and column labels in the table and the collections of strings that provide the text for those labels. The relationship between the instances of these classes is shown in the following diagram:

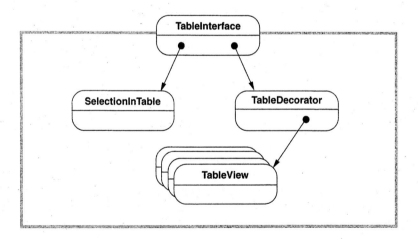

Related Patterns

Facade versus Adapter

A Facade is similar to an Adapter (105). Whereas an Adapter converts the interface of a single object, a Facade combines and converts the interface for multiple objects. An Adapter provides most, if not all, of the behavior of its Adaptee. A Facade provides a simplified subset of its objects' behavior.

FLYWEIGHT (DP 195)   Object Structural

Intent

Use sharing to support large numbers of fine-grained objects efficiently.

Structure

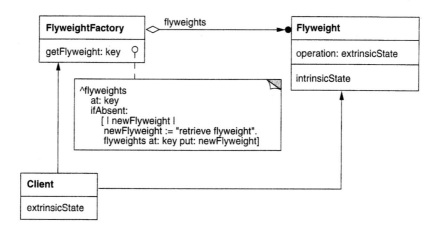

The following instance diagram shows how flyweights are shared:

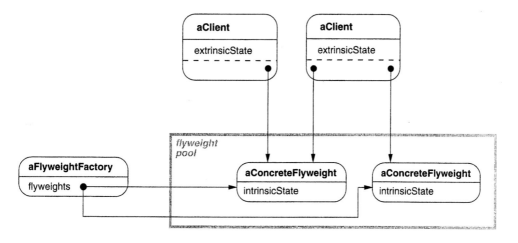

Discussion

When a class is implemented as a Flyweight, no two instances of the class represent the same entity. When two clients independently derive instances of a Flyweight class and the two instances have the same value, then the two clients are really sharing the same Flyweight instance. The clients may be unaware that the class is a Flyweight, so each thinks it has its own independent instance, but the Flyweight class's implementation ensures that the clients are using the same instance.

Flyweights can be shared because they divide their intrinsic and extrinsic state. **Intrinsic state** is the sharable state that is the Flyweight's internal state. **Extrinsic state** is the state that would normally be stored in the Flyweight, but is not sharable because different clients expect the same Flyweights to have different values for this state, so it is stored in the clients instead. Some Flyweight operations may require access to the extrinsic state, so they accept it as parameters.

A typical class provides instances on demand, whenever a client sends the class new, but a Flyweight class's instance creation is controlled though a **FlyweightFactory**. A client specifies to the FlyweightFactory which Flyweight it wants, and the factory returns it. The catch is that the factory doesn't necessarily create a new instance. It contains a **flyweight pool** of existing instances; if the specified instance is in the pool, the factory returns an existing instance. Either way, the client is not aware of whether it's receiving a new instance or a previously existing one.

Applying the Flyweight pattern is this process of taking a class whose instances weren't originally designed to be shared and redesigning the class so that its instances can be shared. This involves dividing a class into its shared state that goes into the Flyweight and nonshared state that goes into the client. Each of the Flyweight's operations that require the nonshared state gets a new message signature that adds parameters for the nonshared state. Finally, clients can no longer create Flyweights on demand; they must go though the FlyweightFactory instead.

Symbols

Let's look at an example from Smalltalk, the `Symbol` class. A `Symbol` is an immutable `String`, which means that its characters cannot be replaced or changed. For example, it's simple to take an arbitrary string and capitalize its first letter:

```
| string |
string := 'string'.
string := string, ''.        "Only necessary in IBM Smalltalk."
string at: 1 put: (string at: 1) asUppercase.
^string
```

However, the same thing won't work with `Symbols`:

```
| symbol |
symbol := #symbol.
symbol at: 1 put: (symbol at: 1) asUppercase.
^symbol
```

This code, specifically `Symbol>>at:put:`, will produce an error saying that symbols cannot be modified. Thus symbols are immutable, whereas strings are not.

What good is an immutable string? It allows multiple objects to share the string while guaranteeing that none of the objects will change the string. Sharing any common value involves a level of trust. One of the other objects might do something to the value that you don't like. For example, let's say that you're sharing a string with some other objects, and one of them decides to capitalize it. If you didn't want it capitalized, too bad, because the string's state has now been changed, and you don't even know it. Thus, sharing a value can be risky. Everyone using the value must agree to any changes made to its state. The easiest such agreement says that no one will change the value's state. To guarantee that agreement, it's helpful if the value refuses to allow its state to be changed. Thus, when you try to modify a symbol (`Symbol>>at:put:`), it raises an error. So when you want to share a string but guarantee that no one will change it, share a symbol instead.

Because a symbol never changes state, there's no reason to have more than one instance that contains the same series of characters. With strings, you might want to have your own copy of `'characters'` so that you can change it the way you want, and another object might want to have its own independent copy of `'characters'` so that it can change the string the way it wants. But since neither object can change the symbol `#characters`, there's no reason each needs its own copy, and it's more efficient for the system to store just one copy that the two objects share instead of two copies.

Yet the two objects may not even know about each other, much less that they're using the same symbol and could potentially share it. All each one knows is that it needs a particular symbol, the one that contains a particular series of characters. Since neither object knows about the other, something that knows about both of them must mediate between them, realize that they want to use the same symbol, and give them both the same one so that they'll be sharing it even though they don't even realize it. In the case of symbols, this mediating object is the Smalltalk system itself, specifically the `Symbol` class.

Symbol Creation

There are two ways to create symbols in Smalltalk: source code can contain a symbol literal, and a string can be converted into a symbol:

```
| symbol |
symbol := #characters.
```

```
| symbol |
symbol := 'characters' asSymbol.
```

Either way, a symbol always starts out as a string, because source code is just a string that gets passed into the parser. Both the parser and String>>asSymbol use the Symbol class to create a new instance. Each dialect has its own implementation for converting a string into a symbol, and each is rather complex. However, this code shows the general algorithm that all dialects use:

```
String>>asSymbol
    ^Symbol intern: self

Symbol class>>intern: aString
    "If the symbol already exists, it will be in the
    symbol table, so find it and return it. Otherwise,
    create the symbol, add it to the table, and return it."
    | symbol |
    symbol := self findInTable: aString.
    symbol notNil ifTrue: [^symbol].
    symbol := Symbol privateFromString: aString.
    self addToTable: symbol.
    ^symbol
```

The code depends on a symbol table, a collection that the class uses to store all existing instances. Either the symbol the string represents is in the table, so the class returns that existing instance, or the class creates a new instance, adds it to the table, and returns it. In IBM Smalltalk, the symbol table is the SymbolTable class variable in Symbol. VisualWorks's Symbol class uses two class variables, USTable and SingleCharSymbols.

The symbol table is essentially a giant collection implemented with one or more of the weak collection classes. A weak pointer is one that the garbage collector ignores. As long as an object has a single viable reference pointing to it, the garbage collector won't collect the object because it is still in use. However, an object can have numerous weak references pointing to it, but if it doesn't have any viable regular references, the garbage collector will consider the object unused and reclaim its memory. The symbol table uses weak collections so that symbols that are no longer being used can be garbage collected. Otherwise, once a symbol was added to the symbol table, it would never leave.

Symbol is an example of the Flyweight pattern. Symbol is a Flyweight class because no two separate instances of the class represent the same value (i.e., contain the same series of characters). The uniqueness of each instance is ensured by Symbol's class side, which acts as a FlyweightFactory. Most classes create new instances on demand, ultimately via new, but Symbol's class side creates a new instance only if the symbol table doesn't already contain an instance with that value. Thus, the symbol table, a class variable like SymbolTable or USTable, is a flyweight pool, a collection of all existing instances.

How does the Symbol's class side know what value to look for in the symbol table? The instance creation method isn't a simple one like new that unfailingly instantiates another instance every time it's called. Rather, it's a more complex one like `intern:` that creates new instances conditionally and accepts a parameter that helps it decide what to do. In this case, the parameter is a `String` that describes what `Symbol` it should return. The `String` acts as a key that specifies which instance to return. The FlyweightFactory either finds an instance with that key in the flyweight pool and returns it, or it creates a new instance that corresponds to the key, adds the new instance to the pool under that key, and returns the new instance. Either way, the client gets back an instance corresponding to the key it requested.

Designing a Flyweight

The FlyweightFactory allows multiple clients that don't even know about each other to share flyweights without even knowing it. A client using a flyweight may or may not be sharing it with other clients, but it doesn't know, and it probably doesn't even know that the object is a flyweight and might be shared.

A flyweight can be shared because it only contains state that can be shared. A Flyweight class usually starts out as a regular class that can have duplicate instances, because that's a far easier way to design classes. The regular class contains whatever state it needs to do its job. But then you discover that the system requires an overwhelming number of instances of this class and that there are relatively few unique instances, so the system might as well share a small number of instances that act like a huge number.

The problem becomes how to redesign the class and its client code to make it into a Flyweight class. That requires two main steps: separating out the sharable state from the unsharable state and allowing the class to control its own instance creation.

Multiple clients may appear to use duplicate instances of the regular class, but upon closer inspection, those instances may not all have exactly the same state. Duplicate instances have two categories of instance variables: those that always have the same values (or else their instances wouldn't be duplicates) and those that may not always have the same values. The ones guaranteed to be the same can be shared; those that might vary depending on the client cannot be shared. The variables that cannot be shared must be moved out of the regular class and into the client classes as part of making the regular class into a Flyweight. This is why *Design Patterns* refers to the stared state inside the Flyweight as intrinsic and the unsharable state in the clients as extrinsic (DP 196).

The problem with moving state out of the Flyweight is that its behavior still requires that state. Most classes wouldn't work very well if you removed half of their instance variables, and Flyweights are no different. There are two ways you can resolve this: move the behavior into the clients, or make the clients provide the extrinsic state to the Flyweight's behavior. The problem with moving the behavior into the clients is that you're unencapsulating the Flyweight's behavior and that behavior will probably have to be duplicated in multiple client classes that all use the same Flyweight class. Thus, it's preferable to maintain the Flyweight's encapsulation and provide the extrinsic behavior to the Flyweight behavior that needs it. The way to do this is to change the method signatures of the behavior's operations to add parameters for the necessary extrinsic state and then change the messages sent by the clients to use these new methods. That's why the Flyweight operations in the Structure class diagram require the extrinsic state as a parameter.

The other issue for redesigning the class is allowing it to control its own instance creation. Regular classes ultimately allow instance creation through new, a message that unconditionally instantiates a new instance and returns it. To make the regular class into a Flyweight, the class is going to need more specific instance creation messages that control the process more carefully. That is the purpose of the Flyweight-Factory's getFlyweight: message: like new, it will create a new instance, but only if it doesn't already have an appropriate instance that can be shared.

Class Side Flyweight Factory

Design Patterns shows the FlyweightFactory as a separate class, but in Smalltalk the FlyweightFactory is often the class side of the Flyweight class. This combines Flyweight and FlyweightFactory together into one class with the Flyweight-Factory look-up behavior on the class side. This works well because the class side of any class is already responsible for instance creation (like new), so making it responsible for instance management as well is quite easy.

The FlyweightFactory stores the existing instances in a flyweight pool. This pool is the flyweights collection variable, an instance variable in the Flyweight-Factory, that it uses to reference its Flyweight instances. When implementing the FlyweightFactory on the class side of Flyweight, the instance variable becomes a class side variable.

Whether the class side flyweight pool should be a class variable or a class instance variable depends on how many pools the system needs and what Flyweights it wants those pools to contain. All of the classes in a hierarchy share the same instance of a class variable, but each class in a hierarchy gets its own copy of a class instance variable. So the question is: Should all of the Flyweight instances in the hierarchy be kept in one pool, or should all of the instances for each subclass be kept in its own pool? This is difficult to determine when Flyweight is a single class, not a hierarchy, because then there is no real difference. When in doubt, use a class variable so that all of the Flyweights will be in a single pool.

The name "flyweight pool" might seem to imply that the factory should keep its flyweights in a pool variable, but those two uses of the term "pool" have nothing to do with each other. The factory should use either a class variable or a class instance variable, not a pool variable.[4]

---

[4]Pool variables are specialized global variables in Smalltalk whose uses are rather odd and thankfully rare (Ewing, 1994). Interestingly, one can argue that the items in any pool variable are themselves Flyweights because of the way they're shared, which means that a pool variable *is* a flyweight pool without a FlyweightFactory's interface, but that becomes a rather esoteric discussion that sheds little light on the general nature of the pattern.

The FlyweightFactory is a Singleton (91) that controls access to the Flyweight instances. As that pattern explains, implementing a Singleton on the class side of a class can be shortsighted because you may later discover the need for more than one instance. In this case, the issue is whether one Flyweight class might need multiple flyweight pools. If it does, it will need multiple instances of FlyweightFactory to manage those pools, so FlyweightFactory should be implemented as a separate class instead of on the class side of Flyweight.

Efficient Comparison

One nice side effect of a Flyweight class is that it implements equal (=) efficiently. To compare two strings, you have to compare each pair of characters to make sure they're equal. The longer the strings are, the longer the comparison takes. Comparing two symbols, no matter how long they are, is much faster because they're either the same object or they're not. If they're different objects, they won't contain the same series of characters, so they cannot be equal. Thus, in VisualWorks, Symbol implements equal as double-equal (==) (in Visual Smalltalk, Symbol>>= is implemented by a primitive, which does the same thing as ==):

```
Symbol>>= aSymbol
    ^self == aSymbol
```

Double-equal tests two objects to see if they're the same object, if they occupy the same location in memory. Two instances of a regular class may be equal without being identical because they're two separate objects but have the same state. However, the only way two flyweights can have the same state is if they're really the same object, so equality and identity are the same thing for two flyweights.

This code shows how double-equal works differently for String versus Symbol because String is not a Flyweight but Symbol is:

```
"VisualWorks and Visual Smalltalk"
"(String literals work differently in IBM Smalltalk)"
"line 1"    'String' = 'String'              "Returns true."
"line 2"    'String' == 'String'             "Returns false."

    "VisualWorks, Visual Smalltalk, and IBM Smalltalk"

"line 3"    #Symbol = #Symbol                "Returns true."
"line 4"    #Symbol == #Symbol               "Returns true."
"line 5"    'String' = ('Str','ing')         "Returns true."
"line 6"    'String' == ('Str','ing')        "Returns false."
"line 7"    #Symbol = 'Symbol' asSymbol      "Returns true."
"line 8"    #Symbol == 'Symbol' asSymbol     "Returns true."
```

Two String literals for the same string are equivalent (as shown in line 1) but not identical (line 2). Yet two Symbol literals that contain the same series of characters are both equivalent (line 3) and identical (line 4). This is true not only for literal Strings and Symbols but also for ones created programmatically (lines 5–8). (For more information about the difference between equality (=) and identity (==), see Woolf, 1996.)

Integer, Float, and Character

Integer is not a concrete class; it is an abstract class with multiple concrete subclasses. One of them is SmallInteger, the class for "common" integers roughly in the range of -10^8 to 10^8. Two instances of SmallInteger that represent the same value are indistinguishable; they are double-equal, and they hash to the same value (themselves). Are they really implemented as Flyweights? That's hard to say; the implementation is buried in the virtual machine and primitives. If there's a FlyweightFactory containing a flyweight pool of SmallIntegers, it is not visible from the Smalltalk image. But two instances of the same value are indistinguishable, so Smalltalk code treats them like Flyweights.

Not all Number classes act like Flyweights, just SmallInteger. Other Integer subclasses don't work this way. You might think that SmallInteger is a Flyweight because it wraps an integer data type so that integer math can be performed by the CPU. However, Float also wraps a Real data type for efficiency, yet it is not a Flyweight. Try this in a workspace:

```
"line 1"    4 == 4                    "Returns true."
"line 2"    5 == (2 + 3)              "Returns true."
"line 3"    8589934592 == (2**33)     "Returns false."
"line 4"    4.0 == 4.0                "Returns false."
```

Similarly, Character in Smalltalk is a Flyweight class, just like in the Motivation in *Design Patterns*. Two Characters that represent the same ASCII value are really the same instance.

One shortcoming of Symbol, SmallInteger, and Character as examples of the Flyweight pattern is that they do not really separate intrinsic and extrinsic state. They are used passively by client code, not told to perform actions using extrinsic state that is passed in as parameters by the clients.

Flyweight Pool

Design Patterns mentions that reclaiming the flyweight's storage can be an issue (DP 200). Implementing the FlyweightFactory can be tricky in that once it adds a flyweight to the flyweight pool, the object may never leave. Once clients are no longer using a particular flyweight, it can safely be garbage collected. But should it be? If the flyweight might be used again soon, perhaps the pool should hang on to it until then. On the other hand, if no one is using the flyweight and no one is likely to in the near future, the flyweight pool might as well discard the flyweight to save space. If the flyweight is needed again later, it can be recreated at that time.

The problem is, how does the FlyweightFactory know when a flyweight is no longer being used? It's pointing to the flyweight via the flyweight pool, but who else is? Just as the various clients don't know about each other, the Flyweight-Factory factory doesn't really know about any of them; it just knows about the flyweights. The flyweights also don't know how many clients are using them, if any.

One approach is reference counting, which is commonly used in C++. Whenever a client requests a flyweight, the FlyweightFactory remembers that this client is using this flyweight. When the client no longer needs the flyweight, it must inform the FlyweightFactory. If clients are no longer using a flyweight, it can be removed from the flyweight pool. This approach is rather complex and requires a lot more collaboration between the FlyweightFactory and the clients.

A simpler approach in Smalltalk is to implement the flyweight pool using one or more weak collections. The garbage collector ignores the references of weak collections. If clients are no longer using a flyweight, then the only reference to it will be from the flyweight pool, and that is a weak reference. If the garbage collector runs, it will ignore the weak reference, find that the flyweight doesn't have any other references, and deallocate the flyweight. Symbol uses weak collections to implement its symbol table.

Not Very Common

There are very few examples of the Flyweight pattern in Smalltalk. Symbol, SmallInteger, and Character are commonly used classes, but their implementations do not illustrate the pattern well. The last two classes are implemented primarily in the virtual machine, and none of the classes' operations require extrinsic state as a parameter.

Flyweights are ultimately simple types—fine-grained objects that are used millions of times and yet have few unique values. Smalltalk programmers do not need to implement their own simple type classes; the vendors have already done this. Even if you do implement a new simple type, such as a new Number class, you probably won't need to implement it as a Flyweight.

Sharable

Learning the Flyweight pattern is still helpful even though examples are hard to find because Flyweight is a specialization of a broader pattern we'll call Sharable. Both the principles and the implementation of the two patterns are quite similar, so understanding one makes it much easier to understand the other. Furthermore, although examples of Flyweight are rare, examples of Sharable are more common.

The difference between the two patterns is intent. Flyweight is for fine-grained objects; Sharable can handle anything from the smallest objects to the largest ones. Flyweight requires large numbers of duplicate objects; Sharable requires only enough duplicates that efficiency starts to suffer, which may be as few as two. Flyweight focuses on efficiency, whereas Sharable focuses on consistency and correctness.

Flyweight and Sharable are similarly implemented. Both involve a Sharable-Factory that draws from an object pool of existing instances. Both involve dividing the object into internal state that can be shared and nonsharable state that goes in the clients. In both cases, operations that require the external state must get it via parameters.

Examples of Sharable

A common use of the Sharable pattern in Smalltalk is to share very large objects so as to avoid duplicating them. Here the issue is not that an object might be used by dozens or hundreds of clients; it might have only a couple of clients using it. Nevertheless, it is so large that to duplicate it even a few times is very wasteful. Thus, even on this small scale, sharing is helpful—not because the Sharables are so fine-grained but because they're so large.

Another use of Sharable is to help ensure data integrity and consistency. *Design Patterns* explicitly says this is not the focus of Flyweight (DP 137), but the two purposes are similar. Multiple objects should not represent the same conceptual entity. If the same entity is represented by duplicate objects and their states differ, what is the true state of the entity? Thus these duplicate objects would have to be synchronized to keep their state the same. Rather than constantly resynchronizing them, it is easier to keep just one object and let the clients share it. That way, when one client changes the object's state, no synchronization needs to be done. (As for keeping the various clients in sync with changes in the Sharable, see Observer (305).)

In all three cases—numerous finely grained objects, duplicate large objects, and objects that must consistently store the same state—clients need to be able to share instances rather than duplicate them. This sharing should be transparent. That is, each client uses a central location and standard protocol for acquiring a new one of these Sharables and is unaware of what other clients, if any, are sharing the object. This transparent sharing is the heart of Sharable.

USState

As an example, consider how to implement an object that represents a state in the United States, USState. Since there are only 50 states, the system does not need an unlimited number of USState instances, just one for each state. Each USState may be a rather large object filled with statistics and census information about its state, such as population for each city, lists of telephone area codes and prefixes, and images showing what the state looks like. Thus, not only does the system not need more than one instance for any particular state, multiple instances would waste memory and cause update problems as new statistics became available.

It is not critical that USState be implemented as a Sharable, but it would be helpful. This would ensure that there is only one instance for each state in the Union. The following diagram shows what USState looks like implemented as a Sharable:

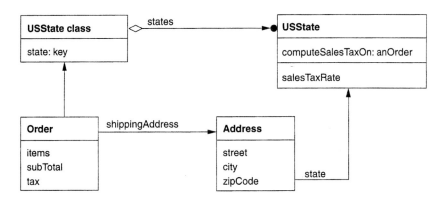

Each state sets its own sales tax rate, so it can be different for all 50 states. When a mail order company ships an order to a customer, the amount of tax depends on what state the customer is in. Furthermore, some items are taxable but others are not, and this varies by state as well. Thus, computing the tax on a rather simple order can be fairly complicated. All of these variations for computing the tax are not really the order's responsibility, and since the specifics vary by state, USState would be a logical place to put this behavior.

To compute the tax, USState would implement a message like compute-SalesTaxOn: that accepts an Order as its argument, as shown in the next diagram on the following page. If the state computed the tax the same on all types of items, it could simply compute the tax based on the order's subtotal. If some item types are taxable but others are not, the state object could calculate the tax on each item and sum them. Either way, the state would then tell the order its tax so that the order could compute its total cost.

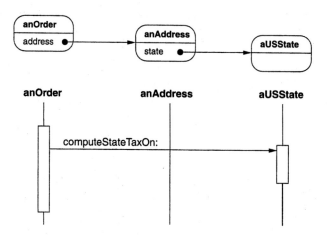

In this example, USState is the Sharable class, and Order is the Client. The state contains the intrinsic state such as the tax tables. Order contains the extrinsic state such as the items to compute the tax on. The tax computation method, USState>>computeSalesTaxOn: anOrder, knows both the state with the tax rates and the order with the items to be taxed. It computes the tax and returns it to the order.

Persistent Objects

Persistent objects—ones stored outside the Smalltalk image in a database or file—should not be duplicated because of integrity and efficiency considerations. The system's interface to the persistent store is a SharableFactory that illustrates how the Sharable pattern can be used to ensure there is only one instance for each conceptual entity.

The architecture of a system using a database, especially a relational database, should include a database layer that allows access to the database and hides these details from the rest of the system (Brown, 1995a). This database layer is responsible for loading the domain objects and committing their changes. When the system needs to access a domain object, it asks the database layer for that object by specifying its keys. To improve performance, the database layer often caches objects it has already read out of the database so that it won't have to load them again. Thus, when one client requests a domain object that another client has already requested, the database layer returns the cached object, and the two clients are now sharing the same object without even knowing it.

This is Sharable. The database layer is a giant SharableFactory, controlling creation of and access to domain objects. The layer's cache is an object pool that contains the domain objects. This makes the domain objects themselves Sharables. The process of separating the domain (persistent) behavior from the application (transient) behavior is similar to that for separating intrinsic from extrinsic state. The result is that the persistent state can be stored without storing the transient state as well. This isn't Flyweight in the *Design Patterns* sense, but the development process, as well as the resulting structure and behavior, are very similar.

Distributed Flyweights

Distributed Smalltalk, or any other kind of distributed object scheme, presents special challenges for any variation of the Sharable pattern, including Flyweight. A distributed Smalltalk image consists of several physical Smalltalk images, each running on a separate machine, that work together as one logical image with a single object space. This allows load balancing because objects can perform their computations on whichever machine has the most available CPU cycles, regardless of the location of the object that expects the result. It also allows geographically dispersed users to share the same objects rather than using duplicate objects that have to be synchronized (see Proxy (213)).

The problem for the Sharable pattern is that an image is supposed to contain only one instance of a Sharable class with a particular value. For example, there is only one capital letter A in the system and only one integer 5. When the image is distributed (logically) across multiple machines, which machine should contain the Sharables? If the integer 5 were stored on one machine and 7 on another, computing 5 plus 7 would suddenly become a lot more difficult because of network communication. If the network were down temporarily, the computation couldn't be performed at all.

To help minimize communication between physical images, heavily used Sharables (mostly Flyweights, such as Characters, SmallIntegers, and Symbols and Singletons (91) such as true, false, and nil) are duplicated across physical images. Thus, two Flyweights with the same value can exist in the same logical image (one distributed across multiple machines) as long as they are in separate physical images (one per machine). Yet these separate Flyweight objects that represent a single value are still logically one object. This is manageable because these Flyweights have an internal (intrinsic) state that does not change. Yet it wreaks havoc with identity messages like double-equal. Comparing two memory addresses to see if they're the same works only if the two addresses are in the same physical memory space, which means they must be on the same machine. Thus, double-equal has to work differently when the two arguments are in separate memory spaces. In fact, the distributed Smalltalk vendors recommend not using double-equal to compare objects that may not be in the same memory space.

Applicability

Once you've decided to apply the Sharable pattern, there are three distinct ways for a system to use it. How the system uses Sharable determines how carefully you must implement them:

1. *Identity uniqueness.* The system assumes that two Sharable instances with the same value are the same object and depends on this assumption. It takes great advantage of double-equal (==) to manage the objects as efficiently as possible. Such a system treats two separate Sharables with the same value as though they're separate values and fails to eliminate duplicates. For example, you can use an `IdentitySet` to eliminate duplicate Sharables, but only if duplicate ones are guaranteed to be identical.

2. *Data integrity.* The system uses Sharables to ensure that each conceptual entity is represented by only one instance. Multiple instances require overhead to keep their state synchronized because unsynchronized instances would cause a loss of data integrity. Duplicates will not cause code to stop working, but they can hurt the reliability of the system's data.

3. *Space saving.* The system uses Sharables to store equivalent instances because duplicate instances are time-consuming to instantiate and consume a lot of memory. Such a system does not assume that the instances are Sharables. Just the opposite: each client assumes that it has its own independent copy and that two instances are unlikely to be the same instance. If a Sharable in this system gets duplicated, that's okay; the system will still work correctly, just a little less efficiently.

Implementation

There are two distinctly different ways to implement a Sharable class and its SharableFactory class. The difference concerns how new Sharable instances are created and affects how they are accessed:

1. *Creation through code.* One way to create a new Sharable is to run a method that does so. Thus, the SharableFactory contains a separate method for creating each Sharable. A SharableFactory that works this way does not need a single look-up method (i.e., `SharableFactory>>getSharable: key`), as *Design Patterns* suggests for Flyweight. Such a look-up method inevitably contains a case statement to match Sharable keys to their creation methods. Instead, the factory should use a separate accessor method for each Sharable (`getSharableA`, `getSharableB`, etc.). This hard-codes the number and variety of available Sharables at compile time, but that is already hard-coded because new Sharables cannot be created at runtime if their creation methods were not implemented at compile time.

2. *Creation by metadescription.* The other way to create a new Sharable is to allow the user to specify new Sharables at runtime. Thus, the Sharable-Factory does not contain code for creating new Sharables, but rather contains an interface that specifies a new Sharable's intrinsic state and creates a new Sharable instance accordingly. These new instances can be created by the user or read in from a persistent store such as a file or database.

One of the attributes to specify is a unique name for the new Sharable that will be used as the key for accessing it. When another part of the system uses the Sharable with a particular name, the system will access the Sharable using the SharableFactory's look-up method (i.e., `SharableFactory>>get-Sharable: key`), where the key is the Sharable's name. Such a Sharable-Factory cannot provide a separate accessor method (`getSharableA`, `getSharableB`, etc.) for each Sharable because the total variety of Sharables is not known at compile time.

Regardless of how new Sharable instances are created, there are several other issues to consider when implementing a Sharable:

1. *Equal is double-equal.* All objects in Smalltalk understand = (equal) and == (double-equal). A Sharable class implements equality to be the same as identity. This is because for Sharables, object identity and equality are the same thing. However, clients taking advantage of this feature must be aware that the objects are Sharables and are being shared.

2. *Copy returns the original.* All objects in Smalltalk understand `copy`. A Sharable class implements `copy` simply to return `self` (the receiver) rather than a duplicate. This is because a Sharable class cannot have two instances with the same value (i.e., duplicates). (For more discussion on `copy`, see Prototype (77).)

3. *Class-side SharableFactory.* In Smalltalk, the SharableFactory is often implemented on the class side of the Sharable class. Whereas the class side is always responsible for instance creation, it is also responsible for instance access as well in a Sharable class.

   It may not always be appropriate to implement the SharableFactory on the class side. The SharableFactory is essentially a Singleton (91), but a system could require a separate SharableFactory class that can have multiple instances. For example, a system might implement separate sessions within a single image. Its Sharables are expected to be unique within a session but can be duplicated across sessions. Thus, each session will need its own SharableFactory to create and manage the Sharables for that session independent of the other sessions.

4. *Persistent Sharables.* Sharables raise special persistence issues. Essentially the way an object database works is to take the binary image of an object and store it. Later, it loads the object by loading the bytes back into the Smalltalk image. Relational database storage is similar but requires converting the object to and from relational form.

   This standard technique may not work for Sharables. Some object databases are careful to preserve object identity so that a single unique object will be loaded into an image only once. However, not all databases are this careful. With them, storing Sharables on demand creates multiple copies of the Sharables, which wastes database space just as it would waste image space. Worse, loading Sharables on demand can load multiple copies of the same Sharable.

Instead, Sharables must be saved persistently in two phases. In the first phase, the Sharables class stores each of its instances persistently as usual. In the second phase, when storing an object and its parts where one of those parts is a Sharable, don't store the entire Sharable; store just its key. Reverse the process to load the Sharables again. First, load the persistent Sharables, taking care to ensure that you don't load a Sharable that duplicates one that is already loaded. Then when loading an object containing a Sharable part, use the key to access the Sharable and link it into the client object. This process ensures that Sharables can be saved persistently and will still be Sharables when they're loaded again.

Finally, the SharableFactory may wish to implement its sharable pool using weak collections. That way, when clients are no longer using a sharable, the garbage collector will ignore the sharable pool's reference and reclaim the sharable's memory.

Sample Code

One common use of the Sharable pattern is to manage graphical icons. Graphical user interface (GUI) windows often display graphical icons as button labels, menu choices, list items, and so on. Often the same icon is used in several places. A Help icon might be displayed on both the "Help" button and the *Help* menu choice. If an icon indicates the state of each item in a list and there are only a few possible states, the same few icons will be used repeatedly throughout the list.

An icon is represented in VisualWorks as an instance from the `PixelArray/ Image` hierarchy, in Visual Smalltalk as an `Icon`, and in IBM Smalltalk as a `CgIcon`. We'll use the VisualWorks `Image` class for this example. An `Image` is rather resource intensive; it consumes a lot of memory—either Smalltalk memory, window system memory, or both. Thus, if you're going to display the same icon in several places and it's going to look the same in each place, it will be more efficient to use the same instance of `Image` in all of those places. This will work because once an `Image` is created, its internal state does not change. The widgets that use the `Image` should not change its state.

Since the `Image` hierarchy already exists, the Sharable classes have already been implemented for you. However, `Image` is not implemented as a Sharable class; it is just a regular class/hierarchy that can have instances with the same value. Thus, to use `Images` as Sharables, you need to implement the SharableFactory.

There are two approaches for implementing the SharableFactory: implement it on the class side of `Image` (or its superclass, `PixelArray`) or as a separate class. Since `Image` is a vendor class, implementing the factory on the class side means modifying vendor code. With ENVY/Developer, you can use a class extension to avoid some changes to the vendor Application, but you may still need to change the class definition to add a class variable. By using a new class, you will be able to avoid modifying the vendor code at all.

Class-Side Factory

Let's look at implementing the SharableFactory on the class side of the Sharable class, Image. First, we'll need a variable to implement the object pool shown in the Structure's instance diagram. It is a class variable that caches all of the Sharable instances in the hierarchy. If we wanted each subclass to be able to cache its instances independent of the other classes, we would use a class instance variable. We're using a class variable for the whole hierarchy, and we'll call it Image-Pool.

Adding a new class variable requires modifying the class definition. However, you should avoid modifying vendor code because it can introduce bugs and makes porting changes forward to new vendor releases more difficult. Adding a class variable requires changing the class, but since Image is a vendor class, we do not want to change it if we don't have to. Thus, instead of using a class variable, we'll use a global variable called ImagePool that is used privately by the class as if it were a class variable.

Since Image now requires a global variable, we need to implement initialize on the class side to create the variable and set its initial value. We'll implement the cache using an IdentityDictionary where each key is a Symbol that specifies the image name and each value is the corresponding Image. Since the keys are Symbols and Symbols are Sharables (Flyweights), we can use an IdentityDictionary, which is a little more efficient than a plain Dictionary.

Why is an IdentityDictionary more efficient than a regular Dictionary? A Dictionary uses the method findIndexOrNil: to look up a key. It uses equal (=) to determine if the key it has found is the same as the key it's looking for. IdentityDictionary works the same as a Dictionary except that it reimplements findIndexOrNil: to use double-equal (==) instead of equal. Since double-equal is more efficient, an IdentityDictionary is also more efficient. Since a Sharable class implements equal and double-equal as the same thing, an IdentityDictionary works just as well as a Dictionary when the keys are Sharables.

Since we're implementing initialize on the class side, we should also implement release to undo the work that initialize does:

```
Image class>>initialize
   "Set the class' initial state."
   "[Image initialize]"
   Smalltalk
      at: #ImagePool
      put: IdentityDictionary new.
   ^self
```

```
Image class>>release
   "Prepare the class to be deleted."
   "[Image release]"
   Smalltalk at: #ImagePool put: nil.
   Smalltalk removeKey: #ImagePool.
   ^self
```

We would then run the `initialize` method to create and initialize the global variable. We should now implement a method to access the global variable:

```
Image class>>imageCache
   "Return the Image caching dictionary."
   ^ImagePool
```

Next we implement the Sharable creation methods. Each one will create and return an `Image`. It's helpful to follow a naming convention like "create<icon name>Icon." For example, if we need icons for the Help function and the Save function, we should name the icon creation methods `createHelpIcon` and `createSaveIcon`.

Let's say that no particular class is responsible for the Help icon. Then we will implement it in `Image` by default. Creating an `Image` instance is fairly detailed and not very important for understanding the Sharable pattern. Suffice it to say that it involves running the method `CachedImage class>> on:extent:depth:bitsPerPixel:palette:usingBits:` with lots of parameters that specify the bitmap for the image and how it should be rendered. For an example, see `VisualLauncher class>>CGHelp32`, a method that creates and returns the help book image displayed on the VisualWorks launcher.

The implementor of `createHelpIcon` would look something like this:

```
Image class>>createHelpIcon
   "Create and return the Image for the Help icon."
   ^CachedImage
      on: ...
      extent: ...
      depth: ...
      bitsPerPixel: ...
      palette: ...
      usingBits: ...
```

However, if you implement all of the icons in the system on the class side of `Image`, the class side will become a dumping ground for orphan icon definitions. It would be better to encapsulate the icon definition with the code that uses it. Let's say that the Save icon is used primarily by the main menu window. Then its class (e.g., `MainMenuUI`) should define the method `createSaveIcon`. It would look like the `Image class>>createHelpIcon` method shown above. `Image` still needs an implementor of `createSaveIcon`, but this method will just forward the request to the appropriate class, `MainMenuUI`. Thus the implementation will look like this:

```
Image class>>createSaveIcon
    "Create and return the Image for the Save icon."
    ^MainMenUI createSaveIcon
```

We now have a SharableFactory on the class side of `Image`, and it has methods for creating the `Image` Sharables. What it now needs is a method or methods for accessing the Sharables. *Design Patterns* suggests using a method like `get-Flyweight: key`. However, when the number of Sharables is fixed, it is easier to implement a separate accessor method for each Sharable. Just as the naming convention for the creation methods was "create<icon name>Icon," the accessing naming convention should be "<icon name>Icon."

Thus we need to implement `helpIcon` and `saveIcon` like this:

```
Image class>>helpIcon
    "Return the Image for the Help icon."
    | cacheDictionary |
    cacheDictionary := self imageCache.
    ^cacheDictionary
        at: #help
        ifAbsent:
            [cacheDictionary
                at: #help
                put: self createHelpIcon]

Image class>>saveIcon
    "Return the Image for the Save icon."
    | cacheDictionary |
    cacheDictionary := self imageCache.
    ^cacheDictionary
        at: #save
        ifAbsent:
            [cacheDictionary
                at: #save
                put: self createSaveIcon]
```

How does `at:ifAbsent:` work? If the dictionary already contains the specified key, the method returns its value. Otherwise, the method runs the absent block. The block obtains the new value by running the create method, adds it to the dictionary at the specified key, and then returns the new value. This causes `at:ifAbsent:` to return the new value as if it were there in the dictionary all along. In this way, `helpIcon` and `saveIcon` always return the specified image whether or not it's already in the cache.

If your Smalltalk dialect implements `Dictionary>>at:ifAbsentPut:`, you can use it in place of `at:ifAbsent:` to simplify the implementations of `helpIcon` and `saveIcon`. VisualWorks doesn't implement it, but VisualWorks with ENVY does.

The implementations of these two methods, helpIcon and saveIcon, are very similar. The common code could be extracted into a common, parameterized method that both of these would use. However, the code for doing that would be somewhat complex and difficult to explain here.

The following code would retrieve the Help icon Sharable: Image helpIcon.

Separate Factory Class

A separate factory class would work a lot like a class-side factory except that it is implemented using Singleton (91). The pattern says: Don't implement a Singleton object on the class side, implement it on the instance side (DP 128). So first we need to create a new factory class. It defines an instance variable for caching the images and a class variable for caching its Singleton instance.

```
Object subclass: #ImageFactory
    instanceVariableNames: 'imagePool '
    classVariableNames: 'Singleton '
    poolDictionaries: ''
```

It defines a class side implementor of initialize to create the Singleton, release to destroy it, and a getter method to retrieve it:

```
ImageFactory class>>initialize
    "Set the class' initial state."
    "[ImageFactory initialize]"
    Singleton := self new.
    ^self

ImageFactory class>>release
    "Prepare the class to be deleted."
    "[ImageFactory release]"
    Singleton := nil.
    ^self

ImageFactory class>>default
    "Return the class' primary instance."
    ^Singleton
```

The instance side implements initialize to set its initial state and an instance creation method (on the class side) to invoke it:

```
ImageFactory>>initialize
    "Set the instance's initial state."
    imagePool := IdentityDictionary new.
    ^self

ImageFactory class>>new
    "Create and return an instance of the class."
    ^self basicNew initialize
```

Now we implement the rest of `ImageFactory` on the instance side the same way the factory was implemented on `Image`'s class side. So, `imagePool`, `createHelpIcon`, and `helpIcon` are defined as instance methods in `Image-Factory`.

The following code would retrieve the Help icon Sharable: `ImageFactory default helpIcon`.

Known Smalltalk Uses

Character, Symbol, and SmallInteger

These system classes are implemented as Flyweights. All are used quite heavily by any code.

Cursor and ColorValue

The `Cursor` class in VisualWorks is an example of the Shared Object pattern. A system can contain as many different cursors as it wants. However, when different parts of the system all use the same style of cursor (e.g., normal, execute, garbage collection), they are all actually displaying the same `Cursor` instance because each style of cursor is cached within the class. Each time you ask the class for a particular style of cursor (such as the execute cursor), you get the same cached instance. This saves time by eliminating the need to create—and later garbage collect—the same cursor repeatedly, and it saves memory by not storing the same cursor in multiple locations.

Unfortunately, `Cursor` does not use a `Dictionary` to cache its instances. Instead, each style of cursor has a corresponding class variable to cache it. This is slightly more efficient than using a dictionary because looking up a variable is faster than looking up a dictionary variable and then retrieving a value from that dictionary. However, using a variable for each style of cursor fails the easy-to-extend criterion. A developer should be able to add a new style of cursor without changing any existing code. He can add the new cursor (such as a Target cursor) by adding a new creation method (such as `initTarget`) and a new getter (`target`). However, to cache the new instance, the developer will need to modify the `Cursor` class definition to add a new `TargetCursor` class variable (although he could use a global variable instead). If the cursors were stored in a dictionary, the developer would not need to modify the class definition.

Similarly, `ColorValue` in VisualWorks caches several standard constants. Each time you run `ColorValue blue`, for example, you might expect to get a different instance, but you actually get the same instance each time. The class implements 31 standard colors, storing each in its own class variable.

RegistrationRecord

Yelland (1996) discusses using the Flyweight pattern as part of an experimental VisualWorks framework for GUI windows. The framework is significant because it accomplishes opposing goals: the GUI windows use host (native) widgets and yet are portable across various windowing systems (Macintosh, MS-Windows 3.x, Windows95, Motif, etc.). The framework implements each GUI widget in two main parts: a Smalltalk object and a host widget. Each Smalltalk widget object has to register a dependency on its corresponding host widget for each event it will react to; this is Observer (305). The events of interest and their corresponding Smalltalk messages are the same for all widgets of a particular type. The only difference is which Smalltalk widget needs to receive the message.

The proposed VisualWorks system implements the dependency with two unspecified classes we'll call RegistrationRecord and RegistrationPair. RegistrationRecord is a Flyweight class that encapsulates the intrinsic state: the events of interest, the corresponding Smalltalk messages, and the mapping of event arguments to message parameters. A RegistrationPair represents the dependency of a Smalltalk widget on its corresponding host widget. It encapsulates the RegistrationRecord Flyweight with its corresponding extrinsic state: the Smalltalk widget that should receive the event messages.

Related Patterns

Flyweight versus Singleton

The Flyweight and Singleton (91) patterns are sometimes confused. A Singleton class has a limited number of instances. This limit is usually one, but it can be any fixed number (see DP 128). A Flyweight class, on the other hand, can have an unlimited number of instances, though no two instances can have the same value. For example, UndefinedObject has only one instance. Symbol can have an unlimited number of instances, but no two instances will contain the exact same series of characters. Thus UndefinedObject is a Singleton, and Symbol is a Flyweight.

This difference can still be confusing when a class seems to have a limited number of instances. Is it a Singleton or a Flyweight? In Singleton, the class's responsibilities limit the number of instances. For example, the ChangeSet class in Visual-Works can have an unlimited number of instances, but the only useful ones are those paired with Projects. In fact, only one ChangeSet is useful at any given time—the one for the current Project—so that ChangeSet is globally available through ChangeSet current. ChangeSet is a Singleton, even though it can have more than one instance, because its implementation limits the number of useful (or active) instances it can have to one. The class SmallInteger, on the other hand, can have an unlimited number of instances. Its range is limited not because of the internal responsibilities of the class, but because it wraps an integer data type whose range is limited. Since the class's range is limited only by the data type and the coupling between the two, SmallInteger is a Flyweight.

FlyweightFactory as Singleton

The FlyweightFactory (*not* the Flyweight) is often a Singleton (91). This is because there is only one set of flyweights, and thus the system needs only one FlyweightFactory. This is why the FlyweightFactory can be implemented as the class side of Flyweight; the class has only one class side, but there will never be more than one FlyweightFactory instance anyway. If the FlyweightFactory is implemented as a separate class, that class can be a true Singleton class. Later, if the system needs more than one FlyweightFactory instance, the class can be converted to allow more than one instance.

Flyweight versus Proxy

Flyweight and Proxy (213) are confused even though they are very different patterns. The name "flyweight" makes developers think of lightweight objects that are loaded as substitutes for real objects. This is a common technique to avoid loading in a huge set of large objects when the user will never use most of them. Instead, they're loaded as lightweight substitutes, and the ones that the user actually uses are then converted into real objects. This is a perfectly valid and common pattern, but it is not Flyweight; it's Proxy. A Flyweight is an object that acts like independent copy when it's really being shared transparently by multiple clients. Flyweight and Proxy are different patterns; don't let the names fool you.

Flyweight and Proxy, Adapter, and Decorator

Flyweights and Proxies to Flyweights often don't mix well. Let's say two variables point to the same object, as shown below. The first variable, t1, points directly to the subject, aRealSubject. The other variable, t2, points to the subject indirectly via the proxy, aProxy. How can code tell that both variables are pointing to the same subject?

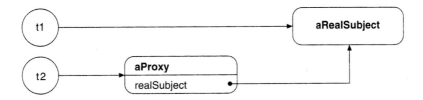

If the code uses equal (=) to compare the two variables, the Proxy class can implement equal to detect this circumstance (which could require double dispatching; Beck, 1996) and return true. Essentially, if the other variable (t1) points to the same subject that the proxy does, the variables are equal.

However, if the subject is a Flyweight and the client code knows it, then the code will probably use double-equal (==) to make the comparison. The two variables are clearly not double-equal, so the test will return false when the client probably expects true. Thus, you can often use double-equal with Flyweights but probably not when using Proxies as well. Similarly, the intermediate object might be an Adapter (105) or Decorator (161) instead of a Proxy (213). Again, although double-equal is often used with the Flyweight pattern, it will not work well with these other patterns.

PROXY (DP 207)   Object Structural

Intent

Provide a surrogate or placeholder for another object to control access to it.

Structure

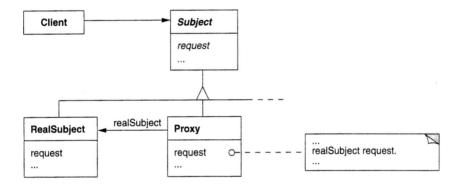

Discussion

A major part of object-oriented design is deciding what objects know about what other objects. In Smalltalk, this connection is usually done through a direct reference to an object or a more generic mechanism like the Observer pattern. However, sometimes you don't even want to reference another actual object at all. Instead, you just want to say, "An object of some kind *should* go here," and reference a surrogate for the actual object. This desire is the motivation for the Proxy pattern.

The key to the Proxy pattern is two objects of the same type, a placeholder and a full-fledged object, where the placeholder controls access to the full-fledged object. The placeholder, a **Proxy,** has the same interface as the full-fledged object, a **RealSubject,** so that the rest of the system thinks it's using the RealSubject but is actually using the Proxy.

The Proxy uses its limited state and behavior to handle as many of the messages as it can, forwarding messages to its RealSubject only when it has to. This allows the Proxy to restrict or optimize the system's use of the RealSubject.

Proxy in Smalltalk

Proxy is a common pattern in Smalltalk, with two main uses:

1. *Persistence Proxy.* Loading an object from a persistent store, such as a relational or object database or a flat file, is often time-consuming. Loading numerous persistent objects, especially ones that never get used, is not only time-consuming but may be wasteful as well. Proxies for persistent objects can avoid loading objects that are never used. Almost every commercial database framework contains at least one occurrence of the Proxy pattern in this form. Many of the object database vendors' Smalltalk language bindings use it as well. This is an occurrence of what *Design Patterns* terms a *virtual* proxy.

2. *Distribution Proxy.* When a logical Smalltalk image is distributed across physical images, each object can exist in only one physical image but must be accessible from all of them. Message sends across physical images are slower than those within an image. A proxy to a remote object can optimize the collaboration by minimizing message sends, thereby making the remote object behave more like a local one. Both distributed Smalltalks on the market, VisualAge Distributed Option and ParcPlaceDigitalk Distributed Smalltalk, use the pattern. *Design Patterns* refers to this as a *remote* proxy (DP 208).

Design Patterns mentions two other types of proxies: protection proxies and smart references. However, these are not as commonly seen in Smalltalk as in other languages. In our discussion we will focus on the two previously mentioned types of proxies.

Implementation

A Proxy That Forwards (Nearly) Everything

There are two main approaches to implementing the Proxy pattern. *Design Patterns* focuses on one implementation approach, where both `RealSubject` and `Proxy` are subclasses of an abstract `Subject` class. `Proxy` supports all of `Subject`'s messages, handling the ones it can and forwarding the rest to its RealSubject.

Smalltalk's dynamic binding offers an alternative that *Design Patterns* touches on (DP 212–213, 215–216). Rather than supporting `RealSubject`'s interface in its entirety, `Proxy` implements only some of them, using `doesNotUnderstand:` to forward other messages to its RealSubject. An important consideration here is that `Proxy` should not inherit messages from its superclass. For every message it might receive, the Proxy should implement a corresponding method or else ensure `doesNotUnderstand:` will be invoked. Unfortunately `Proxy`, like most other classes, is a descendant of `Object`. That means it inherits methods that it probably won't want to reimplement explicitly (like `printOn:`, `inspect`, etc.).

Since the problem lies in `Proxy`'s subclass relationship to `Object`, one way to solve it would be to dissolve this relationship. How is that possible? Subclass

`Proxy` off of `nil`. Yes, this can be done in Smalltalk. After all, what is the super-class of `Object`? It's `nil`. If `nil` can have one subclass, it can have others, but not without consequences.

One of the simple consistencies of Smalltalk is that everything's an object. Not only does this mean that everything's an abstract data type capable of receiving messages, but also that everything is an instance of a class and every class is a subclass of `Object` (except for `Object` itself). This approach to Proxy breaks this simple truth. The Proxies are still objects, but they're not a kind of `Object`.

Messages Not to Forward

In general, defining a class as a subclass of `nil` is risky business, because it breaks many basic assumptions about objects in Smalltalk. Due to a subtle bug in Visual Smalltalk, for example, you won't even see a newly defined subclass of `nil` in the Class Hierarchy Browser until you open a new Browser. As a subclass of `nil`, the only message `Proxy` understands is `==` (double-equal) because it's implemented directly by the virtual machine instead of sent as a message. `Proxy` must implement `doesNotUnderstand:`, or else any message it does not implement would cause an infinite loop.[5] For all messages other than double-equal, the Proxy can choose to implement the message itself or let `doesNotUnderstand:` forward the message to the RealSubject.

These are some other methods `Proxy` may need to implement:

- `isProxy`—This provides a simple way to tell whether an object is a proxy. You can't use `inspect` or rely on `printString`, because both methods will be forwarded to the subject. You'll need two implementors of `isProxy`, one in `Proxy` that returns `true` and one in `Subject` that returns `false`.

- `become:`—This must be implemented if the design wants to switch a Real-Subject for its Proxy (see Swapping a RealSubject for its Proxy below).

- `=` and `hash`—Implement these messages if the Proxies may be compared or stored in a `Set` or other `Collection`.[6]

- `halt` and (in Visual Smalltalk) `vmInterrupt:`—Implement these messages if you plan on debugging the proxies.

- `class`—Implement this message if the Proxy needs access to its class side methods.

To implement these methods, copy the code out of their implementations in `Object`.

---

[5] Actually, in Visual Smalltalk, if you send a message to an object that does not understand `does-NotUnderstand:`, the virtual machine helpfully pops up an error dialog informing you of that fact, but then causes Smalltalk to exit without letting you save the image!

[6] See Woolf (1996) and Equality Method and Hashing Method in Beck (1997) for more information on implementing these two methods.

Swapping a RealSubject for Its Proxy

A drawback of Proxies is the overhead they incur, particularly when they're meant to improve performance. For example, a persistence Proxy actually reduces overhead initially because it avoids loading the persistent object until absolutely necessary. But once the persistent object is loaded, the Proxy just gets in the way. True, the performance hit of every message send being doubled is small, and the Proxy probably doesn't consume much memory. But the overhead may be significant in some applications, and a designer may wish to remove the Proxy once the RealSubject is available.

This can be accomplished using a message called become:. What become: does is change all of the pointers to the receiver to make them point to the object passed as the argument. This is a one-way become: which is used by Visual Smalltalk. So, after execution of the become: method, all objects that used to reference the receiver now point to the argument. In VisualWorks and IBM Smalltalk, become: is two-way, so that it also changes all the references to the argument to point to the receiver: all variables in the system that once pointed to one of the objects now point to the other one. To see this in action, try the following in a workspace:

```
| string1 string2 |
string1 := 'abc' copy.
string2 := 'xyz' copy.
string1 become: string2.
Transcript show: string1.       "Displays 'xyz'"
Transcript show: string2.
    "Displays 'abc' in VisualWorks and IBM"
    "Displays 'xyz' in Visual Smalltalk"
```

What does become: return? The method is essentially a procedure, so it returns self. The question is, What is self? It's not the receiver! All of the pointers to the receiver now point to the argument, including self, so become: returns the argument because it returns the receiver, and the receiver is now the argument:

```
| string1 string2 string3 |
string1 := 'abc' copy.
string2 := 'xyz' copy.
string3 := string1 become: string2.
string3 printString            "Returns 'xyz'"
```

If you have a Proxy to a RealSubject and you want to get rid of the Proxy to use just the RealSubject, you can use become: to swap them:

```
aProxy become: aRealSubject
```

After this, all of the Proxy's clients now reference the RealSubject. If the become: is one way, the Proxy still references the RealSubject as well. If the become: is two-way, the Proxy now references itself as its RealSubject! In any event, if the Proxy contained the only reference to the RealSubject before the become:, then nothing references the Proxy now, and so it will be garbage collected.

Implications of doesNotUnderstand: and become:

Both doesNotUnderstand: and become: have a significant impact on a design, for better and worse. As Beck (1997) mentions, become: should generally be avoided because it makes design harder to understand and code more difficult to debug. The same can be said for doesNotUnderstand:. These are not very fast messages, moreover, so there is a cost in performance.

There are two benefits to using doesNotUnderstand: with Proxy:

1. It simplifies code in the Proxy, so there is less code to write.

2. It is flexible and transparently handles interface changes.

There are also two drawbacks:

1. It is difficult to debug. It can be disconcerting to see messages handled by objects that don't implement them.

2. It is slower than a direct message send.

Programmers entranced with the power of doesNotUnderstand: tend to overuse it, with overly general and inefficient results. Remember that Smalltalk is optimized for message sends; use them whenever possible. There may be a substantial performance penalty for using doesNotUnderstand: instead of a normal message send. The difference is slight in Visual Smalltalk, but doesNotUnderstand: is about three times slower in IBM Smalltalk; in VisualWorks it is almost six times slower.

The become: method can be slow as well. In fact, it is significantly slower in Visual Smalltalk than in either VisualWorks or IBM Smalltalk. In one test of using become: to swap two objects with only one reference, we found that Visual Smalltalk's become: took over 100 times longer than either of the other two dialects. The total time spent in each become: method was several hundred milliseconds on our test machine. If you are using Visual Smalltalk, avoid become: if you're at all concerned about performance.

Also, we have found that in IBM Smalltalk, the speed of each become: depends on the total number of references to the objects being swapped. Although it is quite efficient on objects with only a few references, it can take up to several seconds to do a become: on objects with a several thousand references.

Retaining the Proxy

Using become: to eliminate a Proxy may seem attractive. However, one advantage of keeping the Proxy between the client and the RealSubject is that the Proxy can decide that its RealSubject is no longer needed, release it, and let it be garbage collected. This can be a useful feature in memory-constrained systems.

Sample Code

We'll begin by examining the implementation of a standard Virtual Proxy in Smalltalk, and then consider a Swapping Proxy.

Standard Structure

Here's a simple example of a Virtual Proxy in VisualWorks. It's equivalent to the *Design Patterns* Sample Code in C++ (DP 213–215).

```
VisualComponent subclass: #ImageProxy
   instanceVariableNames: 'image fileName extent '
   classVariableNames: ''
   poolDictionaries: ''
```

VisualWorks's `displayOn:` method corresponds to the `Draw()` member function (DP 208). If the Proxy does not yet reference its image, it loads it; otherwise it forwards the message to its image:

```
ImageProxy>>displayOn: aGraphicsContext
   "Display the receiver on aGraphicsContext. This proxy
   forwards display requests to its image."

   image == nil
      ifTrue: [image := self loadImage].
   ^image displayOn: aGraphicsContext
```

The `loadImage` method corresponds to the `Load()` member function (DP 215):

```
ImageProxy>>loadImage
   | newImage |
   newImage := CachedImage on:
         (ImageReader fromFile: fileName) image.
   ^newImage
```

Finally, `preferredBounds` in VisualWorks is equivalent to the `GetExtent()` member function. This message is answered without consulting the RealSubject:

```
ImageProxy>>preferredBounds
   ^0@0 extent: self extent
```

Swapping Proxy

A swapping version of the image Proxy offers a simpler approach. This Proxy uses `doesNotUnderstand:` to capture the first message sent to the subject. Thereafter the Proxy "becomes" the subject so that all subsequent messages are sent directly to the subject. This implementation would look like the following:

```
nil subclass: #ImageDNUProxy
   instanceVariableNames: 'fileName '
   classVariableNames: ''
   poolDictionaries: ''
```

Note that `ImageDNUProxy` does not need an `image` instance variable to point to its RealSubject. That's because instead of pointing to the subject, the Proxy will *become* the subject:

```
ImageDNUProxy>>doesNotUnderstand: aMessage
   "This demonstrates the use of a Smart Pointer proxy.
   This object will create its RealSubject and then
   immediately swap itself out for that RealSubject."
   | image |
   image := CachedImage on:
      (ImageReader fromFile: fileName) image.
   self become: image.    "here, self is the Proxy."
   ^self                  "self now refers to the image."
      perform: aMessage selector
      withArguments: aMessage arguments
```

As discussed, the implementations of =, `hash`, `class`, and `become`: would need to be copied from those found in `Object` to make the swapping proxy work.

Known Smalltalk Uses

VisualWorks ExternalLibraryHolder

A classic Virtual Proxy can be found in the VisualWorks class `External-LibraryHolder`, which is part of a subsystem for dealing with external link libraries written in other languages. When an `ExternalInterface` (the Facade of this subsystem) is told to load a particular set of library files, it doesn't load and link those libraries immediately; instead it creates an `ExternalLibrary-Holder` to stand in for each of the files.

`ExternalLibraryHolder` will defer loading an `ExternalLibrary` object to the time an external call occurs. More specifically, the library will load when an `ExternalMethod` object must map the address of an external call using `map-Address:`. Any subsequent calls to `mapAddress:` will be sent to the cached `ExternalLibrary` held in the `ExternalLibraryHolder`. Thus, only libraries that are used get linked into an image.

VisualWorks RemoteString

Also in VisualWorks, instances of the class `RemoteString` act as persistence/ virtual proxies. In a base VisualWorks image, a `RemoteString` holds the file reference to a class comment or any other piece of executable text within a file (such as the sources or changes file). The problem here that warrants the use of a Proxy is that the position of the text itself in the file may change as code is added or rewritten. Rather than hold onto a potentially incorrect piece of source text, clients hold onto a `RemoteString` instead, which can recreate the source text on demand by looking it up at the most recent location in the sources or changes file.

Distribution Proxies in IBM Smalltalk

In the IBM Smalltalk Distributed Option, instances of `DsRemoteObject-Pointer` represent objects in a remote object space. A `DsRemoteObject-Pointer` uses the `doesNotUnderstand:` message to forward messages to objects in a remote Smalltalk image. Certain messages (`become:`, `isKindOf:`, `isNil`, etc.) are handled locally to reduce overall network traffic and to ensure the integrity of the two object spaces (local and distributed).

VisualWorks ObjectLens Proxies

VisualWorks uses two types of swapping proxies that illustrate the various trade-offs in implementing proxies in its ObjectLens database system.

Lens proxies are rooted on an abstract class `LensAbsentee` that forms a separate root hierarchy apart from `Object`. The class `LensAbsentee` implements a minimal Proxy protocol. `LensAbsentee` has a single subclass, `LensAbstract-Proxy`, that implements the common methods in its two concrete subclasses, `LensProxy` and `LensCollectionProxy`. Both classes reimplement `does-NotUnderstand:` to instantiate the subject, and both `become:` that subject before forwarding the original message.

Related Patterns

Proxy versus Decorator

These two patterns look similar but behave differently. Both a Decorator (161) and a Proxy are the same type as their subject, so they have the same interface, and a client can use them transparently instead of the subject. Both implement their interface primarily by forwarding their messages to their subjects.

The main difference is that Decorators can be nested, but there's not much point in nesting Proxies. Each Decorator adds behavior when nested. Once one Proxy defers loading an object, another one is not useful. Multiple distribution/remote proxies can be nested to bounce a message from one object space to another to another, but this would be rather inefficient.

Proxy and Template Method

One problem with the "forwarding" patterns like Proxy (and Decorator) is that the more messages the abstract class implements, the more messages the forwarding subclass must implement to forward. A partial solution is to use the Template Method (355) pattern aggressively in the superclass. Then the only methods that the subclasses need to implement are the primitive operations. This way, the forwarding subclass doesn't have to forward every message defined in the superclass, just the primitive ones.

Chapter 5

Behavioral Patterns

Chain of Responsibility (225) Avoid coupling the sender of a request to its receiver by giving more than one object a chance to handle the request. Chain the receiving objects, and pass the request along the chain until an object handles it.

Command (245) Encapsulate a request or operation as an object, thereby letting you parameterize clients with different operations, queue or log requests, and support undoable operations.

Interpreter (261) Given a language, define a representation for its grammar along with an interpreter that uses the representation to interpret sentences in the language.

Iterator (273) Provide a way to access the elements of an aggregate object sequentially without exposing its underlying representation.

Mediator (287) Define an object that encapsulates how a set of objects interact. Mediator promotes loose coupling by keeping objects from referring to each other explicitly, and it lets you vary their interaction independently.

Memento (297) Without violating encapsulation, capture and externalize an object's internal state so that the object can be restored to this state later.

Observer (305) Define a one-to-many dependency between objects so that so that when one object changes state, all its dependents are notified and updated automatically.

State (327) Allow an object to alter its behavior when its internal state changes. The object will appear to change its class.

Strategy (339) Define a family of algorithms, encapsulate each one in a separate class, and define each class with the same interface so they can be interchangeable. Strategy lets the algorithm vary independently from clients that use it.

Template Method (355) Define the skeleton of an algorithm in an operation, deferring some steps to subclasses. Template Method lets subclasses redefine certain steps of an algorithm without changing the algorithm's structure.

Visitor (371) Represent an operation to be performed on the elements of an object structure in a class separate from the elements themselves. Visitor lets you define a new operation without changing the classes of the elements on which it operates.

CHAIN OF RESPONSIBILITY (DP 223)   Object Behavioral

Intent

Avoid coupling the sender of a request to its receiver by giving more than one object a chance to handle the request. Chain the receiving objects, and pass the request along the chain until an object handles it.

Structure

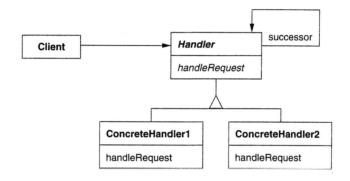

A typical object structure and message interaction might look like this:

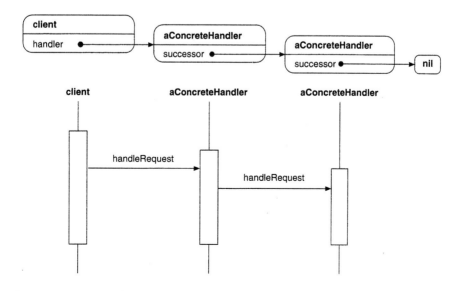

Discussion

In Chain of Responsibility, a chain of objects, each linked by a reference to the next, pass a request from one object to the next until one of them decides to handle the request. The client that initiated the request does not know which object, or **handler,** eventually handles the request. This enables the chain to be rearranged and the responsibilities redistributed along the chain without affecting the client.

The chain can be a simple linked list, but it is usually part of a tree. (For a discussion of tree structures, see Composite (137).) The chain is the path from the client's handler up to the root of the tree. This diagram shows a typical tree and a client pointing to its handler; the Chain of Responsibility path from the client's handler to the root is shown in bold:

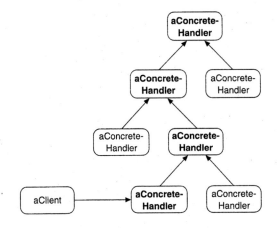

A Chain of Responsibility tree is not just any tree structure, but one whose levels represent levels of specificity, from most general to most specific:

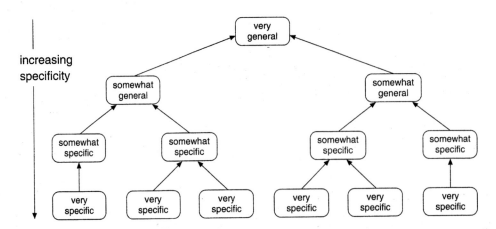

When a client sends a request to its handler, it is asking for the most specific response possible. Thus, the client's handler should be very specialized. If the handler can't handle the request, it will pass the request to its successor, a somewhat more general handler, and so on, until a handler handles the request and returns a response. Because the tree is organized from the most general handler at the root to the most specific handlers at the leaves, the handling of the request will be the most specific handling possible for that client.

Think of the Military

A good example of Chain of Responsibility is one that has nothing to do with object-oriented programming: the chain of command in the military. Imagine a private in the army who needs approval before taking action, so he requests authorization from his sergeant. The sergeant may also lack authority, and so passes the request to his superior, who passes it to his superior, and so on, until someone finally makes a decision. Then the decision passes back down, eventually reaching the private. The private is unaware of what level made the decision; it may have been his sergeant, or the request may have gone all the way to the Joint Chiefs of Staff. Some requests are simple and don't travel too far up the chain of command; others are more complex and travel to the highest levels of the military.

This chain of command is not a static, unchanging structure. The participants in this chain and their arrangement change as people retire, get promoted, and are reassigned. The level at which certain decisions are made can change based on the authority of the people in those positions at the time and whether the unit is operating in battle, a training exercise, or standdown. Thus, the chain can respond dynamically to changing conditions and redistribute authority for making decisions accordingly.

This is Chain of Responsibility in a nutshell. When someone says Chain of Responsibility, think chain of command, and you'll have a good example of the pattern.

Class Hierarchy

The Smalltalk class hierarchy is an excellent example of how Chain of Responsibility works, but not how to implement the pattern. Its root is Object, the most general class there is, and successive subclasses are increasingly specific. Each class knows about its superclass and inherits behavior from that superclass that it does not otherwise implement itself.

Consider what happens when an object is sent a message and must find the method to run in response. (This describes how method look-up behaves logically; Smalltalk actually implements it more efficiently.) Let's say you have four classes—A, B, C, and D—where D subclasses C, which subclasses B, which subclasses A. Let's say B implements operation and C and D inherit that implementation unchanged (see following page):

```
┌─────────────┐
│ A           │
├─────────────┤
│ operation   │
└─────────────┘
       △
┌─────────────┐
│ B           │
├─────────────┤
│ operation   │
└─────────────┘
       △
┌─────────────┐
│      C      │
└─────────────┘
       △
┌─────────────┐
│      D      │
└─────────────┘
```

If a client sends the operation message to an instance of D, aD, how does the method in B ultimately get invoked? The receiver, aD, asks its class, D, for its implementation of the message, operation. Since there is no operation method in D, that class asks its superclass, C, for its implementation. Since C does not implement operation either, it asks its superclass. Finally, an implementation of operation is found in B, so the class returns the method. C gets the method from B, passes it on to D, which passes it on to aD, which invokes the method. Notice that whether A also implements operation is irrelevant in this example since the request for an implementor of operation never gets passed to A.

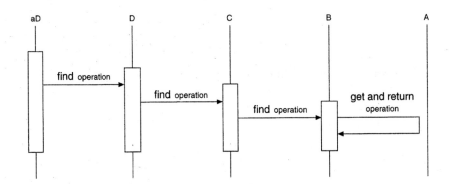

This illustrates how Chain of Responsibility works. The client, aD, makes a request: find an implementation of operation. The client sends that request to its handler, D. That handler, unable to handle the request itself, passes the request to its successor, C, which passes the request to its successor, B. That handler, B, can handle the request, and so it does. As the request path unwinds, the response goes from B to C to D to aD, the client that originally made the request and now has the response without knowing what handler actually handled the request.

Although method look-up in the class hierarchy shows how Chain of Responsibility works pretty well, it is a weak example of the pattern itself because the pattern's chain is supposed to be a chain of instances, not classes. The second consequence of the pattern says that the chain can be dynamically changed at runtime (DP 226). Classes and the methods they implement tend to be rather static at runtime; they don't change without recompilation. A true Chain of Responsibility tree is a structure built at runtime, not hard-coded at compile time like the class hierarchy.

Signal Tree

So what's a good example of an object tree where the tree levels represent increasing levels of specificity? The VisualWorks exception-handling mechanism contains one. Each type of error that can occur—message not understood or key not found, for example—is represented with an instance of `Signal` that describes the error.

`Signal` instances form a hierarchy whose root, `Signal genericSignal`, represents all signals. Its main child, `Object errorSignal`, represents all runtime code error signals. Successive children represent progressively more specific types of errors until the descriptions are specific enough to tell the programmer exactly what went wrong. The diagram below shows part of the standard signal tree, the branch for not-found errors:

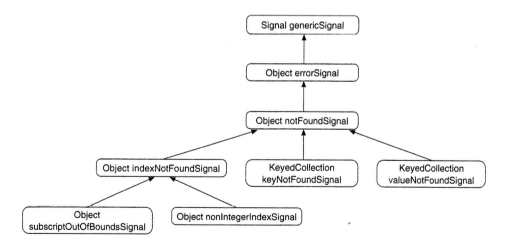

This is a good example of a Chain of Responsibility tree because the most general objects are at the top and the most specific ones are at the bottom. This is sort of an object (as opposed to class) version of inheritance, where each child receives the properties of its parent but specializes them.

Yet the exception-handling framework doesn't really use the Chain of Responsibility pattern, even though it has the perfect tree for the pattern. The closest example of Chain of Responsibility in `Signal` is its implementation of `accepts:`. It is sort of the `isKindOf:` of signal trees in that you're testing whether a signal belongs to a particular signal hierarchy. For example,

```
Object notFoundSignal accepts: Object nonIntegerIndexSignal
```

is true because not-found is an ancestor of non-integer-index. Similarly, `Object errorSignal` accepts all error signals for coding mistakes, but not other kinds of signals (such as user-interrupt).

The `accepts:` method is implemented like this:

```
Signal>>accepts: aSignal
    ^aSignal inheritsFrom: self

Signal>>inheritsFrom: aSignal
    ^aSignal == self or:
        [parent notNil and: [parent inheritsFrom: aSignal]]
```

The receiver accepts aSignal if the receiver is that signal or if one of its ancestors is. Thus any time `accepts:` is run, either one of the signals returns true or ultimately the root signal returns false. The other signals in the path decide whether to handle aSignal, decide not to, and pass the buck to their parent. This is essentially Chain of Responsibility, but not a very exciting example of it.

Another disadvantage of the signal tree as an example of Chain of Responsibility is that the tree does not change its structure or redistribute its responsibilities at runtime. Conceivably, the system might discover the need to detect new types of errors while it is running, and so it would add those error types to the signal tree. For example, only certain operating systems support files that are symbolic links. When VisualWorks detects that it's running on one of those operating systems, it might load a signal for detecting invalid-symbolic-link; when it switched to another operating system, it could unload the signal. Although VisualWorks could work this way, it doesn't. The signal tree's structure is static while the system is running.

Not Very Common

There are very few examples of the Chain of Responsibility pattern in Smalltalk. It requires a linked-list or tree that is organized by specialization, one that may be dynamically reconfigured and its responsibilities redistributed while the system is running, and each piece of behavior must be implemented in one handler of a chain whereas the others simply pass the buck. Trees like this are rare, and behavior implemented this way is even rarer.

Object-Oriented Recursion

Learning the Chain of Responsibility pattern is still helpful even though examples are hard to find because Chain of Responsibility is a specialization of a broader pattern we'll call Object-Oriented (OO) Recursion. The implementation of the two patterns is rather different, but the principles behind them are quite similar, so understanding one makes it much easier to understand the other. Furthermore, although examples of Chain of Responsibility are rare, examples of OO Recursion are plentiful.

In Chain of Responsibility, a handler can only do one of two things: (1) handle the request completely and return the chain's response to the request, or (2) pass the request to the successor without doing anything else to help handle the request. This means that only one handler in the chain, a true handler, actually handles the request; all of the other handlers in the chain between the client and this true handler are merely potential handlers that ultimately do nothing but convey the request and forward the response.

There are few examples of this Chain of Responsibility behavior. Whenever one object forwards requests to another, rarely does it do nothing other than forwarding the request. If it consistently did so, it wouldn't be a very valuable part of the chain. Instead, whenever one object forwards requests to another, it tends to enhance that request with a little extra behavior before or after the request.

When the handlers do a little extra work while forwarding the requests, this is an example of the OO Recursion pattern, also called **recursive delegation.** In procedural recursion, a function calls itself with a different parameter each time. Eventually the parameter is a base case that the function simply performs, and then the recursion unwinds back to the original call (Sedgewick, 1988, Chap. 5). In object-oriented recursion, a method polymorphically sends its message to a different receiver (which may be another instance of the same class or of a different class of the same type). Eventually the method invoked is a base case implementation that simply performs the task, and then the recursion unwinds back to the original message send (Beck, 1997).

Another important difference between Chain of Responsibility and OO Recursion is that the latter is much less concerned about the levels of specialization in the structure. OO Recursion is not concerned about why the nodes in the structure are arranged as they are, only that the structure can be traversed recursively to fulfill a request. Thus, the tree arrangement may represent specialization, containment, ordering, or some other relationship. Also, recursion can travel not only up the tree but also down it, branching into multiple smaller recursions at the branch nodes. Recursion can travel in any direction that a structure has pointers.

Tree Recursion

OO Recursion (and Chain of Responsibility) behavior occurs along a linked-list structure; the list is the chain. But linked-lists are fairly rare in Smalltalk. However, tree structures are very common, and since the path between the root and any leaf node—in either direction—is essentially a linked-list, OO Recursion is commonly used to pass requests or broadcast announcements up and down the tree. Each path in a graph structure is also a linked-list, but graphs are less common than trees. The pointers between the nodes in a tree or graph may be unidirectional or bidirectional. (See the discussion of tree structures in Composite (137).) The chain is formed by the pointers, so the recursion can travel only in the direction of the pointers.

A linked-list or tree might seem like just another way to collect elements, but these linked structures are quite different from the way most `Collections` are implemented. A typical `Collection` is a two-layer structure where one object, the `Collection` itself, knows what all of the elements in the structure are. Thus, it can easily list how many elements there are, what each of them is, and so forth. For example, an `OrderedCollection` and its elements are related like this:

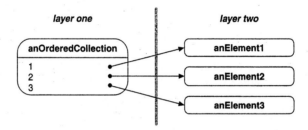

A linked-list or a path in a tree or graph is a multilayered structure where no one node in the structure knows what all of the other nodes are. Instead, each node knows what the next node is, so they can all be traversed eventually. But this makes common tasks like determining how many elements there are and what each one is a multiple step process. This is how the nodes in a linked list are related:

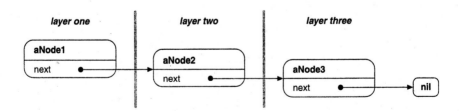

The elements in the linked-list form a chain that OO Recursion recurses through. The elements in a `Collection` do not form a chain, so OO Recursion cannot traverse the elements.

Visual Trees

The visual tree structure used to implement a window in VisualWorks contains several examples of OO Recursion. For more details about the structure of a visual tree, see Composite (137).

When a visual computes its bounds (`VisualComponent>>bounds`), it uses OO Recursion. Most visuals draw themselves as large as necessary to fill the space they're given. Thus, their preferred bounds are unlimited. Yet a visual's actual bounds are constrained by the bounds of its container visual, which is constrained by its container, and so on. Ultimately the window frame constrains the bounds of all of its components.

Because of this container relationship, a visual does not know its own bounds. Its bounds depend on what it's contained in and what the container's bounds are. The diagram below shows a typical example of what happens when a client asks a visual for its bounds:

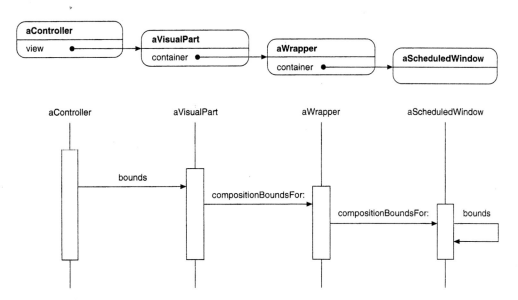

Let's look at the implementation of the messages in the diagram. Sending `bounds` to the visual invokes the implementor in `VisualPart`:

```
VisualPart>>bounds
    "Answer the receiver's compositionBounds if there
    is a container, otherwise answer preferredBounds."
    ^container == nil
        ifTrue: [self preferredBounds]
        ifFalse: [container compositionBoundsFor: self]
```

The instance diagram shows that the `VisualPart`'s container is not nil, so bounds sends `compositionBoundsFor:` to the container. The container is a `Wrapper`, and `Wrapper` inherits `compositionBoundsFor:` from `Visual-Part`:

```
VisualPart>>compositionBoundsFor: aVisualPart
    "The receiver is a container for aVisualPart.
    An actual bounding rectangle is being searched for by
    aVisualPart. Forward to the receiver's container."
    ^container compositionBoundsFor: self
```

This implementor shows the recursion of `compositionBoundsFor:`, which travels up the visual tree via the container relationships. Eventually the recursion reaches a terminating case, a bounding visual such as the window itself. The bounding visual just computes the bounds:

```
ScheduledWindow>>compositionBoundsFor: aVisualComponent
    "Answer the receiver's bounds."
    ^self bounds
```

This finally returns the bounds for the window and the recursion unwinds.

This simple explanation would seem to imply that any visual's bounds are the same as its window's, but this is not the case. Many visual classes, especially `Wrappers` (Decorator (161) visuals), affect their components' bounds. For example, a `TranslatingWrapper` adjusts a visual's offset from its container by translating its coordinates. It does this by specializing the implementation of `compositionBoundsFor:`.

```
TranslatingWrapper>>compositionBoundsFor: aVisualPart
    ^(container compositionBoundsFor: self)
        translatedBy: self translation negated
```

Invalidation and redisplay of a window's graphics also uses OO Recursion. When a client tells a visual to `invalidate`, the message defined by `Visual-Part>>invalidateRectangle:repairNow:forComponent:` recurses up the tree until the window handles it. When a client tells the window to redisplay via `ScheduledWindow>>displayDamageEvent:`, the message defined by `VisualComponent>>displayOn:` recurses down the tree depth-first as each visual redisplays itself.

Finally, VisualWorks also uses OO Recursion to determine which `Controller` in a visual tree wants control. In polling windows, `ScheduledWindow>>sub-ViewWantingControl` initiates a recursion where `VisualPart>>object-WantingControl` and `CompositePart>>componentWantingControl` alternate down the tree. In event-driven windows, `VisualPart>>handler-ForMouseEvent:` recurses down the visual tree as the controller searches for the receiver of a mouse event.

Field Description Trees

The File Reader (Woolf, 1997) reads record-oriented files using a tree of field format objects that describes a record's format. The framework contains a special stream class, `FormattedStream`, that combines a regular stream and a field format tree to read the file and map the records to domain objects. (See Decorator (161) for more details on `FormattedStream`.)

As a `Stream`, `FormattedStream` implements `next` to read the next record from the file. `FormattedStream>>next` initiates the recursive message defined by `FieldFormatDescription>>readObjectFrom:into:`. The message recurses down the field format tree and reads the record into a domain object. The way `next` initiates the read request without knowing which field formats will handle the request is an example of OO Recursion. The nodes in the field format tree form the chain. Each node fulfills its responsibility for reading its part of the record.

`FormattedStream` also implements `nextPut:` to write a domain object to the file as a record. `nextPut:` initiates the recursive message `FieldFormat-Description>>writeObjectIn:to:`. The message recurses down the field format tree and writes the domain object into the record. This recursive implementation of `nextPut:` is another example of OO Recursion. The field format tree nodes are the tree, and each fulfills its responsibility for writing the object into the record.

For more details about how the field format tree works, see the Sample Code section.

Interpreter Trees

An Interpreter traverses an expression tree to evaluate the regular expression that the tree represents (DP 244). To traverse the tree, a client sends an interpret message to the root node in the tree. The node interprets itself by interpreting its children, which in turn interpret their children. The way the interpret message recurses through the tree is an example of OO Recursion.

OO Recursion in Class Hierarchies

A less obvious example of OO Recursion is messages implemented up through classes in a hierarchy. Once again, the class tree is a static tree that does not change at runtime, but it is still a tree, a set of chains, and so it can still implement OO Recursion.

The implementation of `initialize` is a good example of OO Recursion in a class hierarchy. Imagine class `D` is a subclass of `C`, which subclasses `B`, which subclasses `A`, and all four classes implement `initialize`. Each implementation would send `super initialize` except the one in `A`:

```
A class>>new
    ^self basicNew initialize

A>>initialize
    ...
    ^self

B>>initialize
    super initialize.
    ...
    ^self

C>>initialize
    super initialize.
    ...
    ^self

D>>initialize
    super initialize.
    ...
    ^self
```

When a client creates an instance of D and new runs `initialize`, the `initialize` method in D will run the one in C, which in turn runs the method in B, which runs the one in A. This way, each class takes responsibility for initializing its own part of the object. This is OO Recursion, statically coded within a class hierarchy.

Equal, Hash, and Copy

Many common messages in Smalltalk are often implemented using OO Recursion. The messages `equal` (=), `hash`, and `copy` are three examples.

The default implementation of equal in `Object` is not very interesting. By default, equal is implemented as double-equal (==). However, structurally complex classes like those for domain objects often implement equal in a much more interesting way. Let's consider how a stereotypical `Person` object would implement equal. For the example, let's say that two `Persons` are equal if their names are equal:

```
Object subclass: #Person
    instanceVariableNames: 'name address phoneNumber'
    classVariableNames: ''
    poolDictionaries:''

Person>>= aPerson
    "Two Persons are equal if their names are equal."
    (aPerson isKindOf: Person) ifFalse: [^false].
    ^self name = aPerson name

Object subclass: #PersonName
    instanceVariableNames: 'firstName lastName'
    classVariableNames: ''
    poolDictionaries:''
```

```
PersonName>>= aPersonName
    "Two PersonNames are equal if their
    first names and last names are equal."
    (aPersonName isKindOf: PersonName) ifFalse: [^false].
    ^(self firstName = aPerson firstName)
        and: [self lastName = aPerson lastName]

String>>= aString
    "Two Strings are equal if their characters are equal."
    "This example is from VisualWorks."
    | size |
    aString isString ifFalse: [^false].
    aString isSymbol ifTrue: [^false].
    (size := self size) = aString size ifFalse: [^false].
    1 to: size do:
        [:index | (self at: index) = (aString at: index)
            ifFalse: [^false]].
    ^true
```

As this code shows, two `Persons` are equal if their `PersonNames` are equal, which are equal if their first and last name `Strings` are equal, which are equal if their `Characters` are equal. This delegation of equal from `Person` to `PersonName` to `String` to `Character` is OO Recursion. Each object takes responsibility for its part of the computation and then delegates the rest of the responsibility to its appropriate attributes.

Any class that implements equal should also implement `hash` (Beck, 1997; Woolf, 1996). A class's implementor of `hash` works by delegating to the same attributes it delegates equal to. For example, since our `Person` class delegates equal to its name attribute, it should do the same for `hash`:

```
Person>>hash
    "A Person's hash value is the same as its
    name's hash value."
    ^self name hash
```

Since `PersonName` uses two attributes for equality, both of them must be hashed and combined:

```
PersonName>>hash
    "A Person's hash value is a combination of its
    parts' hash value."
    ^self firstName hash bitXor: self lastName hash
```

So, like equal, `Person` implements `hash` using OO Recursion, delegating to its `PersonName`, which delegates to its first and last names.

The basic algorithm for an object to create a deep (i.e., fully independent) copy of itself is this: the object copies itself and all of its parts, which copy themselves and all of their parts, and so on. This is OO Recursion as well. For a fuller discussion of implementing `copy`, see Prototype (77).

Object-Oriented Trees

One of the most common and powerful techniques you can learn in object-oriented programming is how to implement object-oriented trees. These trees combine three design patterns: Composite (137), Decorator (161), and OO Recursion. Composite is the Structural pattern that creates trees out of polymorphic nodes. Decorator refines the structure to enable additional behavior to be added to either a branch or leaf node. And OO Recursion provides behavior to request that the tree perform a function without having to know the tree's structure.

Most Composite structures also contain Decorators. Because Composite breaks a Component's implementation into two subclasses, Composite and Leaf, it is difficult to add behavior to the Component through subclassing. Subclassing Component won't work because the subclass won't affect Composite or Leaf. If you subclass Composite or Leaf to add the behavior, you'll also have to subclass the other and duplicate the code. Instead, Decorator is a flexible alternative to subclassing that allows additional behavior to be added to nodes in a structure dynamically. Thus, by implementing the extra behavior in a Decorator subclass of Component, you can add the behavior as a Decorator to a Composite or a Leaf.

Not only are Composite and Decorator convenient to use together; their designs fit together well. This book's sections on Composite and Decorator discuss how the Component superclass declares the subclasses' core interface. The discussions also caution against extending the core interface in subclasses because doing so can ruin the polymorphism that the client expects. Because of this, classes in either a Composite or Decorator class tend to have a fairly limited interface that nevertheless provides a full set-of functionality. Narrowing the Component's interface to apply the first pattern (either Composite or Decorator) is difficult, but once it has been done, applying the second pattern is much easier. Usually Composite is applied first to define the tree structure. After that, applying Decorator is relatively easy because Composite has already defined Component's limited core interface.

It is difficult to request a tree to perform a function. A tree is not one object; it is a collection of objects arranged in a hierarchical fashion. Thus, for the tree as a whole to perform a function, it must tell each of its nodes to perform that function. The procedure to perform the function on all of the tree's nodes cannot make many assumptions about the tree's overall structure since that structure can easily change. Thus, the procedure should let the tree structure itself perform the function on each node. A procedure that defers to the tree structure is an example of the OO Recursion pattern.

Thus the Composite, Decorator, and OO Recursion patterns are often used together. Composite defines object-oriented trees. Having done so, Decorator and OO Recursion enhance the trees' functionality and flexibility.

Applicability

There are two constraints on applying the Chain of Responsibility and OO Recursion patterns:

1. *Chain already exists.* The pattern does not create a chain where there was none. *Design Patterns* says it can (DP 226), but it's more accurate to say that the chain comes from applying a Structural pattern that creates the links the Behavioral pattern will traverse. The chain is either a linked-list or a path in a tree or graph. If each node in the chain is more general than the last, the chain can be used for Chain of Responsibility. Otherwise, its use is the more general pattern, OO Recursion.

2. *Collections are not chains.* A `Collection` (e.g., an `OrderedCollection` or an `Array`) is not a chain in the sense of this pattern. As the diagrams showed, each node in a chain points to its successor. In a `Collection`, the elements are not aware of each other, and so no element knows what the next one is. Chain of Responsibility and OO Recursion cannot traverse a `Collection` structure; the client must use Iterator (273) instead.

Implementation

There are several issues to consider when implementing the Chain of Responsibility and OO Recursion patterns:

1. *Automatic forwarding in Smalltalk.* This technique, described in *Design Patterns* (DP 229), seems simple but should be avoided. Rather than forwarding each message individually to its successor, a handler can simply implement `doesNotUnderstand:` to forward any message that the handler does not understand to its successor. This technique is extremely flexible but also quite haphazard. For more details about this implementation technique and its dangers, see Proxy (213).

2. *Do work, pass the buck, or both?* *Design Patterns* implies that each handler in the chain either handles the request completely and stops the chaining, or passes the request to its successor without doing anything. That's Chain of Responsibility. Smalltalk commonly uses a third option where a handler will handle the request partially but also pass the request to its successor. This way the work of handling the request is spread through the handlers. This is OO Recursion.

3. *Placement of recursion methods.* The recursion in OO Recursion consists of three methods: an initiator, a recurser, and a terminator. Since the terminator method is the base case of the recurser method, they are polymorphic. The initiator method cannot be polymorphic with the recurser and terminator because the message that initiates the recursion must be different from the recursive message itself. As shown in the table on the next page, where you implement these messages depends on which direction the recursion is traveling in:

| | Method's Class | | |
Direction	Initiator	Recurser	Terminator
Up the tree	Leaf, Component, or Client	Component	Component
Down the tree	Component or Client	Composite	Leaf

- *Recursing up a tree.* A path from a leaf node to the root node in a tree is a linked-list. The initiator node is a leaf, so the initiator method is implemented in the Leaf class. If the recursion can start with any node, the initiator method is implemented in the Component class. The initiator method can also be implemented in a Client class. Since the recursion can travel through any node, the recurser method is implemented in the Component class. Since any node can act as the root, the terminator method is also implemented in the Component class.

- *Recursing down a tree.* Recursing down a tree from the root node to the leaves traverses the entire tree, usually depth-first. Thus, recursion branches when it hits a Composite node; it recurses the path for one child, unwinds, recurses the path for the next child, unwinds, and so forth for the rest of the children. If the recursion can start with any node, the initiator method is implemented in the Component. It can also be implemented in a Client class. The recurser method is implemented in the Composite class; it continues the recursion by running the recursion on each of its branches. The terminator method is implemented in the Leaf class; there is usually no reason to move it up into the Component class.

Sample Code

The File Reader (Woolf, 1997), discussed above, implements a couple of examples of OO Recursion. It creates a tree to describe the mappings of a record's fields to a domain object's structure and uses a special stream to read in the records as domain objects.

As a `Stream`, `FormattedStream` implements `next` to read the next record from the file. `next` initiates the recursive message `readObjectFrom:into:`, which recurses down the field format tree and reads the record into a domain object:

```
Stream subclass: #FormattedStream
    instanceVariableNames: 'dataStream streamFormat ...'
    classVariableNames: ''
    poolDictionaries: ''

FormattedStream>>next
    "See superimplementor."
    ...
    ^streamFormat readObjectFrom: dataStream
```

```
Object subclass: #StreamFormatDescription
   instanceVariableNames: 'dataFieldFormat resultChannel ...'
   classVariableNames: ''
   poolDictionaries: ''

StreamFormatDescription>>readObjectFrom: dataStream
   ...
   dataFieldFormat
      readObjectFrom: dataStream
      into: resultChannel.
   ^self result

Object subclass: #FieldFormatDescription
   instanceVariableNames: ''
   classVariableNames: '...'
   poolDictionaries: ''

FieldFormatDescription>>readObjectFrom: dataStream into:
aValueModel
   "Reads the field that the receiver describes from
   dataStream and stores the field's value in aValueModel."
   self subclassResponsibility
```

Each kind (subclass) of field format has a different procedure for reading its data out of the data stream. In the simplest case, a leaf field format reads the data from the next field, converts them, and stores them in the return object:

```
FieldFormatDescription subclass: #LeafFieldFormat
   instanceVariableNames: 'readSelector writeSelector'
   classVariableNames: ''
   poolDictionaries: ''

LeafFieldFormat>>readObjectFrom: dataStream into: aValueModel
   "See superimplementor."
   | bytes fieldValue |
   ...
   bytes := self readFieldFrom: dataStream.
   ...
   fieldValue := bytes perform: readSelector.
   aValueModel value: fieldValue
```

A composite field format reads itself out of the record by recursively reading each of its child fields out of the record:

```
FieldFormatDescription subclass: #CompositeFieldFormat
   instanceVariableNames: 'fieldFormats resultChannel
fieldAdaptors'
   classVariableNames: ''
   poolDictionaries: ''
```

```
CompositeFieldFormat>>readObjectFrom: dataStream into:
aValueModel
    "See superimplementor."
    ...
    self readFieldsFrom: dataStream

CompositeFieldFormat>>readFieldsFrom: dataStream
    "Read the fields out of dataStream into the result object."
    1 to: self numberOfFields
      do:
        [:i |
        | field adaptor |
        field := self fieldAt: i.
        adaptor := fieldAdaptors at: i.
        field readObjectFrom: dataStream into: adaptor]
```

A decorator field format simply forwards the read request to its component:

```
FieldFormatDescription subclass: #FieldFormatDecorator
    instanceVariableNames: 'fieldFormat'
    classVariableNames: ''
    poolDictionaries: ''

FieldFormatDecorator>>readObjectFrom: dataStream into:
aValueModel
    "See superimplementor."
    fieldFormat readObjectFrom: dataStream into: aValueModel
```

`FormattedStream` also implements `nextPut:` to write a domain object as a record using the recursive message `writeObjectIn:to:`.

```
FormattedStream>>nextPut: anObject
    "See superimplementor."
    streamFormat writeObject: anObject to: dataStream

StreamFormatDescription>>writeObject: anObject to: dataStream
    ...
    resultChannel value: anObject.
    dataFieldFormat writeObjectIn: resultChannel to: dataStream

FieldFormatDescription>>writeObjectIn: aValueModel to:
dataStream
    "Writes the value in aValueModel to sourceStream
    using the field format described by the receiver."
    self subclassResponsibility
```

The recursion of `writeObjectIn:to:` is implemented just like `readObjectFrom:into:`. Since it also recurses down the tree, its key implementors are in `CompositeFieldFormat` and `LeafFieldFormat`. `FieldFormatDecorator` just forwards the message.

The Sample Code section in Composite also demonstrates OO Recursion.

Known Smalltalk Uses

Chain of Responsibility is rarely used in Smalltalk. Most trees are organized by composition, not specialization. Most handlers do some work *and* delegate, not just one or the other.

OO Recursion is very common in Smalltalk. While linked-list structures are rare in Smalltalk, tree structures are common. Virtually every tree structure in Smalltalk uses OO Recursion to distribute behavior.

Related Patterns

OO Recursion and Composite, Decorator, and Adapter

When a Composite (137) delegates a message to its children or a Decorator (161) delegates to its component, this is OO Recursion. Similarly, an Adapter (105) delegating to its adaptee is also OO Recursion, although the chain is not polymorphic. All of these examples are rather degenerate because one object delegating to its collaborator is not a very extensive chain.

The better example of OO Recursion is when a series of Composites, Decorators, and Adapters form a chain. Then a message that starts at the beginning of the chain travels through the chain looking for handlers to handle it. The client doesn't know which nodes will handle the request. The Structural patterns form the chain, but the behavior of the message traversing down through the nodes is OO Recursion.

OO Recursion versus Iterator

Iterator (273) allows each node in a structure to be considered so that functions may be performed on it in isolation from the other nodes in the structure. The Iterator knows which node will handle each request; it is the node that is currently being iterated on. The Iterator ensures that each node is considered in turn.

OO Recursion does not consider each of the structure's nodes in isolation. Instead, a client makes a request of one of the nodes, and that node passes the request to other nodes, until one of them handles it. All of the nodes in the structure may be involved, or only the first one may participate. Either way, the client is unaware of which nodes are ultimately involved.

OO Recursion and Iterator

Although they are different patterns, an example of Iterator may be implemented using OO Recursion. Consider how a subclass of `Collection` implemented as a tree would implement `do:`. The root node would recursively pass the `do:` block to each node in turn so that the node could evaluate the block on itself. Each composite node would evaluate the block on itself and recursively pass the request to its children. Each leaf node would simply evaluate the block on itself and be done. In this way, iterating through a tree is implemented as a recursion from the root that always traverses all of the nodes.

OO Recursion and Interpreter

Interpreter uses the interpret message to traverse an abstract syntax tree. This traversal is an example of OO Recursion.

COMMAND (DP 233)   Object Behavioral

Intent

Encapsulate a request or operation as an object, thereby letting you parameterize clients with different operations, queue or log requests, and support undoable operations.

Structure

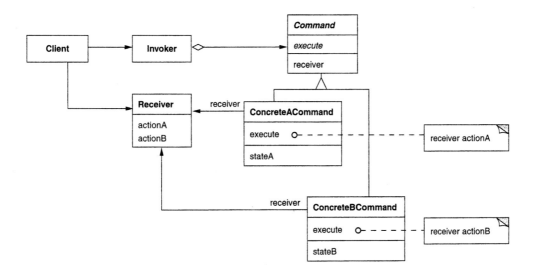

Discussion

Sometimes it's necessary to send messages to an object in a generic fashion without actual knowledge of the message selector or perhaps even the receiver. To the novice, this may sound more or less impossible. After all, how can one object send a message to a second object without knowing what message to send or which object to send it to? In this pattern, we'll show you how.

User interaction with interface widgets provides one example of why we need such a facility. When a user clicks on a button or a menu item, *something* happens in response. In the Model-View-Controller paradigm or in the condensed model-pane scheme in Visual Smalltalk and older Digitalk environments, these widgets (views, panes) are attached to an underlying model or application. The action taken in response to a button press or menu selection is the responsibility of the application. For example, if the user selects the *Cut* menu item in a text editor, the application deletes the currently selected text. The user interface widgets do not themselves know what to do in response to a user interaction event. Neither do they know which message to forward to an application when an event occurs because that is application-specific; to be reusable by any application, widgets are implemented in a generic fashion. The upshot is that we need a mechanism that allows a non-application-specific widget to forward a specific message to the application.

One such mechanism is provided by the Command pattern. It allows us to represent a messaging request as an object that can be referenced by other objects and passed around among objects. This is one solution, and we'll show how it can be implemented in Smalltalk. However, with regard to a mechanism by which generic widgets can invoke specific functionality in their models, Visual Smalltalk and IBM Smalltalk offers another solution; we'll describe that solution as well.

Implementation and Sample Code

A Command object may hard-code the message it forwards, or it may be parameterized at runtime. We call the latter a Pluggable Command. In this section, we'll discuss and show how to implement both varieties here. We'll also show how the Command pattern enables an undo-redo facility. And, as we noted above, we'll describe an alternative approach to the problem of configuring widgets to send application-specific messages as events occur.

Hard-Coded Commands

Although Smalltalk provides an alternative solution, the Command pattern as implemented in *Design Patterns* is useful for purposes such as undo and redo facilities. It is also used by major application frameworks, such as MacApp (Schmucker, 1986; Collins, 1995).

Continuing our user interaction example, Command objects may sit between a screen widget and some other object—usually the application itself—that knows how to perform the operations associated with the widget. For example, if the widget is a button whose text reads "Cut," the object on the other side of the Command object is the one that knows how to perform the cut operation.

Each widget is told by the application which Command instance to hook up to. The Command knows two things: (1) a particular object to which it should forward messages (the Command's receiver) and (2) exactly which messages to send to that object when told to. The widget only knows about its Command object; it has no knowledge of the messages the Command sends or the object it sends them to. When a widget event occurs (e.g., a button is clicked), the widget simply sends the generic execute message to its Command object. At this point, the Command redirects a different message or messages to its receiver (in MacApp, the message sent to the command object is DoIt).

Thus a Command represents a receiver-action pair. The receiver is set by the application and maintained in an instance variable within the Command object. The action derives from the specific message or messages sent to the Command's receiver by the execute method. These messages are hard-coded in execute. Hence, a concrete Command subclass is required for each specific operation: a CutCommand object might send the cut message, and a RevertCommand instance might send a sequence of messages, such as selectAll, delete, reopenFile to have an edited file revert to its previously saved state. An instance of CutCommand can be used to link a *Cut* button to an application, a *Revert* menu item is handled by a RevertCommand object, and so forth.

Here is a small interaction view showing how a Command fits between a widget and an application object, decoupling the two, and translating a generic message (execute) from the former to an application-specific message sent to the latter:

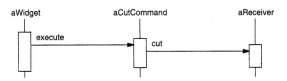

The full example is portrayed from a higher level in the following structure diagram. The application configures the MenuItem objects with specific Command instances. When the user selects a menu item, the corresponding MenuItem instance sends execute to its Command object:

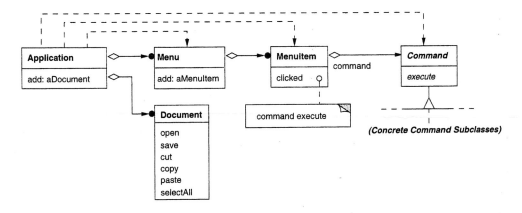

Let's look at sample code for this example. First we define the abstract Command class:

```
Object subclass: #Command
    instanceVariableNames: 'receiver'
    classVariableNames: ''
    poolDictionaries: ''
```

And we need an instance creation class method:

```
Command class>>for: aReceiver
   "Create a new instance and set its receiver
    to aReceiver."
   ^self new receiver: aReceiver
```

We also need a getter-setter pair of methods for the instance variable:

```
Command>>receiver
   ^receiver

Command>>receiver: anObject
   receiver := anObject
```

Here's the method that is the core of the Command object:

```
Command>>execute
   "I'm an abstract class; subclasses must override this."
   self subclassResponsibility
```

Now we can define some concrete subclasses with concrete implementations of the execute method:

```
Command subclass: #CutCommand
   instanceVariableNames: ''
   classVariableNames: ''
   poolDictionaries: ''

CutCommand>>execute
   receiver cut

Command subclass: #PasteCommand
   instanceVariableNames: ''
   classVariableNames: ''
   poolDictionaries: ''

PasteCommand>>execute
   receiver paste
```

In this example, execute sends a sequence of messages to the receiver:

```
Command subclass: #RevertCommand
   instanceVariableNames: ''
   classVariableNames: ''
   poolDictionaries: ''

RevertCommand>>execute
   receiver
      selectAll;
      delete;
      reopenFile
```

Thus, each subclass of Command implements its own version of execute by sending different application-specific messages to the receiver. The fact that we require a new Command subclass for each operation, however, is a drawback of this approach. But a specific class for each operation means that each class can be programmed with the precise messages required to undo the execute operation. Further, implementing undo functionality in Command objects often implies the need to save information about the state of its receiver before execute sends messages that change that state; thus, each specific Command class can know precisely which state information must be remembered for *its* operation.

For example, a CutCommand would have to save information regarding the current selection before forwarding the cut message to its receiver. It would then implement an unexecute method to effect the undo (in MacApp, the undo method is named UndoIt). In the following example code, we return to the Cut-Command class to effect the changes required for unexecute. In the code, we make a couple of simplifying assumptions: (1) there is a single contiguous selection, and (2) asking the editor for its current selection retrieves a single object that includes the actual text or objects that are currently selected, as well as information about the location of the selection within the document (for example, in Visual Smalltalk, a TextSelection object encapsulates several pieces of information regarding selected text, such as its start and end positions and the text pane in which the text appears):

```
Command subclass: #CutCommand
    instanceVariableNames: 'selectionBeforeCut'
    classVariableNames: ''
    poolDictionaries: ''

CutCommand>>execute
    selectionBeforeCut := receiver currentSelection.
    receiver cut

CutCommand>>unexecute
    receiver
        selectBefore: selectionBeforeCut origin;
        paste: selectionBeforeCut text
```

Now an application can hook together a widget, say a button, with a Command in the following fashion:

```
AnApplication>>open
    ...
    self addSubpane:
        (Button new
            contents: 'Cut';
            command: (CutCommand for: self);
            ...)
```

The following interaction diagram portrays the collaborations involved in this pattern:

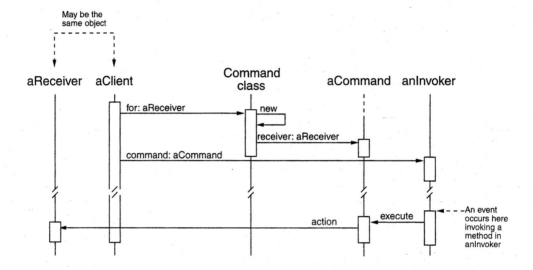

Note that aReceiver may be an object separate from aClient or a single object may fulfill both roles; it's up to the client to decide, and inform aCommand, who the command object's receiver is. The object labeled anInvoker would be a widget in our previous examples. There's also a language-based difference between our diagram and the one on page DP 237. In *Design Patterns,* the code new Command is shown; this portrays an instance creation statement intrinsic to the C++ language and resulting in the instantiation of aCommand. In Smalltalk, the Command instance creation occurs as the result of sending the new *message* to an object, the Command class object (this occurs during the Command class's response to the for: instance creation message).

An Undo-Redo History List

One significant implication of the Command pattern is that it allows us to maintain a history of all the operations performed by a user. For each user action, the application can add the associated Command object to a **history list**. Then we have the means to implement a multilevel undo-redo facility. To undo an operation, we retrieve the previous Command from the history list and send it the unexecute message. To redo an operation that has been undone, we retrieve the same Command object and send it execute again. In the Iterator pattern, we provide a detailed explanation and implementation of a history list class named HistoryStream, along with the mechanisms we need for traversing the list in the backward direction for undo and forward for redo. Here we'll sketch how an application might make use of a history list for undo-redo.

Let's assume that our application class, AnApplication, defines an instance variable named historyList:

```
AnApplication class>>new
   ^self basicNew initialize

AnApplication>>initialize
   historyList := HistoryStream new.
   . . .

AnApplication>>saveForUndo: aCommand
   historyList nextPut: aCommand deepCopy
```

We save a copy of the Command object for undo because it can contain state information snapshotted from its receiver object, and this information will change the next time it's invoked (which, of course, may be prior to performing an undo operation).

The saveForUndo: method implies some coupling between the application and the Command objects (Commands have to know about the application in order to send it the saveForUndo: message). If we add an instance variable to the Command class definition, we can provide each Command with knowledge of its application at instance-creation time. Note that we cannot use the Command's receiver instance variable for this purpose because that may or may not point to the application. So we return to the Command definition to add the application variable and an associated setter method, change the instance creation method, and redefine the execute method:

```
Object subclass: #Command
   instanceVariableNames: 'receiver application'
   classVariableNames: ''
   poolDictionaries: ''

Command>>application: anObject
   application := anObject

Command class>>receiver: aReceiver application: anApplication
   "Instance creation."
   ^self new
      receiver: aReceiver;
      application: anApplication

Command>>execute
   "Here in the abstract superclass we define execute as a
   Template Method. First, invoke handleExecute and then
   save the Command object in the history list. This way,
   subclasses just override handleExecute and get history
   list behavior for free."
   self handleExecute.
   application saveForUndo: self
```

Concrete `Command` subclasses now define their own `handleExecute` method:

```
CutCommand>>handleExecute
    selectionBeforeCut := receiver currentSelection.
    receiver cut
```

As we saw earlier, concrete subclasses also implement their action-specific undo behaviors in their `unexecute` methods.

Once we have the Command classes defined, we can implement the application's undo and redo operations:

```
MyApplication>>undo
    | aCommandOrNil |
    "If there are no previous Commands to undo, exit:"
    (aCommandOrNil := historyList previous) isNil
        ifTrue: [^Screen default ringBell].
    aCommandOrNil unexecute

AnApplication>>redo
    | aCommandOrNil |
    "If there are no redo-able Command objects in the
     history list, exit:"
    (aCommandOrNil := historyList next) isNil
        ifTrue: [^Screen default ringBell].
    aCommandOrNil handleExecute
```

Notice that `redo` sends `handleExecute` to the `Command` rather than `execute`. For redo, we don't want to add a new `Command` to the history list here; that is done in `execute`, which is called when the user performs a new operation. We just want to reexecute the operation already in the list.

We've shown the undo-redo facility implemented by the main application object. In practice, an application often employs a separate undo manager object for this purpose. This approach is used in WindowBuilder and EFX (Alpert et al., 1995), for example. The application maintains an instance variable pointing to its undo manager, and the latter maintains the history list and invokes the undo-redo functionality as requested by the user.

Pluggable Commands

In the previous version of Command, we hard-coded the message(s) to be forwarded to the Command's receiver in each Command's `execute` method. As a result, we need a different Command class for every possible user action: one for cut, another for copy, another for paste, and on and on.

Also, notice that in the C++ version of Hard-Coded Commands, the instance variable referencing the Command's receiver is declared in the concrete Command subclasses—in the `OpenCommand` class (DP 239), it was named `_application` and its type was `Application`; in `PasteCommand` (DP 240) it was `_document`, declared to be of the `Document` class. On the other hand, we declared a generic `receiver` instance variable in the abstract `Command` class. In C++, with its strong typing, we do not want to commit the Command's receiver to be of a specific type; it may vary depending on the particular Command types. In Smalltalk, this issue is greatly simplified. Without typing, the `receiver` variable may reference a variable of any class at runtime.

Design Patterns discusses a C++-flavored way around some of these difficulties. It considers the notion of parameterizing the Command's receiver using C++ templates. In this way, we can define a single `SimpleCommand` class (DP 240–241) and instantiate it using different types of receivers. The `SimpleCommand` class also has an instance variable that points to a member function. Hence, this version allows the behavior of `execute` to be parameterized as well. We pass a pointer to the appropriate method when instantiating the class, and `execute` simply invokes this parameterized method.

We can parameterize the behavior of `execute` in other ways as well. A Command object is really just an Adapter with a specialized role; it adapts the single generic `execute` message, sent by widgets, to an application-specific message (or messages); the Adaptee is the Command's receiver. Since it's an Adapter, we can define a single Pluggable or Parameterized Adapter/Command class to forward a client-supplied message to the receiver or execute a client-supplied block using the receiver as an argument. We showed how to do both of these in the Adapter (105) pattern, and below we demonstrate another Smalltalk-flavored version of a pluggable message-forwarding Command.

However, the advantage to the action-specific hard-coded Command implementation—where we have a specific class for each user action—is that these classes know exactly what information and receiver state to save for an undo operation. A cut operation needs to save different state from a paste, for instance. There's no way to know how to do this generically, so a pluggable Command cannot be used when we want Commands to participate in an undo-redo facility.

A Smalltalk-Flavored Pluggable Command. Here we present another approach for implementing a single generic type of `Command` object rather than one type per operation. This Command lets us forward a single message selector to the receiver, like a Pluggable Adapter, and also allows us to remember arguments to be passed along with the forwarded message, something Pluggable Adapters do not do for us:

```
Object subclass: #PluggableCommand
    instanceVariableNames: 'receiver selector arguments'
    classVariableNames: ''
    poolDictionaries: ''
```

Assume we've also written accessor messages for each of the instance variables. Instance creation would then look like this:

```
Command class>>receiver: anObject
               selector: aSymbol
               arguments: anArrayOrNil
   "Instance creation."
   ^self new
      receiver: anObject;
      selector: aSymbol;
      arguments: (anArrayOrNil isNil
                     ifTrue: [#()]
                     ifFalse: [anArrayOrNil])
```

The application then instantiates PluggableCommand and plugs it together with a widget, much as we've done above. The difference is that the application would specify not only the Command's receiver but its selector and, optionally, arguments as well:

```
AnApplication>>open
   | command |
   ...
   command := PluggableCommand
                  receiver: self
                  selector: #cut
                  arguments: (Array with: myTextPane).
   self addSubpane:
      (Button new
         contents: 'Cut';
         command: command;
         ...)
```

Now when the widget sends the generic execute message to its Command object, the following code is invoked:

```
PluggableCommand>>execute
   "Answer the result of sending the selector to
    the receiver along with any arguments."
   ^self receiver
      perform: self selector
      withArguments: self arguments
```

The class we have just defined is virtually identical to the existing Visual Small-talk Message class. (In IBM Smalltalk and VisualWorks, the Message class contains only two instance variables, corresponding to selector and arguments. Their respective subclasses, however, add the receiver variable, as in Visual Smalltalk's Message class. In IBM Smalltalk, that subclass is named Directed-Message, and in VisualWorks, it is named MessageSend. For Visual Smalltalk Message instances, the execute message is actually named perform; in IBM's

DirectedMessage, it is called `send`; and in VisualWorks's `MessageSend` class, it is `value`. In the ensuing discussion, we'll refer only to the `Message` class, as in the Visual Smalltalk implementation.) `Message` instances are reifications of the messages that objects send to one another. `Messages` and `perform:` allow us, in a very general way, to create, store, and send any message to any object. Thus, in Smalltalk, it is possible to replace a hierarchy of Command objects with a single, parameterized `Message` object.

Event-Driven Interactive Applications

A shortcoming of the Command pattern as implemented above is that it allows us to associate only one operation, and thus one command, with each widget. This is fine for a menu item. When the item is clicked, we want to invoke a single specific operation in the application. However, many widgets have a number of events associated with them, such as left-button mouse click, right-button click, double-click, and mouse-move over the widget. We would like to be able to associate a message-receiver pair with each of these events for every widget. Both IBM Smalltalk and Visual Smalltalk allow us to do just that. Both approaches are discussed in greater detail in the Observer pattern (see SASE in Visual Smalltalk, page 314, and SASE in IBM Smalltalk, page 317); here we'll briefly consider the basic concepts in Visual Smalltalk's implementation.

Every Visual Smalltalk pane has multiple events associated with it. As a simple example, a `RadioButton` generates one event when the user clicks on it to turn it on and a different event when the button is turned off. When an interactive application builds a window, it tells each pane what to do when specific events occur. Essentially, it associates a `Message`—that is, a message selector, receiver, and, optionally, arguments—with each of these events. (In fact, there are other alternatives besides a `Message` per se—for example, a block may be used—but here we'll discuss the plain vanilla message case.)

When an application is building a window, it can tell each widget what to do when specific events occur. Let's say we have a point-of-sale application whose screen interface includes a set of radio buttons to indicate which credit card the customer is using:

```
PointOfSale>>open
  . . .
  self addSubpane:
    (RadioButton new
      contents: 'American Express';
      when: #turnedOn send: #americanExpressPicked to: self;
      . . .
```

The `when:send:to:` message means, "When your `turnedOn` event occurs, send me the `americanExpressPicked` message." Every pane has an instance variable named `handlers`, which is a dictionary whose keys are event names and whose corresponding values are the actions to take when an event occurs. The `when:send:to:` message, and its variants, set the entries in this dictionary. The `when:` argument specifies the event name (the key), and the `send:to:` parameters specify the selector and receiver for the associated `Message` object (the value). When an event occurs, the associated `Message` is retrieved from `handlers` and is told to execute.

There are a number of variations of `when:send:to:`, including, most notably, `when:send:to:with:`, where the `with:` parameter specifies the argument (or multiple arguments) to be sent with the message when the corresponding event occurs. (Another variation allows you to specify a block to be evaluated when the event occurs, but for clarity we're focusing here on the `Message` version.)

The main points of this approach are these:

- We can use a `Message` as a Command object, providing a generic mechanism for linking a user interface widget to an application object—more specifically, for linking each pane event to a message sent to the application object or any other receiver, of the application's choice. The message may include arguments as well.

- The approach permits us to build real event-driven interactive applications because it permits multiple events to be associated with each widget and each of those events to be associated with a different Command.

- Since there are multiple events per widget, we need a mechanism for keeping track of all of the event-to-action mappings. In Visual Smalltalk the implementation is table driven, with a dictionary in each widget keyed by event name.

Known Smalltalk Uses

Visual Smalltalk and IBM Smalltalk Interactive Applications

All user interface applications built in Visual Smalltalk—that is, applications that incorporate interactive windows—use the event-driven, multiple Command per widget approach described above. Although messaging details are different, IBM Smalltalk adopts a similar approach. As in Visual Smalltalk, IBM Smalltalk applications tell each widget what application-specific messages to send when particular events occur, and there are multiple events associated with each widget (some events are common to all widgets, some are widget-specific). You can thus configure multiple Commands per widget.

Visual Smalltalk MenuItems

In Visual Smalltalk, `MenuItem` instances act as Command objects. Suppose we have a pull-down menu that looks like this:

We can build this menu in a number of ways; here's one:

```
AnApplication>>buildEditMenu
    | menu |
    menu := Menu new.
    menu
        appendItem: 'Cut' selector: #cut;
        appendItem: 'Copy' selector: #copy;
        appendItem: 'Paste' selector: #paste;
        appendSeparator;
        appendItem: 'Revert' selector: #revert;
        owner: self;
        title: 'Edit'.
    ^menu
```

This results in a Menu containing four MenuItem objects. Each of the MenuItems has an instance variable referencing a selector; when the menu item is selected by the user, the message selector is forwarded to the Menu's owner (using per-form:). Hence when the user selects the *Cut* item, the cut message is sent to AnApplication.

We can alternatively associate a Message object with any menu item. Hence we can set up a MenuItem to send a message to any receiver and include arguments. For instance, we could add the following to buildEditMenu:

```
menu
    appendItem: 'Insert Date'
    action:
        (Message
            receiver: myTextPane
            selector: #paste:
            arguments: (Array with: Date today printString)).
```

Delayed Database Updates

One of us has used the Command pattern to maintain a list of user changes to a relational database and perform a delayed batch update of the database as a single transaction. The application allowed users to retrieve a database schema from disk, which caused it to be converted into an internal Smalltalk representation. The user could rename columns, drop and add columns, and so on, and these operations would change only the Smalltalk representation of the schema (not the database on disk). Each change was recorded as a command object in a history list. The user could undo and redo changes from this history of operations, but only the Smalltalk "copy" of the database was altered. At the end of the user's interaction, the command objects would generate the appropriate SQL code corresponding to their operations and execute that code on the actual physical database schema. Thus, the Command pattern was used to remember changes and delay applying them until all such modifications were finalized.

Undo in an Object-Oriented Database

In another project, one of us has again used the Command pattern for a similar purpose. Here, the application includes specialized editors, which must implement an undo capability; the problem, however, is that all changes to objects are immediately updated in the application's object-oriented database, and backing them out (for undo) is nontrivial. What we've done instead is to make a deep copy of an object when a user begins to edit it. Then all editing changes are applied to this copy *and* saved in a history list of commands. In this case, the command objects are basically `Message` objects that record those messages sent to the object copy by the editor. When the user is finished editing, she has the choice of committing the changes she made or discarding them. In the former case, the messages saved in the history list are reapplied to the original object; for the latter choice, the object copy and history list are discarded, and the original object is left unchanged.

WindowBuilder

WindowBuilder, the user interface builder from ObjectShare Systems, uses a variation of the Command pattern along with an undo-redo history list. When an operation is performed by the user in the interface builder window, the `Window-Builder` object adds a `WBUndoAction` instance to the history list in its `WBUndoManager`. A `WBUndoAction` is pluggable. Rather than hard-coding the statements to execute, `WBUndoAction` objects allow their clients to supply the code to perform both undo and redo actions. Rather than saving a single selector for each action, both are supplied and stored as blocks.

Related Patterns

Adapter

A Tailored Adapter (106) is quite similar to our first implementation of Command (described in the Hard-Coded Commands section). A Tailored Adapter sits between two other objects and knows how to translate a message from one of these objects to a different message, which it forwards to the second. It looks a lot like the Command object in the following interaction diagram:

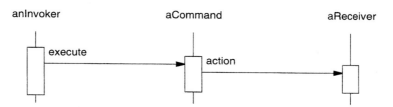

We can consider this Command implementation to be a Tailored Adapter that knows how to translate the execute message. In the Command object, the "Adaptee" to which the converted message is sent is maintained in the receiver variable. In both the Tailored Adapter and the Hard-Coded Command, the message to be forwarded is hard-coded (in the Command's execute method and in the Adapter's value and value: methods). Rather than being competing patterns, we might say that the Adapter pattern is used in service of the Command pattern.

Our Pluggable Command is basically a Pluggable Adapter (107). This Command object is told what message to forward to its "Adaptee" (receiver) when it receives the execute message. It stores the to-be-forwarded message internally and thus implements a generic translation mechanism rather than the hard-coded version above.

Observer

The Visual Smalltalk event-driven mechanism we described is a variation on the Observer pattern (305). It is used when we want widgets to notify other objects when specific events, or even a generic change, occurs.

INTERPRETER (DP 243)   Object Behavioral

Intent

Given a language, define a representation for its grammar along with an interpreter that uses the representation to interpret sentences in the language.

Structure

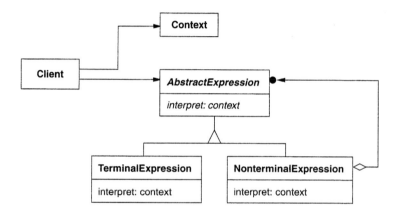

Discussion

The Interpreter pattern deals with defining a grammar for a simple language, representing expressions in that language, and interpreting, or evaluating, those expressions. Interpreter is useful whenever you need to do something at runtime that would seem to necessitate the use of the compiler. This includes the evaluation of arbitrary Smalltalk expressions composed at runtime—that is, not known at compile time. Of course, each Smalltalk environment includes the classes that make up the compiler, and they are fully available in the development environment. But the Smalltalk vendors charge substantial runtime fees for the use of the compiler in a deployed image, making it difficult to justify the expense in most systems. For this reason, use the Interpreter pattern when financial considerations outweigh the additional flexibility gained from the full Smalltalk compiler.

Central to the Interpreter pattern is a set of **Expression** objects that can be constructed into a tree to express any statement in a simple language. These Expressions are instances from an AbstractExpression hierarchy that has subclasses for each different Expression type. Each Expression can interpret itself and return the value it represents. Some Expressions may be like variables; their value depends on the Context in which the tree is currently being interpreted. Thus, the Client that requests the interpretation may need to provide the Context to the interpretation.

Domain Architectures and Interpreter

Interpreter is a hard pattern to classify. It's applicable "when there is a language to interpret, and you can represent statements in the language as abstract syntax trees" (DP 245). One of the more difficult parts of applying the Interpreter pattern is recognizing that you *have* a language to interpret. We have found that unless a developer has formal training in compiler construction, this pattern may not be seen as a potential solution to many problems to which it could be applied.

On the other hand, when you recognize that your particular problem domain can be represented by a language, this pattern can form the core of the architecture of an entire system. Certainly this gets into a gray area between generic and application- or domain-specific patterns. The investment in understanding the pattern and its application may be high, but the potential rewards are huge.

Dynamic Query Language

Applications often need the ability to perform arbitrary queries against a database and display the results. This is especially common in decision-support systems that do data analysis. In some cases, the application can simply allow the user to write SQL code and pass that on to a relational database for interpretation. However, this is more difficult if the data are stored in an object-oriented database or flat file. Even when a system uses a relational database, exposing the user to raw SQL is often not desirable. The user may not know SQL, or the application may want to limit the data that the user can see and change.

This is a good candidate for a simple query language, an editor to allow the user to create queries, and an interpreter to execute those queries. The language expresses the query in a simple, user-friendly manner. The editor helps the user build queries that are syntactically correct. Users are often very impressed with the interpreter's ability to find problems in the queries. Not only can the interpreter execute the query, it can also validate the query and verify that it does not violate any security considerations.

Scripts and Macros

Another possible application of a runtime interpreter-evaluator is an end-user scripting language. Many commercial productivity software products contain a scripting language. Visual Basic for Applications and its kin have built an expectation in customers that they should be able to control their own software tools the way they want.

Still another application of the pattern is macro development. Some tools allow the user to define a series of steps of an operation that is performed often, assign the series to a hot key, and execute the series at the press of a button. For example, most word processors provide the ability to define macros like this.

Macros can be an example of the Interpreter pattern or the Command pattern. If the user uses a macro editor to develop a macro abstractly using a textual language, this is an example of Interpreter. On the other hand, the user can often create a macro by performing a series of actions and recording them. That technique involves the Command pattern, where each action is captured as a Command and the series as a whole is captured as a composite Command (245). Of course, the two techniques can be combined, so one does not necessarily rule out the other.

Beyond Scripting

The Interpreter pattern provides a guide for developers seeking to develop their own small scripting tools, but it is not limited to solving these kinds of problems. As stated above, one of the trickier points of applying the Interpreter pattern is in realizing that you have a language for which you can write an interpreter. Identifying the language in question and then building a class hierarchy of parse nodes to represent the language is one key to the Interpreter pattern.

Design Patterns shows the Interpreter pattern being applied to two common types of languages: regular expressions and boolean expressions. Although these simple languages make excellent examples, it is unfortunate that many readers of *Design Patterns* will not see that they can apply the pattern to other types of languages. It is one of the hallmarks of experienced designers that they can see "outside the box" and understand that they can express many kinds of problems in terms of domain-specific languages.

Parsers

The Intent of Interpreter states two distinct parts to the pattern:

1. Define a representation for a grammar.

2. Develop an interpreter to evaluate expressions in that representation.

As we've noted, a program that uses Interpreter may also involve *parsing* high-level expressions into an underlying representation. Parsers per se don't "count" as Interpreters, however, because they don't interpret or evaluate expressions after parsing. This is a common misunderstanding regarding the Interpreter pattern. Nonetheless, parsers use classes and structures isomorphic—or identical—to those of the Interpreter pattern to represent high-level expressions in an underlying form.

The various Smalltalk compilers, of course, incorporate parsers to decompose Smalltalk expressions into lower-level tree structures. Many other Smalltalk systems also incorporate parsers, which use the same class structure as Interpreter; we'll mention a few of these here. The TGen parser generator program is available for free from the UIUC Smalltalk Archives.[1] Dave Collins of Outback Software

---

[1] The UIUC (University of Illinois at Urbana-Champaign) Smalltalk archives, maintained by Ralph Johnson and his graduate students, contain free Smalltalk code for various dialects. You can visit the archives at http://st-www.cs.uiuc.edu/.

wrote a regular expression compiler-recognizer named RegExp which understands expressions written in the syntax of Perl, Lex, and other languages. ParCE (Alpert & Rosson, 1992) was a context-free parser aimed at decomposing natural language sentences into underlying tree structures composed of nonterminal (noun phrase, prepositional phrase, verb phrase, etc.) and terminal (noun, verb, preposition, determiner, etc.) sentence constituents.

Sample Code

Let's look at a simple example of how to develop an arbitrary query language. Say we are dealing with a health insurance application that maintains a list of patients. We define the patient in Smalltalk by the following class definition:

```
Object subclass: #Patient
   instanceVariableNames: 'name streetAddress city state
       zip sex dateOfBirth policy'
   classVariableNames: ''
   poolDictionaries: ''
```

The application may need to retrieve all patients whose attributes match a specific value. For example, you may want to find all patients who live in Cleveland. Once we have a list of patients, this is easy to do in Smalltalk without Interpreter. We simply use the `select:` method defined in `Collection` (see Iterator (273)).

```
aCollectionOfPatients select:
   [:each | each city = 'Cleveland']
```

Even more complex queries are easy to accomplish with simple Smalltalk code. For example, the following code retrieves all of the patients in the list who live in Cleveland, Ohio (as opposed to Cleveland, Michigan, or Cleveland, Indiana):

```
aCollectionOfPatients select:
   [:each |
   (each state = 'OH')
      and: [each city = 'Cleveland']]
```

This is all well and good so long as you know all of the required queries before writing the code. But what if the user needs to specify new queries at runtime? The Interpreter pattern solves this problem.

What we want to specify is, in effect, a simple query language like the WHERE clause of an SQL statement. We need a way to specify what objects to select from a collection based on their attributes. More complex queries are formed by joining together multiple simple queries with boolean operations (like AND and OR).

Simple Query

Let's start with a simple query. Say we want to select only objects whose attributes match a specific value. We will need to be able to obtain the value of any attribute of an object. This is straightforward if that object's class implements getter methods for the attributes in question. If we know the name of the getter method, we can find the value of that attribute by using the method `perform:` to execute the method—for example, `aPatient perform: #name` will return the name of a `aPatient`. Since the argument to `perform:` is a `Symbol`, we do not need to know the name of the attribute ahead of time. We can request it from the user when it is needed.

This brings us to the simplest part of our query language: equality tests. Let's say in our language we want to interpret sentences of the form `aspectName = someValue`—for example, `city = 'Cleveland'`. Using the Interpreter pattern, we can deal with sentences like this by implementing the following class hierarchy:

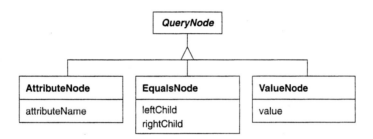

The class `QueryNode` defines the message `evaluateAgainst:`; all of the concrete subclasses must override this message. The basic idea is that you will construct parse trees at runtime from expressions or sentences composed using your query language and then evaluate (or interpret) the query represented by a parse tree. In our example, the interpretation phase is handled by sending the root node of a parse tree the message `evaluateAgainst:`, which says, "Go figure out what your value is in this particular context." To understand this more fully, let's look at the implementations of the three classes shown in the diagram above:

```
Object subclass: #QueryNode
    instanceVariableNames: ''
    classVariableNames: ''
    poolDictionaries: ''

QueryNode>>evaluateAgainst: anObject
    "Return the result of evaluating myself
    against anObject."
    ^self subclassResponsibility
```

An `AttributeNode` implements `evaluateAgainst:` to return the result of sending `perform:` to the message's argument, `anObject`. The message to be performed is held in the node's `attributeName` variable. This is the simplest case; a more complicated case would involve sending additional parameters with `perform:with:` or `perform:withArguments:`.

```
QueryNode subclass: #AttributeNode
    instanceVariableNames: 'attributeName'
    classVariableNames: ''
    poolDictionaries: ''

AttributeNode>>evaluateAgainst: anObject
    "Return the result of sending anObject the message
    selector contained in my attributeName variable"
    ^anObject perform: attributeName
```

When a `ValueNode` is evaluated against an object, it simply returns the value of the constant that it contains. It would also implement accessor methods for its `value` instance variable:

```
QueryNode subclass: #ValueNode
    instanceVariableNames: 'value'
    classVariableNames: ''
    poolDictionaries: ''

ValueNode>>evaluateAgainst: anObject
    "Return my value. I do not care about
    anObject since I'm a constant."
    ^value
```

An `EqualsNode` has two children. It evaluates each against `anObject` and then compares the results for equality:

```
EqualsNode>>evaluateAgainst: anObject
    "Answer whether my two children produce equal results
    when evaluated against anObject"
    ^(leftChild evaluateAgainst: anObject)
      = (rightChild evaluateAgainst: anObject)
```

To see how this works, let's take the example from above and see how to construct a parse tree for that statement:

```
| equals value attribute patients|
"Get a list of patients."
patientList := Patient examplePatients.
equals := EqualsNode new.
value := ValueNode new.
attribute := AttributeNode new.
attribute attributeName: #city.
value value: 'Cleveland'.
equals
    leftChild: attribute;
    rightChild: value.
```

```
^patientList select:
    [:each | equals evaluateAgainst: each]
```

The following diagram shows the structure of the previous example code:

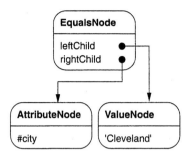

From the above code, you might assume that you must know the structure of a query ahead of time and that this is no better than coding a `select:` statement directly. However, this is not really true. Another idea crucial to the Interpreter pattern is that once you have set up the classes for the nodes, the actual building of the parse tree can be deferred until runtime. In actuality, you would have to build a parser that could read some user-provided representation of the query (say the text of the query) and generate the appropriate parse-tree nodes from that representation. If your language is sufficiently simple, then hand-coding such a parser is pretty straightforward. If it gets more complicated, you may want to look into using something like the TGen parser generator.

Complex Query

The above solution works fine for the simple queries of the type defined earlier. If we wanted to handle more complex queries involving AND and OR, we would need to refactor and expand our design to the following one:

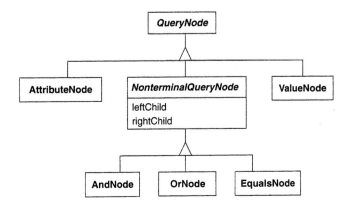

This new design has a simple division between terminal and nonterminal nodes, with each nonterminal being a binary node having a left child and a right child. We achieve this by adding the class `NonterminalQueryNode`. Subclasses of this class inherit the instance variables `rightChild` and `leftChild`, to represent the child nodes.

The classes `AndNode` and `OrNode` have implementations of `evaluateAgainst:` that are nearly identical to the one previously shown for `EqualsNode`. The `AndNode` class evaluates both nodes and returns the result of combining them using `and:`. The `OrNode` class does the same using `or:`. Neither class adds any additional instance variables:

```
AndNode>>evaluateAgainst: anObject
    "Evaluate both of my child nodes against anObject and
    then return the logical AND of these evaluations."
    ^(leftChild evaluateAgainst: anObject)
        and: [rightChild evaluateAgainst: anObject]

OrNode>>evaluateAgainst: anObject
    "Evaluate both of my child nodes against anObject and
    then return the logical OR of these evaluations."
    ^(leftChild evaluateAgainst: anObject)
        or: [rightChild evaluateAgainst: anObject]
```

To see how this would work, consider the following example that uses a boolean node:

```
| cityEquals cityValue cityAttribute stateEquals stateValue
stateAttribute andNode |
"Get a list of patients."
patientList := Patient examplePatients.

cityEquals := EqualsNode new.
cityValue := ValueNode new.
cityAttribute := AttributeNode new.
cityAttribute attributeName: #city.
cityValue value: 'Cleveland'.
cityEquals leftChild: cityAttribute;
    rightChild: cityValue.

stateEquals := EqualsNode new.
stateValue := ValueNode new.
stateAttribute := AttributeNode new.
stateAttribute attributeName: #state.
stateValue value: 'OH'.
stateEquals leftChild: stateAttribute;
    rightChild: stateValue.

andNode := AndNode new.
andNode leftChild: cityEquals;
    rightChild: stateEquals.
^patientList select: [:each |
    andNode evaluateAgainst: each].
```

The following diagram shows the structure of the previous example:

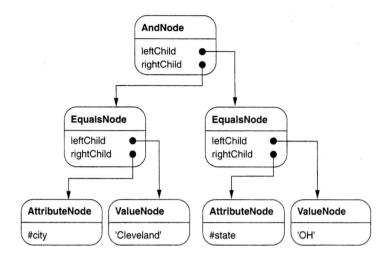

You may have noted that in the above design, the only comparison operator we have is equality. Adding more comparison operators is straightforward. `Less-ThanNode`, `GreaterThanNode`, and `NotEqualsNode` are simple to implement and similar to `EqualsNode`. Note that if you introduce less than and greater than you need to have some level of type checking to make sure that you don't get type conflicts. The Visitor pattern in *Design Patterns* (DP 331) provides information on how to do this.

This query language is not restricted to being used in `select:` statements. If the classes `LessThanNode` and `GreaterThanNode` are added, then it can also be used to form sort blocks. One possible extension to this example might be a visual builder that constructs expressions on the fly. An alternative would be a parser to parse expressions in the grammar into the appropriate nodes.

Known Smalltalk Uses

Factory Scheduling System

One of the hardest parts of applying the Interpreter pattern lies in recognizing that a particular problem can be represented by a domain-specific language. We have used Interpreter in a factory scheduling system for resource scheduling from pools of available resources. The basic problem was this. There were three types of resources we wanted to build schedules for: Labor, Machines, and Tools. To perform a certain type of job, a particular combination of Labor (drawn from a pool of skilled operators), Machines (drawn from a pool of identical machines), and Tools (drawn from a pool of identical tools) must be available at the same time.

For example, to make a Widget, we need a drill press (of which our factory has two), a 10-mm drill bit (of which our factory has three), and a drill press operator (a qualification that two different people in our factory have). Let's think of each object in our system as having a calendar made up of day-long slots. Each slot is either filled (reserved) or empty. Part of scheduling a job is to evaluate the various combinations of labor, machines, and tools that are available. We understood that evaluating the combinations was the role of a set of rules, but we needed to be able to represent the search space that these rules would evaluate. To do this, we used a hierarchy that looked like the following:

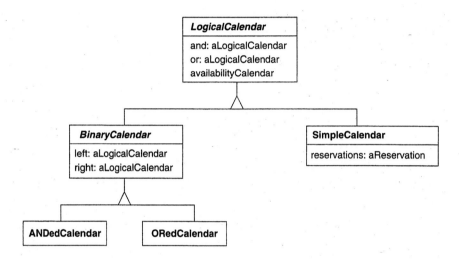

Each object in the system (Labor, Machine, or Tool) has as one of its instance variables an instance of `SimpleCalendar`. Since scheduling occurs on week boundaries, the `SimpleCalendar` contains an array representing the days in a week. The index of the array for each day either contains an instance of `Reservation`—indicating that that object was reserved for that day—or nil.

Now, a problem arose in representing our scheduling problem for Widgets in terms of calendars. In our case the code would resemble the following:

```
availabilityCalendar :=
    ((drillPressOne calendar or: drillPressTwo calendar)
        and: ((bitOne calendar or: bitTwoCalendar)
            or: bitThree calendar)
                and: (bob calendar
                    or: steve calendar)) availabilityCalendar
```

This method in effect constructs a parse tree of nodes. The interesting part comes when the availability calendar is asked to evaluate itself. In this case that means constructing an availability calendar from its component parts. The `ANDedCal-endar` and `ORedCalendar` do different things in this construction. An `ORed-`

`Calendar` will return a concatenation of all of the calendars for the resources in its left and right calendars. An `ANDedCalendar` will instead combine the results of its left and right calendars into a permutation of all the possible time slots in its left with all of the possible time slots in its right. So at the top level, the `ResourceScheduler` receives a collection of all possible combinations of labor, machine, and tool that its rules can evaluate for the "best" combination.

The structure of this solution makes it easy to prune the solution space by removing unnecessary paths. For instance, if one tool in our example is already reserved for the entire week, the `ORedCalendar` that contains its calendar can detect that fact and decline to include it in its concatenation.

Smalltalk as a Rule Engine

Davidowitz (1996) shows how to use the Smalltalk interpreter to build a rule language for externalizing business rules from business objects. Davidowitz also mentions a use of the Decorator pattern to extend the program nodes provided by the VisualWorks Smalltalk compiler.

VisualWorks UIBuilder

An unusual use of Interpreter is in the VisualWorks UI Builder system. Yelland (1996) contends that the way in which the UI Builder operates is an Interpreter in that it has a three-step process for instantiating a user interface from an abstract specification. The steps are:

1. The `UIBuilder` reads out a literal array of strings from a `windowSpec` method.

2. The literal array is used to construct a tree of parse nodes (instances of `UISpecification` subclasses)

3. The `UISpecification` nodes are asked to build their representations of themselves in conjunction with a `LookPolicy` and a `UIBuilder`.

Whether this is actually a use of the pattern is open for debate. The key missing element is that there is no actual language that is ever parsed. Instead, the composite structure of a VisualWorks window as built in the UI Builder is stored as arrays of `Strings` in the `windowSpec` method for the sole purpose of reconstructing it later.

The question is: Does the way in which the `UISpecifications` are asked to build their representations constitute a use of Interpreter or Composite? It could be taken either way. If you view the array as a "language" of sorts, then this fits the definition of Interpreter. If, on the other hand, you don't feel that it is a language, then it doesn't quite fit the definition of the pattern and should instead be considered a use of Composite.

ITERATOR (DP 257)   Object Behavioral

Intent

Provide a way to access the elements of an aggregate object sequentially without exposing its underlying representation.

Structure

Internal Iterator

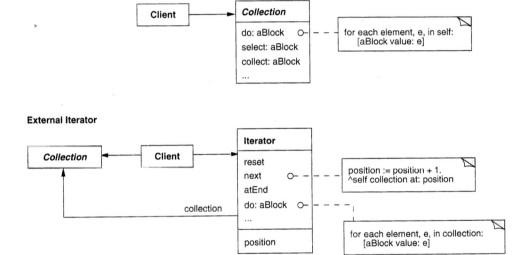

External Iterator

Discussion

The ability to iterate over a list or collection of objects provides an excellent example of reuse in the Smalltalk environment. Reuse, or the potential for reuse, occurs in a number of situations in an object-oriented programming environment, but the simplest form is the use of an existing class, as is, for new problems. Of course, this occurs in reusing the basic abstract data types provided by the base class library. The Iterator pattern demonstrates a couple of excellent examples of this most basic form of reuse.

As we mentioned in our introduction, the Smalltalk *language* doesn't include much. Rather, one of the benefits of the major Smalltalk environments is their extensive sets of base classes. It turns out that the "implementation" of an Iterator is merely a case of reusing functionality extant in the base Smalltalk libraries. We need not reinvent the wheel (a potentially buggy version of the wheel, that is) when we can simply use a wheel that we know works well. With regard to iteration specifically, we need not reimplement a set of Iterator classes because the `Collection` classes provide a public interface that includes a variety of iteration and filtering facilities.

Internal Iterators

For simply iterating linearly over a collection of objects, the `Collection` classes implement the `do:` method. `do:` takes a block as an argument and iteratively binds each entry in the collection to the block's local variable, enabling the block to perform some operation on or involving each object in the collection. Thus performing some operation on each element in a collection is accomplished simply as follows:

```
partsCollection do: [:part | part draw]
```

Similarly, iterating over all of a collection's objects in reverse order may be accomplished like this:

```
undoMessages reverseDo: [:msg | msg perform]
```

Smalltalk's **Internal Iterators**—that is, Iterators intrinsic to the object being iterated over—are made possible by blocks. Blocks allow us to pass the code that is going to be iteratively evaluated *to* the collection object.

`Collection` is an abstract class. Its concrete subclasses (excluding a couple of special-case, special-use classes) can contain objects of any single class as well as heterogeneous aggregations (the elements need not all be of the same class). Further, all `Collections` respond to the `do:` message: `Collection` implements the generic method, and each concrete subclass implements its own version if necessary. Thus, there is no need for a different Iterator, or iteration operation, depending on the type of collection. In the above examples, we really don't care what sort of collection we're traversing or what kinds of objects it contains. All that is required is that each element be capable of responding to the `draw` message (in the `partsCollection` case), but of course `draw` may be implemented polymorphically. This differs markedly from the C++ examples provided in *Design Patterns*, where (1) the client performing the iteration must know what *type* of list it is traversing and instantiate the appropriate Iterator class, or (2) the client must ask the list itself for an Iterator appropriate for the list, or (3) we must implement another class as a Polymorphic Iterator (DP 258).

Filtering Iterators

Design Patterns also speaks of a `FilteringListIterator` (DP 258, 269–270). Here the Iterator returns only those elements of the collection that satisfy specific criteria or constraints. The `Collection` classes also provide intrinsic methods for such filtering purposes, although iterating over the resulting list requires an additional message-send. One of these filtering messages is `select:`. Like `do:`, `select:` takes a block argument; each element in the collection is bound to the block's local variable and is then tested by the code in the block. The test itself is a boolean expression, typically a message sent to the current collection entry. The result of `select:` is a collection of only those elements that satisfy the test. Iteration over this resultant collection simply requires an additional `do:`. Here's an example:

```
(timers select: [:aTimer | aTimer isActive])
    do: [:timer | timer tick]
```

To make the code clearer, we might write this as:

```
activeTimers := timers select: [:aTimer | aTimer isActive].
activeTimers do: [:aTimer | aTimer tick]
```

First, `timers` is filtered to just the active entries (that is, those that return `true` for the message `isActive`). Then the filtered list is traversed.

The `Collection` classes also implement a `reject:` message, which is merely the logical inverse of `select:`. Thus, after executing the following code, `dormantTimers` will reference a collection of all timers that are *not* active:

```
dormantTimers := timers reject: [:aTimer | aTimer isActive]
```

Adding and Removing Elements During Iteration

A common error by Smalltalk novices is iterating over a collection and, based on some test, adding or removing elements along the way (see DP 261). However, if we iterate over a collection using, say, `do:`, and add or delete elements during the iteration, the results may not be as expected. The `do:` method accesses each element in the collection using an index that gets incremented in a loop—so if we delete an element, we may end up missing an entry completely; if we add an entry, we may wind up accessing a particular entry twice. Here is an example of the problematic code:

```
"Don't do this!"
timers do: [:aTimer |
    aTimer isActive ifFalse: [timers remove: aTimer]]
```

So, we need a way to add or remove entries of a collection while iterating over it and have the iteration access each and every element in the original collection just once. The idiomatic way of dealing with this situation is to iterate over a *copy* of the collection, while performing additions or deletions on the original, as follows:

```
"Do this"
timers copy do: [:aTimer |
    aTimer isActive ifFalse: [timers remove: aTimer]]
```

External Iterators

Okay, collections provide their own interface (and internal code) for iteration. But suppose we wish to maintain separate pointers (position markers) into a collection. We might, for example, wish to have multiple pointers into a single list such that more than one traversal may be pending at any time on that list. Or we may need to perform different parts of an iteration in multiple objects or methods; hence we need to be able to pass an Iterator around. The way to maintain such position markers would be to use an object external to the list itself. Such **External Iterators** can also provide clients finer control over the iteration process than the iteration methods intrinsic to `Collections`. The minor trade-off is that External Iterators require an additional object per Iterator.

An object that maintains a positional pointer into a collection simply needs one instance variable referencing the collection and a second variable for the index of the current element. Then, making this object a forward Iterator, that is, one that traverses its collection in a forward direction, would require methods such as `first`, `currentItem`, `next`, and `isDone` (DP 257).

We could, as in *Design Patterns*, have `next` and `first` merely manipulate the position marker and have `currentItem` actually return the current entry from the collection. Instead, to simplify the interface for traversal, we can eliminate `currentItem` and have `next` update the position marker *and* return the entry currently pointed to. So, we're left with `first`, `next`, and `isDone` for forward traversal through a collection.

It turns out that again the Smalltalk base class library includes a subhierarchy of classes that provide precisely this functionality (although with slightly different message names). Several concrete subclasses of the abstract class `Stream` can be used to "stream over"—that is, traverse—collections of elements.

The concrete subclasses of `Stream` include `ReadStream`, for reading objects from a collection; `WriteStream`, for storing objects into a collection; and `ReadWriteStream`, for doing both. Since we need to retrieve items from an existing collection, `ReadStream` is the most appropriate. A `ReadStream` is instantiated and associated with a collection as follows:

```
stream := ReadStream on: aCollection
```

The collection may then be traversed using the following messages: `next` increments the position marker and returns the current entry; `reset` sets the position marker before the first entry so that a subsequent `next` will return the first entry; and `atEnd`, provides the same functionality as `isDone`, that is, it tests whether we've already seen the last element in the collection. So, `stream` can be traversed start to end as follows:

```
stream reset.
[stream atEnd] whileFalse:
   [entry := stream next.
    "do some processing with 'entry'"]
```

It also turns out that for linear traversal performed in one go, from one location in the code, `Stream` implements `do:` as well. Each entry provided to the `do:`'s block argument is the next entry in the Stream's collection. `do:` takes care of the `atEnd` condition, but not the `reset`—that is, it will iterate from the current position to the end of the collection. Hence `stream` could also be traversed as follows:

```
stream
    reset;
    do: [:entry | "do something with 'entry'"]
```

In both examples, the `reset` message is unnecessary if the stream had just been instantiated. That is, at creation time, the stream sets its `position` to 0.

It's important to repeat that a `Stream` doesn't care what sort of collection it is streaming over. The `next` message, for example, will return the next object in the collection regardless of the type of collection or type of object. Thus, there is no requirement for a one-to-one mapping of Iterator classes to `Collection` classes. We need not provide a different type of Iterator for each `Collection` subclass, nor do we need a factory method to ask the collection for the appropriate type of Iterator to instantiate. As a result, when programming the client, we have one less concern.

We can use an external (Stream) Iterator as follows. As on page DP 265, assume we have a `Collection` of `Employee` objects, and the `Employee` class supports the `print` operation. To print the list, an application might define a `printEmployees:` method that takes a `Stream` as an argument:

```
EmployeeApplication>>printEmployees: aReadStream
    aReadStream reset.
    [aReadStream atEnd] whileFalse:
        [aReadStream next printDetails]
```

To print all employees, we would code:

```
EmployeeApplication>>printAllEmployees
    | stream |
    stream := ReadStream on: employees.
    self printEmployees: stream
```

The advantage to having the stream passed as an argument to `printEmployees:` is that we can pass in another sort of stream and `printEmployees:` doesn't care, as long as the stream adheres to the core `ReadStream` protocol. So if we had a reverse traversal stream class named `ReverseReadStream`, we could print all employees in reverse order using the same `printEmployees:` method:

```
EmployeeApplication>>printAllEmployeesReversed
    | stream |
    stream := ReverseReadStream on: employees.
    self printEmployees: stream
```

Iterating over Strings

In Smalltalk, a String is a collection of Characters. Hence we can use the Collection iteration operations to obtain and work with the individual Characters in a String.

First, with an internal Iterator, we can apply Character messages to each element in the String:

```
aString do: [:aCharacter |
    fileStream nextPut: aCharacter asUppercase]
```

More important, the Stream classes include several methods specific to Strings, such as simple parsing operations that can be used while iterating over a String (nextWord, nextLine), as well as general collection-handling methods that facilitate string manipulation, such as operations that traverse a collection searching for a particular object. For example, to remove comments (paired double quotes) from a string, we could implement the following method:

```
String>>withoutComments
    | inStream outStream |
    inStream := ReadStream on: self.
    outStream := WriteStream on: String new.
    [inStream atEnd] whileFalse: [
        "Copy all characters up to the first double-quote:"
        outStream nextPutAll: (inStream upTo: $").
        "Skip all until (and including) the next double-quote:"
        inStream skipTo: $"].
    ^outStream contents
```

Iterating over Composites

So far, we've shown operations and methods for traversing flat collections. But of course we may need to iterate over more complex, hierarchical structures such as Composite (137) trees. Let's look at traversing a pure tree structure with a single root node. This structure's root node has zero or more child nodes; each of these children is recursively defined in the same manner. So we have a structure that looks something like this:

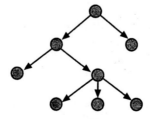

Let's define a class named `Tree`. Each element in the above structure is an instance of this class. The leaves in the structure are `Tree`s with 0 children:

```
Object subclass: #Tree
    instanceVariableNames: 'children name'
    classVariableNames: ''
    poolDictionaries: ''

Tree class>>named: aSymbol
    "Instance creation method."
    ^self new
        name: aSymbol;
        children: OrderedCollection new

Tree>>addChild: aTree
    children add: aTree
```

Assume accessor methods for `children` and `name`. Now, to permit iteration over a `Tree` structure in a generic fashion, passing a block as in `do:`, we can define the following method. This code implements a depth-first traversal of the tree:

```
Tree>>recursiveDo: aBlock
    self children do: [:aTree | aTree recursiveDo: aBlock].
    aBlock value: self
```

Traversing a `Tree` is initiated by sending `recursiveDo:` to the `Tree`'s root node:

```
| top middle bottom |
top := Tree named: #Top.
middle := Tree named: #Middle.
bottom := Tree named: #Bottom.
bottom  addChild: (Tree named: #D);        "a leaf"
        addChild: (Tree named: #C).
middle  addChild: bottom;
        addChild: (Tree named: #B).
top addChild: middle;
    addChild: (Tree named: #A).
top recursiveDo: [:aTree |
    Transcript cr; show: aTree name asString].
```

Running this code results in the following output in the Transcript:

```
D
C
Bottom
B
Middle
A
Top
```

A History List

For the Command (245) pattern, we need a special-case traversal object that allows us to access list entries by moving forward or backward as necessary and lets us add new entries at any time. Our list is ordered temporally and contains Command objects that represent the actions and operations performed by the user. Having such a history list will allow us to implement the multilevel undo-redo facility discussed in the Command pattern. When the user chooses to undo an operation, we will retrieve the latest Command and tell it to unexecute. If another undo is then requested by the user, we'll retrieve the previous Command, and so on. If the user decides to redo operations that were undone, we will travel in a forward direction. For each redo, we'll retrieve the next Command object in the list, relative to the current position indicator, and ask it to execute.

Our first, very easy, decision is to represent the list itself by an OrderedCollection. Next, we need a special kind of Iterator to effect the behavior described above. We'll start by defining HistoryStream as a subclass of ReadWrite-Stream in the VisualWorks image. (As of this writing, ReadWriteStream in Visual Smalltalk and IBM Smalltalk displays behavior inconsistent with the VisualWorks implementation. In VisualWorks, we can add new entries to the stream's collection by sending messages to the stream, whereas in the other environments, attempting to do so results in an error; we are thus forced to break encapsulation and add entries to the stream's collection using messages sent directly to the collection. Thus, in VisualWorks the following works fine:

```
| myColl myStream |
myColl := OrderedCollection new: 10.
myStream := ReadWriteStream on: myColl.
myStream nextPut: 1
```

In the other Smalltalk dialects, this code causes a walkback due to attempting to index beyond the size of myColl (a Collection's size depends on the number of objects contained therein, not on the number of entries requested with new:). The VisualWorks implementation takes care of extending the size of the collection if and when necessary. As a result, we've chosen to offer the sample code for HistoryStream as a VisualWorks implementation.)

A HistoryStream—like all other Streams—will maintain a current position indicator; however, in the case of HistoryStream, it will always point to the next available slot, that is, the position at which a new Command will be inserted into the list. As a user interacts with the application, we add new Commands to the history list at the current position. If we travel back in time by undoing several operations, the next user action must be inserted in the list *at that point in time*, not at the list's end.

Let's consider a user interaction scenario. At the same time, we'll graphically portray the associated behavior of the history list. This will reify our understanding of the implementation requirements. In the following diagrams, circles represent Command objects in the list, the arrow indicates where the history list's position marker is pointing, and the number indicates the current value of the position marker.

Beginning our scenario, the user performs a single operation. After the application processes the user request, it adds the appropriate Command to the history list. Since the indexing scheme inherited from Stream is 0-relative, after adding a single Command, the position pointer has been incremented to 1.

Next, the user performs a second action; the history list now looks like this:

The user now selects the *Undo* menu item. We need to retrieve the previous Command from the history list, so we decrement the position pointer and return the corresponding collection entry (the second one, corresponding to index 1). We leave the position marker at that point. So, after the first undo:

A second undo request occurs: the history list returns the first entry. After the second undo:

The user now requests *Redo*, meaning, "redo the most recent undo." Thus, we need to return the first Command in the list—so the application can send it the execute message—and increment the position pointer. After the redo:

In all cases, the position pointer indicates where a *new* entry should be inserted. Suppose, for example, our user now performs a new operation. We want the new Command object to be inserted in the history list after the first entry. That is, we want to eliminate the second Command; it is no longer a part of the user's interaction history because it was undone (and not redone). History gets "rewritten" so that the next Command available for undo is the one representing the user's latest action. So, after inserting the new Command, the history list looks like this:

Here is the code. Notice that we can implement all of the above behavior by defining just a small set of methods and reusing existing functionality in the Stream library. HistoryStream inherits the position, readLimit, and collection instance variables from ReadWriteStream:

```
ReadWriteStream subclass: #HistoryStream
    instanceVariableNames: ''
    classVariableNames: ''
    poolDictionaries: ''
    category: 'Undo-Redo'
```

We implement HistoryStream such that its client knows nothing about the actual Collection encapsulated within the history list; all client interaction will be with the HistoryStream object:

```
HistoryStream class>>new
    ^self on: OrderedCollection new
```

Adding new Commands to the list is accomplished by sending the standard WriteStream message, nextPut:. It returns the added Command so it is consistent with all other nextPut: implementors:

```
HistoryStream>>nextPut: aCommand
    "Add aCommand at current 'point in time' and eliminate
     any entries after it."
    super nextPut: aCommand.
    self truncate.
    ^aCommand

HistoryStream>>truncate
    | prevReadLimit |
    prevReadLimit := readLimit.
    "Logically remove entries after the current position:"
    readLimit := position.
    "Physically remove them too so they can be garbage-
     collected:"
    prevReadLimit > readLimit
        ifTrue:
            [readLimit to: prevReadLimit do:
                [:indx | collection at: indx + 1 put: nil] ].
                "add 1 to indx because Streams are 0-relative
                 and Collections are 1-relative."
```

When we want to undo an operation, we retrieve the Command prior to the current point in time in the history list:

```
HistoryStream>>previous
    "Return the Command prior to the current position.
     Return nil if we're already at the start."
    self position = 0 ifTrue: [^nil].
    self position: self position - 1.
    ^self peek
```

We let `HistoryStream` inherit `next` from `ReadWriteStream`. We send `next` to a `HistoryStream` when we need the Command beyond the current position for redo. That assumes there *is* a Command logically after the current point in time; `next` will not return any entries beyond the logical boundary maintained in `readLimit` (it increments `position` and returns `nil` if `position` then points beyond `readLimit`). This is why `truncate` as defined above works.

For details on how to use a `HistoryStream` for an undo-redo facility, refer to the Command (245) pattern.

Implementation

The following issues—and nonissues—apply when using Iterators in Smalltalk.

1. *Iterating over mixed aggregations.* Unlike Iterators in a strongly typed language like C++, Smalltalk Iterators don't care about the precise classes of objects in the collections they traverse. In C++, a list is declared to contain objects of a certain type, meaning objects of a specific class or its subclasses only. In Smalltalk, this is a nonissue. A Collection may contain any sort of object. The only thing we care about when iterating over a Collection and sending messages to each of its elements is that each element understand those messages, and, of course, any class may polymorphically implement the identical message interface.

2. *Different Iterators for different collection types?* The C++ version of Iterator as in *Design Patterns* defines an abstract Iterator class and concrete Iterator subclasses for each type of aggregate we wish to traverse. Thus, we have the `ListIterator` class for `Lists`, `SkipListIterator` for `SkipLists`, and so on (DP 258). We have no such requirement in Smalltalk because (1) for internal Iterators, all `Collection` subclasses implement the same iteration protocol, and (2) external Iterators—`Streams`—implement the same iteration protocol as well.

3. *Internal versus External Iterators.* When do we choose to use an External Iterator instead of an Internal Iterator? An important reason to use an External Iterator is that it can easily be shared among methods or passed around among objects. External Iterators provide clients with finer control over the iteration and the ability to invoke steps of the iteration from multiple code locations as needed rather than one-shot internal iteration messages sent

from a single location in a single client method. A further reason in Small-talk is that the external Iterator `Stream` classes provide a number of string manipulation methods.

Let's look at a concrete example. Suppose we wish to parse a string, say a record from a file. Let's say the string contains various fields about an employee, and we wish to validate the information in each field. The first field is the employee name, the second is the department number, and so on, and each field is delimited by a semicolon. We might implement this as follows:

```
EmployeeRecordValidator>>validateRecord: aString
"The record has already been read and is in aString.
 Validate each field."
   | stream |
    stream := ReadStream on: aString.
    self
       validateEmployeeName: stream;
       validateDepartmentNumber: stream;
       . . .

EmployeeRecordValidator>>validateEmployeeName: aStream
    | name |
    name := aStream upTo: $;.
    "Perform the validation now:"
    . . .

EmployeeRecordValidator>>validateDepartmentNumber: aStream
    "The stream is already positioned to point at the
    department number; get it from the stream and
    validate it."
    | dept |
    dept := aStream upTo: $;.
    "Perform the validation now:"
    . . .
```

We could have maintained our own explicit index into the string, performed our own string traversal to extract fields ending with a semicolon, and passed around two arguments to each method, the string and its index. However, a `Stream` composes these two arguments—a collection and a current position pointer—in a single object, making them simpler to share.

4. *Procedural abstractions.* In addition to straightforward iteration methods, the internal and external Iterators in the Smalltalk base libraries provide several procedural (method-level) abstractions for other common iteration scenarios. For example, when we want to calculate a sum based on each subelement in a collection, we can send the `inject:into:` message rather than doing all the work ourselves within a `do:` iteration (see the Sample Code section); when we want to create a new collection containing the results of performing an operation on each element, we can use the `collect:` message; when we want to traverse a string until a specific character is encountered, we can

use the `Stream>>upTo:` message. When we use these abstract methods, the overall amount of code that gets executed is not any less, but we as programmers have fewer details with which to bother ourselves (the entire reason for the notion of abstraction).

5. *Filtering Iterators.* The Iterators in the Smalltalk libraries offer several abstractions for filtering the elements of a collection. When we wish to perform an operation on a logical subset of a collection, for example, we can choose those elements by sending the `select:` or `reject:` messages.

Sample Code

We've already seen a lot of Iterator code. But for readers who want a quick glance at the basics, we provide brief and simple examples here.

In a business financial analysis application, one of the tasks might be to calculate how much the company is spending on employee salaries. Supposing the application already has in hand a collection of `employee` objects, we can perform this calculation by iterating over this collection in a number of ways.

First, traverse the collection using its own internal iteration facilities:

```
FinancialAnalyst>>calculateTotalSalaries: employees
   "Sum the salaries of all employees."
   | total |
   total := 0.
   employees do: [:anEmployee |
      total := total + anEmployee salary].
   ^total
```

Since summing-while-iterating operations of this sort are so commonly required, the Smalltalk `Collection` classes provide a procedural abstraction for just this purpose:

```
FinancialAnalyst>>calculateTotalSalaries: employees
   ^employees
      inject: 0
      into: [:total :anEmployee |
               total + anEmployee salary].
```

We can also perform the same task with an external Iterator, a `ReadStream`:

```
FinancialAnalyst>>calculateTotalSalaries: employees
   | stream total |
   stream := ReadStream on: employees.
   total := 0.
   [stream atEnd] whileFalse:
      [| anEmployee |
       anEmployee := stream next.
       total := total + anEmployee salary].
   ^total
```

Streams also support the do: method for one-shot traversal:

```
FinancialAnalyst>>calculateTotalSalaries: employees
   | stream total |
   stream := ReadStream on: employees.
   total := 0.
   stream do: [:anEmployee |
      total := total + anEmployee salary].
   ^total
```

Known Smalltalk Uses

Iterator is one of those patterns that has probably been used in every application ever written in Smalltalk. We'll leave the list up to you!

Related Patterns

The History List variation on Iterator is used in conjunction with the Command (245) pattern. A History List can store Command objects representing user-initiated operations in an interactive application, and the History List allows for multilevel undo and redo.

Iterating over a tree structure implicitly involves the Composite (137) pattern to represent the tree and its component objects.

MEDIATOR (DP 273)   Object Behavioral

Intent

Define an object that encapsulates how a set of objects interact. Mediator promotes loose coupling by keeping objects from referring to each other explicitly, and it lets you vary their interaction independently.

Structure

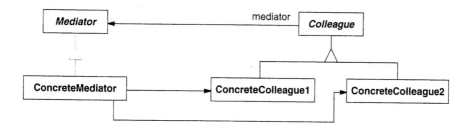

Discussion

Object technology helps designers manage complexity better than traditional design methods. Good object-oriented design increases cohesion within objects and decreases coupling between them. It composes a system of collaborating objects, each with distinct responsibilities, whose configuration dictates how they will work together. The problem is: Where's the behavior? It's not in one object or another; it's between the objects. This is very flexible when each object has a few interactions with a couple of collaborators, but it can lead to designs where the objects are so highly dependent on each other that changes in any one can affect all of the others. When this happens, each object manages itself well, but managing these complex connections becomes a problem. Mediator can solve this problem.

The key to the Mediator pattern is a set of objects that need to collaborate but shouldn't know about each other directly, so instead they all collaborate with a central object that keeps them coordinated. This coordinating object is called a **Mediator.** The objects the Mediator is coordinating are called its **Colleagues.** Events in one Colleague potentially affect many others, but for all of them to collaborate together directly would become exponentially complex. Their design would become dependent on each other such that removing any one of them would require redesigning the others. Instead, all of the Colleagues collaborate with the Mediator, which in turn collaborates with the Colleagues. If one Colleague is removed from the design, the Mediator is redesigned accordingly, and the other Colleagues remain unchanged.

Many problem domains involve complex connections between the various objects of the system. Handling these complex interactions is difficult. For example, let's consider a semiconductor manufacturing system.

Semiconductor Manufacturing

On a factory floor, many different machines work on semiconductor wafers in various stages of production. The machines are connected in an assembly line so that wafers pass from one stage of production to the next. Semiconductor manufacturing is a complex process. Some of the steps in the process must occur within very fine time tolerances. If these tolerances are not met, thousands of dollars worth of materials are lost.

What happens when something goes wrong at a machine? A photolithography machine's alignment sensors can drift out of spec, or a doping station might run out of chemicals, or a baking station's ovens could fall below the minimum acceptable temperature. If this happens, the other machines in the line must adjust their operations, perhaps even shutting themselves down completely, but in an orderly fashion.

One potential solution is to interconnect all of the machines in the assembly line together, as shown in the following diagram. That way, if one raises an alarm, it will notify all of the rest.

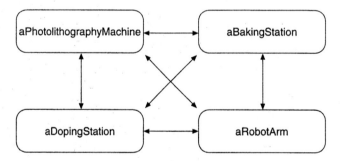

However, this approach presents a few problems:

- Some of the machines are not affected by certain alarms, yet precious time is spent notifying every machine about every alarm. Worse, the machines that need to respond first may not be notified in time.

- Knowledge of how the machines connect is spread and duplicated throughout the system. If a new machine is added or the manufacturing process changes, then code spread throughout the system must be changed.

Another solution is to introduce a new object, an Alarm Supervisor, as shown below. This object's responsibility is to listen for and respond to alarms. It notifies only those machines that are affected, and does so in the optimal order. This way, each machine can concentrate on performing its own tasks independent of the others. It need only inform the Alarm Sensor, and only when one of its alarms goes off.

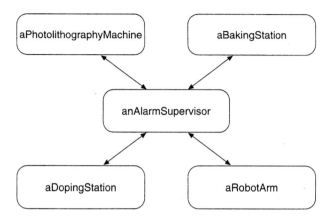

The heart of the Mediator pattern is this approach of taking a number of complex relationships between objects and reifying them into another, distinct object. Mediator avoids the problems of complex interconnection by encapsulating the connection behavior into a separate Mediator object. It is responsible for coordinating the interactions of the objects in the group. Each object in that group, a Colleague, knows only about the Mediator, not about the other members in the group. The Colleagues send requests to the Mediator, who notifies the other Colleagues as necessary.

A Warning About Mediator

Mediator is often abused. Misapplication of the pattern "can make the mediator itself a monolith that's hard to maintain" (DP 277). Novice object-oriented designers often take the Intent of the mediator too literally, trying to encapsulate every set of object interactions. They use the pattern to justify a poor factoring of responsibilities.

Many novice designers create designs containing a large number of "data holders"—objects that have little behavior other than getter and setter methods. They then find that these objects are too simple to perform the system's work. To remedy this, the designer creates a set of Manager objects that contain all of the functionality of the system and operate on the "data holders." To call such objects "mediators" is a misuse of the term.

The purpose of a Mediator is to manage the relationships among numerous objects so that each can focus on its own behavior independent of the others. A Manager object, on the other hand, tends to extract state out of one object, manipulate it, and plug the result into another object. The objects do not encapsulate their own behavior; the Manager does that for them and makes them passive. You should strive to make your objects responsible for their own behavior and to coordinate with each other as necessary. Then you will not need a Manager object. If the objects' coordination becomes overly complex, introduce a Mediator to manage their coordination but not to manage their fundamental behavior.

Sample Code

A layered architecture is a common architectural choice in many applications. Understanding the roles of different objects in an application and the way control and information flow between them is crucial to having a high-level understanding of a complex application. Brown (1996) describes a layered architecture for Smalltalk applications that consists of four layers. The layers are (in order from the top) the View layer, the Application Model layer, the Domain layer, and the Infrastructure layer. Buschmann et al. (1996) describe a similar architecture for IS systems that parallels this division. To understand why this division of roles is necessary, we have to examine the evolution of the Model-View-Controller (MVC) application framework.

Application Model and Domain Model

In the original MVC framework, Models have two roles: (1) representing a domain object and storing its state and (2) supporting the View's display of that state. The early examples of MVC (Krasner & Pope, 1988) showed their Model objects opening Views on themselves and coordinating their display, as well as handling domain-specific behavior. Over time, developers began to realize that this was a lot of responsibility for one object. As Models evolved to support several different types of Views, they became increasingly complex and difficult to implement and maintain. As a result, the MVC framework evolved to factor the Model into two parts, the Domain Model and the Application Model (Woolf, 1995a).

The separate Domain and Application Models simplify the Model concept. Each domain model (also called a domain object) represents an object in the domain. These are the business objects, the classes in the object model. They know nothing about the user interface or how it will display them, if at all. They work just fine even if there is no user interface.

The application model provides the user interface support. The View still does the display, but the application model provides the support it needs. An application model does not contain much state. Instead, it derives its state from one or more domain models. As Brown (1996) demonstrates, the Application Model fulfills two roles. First, it acts as an Adapter to convert the domain's interface into the interface that the View expects. In the process, the application model provides resources that are not part of the domain, such as menus. Second, it acts as a Mediator to coordinate the widgets in the View.

As an example, look at the user interface example diagram in the Motivation for Observer (DP 293). It shows a set of data and three different views of those data: a spreadsheet, a bar chart, and a pie chart. In this enhanced MVC framework, the objects would be a domain object that contains the data, three application models to display the data, and one window for each of the application models:

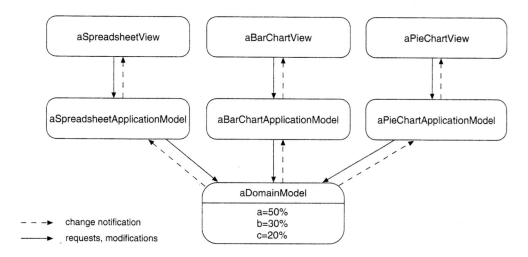

Notice that the diagram shows that each different View would have its own specific Application Model. In actuality, each Window in a user interface would have an underlying application model that coordinated multiple views. This coordination of Views is what makes the Mediator pattern so crucial to understanding the Smalltalk window system architectures.

Design Patterns mentions that Visual Smalltalk uses the Mediator pattern in its application architecture (DP 281). In fact, all three major dialects of Smalltalk use it in nearly the same way. Let's look at how their implementations differ by examining a common example in all three dialects.

Our example is a simple Login dialog, shown in the figure below, used to obtain a user name and password for a mainframe or relational database (Hendley & Smith, 1992). There are three types of collaborations between user interface (UI) widgets in an application model:

1. Simple actions that affect only one UI widget and not the domain model.

2. Complex actions that affect multiple UI widgets.

3. Simple actions that affect both the UI and domain model.

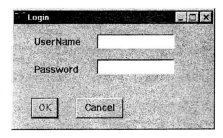

The three major dialects handle these collaborations differently, as this example will show. In our example, we will look at three different interactions that occur within the dialog:

1. The Password Field is disabled until the user begins typing in the User Name field.

2. The OK button is disabled until the user has entered something into both the User Name and Password fields.

3. The OK button causes the domain model to verify the user name and password. If the pair is valid, the window closes. Otherwise, the window displays a message indicating that the user name/password pair entered is not valid.

Mediator in Visual Smalltalk

Design Patterns describes the Visual Smalltalk application architecture in detail (DP 281). It discusses the event mechanism used to communicate between the panes in a window and their Mediator, a `ViewManager`. Our Observer (305) discussion documents this mechanism as the SASE variation of the Observer Pattern.

`ViewManager` is part of the older Smalltalk/V application architecture and is maintained for backward compatibility. Applications may now alternatively use a new Mediator class, `ApplicationCoordinator`. The differences between `ApplicationCoordinator` and `ViewManager` are minor and not relevant to this discussion. For more information, see the *Visual Smalltalk User's Guide*.

The most interesting interaction in the example is the requirement that the OK button be disabled until the user has entered something into both the User Name and Password fields. To accomplish this, we have to check that there is something in both fields before we enable the button. The easiest way to do this is to connect the #textChanged event on both entry fields to a method in the `ViewManager` that looks at the contents of both before enabling the button. To see how this is accomplished, look at the following code snippet from the method in `LoginViewManager` that sets up the panes:

```
LoginViewManager>>someMethodName
    . . .
    userNameEF "an EntryField"
       owner: aModel;
       setName: 'userNameEF';
       when: #textChanged: send: #tryToEnableOK to: self.
    passwordEF "an EntryField"
       owner: aModel;
       setName: 'passwordEF';
       when: #textChanged: send: #tryToEnableOK to: self.
    . . .
```

As described in Observer, the message when: anEvent send: aSelector to: aReceiver creates a Message object. When anEvent occurs in the pane, the message whose selector is aSelector is sent to aReceiver. In this case, the event is each field's text changing, the message is tryToEnableOK, and the receiver is the LoginViewManager.

This code shows how tryToEnableOK works:

```
LoginViewManager>>tryToEnableOK
    | test1 test2 |
    test1 := (self paneNamed: 'userNameEF') contents isEmpty.
    test2 := (self paneNamed: 'passwordEF') contents isEmpty.
     (test1 or: [test2])
        ifFalse: [(self paneNamed: 'okPB') enable].
```

In this case, the Mediator pattern is critical. The ViewManager does not need to handle all of the user interface actions in the Visual Smalltalk framework. The receiver of the SASE can just as easily be another pane. In fact, it is sometimes easier to set up such connections in very simple cases. For example, if enabling the OK button depended on just the user name field, we could have set up the field's text changed event to *directly* enable the OK button:

```
userNameEF "an EntryField"
    owner: aModel;
    setName: 'userNameEF';
    when: #textChanged: send: #enable to: okPushButton
```

However, when an interaction requires that two or more panes be involved, sending messages to the ViewManager is the cleanest solution. This is the Mediator pattern. When we look at the implementation of the Mediator pattern in IBM Smalltalk and VisualAge for Smalltalk, this becomes even more apparent.

Mediator in IBM Smalltalk and VisualAge for Smalltalk

Unlike the other Smalltalk dialects, IBM Smalltalk does not supply an abstract application model class that serves as a Mediator. IBM Smalltalk's windowing system is based on OSF Motif, and Motif does not use Mediator. Instead, to implement a Mediator, you subclass it directly off Object. This is a valid implementation choice documented in *Design Patterns* (DP 278).

VisualAge for Smalltalk, a visual programming environment built on top of IBM Smalltalk, adds an abstract application model class, AbtAppBuilderView. Windows built in VisualAge are subclassed from that class. However, VisualAge application models do not really incorporate the Mediator pattern directly. Instead, VisualAge encourages direct connections between UI widgets.

As an example, let's look at a diagram of the Login window as implemented in VisualAge. Below is an example of the VisualAge Composition Editor. It has four types of connections that can be made between objects ("parts") on the screen:

- *Attribute-to-Attribute*—These connections link data items directly.

- *Event-to-Action*—These connections link events to actions (predefined methods) of some object.

- *Event-to-Script*—The occurrence of an event triggers the running of a script (a user-defined method).

- *Attribute-to-Script*—A script executes to calculate a value for the attribute; this is a form of lazy initialization.

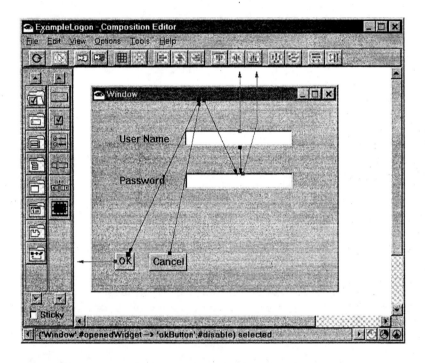

IBM Smalltalk and VisualAge for Smalltalk use the same sort of event mechanism as Visual Smalltalk. Events trigger corresponding methods that react to the event. This is the SASE variation of Observer (305). All four types of connections in VisualAge use SASE (through callbacks) to send a `DirectedMessage` from one part to another when an event occurs.

Attribute-to-Attribute and Event-to-Action connections link two parts together directly. In terms of the Mediator pattern, this is communication between Colleagues. The other two types of connections, Event-to-Script and Attribute-to-Script, are links between the parts and the Mediator (or "visual part") that the user is building. An Event-to-Script connection is an instance of a Colleague informing the Mediator of an event. Each Attribute-to-Script connection (which should actually be called Script-to-Attribute) is an instance of the Mediator communicating with a Colleague, presumably in response to an event.

Therefore, an Event-to-Script connection is the true example of Mediator. Although another form of connection may be visually cleaner and simpler to use, it will not be as easily extendable.

For example, to implement the login example in VisualAge, we create two Event-to-Script connections. They go from each entry field to the script named `tryToEnableOK`. This is the code for that script:

```
LoginDialog>>tryToEnableOK
    | test1 test2 |
    test1 := (self subpartNamed: 'userName') string isEmpty.
    test2 := (self subpartNamed: 'password') string isEmpty.
    (test1 or: [test2])
       ifFalse: [(self subpartNamed: 'okButton') enable]
```

As you can see, the VisualAge implementation is very similar to the Visual Smalltalk implementation.

Mediator in VisualWorks

VisualWorks uses a `ValueModel` as an intermediate object that reduces the total overhead of change notifications to dependents. The `ValueModel` sits between a View and an application model and encapsulates an aspect in the application model. The View is an Observer of the `ValueModel`. The application model may also observe the `ValueModel` using a `DependencyTransformer`. This additional layer of objects decouples the Views from the domain models even further.

The next figure shows the connections between the objects in our example as implemented in VisualWorks. The Button has been left out for simplicity, but it is also connected to the `LoginAppModel` through a `ValueModel`, a `Pluggable-Adaptor`.

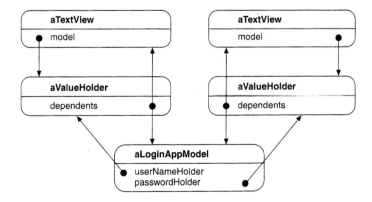

This code shows the class definition for the example in VisualWorks. The Visual-Works UI Builder automatically adds the instance variables `userNameHolder`

and `passwordHolder`. The UI Builder automatically adds lazy initialization code to set these instance variables to hold a `ValueHolder` on an empty `String`:

```
SimpleDialog subclass: #LoginAppModel
    instanceVariableNames: 'userNameHolder passwordHolder'
    classVariableNames: ''
    poolDictionaries: ''
```

The connections between the two `ValueHolders` and `LoginAppModel` are made in `initialize`, as shown below. This method is automatically called when the `LoginAppModel` is created. The method `onChangeSend:to:` will create a `DependencyTransformer` that will send the message specified by the `onChangeSend:` parameter whenever the value of that `ValueHolder` changes:

```
LoginAppModel>>initialize
    super initialize.
    self userNameHolder onChangeSend: #tryToEnableOK to: self.
    self passwordHolder onChangeSend: #tryToEnableOK to: self
```

Now that the `ValueHolders` are set up, the message `tryToEnableOK` is run whenever the value of either `ValueHolder` changes. The method is shown below. As you can see, its implementation is similar to the two previous ones:

```
LoginAppModel>>tryToEnableButton
    | button test1 test2 |
    button := self builder componentAt: #okButton.
    button isNil ifTrue: [^self].
    test1 := self userNameHolder value isEmpty.
    test2 := self passwordHolder value isEmpty.
    (test1 or: [test2]) ifFalse: [button enable]
```

Known Smalltalk Uses

Although Mediator is commonly seen in Smalltalk designs in the application frameworks described earlier, its use is by no means restricted to user interface programming. Brown et al. (1994) describe a class named `HostTransaction` in the design of a framework for mainframe communications. `HostTransaction` acts as a mediator between `HostScreen` objects, which represent individual mainframe terminal screens in a transaction. The `HostTransaction` coordinates the navigation between the `HostScreen` objects and controls the flow of information between them.

The semiconductor manufacturing example discussed in the first section is drawn from a prototype system developed by Knowledge Systems Corporation for a semiconductor equipment manufacturing company. It is similar to code used in the WORKS system developed by Texas Instruments for semiconductor fabrication facility automation.

MEMENTO (DP 283)   Object Behavioral

Intent

Without violating encapsulation, capture and externalize an object's internal state so that the object can be restored to this state later.

Structure

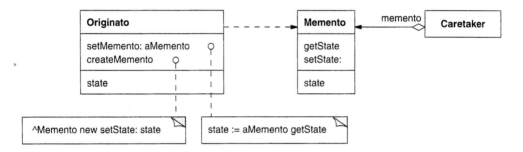

Discussion

A fundamental concept in computer science, and especially business applications, is the idea of a **transaction.** A transaction is an operation or series of operations on a computational entity (an object, a file, a database) that is to be considered a single reversible modification to the entity. A transaction has the property that either all of its operations succeed, and the entity's state is updated, or if any of them fails, the results of all the other operations are discarded and the entity's state remains the same as before the transaction began. Transactions are such a basic concept that they are assumed to be part of the landscape of any database system. However, the Memento pattern is about transactions against objects, even though there may be an associated, secondary transaction to a database. A problem arises when a transaction involves several updates to an object. If something fails after one or more updates have been performed, how do we roll back the object to its previous state?

Similarly, in interactive applications, users often wish to undo actions or operations they have performed at the user interface. Once the user sees the results of her actions or has time to reflect on an operation she has just performed, she may wish to reverse that operation and have the object(s) of interest revert to a previous state. This means being able to reverse a transaction even though it had not failed.

Therefore, we need a way to roll back or restore the state of an object. This desire to be able to restore an object to a previous state is the motivation for the

Memento pattern. This desire is complicated by another fundamental object-oriented concept, encapsulation. In object-oriented systems, allowing one object to meddle directly with the internal state of another object is a poor design choice. So we are caught on the horns of a dilemma: how do we preserve encapsulation, yet allow an object's internal state to be saved and restored later when a rollback is needed? The Memento pattern provides a solution to this problem by defining three roles.

1. The **Originator** is the object whose state is to be saved and possibly restored.

2. The **Memento** is another object that "remembers" the previous state of the Originator.

3. The **Caretaker** is an object that keeps track of the Memento for the Originator. It tells the Originator when to create a Memento and informs the Originator when it should restore its state from the Memento.

Implementation

There are a few issues to consider when implementing Memento that are specific to Smalltalk:

1. *Encapsulation boundaries. Design Patterns* states that Memento has the positive consequence of preserving encapsulation boundaries (DP 286). It also mentions that "it may be difficult in some languages to ensure that only the originator can access the memento's state." Smalltalk is one of these languages, and it can be challenging to achieve the desired result of hiding implementation details. In C++, we have the option of defining different interfaces for different external objects; we can define a wide interface for *friends* of a class and a narrow interface for all others, for example. We have no such language-based capability in Smalltalk. The preservation of the two interfaces must be left up to the discipline of the programmer.

   In the *Design Patterns* version of the pattern, the Memento object presents two interfaces to the outside world. The Originator is allowed access to the methods necessary to save and restore its state (a "wide" interface). These methods are named `setState` and `getState`, respectively. No other object in the system should be allowed access to these methods. The Caretaker, according to *Design Patterns*, sees a "narrow" interface, but it's really not an interface at all. The Caretaker merely holds onto the Memento for the Originator; it obtains the Memento by telling the Originator to create it and passes it back to the Originator when the rollback is required. So, its "interface" is really just being able to pass around the Memento to other objects.

2. *State access. Design Patterns* is somewhat vague about how to implement the messages `Memento>>getState` and `Memento>>setState`. For example, it shows no sample code for either of these methods. Nevertheless, we would like to present at least one example of how these methods might

work in Smalltalk. In Smalltalk, we would need at least the Memento to implement getter and setter methods for its internal values.

The Memento's `setState` message (DP 285) is apparently a misnomer because it takes no parameter. For the Originator to save state in the Memento, it must pass some information in the form of message arguments. For example, one way to set things up would be to pass the Originator itself as a parameter and let the Memento obtain the information it needs via messages to the Originator object. In this case, the method signature would be `setState:`, as follows:

```
Originator>>createMemento
   "Create a snapshot of my current state."
   | memento |
   memento := Memento new.
   memento setState: self.
   ^memento

Memento>>setState: anOriginator
   "Get state from anOriginator."
   self
      stateVariable1: anOriginator stateVariable1;
      stateVariable2: anOriginator stateVariable2;
      stateVariable3: anOriginator stateVariable3
```

This approach, however, breaks encapsulation in the application-specific Originator object; we have to implement methods (such as `state-Variable1`) that provide access to the Originator's state. We'd rather have the less "well-known" Memento present this sort of interface than an object that participates in the application per se (the Memento is known only to the Originator and the Caretaker). Then only the Memento need implement accessor messages, not the Originator (at least not for purposes of the Memento pattern implementation). Here, `Memento` would implement the `stateVariableN:` setter messages:

```
Originator>>createMemento
   "Create a snapshot of my current state."
   | memento |
   memento := Memento new.
   memento
      stateVariable1: stateVariable1;
      stateVariable2: stateVariable2;
      stateVariable3: stateVariable3.
   ^memento
```

We would have similar concerns for implementing `Memento>>getState`.

3. *Combination Originator and Memento.* An implementation choice that can simplify the application of this pattern in Smalltalk relies on removing the distinction between the Originator and Memento classes. There's no specific

requirement that the Originator and Memento be instances of distinct classes; in fact, it often makes sense to have the Originator and Memento be roles played by different instances of the same class. That is, while the Originator and Memento will be different objects, these objects may be members of the same class.

Smalltalk makes this solution easy by providing the `copy` method, which is implemented in `Object` and returns a "shallow copy" of the receiver. In many cases, a shallow copy of the Originator is all that is needed as a Memento. If more than a shallow copy is needed to represent and safely store the state of the Originator, a deep copy may be required. (If changes are made to the Originator's instance variables as the result of messages sent to them after the Memento is saved off, then these messages will modify a shallow-copied Memento as well! We want the Memento to snapshot the state of the Originator at a specific point in time; if changes to the Originator also change the Memento, we cannot roll the Originator back to its previous state. See further discussion on `copy` versus `deepCopy` in the Prototype (77) pattern.)

Note this, however, relating this solution to point 2: the Memento object must implement getter access methods to enable the Originator to retrieve the individual portions of its state (see `setMemento:` in the sample code below) *and* the Memento and Originator objects are instances of the same class; we thus wind up exposing the internal instance variables of the Originator (read, domain or application) object. However, we are making only getter messages available to external objects; we do not make any setter messages public (thus, in this implementation, outsiders still may not set internal variables).

4. *Complex object nets.* A pernicious problem with applying the Memento pattern to complex object networks is that of reconstructing them exactly as they are at a specific point in time. If multiple objects have dependencies on each other, they may all need to be saved at once. This can be complicated, especially in light of the `copy` versus `deepCopy` issues discussed in the previous point. In some cases you may only want to record the fact that an object has a reference to a particular object but not the actual object that is referenced. This will prevent new information from being overwritten with an older copy when an associated Memento is restored. In cases like this, the Proxy pattern can provide a solution: the Memento will hold a proxy to an object, and not the actual object itself, so that dependencies can be resolved later when the Memento is restored.

Sample Code

Let's look at a simple example that has the Memento and Originator represented by the same class. In the example, the object that we will want to restore to its original value is an instance of `Client`, representing a client of an insurance company as in Chapter 2:

```
Object subclass: #Client
   instanceVariableNames: 'name address phone'
   classVariableNames: ''
   poolDictionaries: ''
```

The class must implement only a little additional protocol to support the Memento pattern. That protocol is the external protocol of Originator, the methods createMemento and setMemento: (as shown on DP 286):

```
Client>>createMemento
   "Save my current state in a memento (copy) of me."
   ^self copy

Client>>setMemento: aMemento
   "Set my state to the state saved in aMemento."
   name := aMemento name.
   address := aMemento address.
   phone := aMemento phone.
```

The Caretaker sends these two messages, respectively, to create a Memento and restore the state of an object from the Memento. (By the way, the message name setMemento: may be confusing; perhaps a better name would be restore-FromMemento:.) Note that having the Memento merely be a copy of the Originator also eliminates the need for the setState message sent by the Originator to its Memento in the *Design Patterns* version of the pattern.

For this example, we will make the Caretaker be an application model that represents a Client editor. The newSelection method in the application model is invoked whenever the user selects a new client from a list; at this time, the application model creates a new memento to save off the client's state prior to any user modifications to it. An *Undo* menu selection calls the undoChanges method to reverse user-performed edits:

```
ClientListHolder>>newSelection
   "Tell the newly selected Client (if any) to save off
   its state before the user edits it."
   self domainObject notNil ifTrue:
      [self memento: self domainObject createMemento].
   ...

ClientListHolder>>undoChanges
   (self domainObject isNil
      or: [self memento isNil]) ifFalse:
         [self domainObject setMemento: self memento].
```

That is all that is needed to restore the state of the domain object. Other code may be needed to restore the state of the user interface to show the newly changed domain object.

The structure diagram for this example looks like:

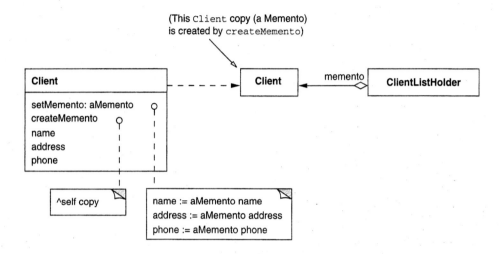

Known Smalltalk Uses

Order Management System

Brown (1996) describes a use of the Memento pattern where one class implements all three participants: Caretaker, Memento, and Originator. This may be the pattern's most degenerate case. However, it does have the distinct advantage of completely preserving encapsulation. No outside object need be aware of the existence of the Memento, and we eliminate the need for accessor messages whose only purpose is to implement the external-Memento version of the pattern.

Refactoring Browser

The Smalltalk Refactoring Browser (Roberts, Brant, & Johnson, 1997a, 1997b), a tool for refactoring Smalltalk class hierarchies, uses Memento to switch between editing buffers. Its implementation is noteworthy in that it can use several Mementos at once, with each buffer state being a different editing session.

GF/ST Graphics Framework

GF/ST, a commercial Smalltalk framework for direct-manipulation graphics developed by Polymorphic Software (now a division of ParcPlace-Digitalk), implements its undo facility with the Memento pattern. The Memento implementation maintains some of the privacy constraints that are maintained in C++. The Memento class includes an additional variable, accessKey, that determines which objects can be restored from a memento. If accessKey is nil, then the object to be restored must be the originator (they must be ==). Otherwise, accessKey contains a symbol that is a message selector. Both the originator and the object to be restored must respond to the message, and the values they return must be equal.

GF/ST's Memento implementation uses `Object>>perform:with:` to restore the state of the originator. The memento "remembers" both the state values and the message used to restore each value. It then uses `perform:with:` to invoke each restore message with its corresponding value.

This code (provided by Jasen Minton of ParcPlace-Digitalk) demonstrates how this Memento works:

```
| aMemento |
someRectangle := Rectangle origin: (0@0) extent: (25@50).
aMemento := Memento
              originator: Rectangle new
              state: someRectangle extent copy
              type: #extent:
              accessKey: #class.
```

The `Rectangle` in `someRectangle` can now be modified, mutated, or garbage collected. At any later time, however, an equivalent `Rectangle` object can be reinstated from the memento. Assuming `anotherRectangle` is a `Rectangle` (it doesn't matter what its current instance variables are set to), the following line of code will restore it to its original state:

```
aMemento restore: anotherRectangle
```

Related Patterns

Memento and Command

Sometimes the Memento pattern might not be the best solution to an undo problem. If a change to an object may have significant side effects, perhaps necessitating a `deepCopy` of its state, Memento might be more trouble than it is worth. In these cases, the Command pattern may provide a better solution. (See the discussion regarding an undo-redo list in the Command pattern (245).)

"What If?" Protocol

The "What If?" protocol (Griffin, 1993) is a sophisticated variation of Memento. To understand this variation, consider that the Memento pattern roughly assumes the following order of operations:

1. Make the Memento of the Originator.

2. Perform some operations on the Originator that may need to be backed out of.

3. Validate the state of the Originator (this may be an internal validation, or an external validation by the user).

4. If necessary, restore the state of the Originator from the Memento.

Griffin describes a slightly different approach that is particularly useful when there are complex validations of the target object or when performing the operations on the target object might make it difficult to restore later. Griffin proposes the following alternate sequence of operations:

1. Make a copy of the Originator.

2. Perform the operations on the copy.

3. Determine if the operations invalidate the internal state of the copy.

4. If so, discard the copy and raise an exception (and leave the Originator unchanged!).

5. Else, perform the operations on the Originator.

This alternate sequence has some interesting consequences. The primary benefit is that the Originator is never in an inconsistent state, and its identity and the identity of its contained objects are maintained. This is especially important when persistence mechanisms depend on the identity of related objects being maintained. Unfortunately, you perform each successful operation twice. This approach is like the Command pattern but differs in that only one operation at a time is ever performed on the target object.

OBSERVER (DP 293) Object Behavioral

Intent

Define a one-to-many dependency between objects so that when one object changes state, all its dependents are notified and updated automatically.

Structure

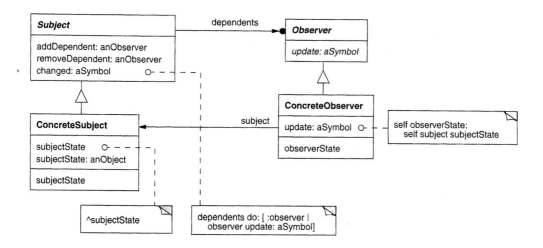

The interaction diagram on the following page illustrates the collaborations between a subject and two observers:

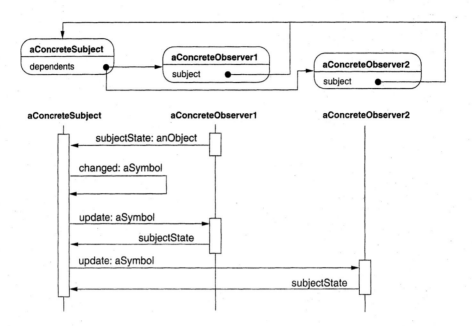

Discussion

Object-oriented techniques encourage the designer to break a problem apart into pieces—objects—that have a small set of responsibilities but can collaborate to accomplish complex tasks. This makes each object easier to implement and maintain, more reusable, and the combinations more flexible. The downside is that any simple behavior is so distributed across multiple objects that any change in one object often affects many others. All changes could be implemented to affect all relevant objects directly, but that would bind the objects together and ruin their flexibility, so objects need an easy, flexible way to tell each other about changes and events. This is the spirit of the Observer pattern.

The key to the Observer pattern is two objects, one of which holds the state that the other needs to share. We call them **Subject** and **Observer**, where a Subject holds the state and an Observer shares it. The Subject's collaboration with its Observer is very indirect so that the Observer may be optional. This way, the Subject can support multiple Observers just as easily as one or none at all. The Subject is unaware of whether it has any Observers, so it always announces changes in its state just in case. Each object that wishes to be an Observer registers its interest with the Subject so that it will receive these change announcements. While otherwise performing its duties, each Observer waits for notification from the Subject that its state has changed. We call it an Observer because of this way that it observes the Subject for state changes and keeps itself synchronized with its Subject. When it receives notification of a change, each Observer reacts in its own appropriate way, which can include ignoring irrelevant changes. Meanwhile, the Subject is unaware of what Observers it has or how various ones react to particular changes. This observation relationship allows the Subject to concentrate on its own behavior and distributes the synchronization responsibilities to the Observers.

One confusing aspect of the Observer pattern in Smalltalk is that both the Subject and Observer protocols are implemented in one class, `Object`. This means that any object can serve as a Subject, an Observer, or both. Thus, when the pattern refers to a Subject or an Observer, remember that this is a distinction of the object's role, not its class. The object is not an instance of `Subject` or `Observer`; it is just an object.

Pattern or Language Feature?

As early as Smalltalk-80, Smalltalk had three kinds of relationships between objects (Goldberg & Robson, 1983, p. 240):

1. An object's references to other objects (i.e., its instance variables).

2. A relationship of a class to its superclass and metaclass (i.e., the instance side of a class knows what its class side and superclass are).

3. The ability of an object to register itself as a *dependent* of another object.

This third type, the dependency relationship used to "coordinate activities between different objects," is the Observer pattern. It is used to communicate between layers in an architecture (Brown, 1995a). Its best-known use is in the Model-View-Controller (MVC) framework for implementing the user interface in ParcPlace Smalltalk. MVC factors the interface into two layers of objects: a Model and a View-Controller pair. A guiding principle of MVC is that a Model should be able to support any number of View-Controller pairs, including none at all. Thus, a Model does not collaborate with its View-Controllers directly. It announces changes to its *dependents*—objects that have said they want to be notified of such changes. Each View and Controller registers itself as a dependent of the Model it is displaying. Then when the Model changes, the Views and Controllers get notified. MVC in Smalltalk became the standard from which all other graphical window systems were designed.

As fundamental as Observer appears to be in Smalltalk, it is not a language feature; it is a feature of most Smalltalk libraries. Every dialect implements it differently. The proposed ANSI Smalltalk standard doesn't include Observer at all (X3J20, 1996). Furthermore, window painters and other visual programming tools automate the use of Observer so that programmers often don't use it directly anymore. Nevertheless, Observer is a significant feature in Smalltalk that Smalltalk programmers should understand.

Observer in Smalltalk-80

The Observer pattern is implemented by the change/update protocol, introduced in Smalltalk-80 and still used in VisualWorks today (Woolf, 1994). The

308   BEHAVIORAL PATTERNS

protocol also exists in similar forms in Visual Smalltalk and IBM Smalltalk, but those dialects mostly use the event protocols described later.

The change/update protocol in Smalltalk-80 is implemented in Object as a combination of the Subject and Observer classes. This enables any object to be a Subject, an Observer (which Smalltalk calls a dependent), or both. When the Subject changes, it sends itself one of the change messages. The protocol converts this to a corresponding update message that is sent to each of the Subject's dependents. This is the series of messages:

Subject	changed
Messages	changed: anAspectSymbol
(Change)	changed: anAspectSymbol with: aParameter
Dependent	update: anAspectSymbol with: aParameter from: aSender
Messages	update: anAspectSymbol with: aParameter
(Update)	update: anAspectSymbol

The change/update protocol adds a key extension to the Observer pattern. When a subject announces that it has changed, it also specifies what has changed. When announcing a change, the subject specifies the update aspect that has changed. An *update aspect* is an object, usually a Symbol, that specifies a type of change that can occur in a subject. The subject defines the update aspects for its changes, and the dependents distinguish between those changes by checking the update aspect. If the update aspect is not one that the dependent is interested in, the dependent will ignore the change announcement.

A subject announces a change by sending itself one of the change messages:

- changed—The subject sends itself changed to announce that something has changed without specifying what has changed.

- changed:—The subject sends itself changed: to announce that a specific aspect has changed. The parameter, anAspectSymbol, is typically a Symbol and specifies the update aspect of the aspect that changed.

- changed:with:—The subject sends itself changed:with: to announce not only what specific aspect changed but also some extra information about the change. The second parameter, aParameter, is that extra information and can be any Object. It is often the new value of the aspect that changed.

A dependent receives a change notification by receiving the series of update messages. By default, a dependent will ignore all updates. A subclass that wishes to listen for any change notifications must implement one or more of the update messages to do so:

- update:—The dependent implements this message if it just needs to know what update aspect changed. The parameter, anAspectSymbol, is the update aspect that the subject specified when it made the change announcement. If the subject did not specify an update aspect, the parameter will be nil.

- update:with:—The dependent implements this message if it also needs to know the extra information that the subject specified about the change. The second parameter, aParameter, is the same object as the second parameter in changed:with:.

- update:with:from:—The dependent implements this message if it also needs to know which subject announced the change. The third parameter, aSender, is the subject that sent the change announcement.

Smalltalk-80: Creating Dependencies

A subject does not notify every other object in the image of its changes. That would be inefficient. Instead, an object that wants to receive certain notification registers itself with the object or objects that provide the desired notification. This way, only objects that have said they might want to know about a change are notified. When an object wants to receive notification from another object, it registers itself as a dependent on that object using the message addDependent:, as shown below. When it no longer wishes to receive notification, it removes itself as a dependent using the message removeDependent:, also shown below:

```
aSubject addDependent: aDependent.
...
aSubject removeDependent: aDependent.
```

A subject uses a collection to keep track of its dependents. In Object, this collection is a value in the DependentsFields dictionary. Only objects that have dependents have keys in this dictionary. Model tracks dependents more efficiently with its own dependents instance variable that bypasses Dependents-Fields. Thus, an object that is going to issue change notifications frequently will be more efficient if it is a subclass of Model.

The addDependent: and removeDependent: messages are often sent from the dependent's implementors of initialize and release, respectively. A dependent can register itself as a dependent on the same subject multiple times, creating redundant dependencies. However, redundant dependencies are inefficient and difficult to break because the dependent usually does not realize it has more than one dependency on the same subject. Thus, a dependent should be careful to register itself as a dependent on a subject only once. That way, a single send of removeDependent: will break the one and only dependency between the two objects.

Often dependent objects do not seem to be garbage collected properly. Over time, this will cause the development image to become bigger and slower for no apparent reason. If these objects are no longer in use, why aren't they garbage collected? Because their dependency is still established and their Subject has not yet been garbage collected. A dependent will not be garbage collected until its Subject is. The class variable in `Object` used to track dependents for non-`Model`s (e.g., `DependentsFields` or `Dependents`) can cause similar problems even after the Subject is no longer being used. So when a dependent object will no longer be used, it should release its dependencies so that it can be garbage collected.

Observer in VisualWorks

Since Smalltalk-80 is the foundation of VisualWorks, VisualWorks includes the change/update protocol described above. When VisualWorks introduced the window painter, it also added some new features to its implementation of the Observer pattern.

VisualWorks: DependencyTransformer

With change/update, the dependency relationships between objects are often difficult to follow. A framework might contain several subjects that are issuing numerous change notifications and several dependents that are listening for numerous change notifications. The cause and effect between any one change and its corresponding response is difficult to see, especially in static code. Threads of control that are difficult to follow cannot be maintained well. Thus, change/update needs a better way to implement the relationship between a change in the subject and a corresponding reaction in a dependent.

VisualWorks clarifies this relationship with a class called `Dependency-Transformer`. A `DependencyTransformer` is an Adapter (105) for a dependent that converts the subject's generic `update:` message to a more specific message in the dependent's interface. It acts as a bridge between a change in a subject and a corresponding reaction in a dependent. It encapsulates three items together: the dependent, what aspect it's interested in, and what message to invoke when this aspect changes. This is an example of the Self-Addressed, Stamped Envelope (SASE) pattern discussed below.

Since any object can be a subject, any object can have a `DependencyTransformer`. As shown below, the message for creating a `DependencyTransformer` is `expressInterestIn:for:sendBack:` and for breaking the dependency is `retractInterestIn:for:`. The two messages use `addDependent:` and `removeDependent:` to make the `DependencyTransformer` a dependent of the subject:

```
aSubject
    expressInterestIn: anAspectSymbol
    for: aDependent
    sendBack: aSelector.
 ...
aSubject
    retractInterestIn: anAspectSymbol
    for: aDependent.
```

Like addDependent: and removeDependent:, a dependent often sends these DependencyTransformer messages from initialize and release.

The code and diagram below show how a DependencyTransformer is created, how it sits between the subject and its observer, and the message interaction when the DependencyTransformer fields an update and notifies the observer:

```
ConcreteObserver>>initialize
    ...
    aConcreteSubject
        expressInterestIn: #name
        for: self
        sendBack: #nameChanged.
    ...
```

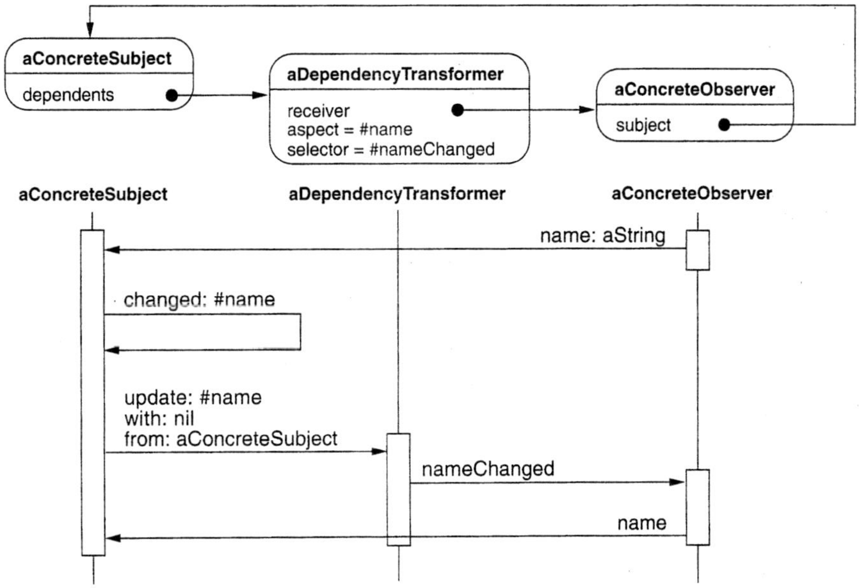

aConcreteSubject
dependents

aDependencyTransformer
receiver
aspect = #name
selector = #nameChanged

aConcreteObserver
subject

aConcreteSubject   aDependencyTransformer   aConcreteObserver

name: aString

changed: #name

update: #name
with: nil
from: aConcreteSubject

nameChanged

name

VisualWorks: ValueModel

Another shortcoming of change/update is that every dependent of a subject is notified of every change in that subject. A change is usually a change in the value of an aspect, which essentially means an instance variable's value has changed. A subject often contains more aspects than a dependent is interested in. Thus, the dependent wastes time receiving notification of changes in aspects it's not interested in. This can even lead to subtle bugs when the dependent misinterprets which aspect changed.

VisualWorks uses ValueModels to encapsulate an aspect and its value as a first-class object. Some languages call this an "active variable." Unlike a plain variable, a ValueModel is itself an object that can be inspected, sent messages, and so forth. One advantage of this encapsulation is that a dependent can register its dependency on a single aspect instead of registering with the container model and all of its aspects. In this way, a dependent can register itself with just the `ValueModels` for the aspects that it cares about.

The dependent usually does not register itself with the `ValueModel` directly. Instead, it uses a `DependencyTransformer`. It creates the dependency on the `ValueModel` using `onChangeSend:to:` and breaks it using `retractInterestsFor:`, as shown below. The two messages create a `Dependency-Transformer` on the `ValueModel` and remove it:

```
aValueModel onChangeSend: aSelector to: aDependent.
...
aValueModel retractInterestsFor: aDependent.
```

As with the other dependency messages, dependencies are usually established in `initialize` and removed in `release`.

VisualWorks: Event

The `Event` hierarchy in VisualWorks is an example of the Observer pattern where the update aspect has been encapsulated as a first-class object. A controller in VisualWorks once polled for input, repeatedly asking the virtual machine if there was any input available for it. Now controllers are event driven. The window's `InputSensor` captures the input as an `Event` that it passes to the window's `Controller`. Thus, in the Observer pattern, `InputSensor` is the Subject, `Controller` is the Observer, and `Event` specifies what change (i.e., input) has occurred.

The SASE Variation of Observer

Design Patterns lists a number of consequences of the Observer pattern (DP 296), one of them being the problem of unexpected updates. Whenever a Subject issues a change notification, it sends `update` to all its dependents, even though some of them may not be interested in this particular change. If a Subject provides change notification for several aspects and it has many dependents, each change notifies several dependents that ignore the notification. The notification would be more efficient if the Subject notified only the dependents that specified they are interested.

Design Patterns also documents that each Observer must implement its own `update` method. This forces the Observer to introduce extra protocol and limits the interface between the Subject and its Observers. The Subject cannot provide optional parameters with the `update` message to the Observers. Also, the Subject cannot send a different message to each Observer; it must send the same `update` message to all of them. Even if an Observer already has a particular method for responding to a change notification, it must still implement an `update` method to send itself that other message.

Seeking to address these shortcomings of the textbook Observer pattern, the Smalltalk vendors developed solutions that are a variation on the Observer pattern. This variation is known as the Self-Addressed Stamped Envelope (SASE) pattern (Brown, 1995b). The pattern works like the traditional postal version of an SASE because the Observer specifies what message the Subject should send, which Observer the Subject should send the message to, and when the message should be sent.

SASE is a combination of the Observer and Command (245) patterns, where the Observer tells the Subject what Command to send it when a particular event occurs. To understand how SASE works, remember that the Observer pattern consists of the following steps:

1. An object registers itself as an Observer on a Subject.

2. Later, the Subject's state changes, so it sends itself `changed:`.

3. The `changed:` method sends `update` to all of the Observers registered on that Subject.

4. When an Observer receives `update`, it determines if the particular `update` applies to it, usually by examining the aspect parameter sent along with the message.

The SASE variation on the pattern takes a slightly different approach:

1. The Observer registers itself on a Subject by providing the Subject with four items:

    *   receiver—the Observer itself.

    *   event—an aspect in the Subject whose change the Observer is interested in.

    *   message—the selector for a message the Subject should send the Observer when the aspect changes.

    *   details—optional parameters the Subject should send along with the message.

    The Subject creates a Letter object, which it uses like an SASE. The Letter, a Command in the Command pattern, knows its receiver, message, and details. The Subject associates the Letter with its event. As a result, the Subject has a list of Letters for each aspect and will mail (execute) them when the aspect changes.

2. Later, an aspect of the Subject's state changes, so it sends itself `trigger-Event:`.

3. The `triggerEvent:` method gathers all of the Letters for that aspect and mails them.

4. Mailing a Letter (executing the Command) involves sending the Letter's message (a Smalltalk message send) to the receiver with the appropriate parameters.

This variation is a combination of Observer and Command patterns. The Letter is a Command, where the Subject is the Invoker and the Observer is the Receiver.

The SASE variation on Observer provides several significant advantages over the textbook Observer implementation:

- *No spurious updates.* With SASE, Observers are notified only when the aspect they are interested in changes; no unnecessary updates occur. This fact alone can greatly increase the efficiency of an application since no time is wasted in unneeded messages.

- *No update implementor.* The Observer is not required to implement `update`. It gets to specify both the selector and parameters that the Subject will use to provide notification. No additional messages are necessary.

- *Simpler Observer code.* The Observer does not need to test the notification and decide how to respond. This makes the Observer code much simpler since it will know by context why it is being called.

The SASE pattern is implemented in VisualWorks as the `Dependency-Transformer` class described above. Visual Smalltalk and IBM Smalltalk implement SASE in a similar way. The implementation is easier to understand in Visual Smalltalk because the messages have better names.

SASE in Visual Smalltalk

Visual Smalltalk uses SASE to connect widget events to corresponding methods in a window's application object. (By *widgets* we mean interactive controls such as text panes, drop-down lists, radio buttons, push buttons, and so on.) When an application constructs a new window (prior to opening it), the application object tells each widget what to do when specific events occur. These widgets are represented by subclasses of `SubPane`, hereafter referred to as panes. Each pane class defines a number of events associated with its instances. For example, a `Button` generates a specific event when the user clicks on it with the left mouse button, a different event for a right-button click, an event whenever the mouse is moving over the button, and several others. The application uses SASEs to connect the events to the application object.

Let's look at an example. The following method resides in a hypothetical text editor application and represents typical Visual Smalltalk code to create the panes of a window:

```
TextEditor>>open
    | pane |
    . . .
    pane := Button new.
```

```
pane
    contents: 'Paste';
    when: #clicked
        send: #pasteButtonClicked:
        to: self
        with: pane;
    when: #mouseMoved:
        send: #mouseIsAt:
        to: self;
    ...
self addSubpane: pane.
...
```

This creates a Button whose label is "Paste." The important statements for our current discussion, however, are the when:send:to:with: and when:send: to: messages. These set up the text editor as an Observer for two aspects of the Button. They tell the Button to inform the TextEditor when the #clicked and #mouseMove: events occur, and exactly how to inform the Observer Text-Editor.

Every object may have an event-action table associated with it. As in the Visual-Works implementation of dependents, there are actually multiple implementations of this event-action table. In general the table is an IdentityDictionary whose keys are events and whose corresponding values are the list of actions to take when the event occurs. Often this list contains only one action for a single Observer, but multiple Observers may be associated with each event. Panes store this table in an instance variable named handlers, as do several other classes; these override the default implementation in Object, where a class variable named EventHandlers is used. EventHandlers is a table of tables, a Dictionary of event tables keyed by the Subject itself.

The when:send:to:... messages set the entries in the event-action tables. The when: argument specifies the event name; the send:to:with: parameters specify the selector, receiver, and arguments that together form the Letter object (the action). For some events—those represented by a keyword message such as mouseMoved:—a specific argument is implied rather than provided. It is through the use of when: that Observers register themselves on Subjects.

This table shows the Button's handlers settings after the code above executes.

Key	Value
#clicked	a Message (selector = #pasteButtonClicked:)
#mouseMoved:	a Message (selector = #mouseIsAt:)

For both of the Message objects, the receiver is the TextEditor that created the Button. For the pasteButtonClicked: message, the argument is an Array with one element, the Button itself. The Message object with selector `mouseIsAt:` has no argument (yet); it will be supplied when the event is actually triggered.[2]

When an event occurs, the pane consults its `handlers` table and sends the appropriate message. Let's look at the mouse move case first. In general, on platforms like Windows and OS/2, when a user interacts with a pane, the operating system sends a message to the application that "owns" the pane. In the case of Windows95, for example, when the user moves the mouse over a pane, Windows sends a `WM_MOUSEMOVED` message to the Smalltalk virtual machine. The virtual machine forwards the event to the appropriate pane object as the Smalltalk message `wmMouseMoved:with:`. The arguments specify, among other things, the point representing the mouse location. After several intervening messages, the pane sends itself:

```
self triggerEvent: #mouseMoved: with: aPoint
```

Triggering the event involves looking up the event name in the `handlers` dictionary and retrieving its associated `Message`—in this case, `mouseIsAt:`. The pane then executes the `Message` using `aPoint` as its argument.

Turning to the button-clicked event, the entry for this event in the `handlers` dictionary references a `Message`. The table shows the `Message`'s settings:

Aspect	Value
selector	#pasteButtonClicked:
arguments	(a Button)
receiver	a TextEditor

When the clicked event occurs, `Message` is evaluated, as above. The result is that the `TextEditor` receives `pasteButtonClicked:` with the `Button` as the argument.

Again, the above scenario does not portray all the precise details, but is slightly simplified for illustrative purposes. Further, there are a number of variations of `when:send:to:with:`, including:

- `when: #event send: #selector`—implies the pane's owner (typically the application) is the receiver.

- `when: #event do: aBlock`—causes the block to be evaluated when `#event` occurs.

---

[2] Actually, for an event whose name is a keyword selector (such as `mouseMoved:`), the corresponding value is an instance of `LinkMessage`, a subclass of `Message`, but we're ignoring a number of details to simplify our example.

The main point with respect to Observer is that the application specifies an action to take place when a particular widget event occurs. This is done up front, before any events actually happen. When a widget event does take place, the SASE mechanism ensures that the action (in the form of a `Message` or a `Block`) is executed.

Notice that the assignment of roles is the reverse of what happens in Visual Works. In the Visual Smalltalk model, the pane is the Subject, and the application object is the Observer. In VisualWorks, the View is the Observer, and the application object is the Subject.

More examples of the Digitalk approach to events and linking panes (widgets) to the underlying application can be found in Shafer, Herndon, and Rozier (1993) and LaLonde and Pugh (1994a, Chaps. 5, 8). These books, however, cover earlier versions of Smalltalk/V (pre–Visual Smalltalk) in which the linking message was slightly different.

SASE in IBM Smalltalk

SASE is used in IBM Smalltalk in nearly the same way as in Visual Smalltalk. In IBM Smalltalk, a `CwWidget` (the closest equivalent in IBM Smalltalk to a Visual Smalltalk `SubPane`) implements two messages: `addCallback:receiver: selector:clientData:` and `callCallbacks:callData:`.

The first message is equivalent to `when:send:to:with:` in Visual Smalltalk. It specifies an event (a Callback Constant), the receiver of a message, the message, and the arguments to the message to be sent when the event occurs. A `CwWidget` triggers events by sending itself `callCallbacks:callData:`. This message is equivalent to `triggerEvent:` in Visual Smalltalk. When events are triggered, notifications will be sent to application objects, just as in Visual Smalltalk.

In addition, IBM Smalltalk uses an almost identical set of methods for communication between objects within the View Layer. `CwWidgets` respond to the message `addEventHandler:receiver:selector:clientData:`, that adds an "event handler" to a `CwWidget` that is called when an event (a mouse movement, expose, or keyboard event) comes in from the underlying window system. Commonly, one of the last things that happens in an Event Handler is to send a call back. In this way a mouse click (say, on a list) will trigger an Event Handler, which will then trigger a Callback so that it can be interpreted by an application object as a list selection.

Implementation

Rather than implementing your own Observer framework, you should use the one Smalltalk already provides.

Design Patterns provides a fairly complete discussion of how to implement the Observer pattern. Each of the following points is relevant to Smalltalk:

1. *Mapping subjects to their observer.* This has already been implemented for you. The `DependentsFields` dictionary in `Object` and the `dependents` instance variable in `Model` store these mappings.

2. *Observing more than one subject.* It is common for an object to depend on more than one subject. The dependent can determine which subject issued the notification by checking the third parameter in `update:with:from:`. However, this often is not necessary unless the subjects duplicate update aspects. The SASE pattern makes this situation easier to handle.

3. *Who triggers the update?* Is it the Subject's state-setting operations or the client code that changes the state? Smalltalk usually uses the first option. The aspect is set through a setter method that accepts the new value as a parameter and stores that value, usually in an instance variable. If the object also needs to notify its dependents when this aspect changes, the change notification should also be sent from the setter method—for example:

```
Subject>>name: aString
    "Set my value for name to aString
    and announce this change to my dependents."
    name := aString.
    self changed: #name with: aString
```

4. *Dangling references to deleted subjects.* This rarely happens in Smalltalk because garbage collection makes object deletion more transparent. A subject's lifetime is usually as long as, if not longer than, its dependents', so it will not be deleted first. If a subject ever were deleted before its dependent, the dependent would probably cease to behave properly because its state just disappeared. The more common problem is for a dependent to be deleted without being disconnected from its subjects. Then it would seem to be gone but could fail to garbage collect. Then when a dependent is through, part of the deletion process should be to break its dependencies on its subjects. This is usually implemented in `release`.

5. *Making sure Subject state is self-consistent before notification.* This is usually not a problem because dependency relationships are usually simple, but complex dependencies could be an issue. The most important consideration is to notify dependents *after* the change has occurred completely. Look at the implementation of the `name:` setter method above. First it sets the instance variable; when that is completely finished, then it notifies dependents.

6. *Avoiding observer-specific update protocols: the push and pull models.* Again, dependent relationships tend to be simple, so observer-specific update protocols are rarely needed. In these simple dependencies, the push and pull models are very similar. The **push model** is to use `changed:with:` where the second parameter is the new value, as shown above. The **pull model** is to announce the change and let the observer fetch it if it wants to, as shown here:

```
Subject>>name
   "Return my value for name."
   ^name

Subject>>name: aString
   "Set my value for name to aString
   and announce this change to my dependents."
   name := aString.
   self changed: #name

Observer>>update: anAspectSymbol
   "See superimplementor."
   anAspectSymbol == #name ifTrue: [self nameChanged].
   ...

Observer>>nameChanged
   "My subject's name has changed,
   so get the new one to update mine."
   | newName |
   newName := self subject name.
   self name: newName
```

7. *Specifying modifications of interest explicitly. Design Patterns* shows how this works in Visual Smalltalk. This is similar to `onChangeSend:to:` in Visual-Works, discussed earlier.

8. *Encapsulating complex update semantics.* This section shows how to implement a `ChangeManager` as a Mediator (287) between a Subject and its numerous Observers. Smalltalk does not provide a class like `ChangeManager`, but you might want to add one if you need to handle the complex dependencies described in *Design Patterns*.

9. *Combining the Subject and Observer classes.* Obviously Smalltalk does this. Both protocols are implemented in `Object` so that any object can be a Subject, an Observer, or both.

Sample Code

The Subject and Observer protocols have already been implemented in `Object` as the change/update protocol.

VisualWorks Application Model

In MVC, the View is a dependent of its Model so that it will receive notification of changes in the Model. In the enhanced MVC described in the section on Mediator (287), the View is a dependent of its Application Model. Yet the Application Models also have to stay synchronized with their Domain Model, so they can be dependents on it. In this way, an Application Model can support any number of Views (including none at all), and a Domain Model can support any number of Application Models (including none at all). The following sample code shows how to implement a typical `ApplicationModel` and domain model pair in VisualWorks.

Let's say you have a domain object called `PhoneNumber` that encapsulates the area code, local number, and extension together. An example might be "212-555-1212 ext. 125." Its class definition and instance creation look like this:

```
Object subclass: #PhoneNumber
    instanceVariableNames:: 'areaCode localNumber extension'
    classVariableNames: ''
    poolDictionaries: ''

PhoneNumber>>initAreaCode: areaString localNumber: localString
extension: extensionString
    "Initialize the receiver with the values
     areaString, localString, and extensionString."
    areaCode := areaString.
    localNumber := localString.
    extension := extensionString.
    ^self

PhoneNumber class>>areaCode: areaString localNumber:
localString extension: extensionString
    "Create and return an instance of PhoneNumber with the
    values areaString, localString, and extensionString."
    ^self new
        initAreaCode: areaString
        localNumber: localString
        extension: extensionString
```

One feature of `PhoneNumber` is that it knows the list of all valid area codes:

```
PhoneNumber>>validAreaCodes
    "Return a list of all valid area codes."
    | validCodes |
    ... code to gather area codes from a database ...
    ^validCodes
```

Another feature of `PhoneNumber` is that when a phone number doesn't have an extension, the `extension` variable is `nil`.

Let's say you need a window that will display objects that have phone numbers and allow the user to edit them (e.g., a window to edit `Employees` or `Customers`). To make editing easier, the phone number widget displays the three parts of the phone number in three separate string fields. The area code field is actually a combo-box widget that limits the user to valid area codes.

Since a phone number will need to be displayed by several different windows, we'll implement the phone number editor in its own `ApplicationModel`, which can be reused by any window. We'll call this class `PhoneNumberAM`. On the canvas, we'll paint a combo-box for the area code and two fields for the number and extension. The reason we use a combo-box for the area code and not just a field is that we'll limit the user to choosing from the list of valid area codes.

The table below shows the settings for the widgets in the phone number window. Once we've applied those, we'll install the class as `PhoneNumberAM`, a subclass of `ApplicationModel`, and define its instance variables and methods.

Widget	Purpose	Property Name	Property Value
Combo box	Area code	aspect	`#areaCodeHolder`
		choices	`#validCodesHolder`
		type	`String`
Input field	Local number	aspect	`#localNumberHolder`
		type	`String`
Input field	Extension	aspect	`#extensionHolder`
		type	`String`

We now have a basic `ApplicationModel`, `PhoneNumberAM`, that can display a phone number but knows nothing about its `PhoneNumber` domain object. So using a code browser on `PhoneNumberAM`, we'll change its class definition to add an instance variable, `domainHolder`, as shown in boldface type below:

```
Object subclass: #PhoneNumberAM
    instanceVariableNames: 'domainHolder areaCodeHolder
validCodesHolder localNumberHolder extensionHolder'
    classVariableNames: ''
    poolDictionaries: ''

PhoneNumberAM>>domainHolder
    "Get and return the value of domainHolder."
    ^domainHolder

PhoneNumberAM>>setDomainModel: aModel
    "Set the domain model to aModel."
    self domainHolder value: aModel.
    ^self

PhoneNumberAM class>>newWithDomainModel: aModel
    "Create and return a new instance of PhoneNumberAM
    whose domain model is aModel."
    ^self new setDomainModel: aModel

PhoneNumberAM class>>openWithDomainModel: aModel
    "Open a new instance of PhoneNumberAM
    whose domain model is aModel."
    ^(self newWithDomainModel: aModel) open
```

Next we'll implement `initialize` to customize the set-up for these variables. `domainHolder` is a `ValueHolder` that holds the domain object, in this case a `PhoneNumber`. The other four variables are `AspectAdaptors`, an object that is like a `ValueHolder` but knows how to extract its value as an aspect from another object called a `subject`. (For more information about how `Aspect-Adaptors` and other `ValueModels` work, see Adapter (105) and Woolf, 1995b.) In this case, the `subject` is a `PhoneNumber` and since it is the domain object, it is accessed from the `domainHolder`:

```
PhoneNumberAM>>initialize
    "See superimplementor."
    super initialize.
    domainHolder := nil asValue.
    areaCodeHolder := self adaptorForAspect: #areaCode.
    validCodesHolder := self adaptorForAspect: #validAreaCodes.
    localNumberHolder := self adaptorForAspect: #localNumber.
    extensionHolder := self adaptorForAspect: #extension.
    ^self

PhoneNumberAM>>adaptorForAspect: aSymbol
    "Create and return an AspectAdaptor for aSymbol."
    ^(AspectAdaptor
        subjectChannel: self domainHolder
        sendsUpdates: true)
        forAspect: aSymbol
```

Notice how `adaptorForAspect:` sets up the `AspectAdaptor:` the adapter gets its subject from the `domainHolder`, which means that its subject will be the domain object, and it expects its subject to send updates. As we'll see, these settings are significant.

Each `AspectAdaptor` has an aspect setting and expects its subject to have getter and setter methods named after the aspect. If the aspect were actually called `aspect`, the getter and setter methods would be called `aspect` and `aspect:`. If the `AspectAdaptor` expects its subject to send updates, it expects the update aspect to be a symbol named after the aspect, such as `#aspect`.

Thus `PhoneNumber` needs several getter and setter methods to support `Phone-NumberAM`'s `AspectAdaptors`. It already implements the `validAreaCodes` getter and does not need a `validAreaCodes:` setter because the combo-box's list will never send the setter message. We need to implement the getter and setter message for the other three aspects.

The getter methods will be very simple; they'll just return the instance variables' values. The setter methods do a little more. They don't just set the instance variables' values; they also notify the domain object's dependents that the instance variable's value has changed. Remember how the `AspectAdaptors` have `sendsUpdates` set to `true`? This means that the adapters will listen for change notification from the domain object, so the domain object's setters must provide that notification:

```
PhoneNumber>>areaCode
    "Get and return the value of areaCode."
    ^areaCode

PhoneNumber>>areaCode: aString
    "Set the value of areaCode to aString."
    areaCode := aString.
    self changed: #areaCode with: aString

PhoneNumber>>localNumber
    "Get and return the value of localNumber."
    ^localNumber

PhoneNumber>>localNumber: aString
    "Set the value of localNumber to aString."
    localNumber:= aString.
    self changed: #localNumber with: aString

PhoneNumber>>extension
    "Get and return the value of extension."
    ^extension

PhoneNumber>>extension: aString
    "Set the value of extension to aString."
    extension:= aString.
    self changed: #extension with: aString
```

Now PhoneNumber is implemented to provide lots of change notification to its dependents. Earlier, the discussion said that a subclass of Object with significant dependency notification will run more efficiently as a subclass of Model. Phone-Number, a domain object, is a subclass of Object that now has significant dependency notification, so it should really be a domain model and a subclass of Model:

```
Model subclass: #PhoneNumber
    instanceVariableNames: 'areaCode localNumber extension'
    classVariableNames: ''
    poolDictionaries: ''
```

Now we can create a PhoneNumber and open an editor on it like this:

```
| phoneNumber |
phoneNumber:= PhoneNumber
                areaCode: '212'
                localNumber: '555-1212'
                extension: nil.
PhoneNumberAM openOnDomainModel: phoneNumber
```

This window *almost* works, but it has one small bug. The extension aspect can be nil, but the extension field is expecting a String, so nil doesn't work. What we need to do is convert nil to a String, such as the empty string. However, we should do this only when the extension is nil; when it's a String, we should use it as is.

Since the field is already using a ValueModel (the AspectAdaptor), the easy way to convert nil to a String is to use another ValueModel designed for this purpose, a TypeConverter. It has a version for making sure that the value is a String created via the message onStringValue:. Thus the initialization code for PhoneNumberAM should use one of the TypeConverters to convert the AspectAdaptor's value. The modified method is shown below with the changes in boldface type:

```
PhoneNumberAM>>initialize
    "See superimplementor."
    | adaptor |
    super initialize.
    domainHolder := nil asValue.
    areaCodeHolder := self adaptorForAspect: #areaCode.
    validCodesHolder := self adaptorForAspect: #validAreaCodes.
    localNumberHolder := self adaptorForAspect: #localNumber.
    adaptor := self adaptorForAspect: #extension.
    extensionHolder := TypeConverter onStringValue: adaptor.
    ^self
```

Now PhoneNumberAM works correctly and can be used as a subcanvas in any ApplicationModel that needs to edit a PhoneNumber.

AspectAdaptor as Observer

The code for PhoneNumber and PhoneNumberAM illustrates the Observer pattern in VisualWorks. The Subject is the instance of PhoneNumber. Its Change messages are each of the setter methods that send changed:with:. The Observers are each of the AspectAdaptors. Their Update message is AspectAdaptor's implementor of update:with:from:.

Let's look at how AspectAdaptor is implemented as a dependent. AspectAdaptor is a subclass of ProtocolAdaptor, and some of the dependency behavior is implemented in the superclass.

ProtocolAdaptor>>hookupToSubject contains the code that actually registers the AspectAdaptor as a dependent of its subject. Notice that it does this only if subjectSendsUpdates is set to true; this is why our AspectAdaptors needed "sendsUpdates: true":

```
ProtocolAdaptor>>hookupToSubject
    "Add the receiver as a dependent of the receiver's subject."
    subjectSendsUpdates
        ifTrue: [subject notNil
                    ifTrue: [subject addDependent: self]]
```

AspectAdaptor then implements update:with:from: to listen for changes in the subject. If the Subject announcing the change is the adapter's subject and if the change being announced is a change in the adapter's aspect, then the adapter concludes that its value has changed and announces this to its dependents:

```
AspectAdaptor>>update: anAspect with: parameter from: sender
    "Propagate change if the sender is the receiver's subject
    and anAspect is the receiver's aspect."
    (sender == subject and: [anAspect == self forAspect])
       ifTrue:
          [dependents
             update: #value with: parameter from: self]
       ifFalse:
          [super
             update: anAspect with: parameter from: sender]
```

Notice that we had to implement the Subject behavior in `PhoneNumber`. On the other hand, `AspectAdaptor` already implemented the Observer behavior for us. This is typical in VisualWorks. We have to implement the Subject ourselves, but VisualWorks has already implemented the Observers.

Observer in Model-View-Controller

The Model-View-Controller framework is the first and best-known example of Observer. Introduced in Smalltalk-80, it lives on in VisualWorks. The main examples of Observer exist between the `ValueModels` and their value-based subviews (Woolf, 1995a). For example, the subview classes for an input field and the field part of a combo-box are `InputFieldView` and its subclass `ComboBoxInputFieldView`.

When a `ValueModel` gets a new value, it announces this to its dependents by sending itself `changed:`.

```
ValueModel>>value: newValue
    "Set the currently stored value, and notify dependents."
    self setValue: newValue.
    self changed: #value
```

When a subview gets notified of a change, it gets its model's new value and displays it. The subview listens for changes in the model by registering itself as a dependent using `addDependent:`. This is implemented in `DependentPart`, the superclass for all views that can have models (such as `View`):

```
DependentPart>>setModel: aModel
    "Set the receiver's model to be aModel."
    ( model == aModel )
       ifFalse: [
          model isNil
             ifFalse: [ model removeDependent: self ].
          (model := aModel) isNil
             ifFalse: [ model addDependent: self ] ].
```

Since a value-based subview has only one model and the model has only one aspect, the subview doesn't even check to see what change is being announced.

The subview assumes that the model's value is what changed and proceeds to get the new value. The subview listens for change announcements by implementing update: to do so:

```
InputFieldView>>update: aSymbol
    "The receiver's model has changed its text.
    Update the receiver."
    self updateDisplayContents
```

In this example, the ValueModel is the Subject and the subview is the Observer. Notice that this ValueModel is in an ApplicationModel and may well be both an Observer on a domain model and a Subject for the subview.

Since VisualWorks already implements both the ValueModel classes and the subview classes like InputFieldView, you do not have to implement any code yourself to use this example of Observer.

Observer in Visual Smalltalk and IBM Smalltalk

For sample code of Observer in Visual Smalltalk and IBM Smalltalk, see the sample code in Mediator (287).

Known Smalltalk Uses

Each dialect implements one or two variations of the changed/update protocol from Smalltalk-80, but these implementations are so fundamental to the language that they're the only ones you need. Most Smalltalk applications contain numerous uses of the changed/update protocol, and each of these is a known use of Observer. Uses of the SASE variation of Observer are also extremely common. The Observer pattern is so fundamental to Smalltalk that it is almost a language feature.

Related Patterns

Many of the classes in the ValueModel hierarchy in VisualWorks are Observer classes. Of those, some are also Adapter (105) classes, so their Subject is also the Adaptee. The others are Decorator (161) classes, so their Subject is also the Component.

An application model, an Observer of its domain model, is also a Mediator (287) for its widgets.

A value-based subview, an Observer of its ValueModel, also uses its Value-Model as a Strategy (339) for accessing its value. The ValueModel also uses the subview as a Strategy for displaying its value.

STATE (DP 305)   Object Behavioral

Intent

Allow an object to alter its behavior when its internal state changes. The object will appear to change its class.

Structure

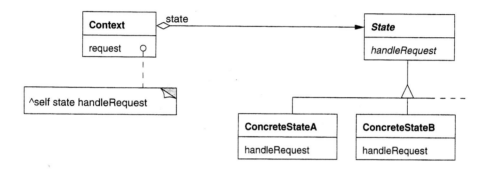

Discussion

In many circumstances, an object's behavior will change over time in response to requests that are made of it. The "history" of the object's life and its current point in that history (that is, its current state) play roles in how the object behaves in the present.

We have all seen code that looks like the following:

```
Order>>submit
    self state == #created
        ifTrue:[^self error: 'Must be validated first'].
    self state == #validated
        ifTrue:[OrderProcessor submitOrder: self.
                ^self state: #submitted].
    self state == #submitted
        ifTrue:[^self error: 'Can''t submit this order twice'].
    self state == #deleted
        ifTrue:[^self error: 'Order has been deleted'].
```

The Order object's behavior depends firmly on its current state but is determined by a poor substitute for a case statement. Superfluous code is executed for each state other than #created because of the multiple tests, and the situation worsens as we extend this code to handle new states. More important, we'll have the same sort of code in other Order methods. Trying to understand, or modify, the overall behavior of Orders for any particular state is therefore a nontrivial task. It requires sifting through multiple case-like methods trying to assemble an overall picture of the state-dependent behavior and, for modifications, splicing code into the appropriate location. So from program understanding, maintenance, and extensibility perspectives, this approach is problematic.

Also note that state *transitions* are encoded in methods like our submit example. Many design methods represent this kind of changing behavior of an object through state transition diagrams that represent the different conditions or states of an object, the events that cause transitions between those states, and the actions that occur when a transition is made. However, while the design diagram may nicely sum up this kind of information, that clarity is usually lost in the translation to code that looks like the previous example.

The State pattern brings this kind of clarity back to the code. With the State pattern, each of the states is represented as a separate object. The Client initializes itself with its initial-state object. To transition to a new state, it replaces its state object with an appropriate new one. When the Client needs to make decisions or provide behavior *based on* its state, it does so by delegating to its State object. In this way, the Client's implementation remains relatively free of state dependencies because it delegates them to its collaborating state objects.

The key to the State pattern lies in separating the state-dependent behavior of the client into a separate set of **State objects.** The State objects implement that part of the system's behavior that is dependent on the current state of the client rather than the client itself. States are defined in a hierarchy where each subclass represents an individual state. The client is implemented in a **Context** class that collaborates with the State hierarchy. When the Context needs to handle a request that is state-dependent, it delegates the request to its current State. Each State subclass implements its handling of the request differently.

Not a Change of Class

The Intent says that the State pattern allows an object to appear to change class when its internal state changes. Some developers may prefer to look at the problem that way, but the truth is simply that the object has a lot of behavior that depends on its internal state—so much so that it acts very differently when its state changes. These differences may be so profound that the object acts like a totally different specialization of its type, but not all examples of the State pattern are quite so dramatic.

The basic issue is not so much that the object appears to change class but that the object's external behavior is highly dependent on its internal state. Most objects have internal state that can change and affect their behavior. The difference with the State pattern is that a Context has a limited number of well-defined states and a consistent set of rules that control the transitions between these states.

The Code Transformation

Applying the State pattern causes a fairly consistent code transformation. Without the pattern, behavior that depends on the states often uses case statements to vary the behavior accordingly:

```
Object subclass: #Context
    instanceVariableNames: 'state'
    classVariableNames: ''
    poolDictionaries: ''

Context>>request
    "Handle the request according to the Context's state."
    self state == #stateA ifTrue: [^self stateARequest].
    self state == #stateB ifTrue: [^self stateBRequest].
    ...
    ^self error: 'unknown state'
```

The *Smalltalk Companion* contains many examples of the evils of case statements and why they should be avoided. In this context, the case statement has two basic problems:

1. The same basic case structure must be duplicated for each public request that a client might make of the `Context`. Each such `request` method will have to test for `#stateA`, `#stateB`, and so on.

2. New states cannot be added without modifying all of the `request` methods.

The State pattern transforms the code to remove the state-dependent code from the `Context`. Various ways of handling each request are implemented polymorphically. The `Context` still knows its `state`, but rather than running it through a case statement, the `Context` delegates to its `state` as a real object:

```
Object subclass: #Context
    instanceVariableNames: 'state'
    classVariableNames: ''
    poolDictionaries: ''

Context>>request
    "Handle the request according to the Context's
    currentState."
    self state handleRequest
```

The `state` object comes from a hierarchy of possible states. The abstract class defines the interface that all states have:

```
Object subclass: #State
    instanceVariableNames: ''
    classVariableNames: ''
    poolDictionaries: ''

State>>handleRequest
    self error: 'Transition not allowed for this state'.
```

Subclasses of State implement different states that the Context can be in. Each subclass implements handleRequest to provide the behavior appropriate to handle the request in that state. If the particular state cannot handle that request, the superclasses' default implementation will raise an appropriate error to that effect:

```
State subclass: #ConcreteStateA
    instanceVariableNames: ''
    classVariableNames: ''
    poolDictionaries: ''

ConcreteStateA>>handleRequest
    "Handle the request one way."
    ...


State subclass: #ConcreteStateB
    instanceVariableNames: ''
    classVariableNames: ''
    poolDictionaries: ''

ConcreteStateB>>handleRequest
    "Handle the request another way."
    ...
```

Other subclasses implement other states. Each subclass encapsulates the behavior for that state so that it doesn't clutter the Context or the other states. Adding new states in the future is easy. The main step is to add a new State subclass that implements the handle messages appropriately.

Changing the Context Class for Real

If the point of the State pattern is to make the object seem as if it has changed its class, why not go ahead and actually coerce the instance to a different class? In languages without reflection, like C++, there is a tendency (almost a necessity) to use somewhat complicated means to do what in Smalltalk is possible with messages that change the identity or class of an object. In all dialects we can use the method become: to change the identity of an object. In VisualWorks we can also use the method changeClassToThatOf: to change its class.

At first glance, the State pattern appears to be another instance of this unnecessary complication. Why not just change the class? Simply, there are two basic problems with using changeClassToThatOf: or another coercion method:

1. All of the instance variables that any of the state classes may want to use must be defined in the superclass. The changeClassToThatOf: method will not work if a subclass defines any additional instance variables. A variant would be to use become: instead of changeClassToThatOf:. However, that would necessitate copying the values of all of the instance variables in the class over to the new instance before the become: is sent. Note that change-

`ClassToThatOf:` does not even exist in Visual Smalltalk or IBM Smalltalk, so the `become:` approach is the only choice in these environments.

2. The bigger, and more central, problem is that we are now precluded from making subclasses of our "Context" object as would have been possible with the State pattern. If we wanted to make a subclass—say, to add an instance variable holding the longest run so far—we would be forced to make additional subclasses of all of the subclasses of the State-Context class. Preventing this class explosion is the biggest reason to use composition as in the State pattern rather than reflective facilities.

So, we have seen that the use of the language-specific features does not add flexibility in this case; it instead makes our design less flexible and harder to reuse. This is an important point to keep in mind when designing an object-oriented program; the "neatest" or "slickest" solution may not necessarily be the best. Often the most straightforward solution is better than those that use special language features.

Applicability

Design Patterns lists a couple of considerations for the appropriateness of the State pattern. Here are some more:

*   The Context must have a limited, well-defined list of possible states. It can have other internal state variables as well, just like any object. But the state that defines its current status can have only a few valid values so that each of those values can be implemented as a State subclass. If the state values can have a virtually unlimited number of valid combinations, then the State class needs a virtually unlimited number of subclasses, so the State pattern is not appropriate.

*   The Context must have well-defined transitions between states. In any possible state, it must be clear when the Context should change to another state and, in each case, what that other state should be. If the transition between states is inconsistent and subjective, the State pattern is not appropriate.

Implementation

One of the Implementation issues deserves further clarification: *Who defines the state transitions?* As *Design Patterns* explains, the State pattern does not specify which participant—the Context or the States—defines the criteria for the transitions from one state to the next. One advantage of the State pattern is that it removes the state-dependent behavior from the Context and encapsulates it in the State objects. Similarly, the pattern may extract the state transition behavior from the Context and distribute it among the State objects. This way, each State knows when it should transition to another State and what other State it should transition to in each case. This requires that each State know what its Context is and have some way to tell its Context to switch to a new State.

Let's consider again the two state classes previously defined. Let's suppose that the two classes, `ConcreteStateA` and `ConcreteStateB`, implement the following state transition diagram:

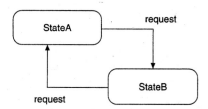

In this example, each request will result in the Context's changing state to the other state. If we choose to have each state control the Context's next state, we would implement the method `handleRequest` in our classes like the following:

```
ConcreteStateA>>handleRequest
   "Handle the request some way."
   … do state specific things …
   context state: (ConcreteStateB new context: context).

ConcreteStateB>>handleRequest
   "Handle the request some other way."
   … do state specific things …
   context state: (ConcreteStateA new context: context).
```

Obviously, there are some other design decisions to be made here:

- Will the Context be held in an instance variable (as in the example above) or be passed in to each method in the state?

- Will new instances of each state be created each time, or will the context be asked for them?

An alternative implementation would be to have the Context switch the state itself:

```
Context>>request
   "Handle the request according to the Context's
   currentState."
   state := self state handleRequest

ConcreteStateA>>handleRequest
   … do state specific things …
   ^ConcreteStateB new
```

A drawback of this implementation is that it precludes the state's handle-Request method from returning any other value.

In some cases it might be convenient to keep all knowledge of the state transitions out of the state classes. For example, if you want to reuse the State classes in several different (but related) finite state machines in different Context classes, this would be appropriate. In that case, you would need to represent the transitions separately from the State classes.

Sample Code

Let's illustrate the code transformation the State pattern introduces by looking at an example from *Design Patterns.*

Without the State Pattern

In our example, we have a class named TCPConnection whose instances represent network connections (TCP stands for Transmission Control Protocol, a standard for network communication). A connection may be in one of several states (e.g., Established, Listen, Closed), and its behavior depends on its current state. For example, when asked to send data, a connection object reacts differently depending on whether it's Established or Closed. These states form a finite state machine that is an implicit part of the connection. The following state transition diagram shows these states and the transitions between them:

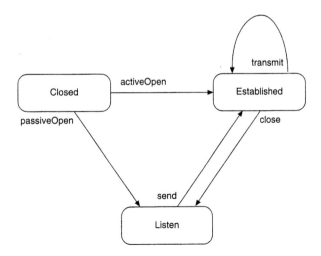

The TCPConnection begins its life in the Closed state. An activeOpen or a passiveOpen command will send it to the Established or Listen states, respectively. Once in the Established state, a close command will send it to the Listen state, while a transmit command will perform an action but keep it in the Established state. In the Listen state, a send command will transfer it to the Established state.

One approach to implementing such state-dependent behavior might be to code a conditional of some sort that, based on the current state, invokes different code or methods within the `TCPConnection` object:

```
Object subclass: #TCPConnection
    instanceVariableNames: 'state'
    classVariableNames: ''
    poolDictionaries: ''

TCPConnection>>activeOpen
    "Open the connection."
    self state == #established ifTrue: [^self].
    self state == #listen ifTrue: [^self].
    self state == #closed ifTrue:
        [^self changeStateTo: #established].
    ^self error: 'unknown state'

TCPConnection>>send
    "Prepare the connection to send data."
    self state == #established ifTrue: [^self].
    self state == #listen ifTrue:
        [^self changeStateTo: #established].
    self state == #closed ifTrue:
        [^self error: 'closed connection'].
    ^self error: 'unknown state'
```

`TCPConnection` implements other requests—`passiveOpen`, `close`, and `transmit:`—in a similar manner. Of course this means if we need to add new states later in the system's life, we'll have to revisit the conditional, adding code to account for these new states.

With the State Pattern

The State pattern offers a cleaner and more easily extensible solution. The structure looks like this:

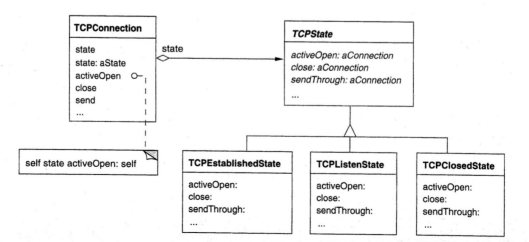

This structure has the finite state machine shown earlier implicit in its design.

Let's assume that you already have the case statement code shown above and you want to convert it to the State pattern structure shown above.

Step 1: Represent the connection's state with a separate object. Thus, TCP-Connection's state variable is not a simple enumeration object, such as a Symbol, but is now a real TCPState object with its own behavior:

```
Object subclass: #TCPConnection
   instanceVariableNames: 'state'
   classVariableNames: ''
   poolDictionaries: ''

Object subclass: #TCPState
   instanceVariableNames: ''
   classVariableNames: ''
   poolDictionaries: ''
```

Step 2: Implement TCPConnection to delegate to TCPState. In this example, we show only the implementation of activeOpen and send. A real framework would also implement passiveOpen, close, and transmit:.

```
TCPConnection>>activeOpen
   "Open the connection."
   self state activeOpen: self

TCPConnection>>send
   "Prepare the connection to send data."
   self state sendThrough: self
```

Step 3: Implement TCPState to accept the delegation:

```
TCPState>>activeOpen: aTCPConnection
   "Open the connection."
   self subclassResponsibility

TCPState>>sendThrough: aTCPConnection
   "Prepare to send data through the connection."
   self subclassResponsibility
```

Step 4: Since TCPState is actually an abstract class, implement a concrete subclass for each possible state:

```
TCPState subclass: #TCPEstablishedState
   instanceVariableNames: ''
   classVariableNames: ''
   poolDictionaries: ''
```

```
TCPState subclass: #TCPListenState
    instanceVariableNames: ''
    classVariableNames: ''
    poolDictionaries: ''

TCPState subclass: #TCPClosedState
    instanceVariableNames: ''
    classVariableNames: ''
    poolDictionaries: ''
```

Step 5: Implement each of the methods appropriately for each of the sub-classes:

```
TCPEstablishedState>>activeOpen: aTCPConnection
    "Do nothing."
    ^self

TCPEstablishedState>>sendThrough: aTCPConnection
    "Do nothing."
    ^self

TCPListenState>>activeOpen: aTCPConnection
    "Do nothing."
    ^self

TCPListenState>>sendThrough: aTCPConnection
    "Prepare to send data through aTCPConnection."
    ^aTCPConnection establishConnection

TCPClosedState>>activeOpen: aTCPConnection
    "Open aTCPConnection."
    ^aTCPConnection establishConnection

TCPClosedState>>sendThrough: aTCPConnection
    "This is an error!"
    self error: 'closed connection'
```

Step 6: Implement the messages that the TCPStates send to TCPConnection. Also, set a TCPConnection's default state to closed:

```
TCPConnection>>establishConnection
    "Establish a connection. Do all of the work necessary
    to properly establish a valid connection and verify
    its success."
    self state: TCPEstablishedState new

TCPConnection>>initialize
    "Set the connection's default state."
    state := TCPClosedState new.
    ^self
```

Here's an example of how you would subsequently use TCPConnection:

```
| connection |
connection := TCPConnection new.
connection
    activeOpen;
    transmit: text;
    close
```

Known Smalltalk Uses

SMTP/Sockets

"A Very Simple VSE SMTP Client" (ParcPlace, 1996) shows a textbook example of the State pattern's use to implement an explicit finite state machine (FSM) in a communications protocol. This article shows how to implement a Simple Mail Transfer Protocol (SMTP) mail system in Visual Smalltalk Enterprise. It represents the SMTP states as State classes that cooperate with a `SocketClient` Context class to send messages to an SMTP server via TCP/IP sockets.

ControlMode

VisualWorks includes an example of the State pattern that is similar to `Drawing-Controller` (DP 313). In VisualWorks, the class `ModalController` is used by the UI Builder framework to handle the positioning and resizing of the different UI components. `ModalController` "redirects mouse-related events to an internally held `ControlMode` object, which may then take some action."[3] A `ModalController` contains (through the intermediary of a `ValueHolder`) an instance of a `ControlMode` subclass that "implements some or all of the basic control sequence of a `ModalController`."[4]

Both the `ModalController`/`ControlMode` combination and the HotDraw example from *Design Patterns* are unusual in that there is no explicit FSM to provide the transitions. Instead the user will, by her actions, determine what the next state will be by picking from the list of possible states. This is an example where the States cannot control the state transitions, so the Context must control them itself.

AlgeBrain

AlgeBrain is an intelligent tutoring system for algebra (being built by Sherman along with colleagues Kevin Singley, Peter Fairweather, and Steve Swerling). It uses State objects to represent the current state of solving an algebraic equation. An `AlgebraTutor` is configured at any point in time with an instance of one of several concrete `AlgebraState` subclasses. Different `AlgebraState` objects know what user actions are acceptable or appropriate given the current state of the problem. Thus, when a user performs an action, the tutor delegates its

---

[3] VisualWorks `ModalController` class comment.
[4] VisualWorks `ControlMode` class comment.

response to its current State object; each of these determines if the user's action is correct and can provide focused, context-dependent error messages. Since each State object knows what it is expecting in the way of user actions, States can be used to provide help regarding what to do next to solve the current problem.

Relational Database Interfacing

Brown (1996) demonstrates the use of the State pattern in an order-processing system. The State objects provide for differing behaviors for saving and deleting objects from a relational database.

Related Patterns

State versus Strategy

State is often confused with its close cousin Strategy (339), and it is sometimes difficult to determine which pattern to use or if an implementation of one is actually the other. A good rule of thumb to follow to distinguish the two is that if the Context will contain only one (of several possible) state or strategy objects during its lifetime, you are probably using the Strategy pattern. If, on the other hand, the Context changes during the normal course of an application so that, over time, it may contain many different state objects, then you may be referring to a State implementation, particularly if there are well-defined orders of transition between the different states. A subtler distinction can sometimes be found in the setting of an object's attributes. An object is usually put into a state by an external client, while it will choose a strategy on its own.

Another distinction is that a Context seems to hide the Strategy it's using, but the State it's using is quite apparent to its Client. For example, when a Client tells a StorageDevice to store some text, the device may use one of several different techniques to compress the text before storing it, including no compression at all. However, the Client doesn't care how the device compresses the text, whether it does so at all, or whether it compresses the text in the same way every time. It just wants the device to store and retrieve the text on command. Because of the way the compression is private to the device and hidden from the Client, the different compression objects are Strategies. On the other hand, once a Client opens a TCPConnection, it certainly expects the connection to behave as if it's open. Once the Client closes the connection, it expects the connection to act as if it's closed. Because the connection's status is readily apparent to the Client, the status objects are States.

STRATEGY (DP 315)   Object Behavioral

Intent

Define a family of algorithms, encapsulate each one in a separate class, and define each class with the same interface so they can be interchangeable. Strategy lets the algorithm vary independently from clients that use it.

Structure

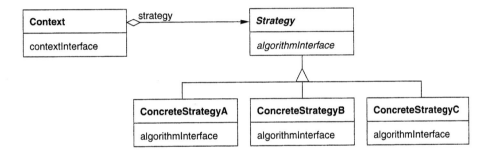

Discussion

Often an application requires a particular service, system function, or algorithm to be performed on its behalf, but there are multiple ways of performing that service. Rather than coding several methods in the main application class to implement the multiple algorithms, we can apply the Strategy pattern to encapsulate the variations in multiple separate classes. Depending on the algorithm—or strategy—choice, only one of these classes is instantiated as the service provider. The application then communicates service requests to this external helper object as needed. The classes that provide the different versions of the same service all polymorphically implement the same service-request interface so the service requester can interact with all of them in the same manner.

When would we need to do this sort of thing? Many systems must choose among multiple strategies based on the context or situation, and many interactive applications allow users to select one of several different algorithmic strategies. For example, video compression programs typically allow users to select one compression algorithm from several possible, based on considerations involving space versus speed or space versus quality trade-offs. Some algorithms retain high-quality video integrity but result in large data files that require high bandwidth playback capabilities, whereas other algorithms may be somewhat lossy yet result in smaller file sizes and simpler playback requirements.[5] So the program must allow users to select the algorithm which best matches their needs.

Here are several example applications that require multiple service providers:[6]

Application	General Service	Ways of Accomplishing Service
Video Compression	Compress video data	MPEG, AVI, QuickTime formats
Car Assembly	Add parts to car/product	Ford, Toyota, Porsche Builders
Product Visualization	Draw assembled car	Ford, Toyota, Porsche renderers
Drawing Editor	Save drawing to disk	BMP, GIF, JPEG formats
File Compression	Compress disk file data	Zip, Huffman, RLE algorithms
Business Graphics	Visualize numeric data	Line plot, bar chart, pie chart
Document Editor	Layout screen contents	Different line-break strategies

Let's consider the last application, fashioned after the *Design Patterns* example on page DP 315. Here, a document editor operates on a composition object containing text and graphics; the composition is responsible for formatting itself for output and can choose among several layout strategies based on user preference. One approach to implementing several strategy choices in such situations would be to "bloat" the implementation of the responsible class itself by implementing the various algorithm choices as individual methods therein; in the composition example, this would mean incorporating the various layout algorithms as distinct methods in the Composition class. Then each time this functionality is required, the composition would invoke the appropriate method using a set of conditional statements. Of course, with regard to extensibility, this implies revisiting this conditional if we add a new strategy in the future.

Instead, we can apply the Strategy pattern to provide a more modular and extensible solution. Here, we'll implement each formatting strategy or algorithm in its own, separate class, and have the composition point to an instance of one of these Strategy classes and call upon this formatter object to perform the layout function. Hence the formatting function is actually performed by an external helper object. The choice of formatting algorithm is effected simply by instantiating one or another of the layout/Strategy classes. This implies the strategy may be changed on the fly by a user (e.g., by menu selection) or programatically based on some changing condition. Doing so entails instantiating a new Strategy object and having the composition point to it. Each time the layout has to be recom-

---

[5] With respect to video compression, "lossy" refers to the loss of some picture data, such as color information or pixels.

[6] The Car Assembly and Product Visualization examples are based on the application described in the Builder (47) pattern.

puted, the client (the composition) sends a single message to its formatter, as opposed to repetitively executing a conditional to decide which message to send itself.

As new formatting requirements arise later in the life of our application, it will be an easier task to implement and integrate such new algorithms since they have been separated into distinct classes. The composition implementation is also easier to understand and maintain because it does not include all of the various formatting algorithms. Instead, in the best tradition of object-oriented design, it merely communicates with *some* line-breaking object using an abstract interface and it really doesn't care what sort of linebreaker it is, as long as it adheres to this interface.

Let's take a quick look at the difference in the code required to invoke the line-breaking functionality (1) if we code the various line-breaking algorithms as separate methods within the Composition class and (2) when using the Strategy pattern. As in *Design Patterns*, the Composition class implements a repair method that is called to update the entire layout of the document and, in turn, invokes the layout code.

Without the Strategy Pattern

Here, Composition contains an instance variable named formatting-Strategy, which determines the algorithm (that is, method) to invoke. We'll look at two different implementation approaches.

Brute Force. The first implementation incorporates a string of if . . . then . . . elses as we might code in virtually any language:

```
Composition>>repair
   "Without the strategy pattern."
   formattingStrategy == #Simple
      ifTrue: [self formatWithSimpleAlgorithm]
      ifFalse: [formattingStrategy == #TeX
         ifTrue: [self formatWithTeXAlgorithm]
         ifFalse: [...]
```

A Smalltalk-Flavored Approach. In Smalltalk, we can also capitalize on the ability to perform: a symbolic representation of a message selector. As we've mentioned elsewhere, this approach is clever but difficult from a program understanding perspective. Even static analysis tools such as code browsers' "senders" and "messages" fail on this code. For example, if you request "messages" sent by the following method, the resulting list would not include formatWithSimpleAlgorithm, formatWithTeXAlgorithm, or any other formatting method selectors programmatically constructed:

```
Composition>>repair
    "Without the strategy pattern, but using perform:."
    | selector |
    "Construct the name of the method to invoke:"
    selector := ('formatWith', formattingStrategy,
                 'Algorithm') asSymbol.
    self perform: selector
```

Using the Strategy Pattern

Here, `Composition` contains an instance variable named `formatter` that points to its layout object. The `Composition` couldn't care less about the exact class of this helper object, merely that it responds to the `format:` message:

```
Composition>>repair
    "With the Strategy pattern."
    formatter format: self.
```

Here's the structure of this application after applying the Strategy pattern:

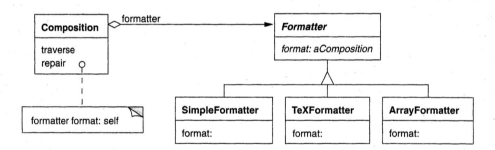

Sample Code

Let's look more in depth at another of the previous examples.[7] Suppose we have a business graphics application capable of interacting with a user to allow visualization of various numerical or financial data. A user can request data for, say, the gross income of a company for the past four quarters, and the application can provide a visualization of those data in various formats: as a bar chart, a line graph, or a pie chart.

We start by implementing a `GraphVisualizer` class. Since the application is interactive, we'll make `GraphVisualizer` a subclass of `ViewManager` (our example will be portrayed with Visual Smalltalk code). The visualizer window will contain a textual entry field for an SQL query; the data to plot will be retrieved from a database based on a user's query. The window will also contain

---

[7]In this pattern, we've switched the order of the Sample Code and Implementation sections. First, we'll present the code for an example application, and in the subsequent section we'll discuss implementation issues raised by this example.

a GraphPane on which the data will be graphed, and a "Graph It" button. When the user selects a graph type, enters a SQL statement, and pushes the button, the application will retrieve information based on the database query and plot it.

```
ViewManager subclass: #GraphVisualizer
   instanceVariableNames: 'graphPane data grapher'
   classVariableNames: ''
   poolDictionaries: ''

GraphVisualizer>>grapher: aGrapher
   grapher := aGrapher
```

The grapher instance variable will point to the object to which the application delegates the task of drawing the graphic visualization. That object will be instantiated from one of the classes in the following Grapher subhierarchy:

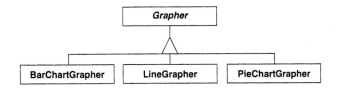

Grapher is an abstract superclass with (currently) three concrete subclasses. When the user requests information to be portrayed as pie charts, GraphVisualizer instantiates PieChartGrapher and installs that instance as its grapher object. The same is true for line graphs and bar charts. When the graph must be drawn, GraphVisualizer sends a message to its grapher to perform this task.

Let's start to define the abstract superclass of the Grapher hierarchy:

```
Object subclass: #Grapher
   instanceVariableNames: 'pen'
   classVariableNames: ''
   poolDictionaries: ''

Grapher>>pen: aPen
   "Draw using aPen"
   pen := aPen
```

All Grapher objects use a Pen instance for their drawing. This works fine for our example application, where graphs are drawn on a GraphPane. We set the Grapher's pen variable to reference the pane's pen. It also means that the Grapher classes can be reused in other applications involving classes that have a Pen, such as Bitmap and Printer.

The visualizer window has a menu that allows users to choose the graph type. When a graph type is selected from the menu, GraphVisualizer instantiates the appropriate Grapher subclass and stores that instance in the grapher variable. The graph selection menu looks like this:

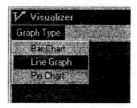

The methods corresponding to these menu items are as follows:

```
GraphVisualizer>>useBarChart
    "The user has selected 'Bar Chart' from the 'Graph
    Type' menu. Create a new BarChartGrapher."
    self grapher:
        (BarChartGrapher new
            pen: graphPane pen)

GraphVisualizer>>useLineGraph
    "The user has selected 'Line Graph'."
    self grapher:
        (LinePlotter new
            pen: graphPane pen)

GraphVisualizer>>usePieChart
    "The user has selected 'Pie Chart'."
    self grapher:
        (PieChartGrapher new
            pen: graphPane pen)
```

When the "Graph It" button is pressed, GraphVisualizer retrieves the appropriate data from the database and tells its grapher to plot it. Here's the method invoked when the button is pressed; it is here that the Grapher (Strategy) object is invoked:

```
GraphVisualizer>>graphIt
    "First, make sure the user has selected a graph type:"
    grapher isNil ifTrue:
        [^MessageBox message: 'Please select a graph type'].
    "Pass the user's SQL query to the database and
     store the result in 'data':"
    data := ...
    "Now plot it:"
    grapher plot: data
```

Now we flesh out Grapher and its concrete subclasses:

```
Grapher>>plot: data
    "Draw the graph for the information in 'data'."
    self implementedBySubclass

Grapher subclass: #BarChartGrapher
    instanceVariableNames: ''
    classVariableNames: ''
    poolDictionaries: ''

BarChartGrapher>>plot: data
    "Draw a bar chart depicting the information
     contained in 'data'."
    ...

Grapher subclass: #LinePlotter
    instanceVariableNames: ''
    classVariableNames: ''
    poolDictionaries: ''

LinePlotter>>plot: data
    "Draw a line plot depicting the information
     contained in 'data'."
    ...
```

Here's what the application looks like structurally:

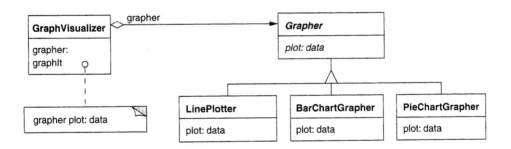

Relating this to the generalized Structure diagram, GraphVisualizer corresponds to Context, and Grapher represents the abstract Strategy, defining the common interface for all concrete Grapher subclasses. LinePlotter, BarChartGrapher, and PieChartGrapher map to ConcreteStrategyA, B, and C.

The important points of this example are that we have a separate Strategy object (instantiated from the Grapher classes) that implements the various graphing strategies, and the application delegates the graphing functionality to this helper object rather than implementing it itself.

Implementation

Here are several implementation issues raised by our example and others.

Coupling the Context and Strategy Objects

When the `GraphVisualizer` needs to graph its data, it calls on its `Grapher` object. An implementation issue that arises here is how to structure the interface between these two objects (and, in the general case, between the Strategy and Context objects) so as to share information. In fact, the issue of how to couple two objects such that they can share information is involved in many of our patterns. As discussed in *Design Patterns*, there are several possible approaches.

In the `GraphVisualizer` case, the information to be shared is the `Pen` with which the `Grapher` should draw and the data to plot. These represent different categories of shared information: static—that which will not change during the running of the application (the `Pen`), and dynamic—that which changes over time (the data). In the static case, we can inform the helper object, in this example the `Grapher`, once and be done with it. On the other hand, we may need to make the helper aware of dynamic information each time the helper is invoked.

Message Arguments.   One possibility is to have the `GraphVisualizer` pass all information to `Grapher` operations in the form of message arguments, thereby keeping the two objects loosely coupled. Thus, a message sent to the `Grapher` might look like this:

```
grapher plot: data using: graphPane pen
```

instead of:

```
grapher plot: data.
```

Of course, in this case, we would have defined the graph-drawing methods in the `Grapher` classes with two arguments:

```
Grapher>>plot: data using: aPen
    . . .
```

However, the `Pen` object is a static bit of shared data. Thus, we can tell the `Grapher` object about this once, up front, rather than each time we draw the graph. This is what we did above. We passed the `Pen` to the `Grapher` as soon as we had instantiated it, as in:

```
GraphVisualizer>>useBarChart
    self grapher:
        (BarChartGrapher new
            pen: graphPane pen)
```

The `Pen` can be set up once; the `graphIt` method passes along the dynamic data object, which *must* be sent each time we draw a graph.

We also could have set this up using an instance-creation method other than `new` in `Grapher`, as follows:

```
Grapher class>>using: aPen
    "Instance creation method."
    ^self new pen: aPen
```

Then passing the `Pen` to the `Grapher` objects at instantiation time would look like this:

```
GraphVisualizer>>useBarChart
    self grapher:
        (BarChartGrapher using: graphPane pen)
```

Self Delegation. Another possible approach would have the `GraphVisual-izer` pass *itself* as an argument to the `Grapher` and let the `Grapher` explicitly request any data it needs from the `GraphVisualizer` by direct message-sends. Beck (1997) refers to this as self delegation. With this approach, when the `Graph-Visualizer` wants to draw a graph, it sends:

```
GraphVisualizer>>graphIt
    ...
    grapher plotFor: self
```

The `Grapher`, thus supplied with a pointer to the `GraphVisualizer`, can send the `GraphVisualizer` messages asking for information such as the data to plot. So we would have defined the graph-drawing methods in the `Grapher` classes with one argument, the `GraphVisualizer`, as in this example:

```
BarChartGrapher>>plotFor: aGraphVisualizer
    | data |
    data := aGraphVisualizer data.
    "Draw the bar chart:"
    ...
```

In fact, if we don't adopt the approach of setting up the `Grapher` object with its drawing `Pen` at instantiation time, this method would look like:

```
BarChartGrapher>>plotFor: aGraphVisualizer
    | data pen |
    data := aGraphVisualizer data.
    pen := aGraphVisualizer penToDrawWith.
    "Now, draw the bar chart:"
    ...
```

Of course, the `GraphVisualizer` class must now define a more elaborate inter-face providing access to its internal objects (e.g., methods such as `data` and `penToDrawWith`). As a result, (1) `GraphVisualizer`'s encapsulation is "weakened" (it now allows any outsider access to its internal objects rather than providing them as arguments in messages it chooses to send) and (2) the Graph-Visualizer and its Grapher are more tightly coupled. Thus, in the current example, this may be a less desirable solution, but in cases where lots of information must be shared, it may be a preferable approach.

Back Pointer.   A slight variation on the self-delegation option would have the Grapher object maintaining a back pointer to the GraphVisualizer in the form of an instance variable. Actually, implementation-wise, it will be a minor variation, but conceptually it's rather different. We can consider the GraphVisualizer itself as a piece of static information to be shared with the Grapher object. Thus, we can share this once, at Grapher instantiation time. Then, any dynamic information the Grapher requires can be requested on the fly. Thus, the Grapher class would be defined with a graphVisualizer instance variable and would implement an associated setter message and a new instance creation method:

```
Object subclass: #Grapher
    instanceVariableNames: 'graphVisualizer'
    classVariableNames: ''
    poolDictionaries: ''

Grapher>>graphVisualizer: aGraphVisualizer
    graphVisualizer := aGraphVisualizer

Grapher class>>for: aGraphVisualizer
    "Instance creation"
    ^self new graphVisualizer: aGraphVisualizer
```

This implementation would, of course, be inherited by Grapher's concrete subclasses. Grapher instance creation in GraphVisualizer now looks like this:

```
GraphVisualizer>>useBarChart
    grapher := BarChartGrapher for: self
```

Now, messages sent by the GraphVisualizer to its Grapher are simpler: they contain no arguments:

```
GraphVisualizer>>graphIt
    grapher plot
```

As in the self-delegation case, the Grapher object requests information directly from its associated GraphVisualizer, but now with messages sent to its graphVisualizer instance variable:

```
BarChartGrapher>>plot
    | data pen |
    data := graphVisualizer data.
    pen := graphVisualizer penToDrawWith.
    "Now, draw the bar chart:"
    ...
```

One potential drawback to this approach is that since the Strategy object (the Grapher) directly points to a single Context object (the GraphVisualizer), the Strategy object can no longer be shared among different Contexts. Therefore, there may exist applications for which self delegation is preferable to a persistent back pointer.

Multiple Simultaneous Strategies, One Active at a Time

Sometimes an application can be linked to multiple Strategy objects simultaneously, although only one is active at any time. That is, rather than creating a new Strategy object each time the algorithm or strategy changes, all of the possible Strategy instances can be created when the application starts, and the application can switch among them. This can be done when the extra instances are not expensive in terms of memory to keep around and is preferable when instantiating and initializing Strategy objects is expensive time-wise. This approach implies some way of "remembering" the instantiated Strategy objects, that is, of keeping pointers to them in the main application. One approach would be to have an instance variable reference a Dictionary containing all of the Strategy objects and another variable to point to the currently active instance.

Exemplifying this approach with the Graph Visualizer, we'll continue to use the grapher variable to point to the active Grapher object. The Dictionary containing all Grapher instances will be referenced by a variable named allGraphers:

```
ViewManager subclass: #GraphVisualizer
    instanceVariableNames:
        'graphPane data grapher graphMessage allGraphers'
    classVariableNames: ''
    poolDictionaries: ''
```

We add a method to initialize allGraphers:

```
GraphVisualizer>>initialize
    "Set up the Dictionary containing all my Strategy objects."
    allGraphers := Dictionary new.
    allGraphers
        at: #BarChart    put: (BarChartGrapher for: self);
        at: #LineGraph    put: (LinePlotter for: self);
        at: #PieChart    put: (PieChartGrapher for: self)
```

And we modify GraphVisualizer instance creation as follows:

```
GraphVisualizer class>>new
    ^super new initialize
```

We also change the `grapher:` setter method to require a `Symbol` as its argument rather than a `Grapher` instance. The `Symbol` specifies the key in the all-Graphers Dictionary:

```
GraphVisualizer>>grapher: aSymbol
    "Change my current graphing strategy."
    grapher := allGraphers at: aSymbol.
```

Finally, when the user selects an item from the "Graph Type" menu, we invoke `grapher:`, as follows:

```
GraphVisualizer>>useBarChart
    self grapher: #BarChart

GraphVisualizer>>useLineGraph
    self grapher: #LineGraph

GraphVisualizer>>usePieChart
    self grapher: #PieChart
```

Domain-Specific Objects as Strategy Objects

A Strategy object need not merely reify a particular algorithm; it may also be a bona-fide application-specific object that also assumes a Strategy role. Here's an example from a financial domain that demonstrates this approach. The application concerns mortgages. A potential customer walks into a bank and wants to know how much her monthly payments would be for a loan of a specific amount. The problem is that there are many different types of mortgages, and each results in different monthly payments for the same principal amount. So, imagine a Mortgage Calculator application. The user interacts with the system by selecting a mortgage type, a down payment amount, and the length of time she wants the mortgage to run, and the application calculates the monthly payments. This sort of application could be used in kiosks on a banking floor or on a bank's Web site. The structure for this application might look like this:

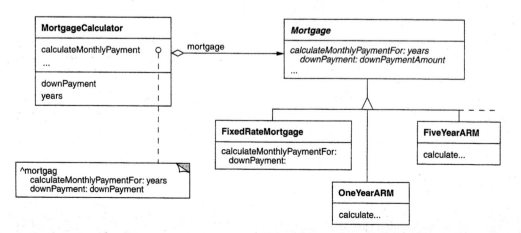

When the user selects a mortgage type, one of the Mortgage subclasses is instantiated (by the way, ARM stands for adjustable rate mortgage). To determine the monthly payments, the Mortgage instance itself acts as a Strategy object for the application and performs the algorithmic calculation. The choice of algorithm is coincident with the choice of mortgage type. So, domain-specific objects that have other responsibilities may also act as Strategies.

Known Smalltalk Uses

ImageRenderer

In VisualWorks, ImageRenderer "is an abstract class *representing a technique* to render an image using a limited palette" (from the class comment, emphasis ours). An ImageRenderer paints an image on a graphics device using an appropriate color palette for that device (e.g., some screens support 256 colors, whereas others support only 16; the ImageRenderer must map colors in the image to those in the supported palette). Concrete subclasses of ImageRenderer encapsulate different rendering algorithms by providing unique implementations of a common rendering message protocol. ImageRenderer subclasses include NearestPaint, OrderedDither, and ErrorDiffusion—again, from the class comment: "Among the subclasses are mapping techniques such as NearestPaint and halftoning techniques such as OrderedDither and ErrorDiffusion." Different graphics devices (e.g., printers and the screen) instantiate different ImageRenderer subclasses to perform rendering depending on their capabilities (gray-scale versus color, color/gray-scale depth), but code that sends messages to these rendering objects doesn't care what type of ImageRenderer it's talking to because they all implement the same message interface.

View-Controller

In the Model-View-Controller framework, the View-Controller relationship is an example of the Strategy pattern. A View instance (representing a screen widget) uses a Controller object to handle and respond to user input via mouse or keyboard. For a View to use a different user interaction strategy, it can instantiate a different Controller class for its controller object. This can even occur at runtime to change the user interaction style on the fly; for example, a View can be disabled (so it does not accept any user input) by instantiating and switching to a controller that ignores input.

Insurance Policy Policies

Philip Hartman of ISSC Object Technology Services used the Strategy pattern in a Smalltalk application for an insurance company to implement different business logic for individual automobile insurance policies. One requirement of the application was that the logic for calculating the cost of insurance had to vary by insurance company subsidiary and/or by the state of residence of the policy holder. For example, points are charged against drivers based on violations and accidents, and different subsidiaries and states use different rules for determining how, and how many, points are assigned. In many cases, the points have a large effect on the premium charged. In the implementation, a `Policy` object represents an insurance policy and points to an instance of one of the concrete subclasses of `PointAssignmentRule`. Each `PointAssignmentRule` subclass encapsulates a different algorithm for assigning points to drivers on the policy. Thus, by instantiating one or another of these classes, the policy logic could be made to vary without varying the code of the `Policy`.

Related Patterns

Builder

The careful reader will notice that the structure diagrams for Strategy are isomorphic to those for the Builder (47) pattern. We might even consider Builder a specialization of Strategy. The difference in the patterns is when and where they are used and the functionality of the helper objects. In the Builder pattern, the helper object has the job of creating a Product in a step-by-step fashion: the Director object iteratively calls on the Builder to add subcomponents and then once for the final Product. In the Strategy pattern, the Strategy object acting as an external helper to a Context object is intended to encapsulate any algorithm—not necessarily for creational purposes but for any runtime service. Multiple algorithms are encapsulated outside of the "main" Context object, and each is reified as an object. The Strategy object is called on periodically, as needed, to perform a complete stand-alone task in one shot.

Abstract Factory

Strategy and Builder are also related structurally and thematically to Abstract Factory (31). In the latter, an external helper object is called on to create some Product on behalf of the main application as well. There may be multiple factory objects to choose from, and they all provide the same abstract interface. Thus, the factory's client doesn't know the exact class of the factory—and doesn't care. It just sends a generic message to its current factory when a particular type of object has to be constructed. Again, this is similar in structure to the Strategy pattern but is divergent in intent and when and where it is used. An Abstract Factory is used for one-shot object creation rather than periodic algorithm execution, as in Strategy.

Admittedly, the lines delineating these patterns are sometimes blurry. In our Graph Visualizer example, the `Grapher` Strategy objects might be said to be producing a product: a graph based on the data it receives. Overall, Strategy may be used for any runtime service when that service may be implemented in multiple ways.

State

Finally, Strategy also bears structural similarity to State (327). See the Related Patterns section in the State pattern essay for more details.

TEMPLATE METHOD (DP 325)   Object Behavioral

Intent

Define the skeleton of an algorithm in an operation, deferring some steps to sub-classes. Template Method lets subclasses redefine certain steps of an algorithm without changing the algorithm's structure.

Structure

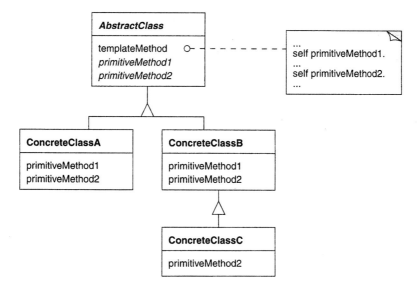

Description

Template Method may be Number 1 on the Design Patterns Pop Charts. Its structure and use are at the heart of much of object-oriented programming. Template Method turns on the fundamental object-oriented concept of inheritance. It relies on defining classes that differ only slightly from an existing class. It does this by relying on the ability of classes to provide for new behavior by overriding inherited methods.

Central to the Template Method pattern is a method that implements a broad message in terms of several narrower messages in the same receiver. The broader method, a **template method,** is implemented in a superclass and the narrower methods, **primitive methods,** are implemented in that class or its subclasses. The template method defines a general algorithm, and the Primitive Methods specify the details. When a subclass wants to use the algorithm but wishes to change some of the details, it can override the specific primitive methods without having to override the entire template method as well.

Reuse Through Inheritance

Code and attribute sharing through inheritance is one of the most maligned techniques in object-oriented programming. It is deceptively easy to use but often difficult to use well. Some authorities have dismissed implementation inheritance as confusing and unnecessary. As early as the first OOPSLA, papers have documented potential problems with inheritance (Snyder, 1986). The object-oriented language SELF does not even support class inheritance; instead, it uses object delegation exclusively. *Design Patterns* advocates favoring object composition over class inheritance (DP 18–21). Many patterns transform code that relies on class inheritance to use object composition instead; State, Strategy, Decorator, Bridge, and Abstract Factory are a few of them.

Nevertheless, inheritance is a fundamental feature of most object-oriented languages, including Smalltalk. Good class hierarchies allow for reuse of abstraction, design, and implementation. Because of inheritance, these hierarchies are easier to understand, maintain, and extend, and their classes are much more reusable. We can define new classes that differ slightly from existing classes by specializing those existing classes rather than starting from scratch. Even as *Design Patterns* shows poor examples of inheritance that work better as composition, it still advocates using inheritance to define and implement interfaces (DP 14–18). Most of the patterns feature at least one class hierarchy with an abstract class at the top that defines an interface and several concrete subclasses that implement it: Adapter's Target hierarchy, Composite's Component hierarchy, State's State hierarchy, and so on.

The Template Method pattern encourages proper use of inheritance. The pattern can also be helpful for refactoring related classes that share common behavior (DP 326). The key to factoring for reuse is to separate the stuff that changes from the stuff that doesn't, and Template Method encourages this by factoring the reusable code into the superclass and the specifics that can change into the subclasses.

How Template Method Works

Abstract classes and the Template Method pattern go very much hand in hand. An abstract class is a superclass that defines the behavior of the classes in its hierarchy while deferring the implementation details to its subclasses. The superclass is abstract because it does not implement all of the behavior it defines. The subclasses are concrete because each one implements all of the behavior, by either inheriting it from its superclasses or implementing the behavior itself.

Template Method is the same technique at the method level instead of the class level. Here is what a Template Method generally looks like:

```
AbstractClass>>algorithmA
    self
        algorithmAStep1;
        algorithmAStep2;
        algorithmAStep3
```

The class defines a method, such as `algorithmA`, for each unit of behavior that it can perform. The method does not do much work; instead, it provides a template listing the steps to be performed and delegates each of the steps back to the receiver (`self`). In this way, the Template Method gets to decide *what* steps are done, but the receiver gets to decide *how* each step is done. This separates the steps that must be performed from how they are performed.

The beauty is that not only can the abstract class define how each of these steps is done, but each concrete subclass has the opportunity to override each of these decisions. If a concrete class generally likes the way `algorithmA` works but not the way `algorithmAStep2` works, it can subimplement (override) `algorithmAStep2` without changing `algorithmA` or the superclass's implementation of steps 1 and 3. This allows the subclass to override just the parts that it needs to while inheriting the rest, which minimizes the amount of code each subclass must implement itself and emphasizes the subclass's differences with its superclass.

Types of Methods

There are four types of methods that the abstract class may implement: template, concrete, abstract, and hook (DP 327–328). The last three are types of primitive methods.

1. *Template.* A template method is one in the abstract class that combines concrete, abstract, and/or hook methods together into an algorithm. Subclasses usually inherit it unchanged, although they may override the methods invoked therein. This is the heart of the template method pattern.

2. *Concrete.* A concrete method is one that the abstract class defines and that subclasses do not override.

3. *Abstract.* An abstract method is one in the abstract class that "declares" a message but defers its implementation to the subclasses. Each subclass *must* override the abstract methods it inherits. (*Design Patterns* refers to these as "Primitive operations." This should not be confused with a "primitive" in Smalltalk, which is a different concept entirely.)

4. *Hook.* A hook method is one in the abstract class that declares a message's behavior and provides a default implementation for it. Sometimes the default is simply to do nothing. Subclasses *may* override the method to change this default.

Design Patterns also lists a fifth type, factory method, but this is really just a special case of a concrete or hook method (see Factory Method (63)).

It is usually easy to identify which methods ought to be concrete. It is more difficult to determine which methods will be abstract and which will be hooks. The
question you need to ask here is whether there is a reasonable default implementation for this method. If so, the abstract class's implementation should be a hook
method. If not, the method will be abstract.

According to *Design Patterns* (329), one design goal is to minimize the number of
primitive operations that subclasses must override. One way to reduce the number of primitive operations (abstract methods) is to implement those messages as
hook methods instead. An abstract method forces a developer implementing a
subclass to override the method. On the other hand, he can choose to inherit a
hook method unchanged. In this way, hook methods make subclassing easier
than abstract methods.

A potential problem with using a hook method rather than an abstract one is that
it may not be obvious to the subclass developer that the method is a candidate for
overriding. Only class or method documentation provides this level of information. If a subclass developer forgets to override an abstract method, he will discover his mistake when he runs the code and gets a walkback from a
`subclassResponsibility` error. Should he inadvertently inherit inappropri-
ate behavior from a hook method, his code will run, but not necessarily correctly.

A "Do Nothing" Hook

A hook method defined in a superclass must provide a reasonable default of an
operation for its subclasses. A special case of a reasonable default is an implementation of the method that does nothing, that is, only returns `self`. This sort
of "do nothing" method is often useful when there is the potential for an operation to occur, but not all subclasses may need that operation. Two examples of
this sort of method are VisualWorks's `ApplicationModel>>preBuildWith:`
and `postBuildWith:` methods. These methods provide hooks for `Applica-
tionModel` subclasses that need to modify the behavior of user interface wid-
gets at two different points in the interface building process. However,
`ApplicationModel` itself does not need to do anything at either stage, so it
implements the messages to do nothing. This default behavior is appropriate for
most subclasses as well.

Another example, from IBM Smalltalk, is `Class>>initialize`. Not all classes
need initialization, so the default implementation is to do nothing. This makes it
possible to use `super initialize` safely in any class's initialization method.
By the way, this is something you should *not* do in class methods in VisualWorks;
in VisualWorks, `Object class>>initialize` has the undesirable side effect
of removing all dependents!

Another example is `Stream>>close` in VisualWorks and Visual Smalltalk. It is
often useful to have clients be unaware of what kind of stream they are using, be
it on an internal collection or an external object (like a socket or file handle). Thus,
the default implementation of `close` is to do nothing. External stream subclasses
redefine this method to clean up external resources.

Designing and Refactoring Hierarchies

When you are refactoring, or initially designing, a hierarchy for reuse, it is often beneficial to move behavior up the hierarchy and state down the hierarchy. Auer (1995) describes this process in four heuristic patterns:

1. *Define classes by behavior, not state.* Initially implement a class to define its behavior without regard to its structure.

2. *Implement behavior with abstract state.* Implement behavior that needs state information to access that state indirectly through messages rather than referencing the state variables directly.

3. *Identify message layers.* Implement a class's behavior through a small set of kernel methods that can easily be overridden in subclasses.

4. *Defer identification of state variables.* The abstract state messages become kernel methods that require state variables. Rather than declaring those variables in the superclass, declare them in a subclass and defer the kernel methods' implementation to the subclass.

This process develops a hierarchy that separates interface from implementation. A superclass abstractly defines the hierarchy's behavior, and one or more subclasses implement it. The superclass is easy to subclass because it uses kernel methods and does not force subclasses to inherit state that they may not need.

This process leads to template methods and primitive methods. The primitive methods are what Auer's patterns call kernel methods. The template methods are the layers that use the kernel methods. What these patterns also show is that the Template Method pattern can be nested; each message layer has its own template-primitive relationship. The primitive messages that a template method sends can themselves be template methods that send other primitive messages.

Here's an example of nested Template Methods from the `Collection` hierarchy in VisualWorks:

```
Collection>>removeAll: aCollection
    "Remove each element of aCollection from the receiver.
     ..."

    aCollection do: [:each | self remove: each].
    ^aCollection

Collection>>remove: oldObject
    "Remove oldObject as one of the receiver's elements. ..."

    ^self remove: oldObject ifAbsent: [self notFoundError]

Collection>>remove: oldObject ifAbsent: anExceptionBlock
    "Remove oldObject as one of the receiver's elements. ..."

    self subclassResponsibility
```

When a `Collection` receives `removeAll:`, the implementation is a template method that delegates to the primitive method `remove:`. However, `remove:`'s implementation is not primitive; it is another Template Method that delegates to `remove:ifAbsent:`. Finally, `remove:ifAbsent:` really is a primitive method, an abstract method that delegates to its subclasses. We'll see another example of this iterative Template Method implementation in the `Window-Policy` example in the Known Smalltalk Uses section.

What to Delegate

When a method is well written, all of its tasks should be performed at the same level of abstraction. That is, its steps shouldn't look like, "Do something general; Do something general; Do something very specific." Instead, the specific code should be factored into another method that this one calls. Then all of this method's steps are at the same level of generality or specificity.

Certain code details jump out as being too specific for general algorithms. These details may include constants, classes, and specific algorithms or portions thereof.

Delegating Constants.   One obvious case for a simple template method is in factoring out the "declaration" of a constant into a separate method rather than hard-coding it in-line. You usually specify constants in Smalltalk through the use of a Pool variable or by defining a separate method that simply returns the constant (a Constant Method, Beck, 1997). Pool dictionaries have many drawbacks. The main arguments against them are that they are poorly supported by the language and class libraries and that they adversely affect reuse (Ewing, 1994). Because of these drawbacks, specifying a method to return a constant is the more flexible approach, because subclasses can implement the method differently to return different constant values. In this way, the methods that *use* that constant are template methods, since the method returning the constant is now a hook.

You can see an example of defining a constant value that differs in various subclasses in the `EtBrowser` hierarchy in IBM Smalltalk. The superclass `EtBrowser` defines the method `classDoubleClickSelector` to return `nil`. This means that nothing special happens when you double-click the selection in the classes list of a browser. Subclasses redefine this method to return a message selector. This message selector is used to do something else: in some classes, double-click means "browse the selected class"; in others, it means "expand or contract the class hierarchy rooted at this class."

Also in IBM Smalltalk, the message `fixedSize` in the `OsObject` hierarchy returns the size (in bytes) of the structure each `OsObject` subclass represents. This use of polymorphism allows Template Methods defined in `OsObject`, like `copyToOsMemory`, to operate on any structure, regardless of its actual size.

Delegating Classes.   Smalltalk classes are a special case of constants. In the Factory Method pattern, a Smalltalk method returns a class, and that class is then used to create instances (see Factory Method (63)). In general, even if you do not wish to use the Factory Method pattern initially, it is a good idea to isolate class names into their own methods to make it easier to maintain the code if the name of a class changes.

Delegating Subparts of Algorithms.   Often you may want to isolate a particular subpart of an algorithm that varies from class to class. Again, this is the main motivation behind the Template Method pattern. Part of the challenge of object-oriented design is finding and setting up such relationships between algorithms and their component subtasks—something that cannot be done in procedural languages because they lack inheritance and delegation.

You can find an example of this in VisualWorks in the `Controller` hierarchy. One of the fundamental parts of the VisualWorks windowing system is the notion of the "control loop" that defines how each `Controller` gains control of the mouse. A template method named `controlLoop`, shown below, implements this notion:

```
Controller>>controlLoop
    [self poll.
    self isControlActive]
        whileTrue: [self controlActivity]
```

The message `controlActivity` is a hook method defined in `Controller` as simply passing control along to the next level of controllers. Subclasses of `Controller` override this method to perform a specific action whenever they receive control. It is interesting to note that one subclass of `Controller`, `ControllerWithMenu`, overrides this method with yet another template method:

```
ControllerWithMenu>>controlActivity
    self sensor redButtonPressed & self viewHasCursor
        ifTrue: [^self redButtonActivity].
    self sensor yellowButtonPressed & self viewHasCursor
        ifTrue: [^self yellowButtonActivity].
    super controlActivity
```

Subclasses of `ControllerWithMenu` can override the messages `redButtonActivity` and `yellowButtonActivity` to perform specific actions while the "Red" or "Yellow" mouse buttons are depressed.

A Case Study in Refactoring

Examining a case study in refactoring can help to clarify how template methods arise during this process and how the issues discussed above play themselves out. Probably the best-known and best-described example of refactoring in Smalltalk was the refactoring of the Smalltalk-80 `View` classes between Objectworks\Smalltalk 2.5 and Objectworks\Smalltalk 4.0.

As both Johnson and Foote (1988) and Rubin and Liebs (1992) describe, the original class `View` in Smalltalk-80 was extremely large and unwieldy. It suffered from trying to be all things to all people. Views were capable of edge decoration (knowing their border thickness and color), containing and managing subviews, and handling their own layout inside a parent view. They were also responsible for communicating with a model (via the Observer pattern) and with their associated controller. As a result, each `View` contained a large number of instance variables; however, each instance used only a subset of those variables.

Objectworks\Smalltalk 4.0 (the precursor to VisualWorks) solved this problem through a significant refactoring of the `View` hierarchy, as described by Rubin and Liebs (1992). Each of the previously listed responsibilities of `View` was refactored into different classes in the `View` hierarchy. There are now three sets of subclasses of the abstract visual superclass `VisualPart`:

1. The `View` hierarchy, consisting of those objects that have a model and controller.

2. The `Wrapper` hierarchy, consisting of those objects that use the Decorator pattern to modify the display or positioning of other visuals.

3. The `CompositePart` hierarchy, consisting of those visuals that use the Composite pattern to combine other visuals.

As a result, the classes are much lighter weight, and a developer can choose more carefully where he will subclass to inherit only those parts that he needs.

One of the other crucial points to emerge during the refactoring was the principle of trading state for behavior in an abstract superclass. In particular, a problem arose when trying to deal with control in the different types of visuals that resulted from the refactoring.

In the refactored hierarchy, the three basic branches described above suffice for most purposes. In most cases, `Views` (visuals with `Controllers`) are the leaves of a visual tree made up of Composites and Decorators. However, there is one case where this breaks down. Occasionally you need a `View` that has a controller but also contains other visuals; this is a `CompositeView`. An example of a `CompositeView` is the VisualWorks canvas editor, which is an instance of `UIPainterView`. The individual views within a `UIPainterView` have their own controllers that describe how they react when they are selected and moved. However, the `UIPainterView` itself also needs a controller to describe how the menu for the canvas as a whole operates. At first glance, this problem of how to give `View` behavior to a subclass of `CompositePart` appears to require multiple inheritance. However, VisualWorks solves it through a clever application of Template Method.

The abstract superclass `VisualPart` implements the method `object-WantingControl` as a Template Method. The method `objectWantingControl` returns the controller in the receiver's visual tree that wants control. The method uses the method `getController`, which is a hook method. Here's the method from the VisualWorks image:

```
VisualPart>>objectWantingControl
    "The receiver is in a control hierarchy and the
    container is asking for an object that wants control.
    If no control is desired then the receiver answers
    nil. If control is wanted then the receiver answers
    the control object."

    | ctrl |
    ctrl := self getController.
    ctrl isNil ifTrue: [^nil].
    "Trap errors occurring while searching for
    the object wanting control."
    ^Object errorSignal
        handle: [...]    "Handle error"
        do: [ctrl isControlWanted
                ifTrue: [self]
                ifFalse: [nil]]
```

The default behavior of `getController`, as defined in `VisualPart`, is to return `nil`, meaning there is no `Controller` that wants control. However, this method is reimplemented as state in the subclasses `View` and `CompositeView` to return their respective controllers. In this way, the objects in both hierarchies can get the behavior they want without unnecessary code duplication.

There are many other uses of Template Method in the VisualWorks visual component hierarchy. Finding them and understanding their use can be an enlightening exercise.

Implementation

Here's one way to implement a complex method that we want to be a template method:

1. *Simple implementation.* Implement all of the code in one method. When trying to factor code, it is often more convenient to just write the code before trying to refactor it. This large method will become the template method.

2. *Break into steps.* Use comments to break the method apart into logical steps. Use a comment to describe each step.

3. *Make step methods.* Make a separate method out of each step in the template method. Put these methods in the same class as the template method. Name each step method based on the comment from step 2 and move its code from the template method. If the step method needs temporary variables from the template method, pass them in as parameters.

4. *Call the step methods.* Simplify the template method to perform each step by calling the corresponding step method. What's left in the template method is an outline of the entire algorithm. This is now a true template method.

5. *Make constant methods.* If the template method still contains literals, class names, or other constants, factor them into separate methods. For each constant, define a method that does nothing but return the constant. Then change the template method to call these methods instead of hard-coding the constants.

6. *Repeat steps 1–5.* Repeat this process for each of the step methods you've created. This will factor them into template methods that call primitive methods. Continue until all of the steps in each method have the same level of generality and until all constants have been factored into their own methods.

Sample Code

One of the more common uses of Template Method (described by Auer, 1995) is to isolate away a default value in a lazy initialization method. Consider the following method:

```
Circle>>radius
    radius == nil ifTrue: [radius := 10].
    ^radius
```

Although this method works fine in a superclass, the problem occurs when subclasses want to substitute a default value for `radius` other than 10. In this case they must reimplement the `radius` method to include all of the above code except for the constant. A better version of this method uses Template Method and defines a hook method called `defaultRadius`. Subclasses can override this default, or they can choose to inherit the superclass's default as is:

```
Circle>>radius
    radius == nil ifTrue: [radius := self defaultRadius].
    ^radius

Circle>>defaultRadius
    "This can be overridden in subclasses."
    ^10
```

Then `BigCircle`, a subclass of `Circle`, can easily change its default radius without having to reimplement the lazy initialization:

```
BigCircle>>defaultRadius
    "Override the inherited default."
    ^100
```

Even if you do not use lazy initialization, the same technique applies in an initialize method. Here's the non–Template Method approach:

```
Circle>>initialize
   radius := 10.
   "other variable declarations"

BigCircle>>initialize
    "Have to re-set the value of variableName in the subclass"
    super initialize.
    radius := 100.
```

A better version of the previous implementation would be:

```
Circle>>initialize
    radius := self defaultRadius.
    "other variable declarations"
```

The implementations of the defaultRadius methods are the same as in the previous example.

Known Smalltalk Uses

The discussion has given many examples of the use of the Template Method pattern in the various Smalltalk dialects. There are several other places the pattern has been used in the Smalltalk base class libraries. We offer these not only as known uses but as additional Sample Code examples for the pattern.

WindowPolicy

In Visual Smalltalk, every window has an associated window policy object, which is called on to decide which (if any) pull-down menus should be added to the window. WindowPolicy defines the interface for all concrete policy classes. Instances of subclass SmalltalkWindowPolicy ensure that the *Smalltalk* pull-down is added to a window's menu bar. Instances of StandardWindowPolicy add the standard *File* and *Edit* pull-downs. And so on. A generic Template Method in WindowPolicy is invoked to add all of the pull-down menus; it looks like this:

```
WindowPolicy>>addMenus
    "Private - add the menus for the window to the
    menu bar."
    ...
    self
       addSystemMenus;
       addStandardLeftMenus;
       addApplicationMenus;
       addStandardRightMenus
```

All of these add...Menus messages are implemented in WindowPolicy as empty methods. Concrete subclasses of WindowPolicy override these implementations as necessary. So, for example:

```
StandardWindowPolicy>>addStandardLeftMenus
    "Private - add the menus that are to be located
    on the menu bar before any application-specific
    menus (File & Edit)."

    self addFileMenu.
    self addEditMenu.
```

Note that this is, in turn, another template method, allowing still lower-level subclasses to determine for themselves which menu items to include on the *File* and *Edit* pull-downs.

Collection Examples

The Collection hierarchies in the various Smalltalk dialects contain examples of all four types of methods found in abstract classes. Let's look at a couple of examples from VisualWorks.

The method collect: is a template method that sends several primitive messages:

```
Collection>>collect: aBlock
    "Evaluate aBlock with each of the values of the
     receiver as the argument. Collect the resulting
     values into a collection that is like the receiver.
     Answer the new collection."

    | newCollection |
    newCollection := self species new.
    self do: [:each |
       newCollection add: (aBlock value: each)].
    ^newCollection
```

The message species returns the class for an object's "kind" rather than its actual class. Since Collection uses it as a primitive message, you might expect to find it implemented in Collection, but Collection actually inherits it from Object:

```
Object>>species
    "Answer the preferred class for reconstructing the
     receiver. ..."

    ^self class
```

This is a hook method because it permits overriding but provides a default implementation that is suitable for most subclasses. One subclass it is not suitable for is `Interval`. It overrides `species` like this:

```
Interval>>species
    "Answer the preferred class for reconstructing the
    receiver, that is, Array."

    ^Array
```

The second primitive method is `do:`. Its default implementation in `Collection` looks like this:

```
Collection>>do: aBlock
    "Evaluate aBlock with each of the receiver's elements
    as the argument."

    self subclassResponsibility
```

It is an abstract method because it does not provide a default implementation and is overridden by numerous `Collection` subclasses. It does not provide a default implementation because the way you iterate through the elements in, say, an `OrderedCollection` versus a `Set` is very different.

The third primitive operation is `add:`. Although it is not actually sent to the receiver (`self`), it is sent to another `Collection` and thus is a primitive part of the larger collecting algorithm. Its base implementation looks like this:

```
Collection>>add: newObject
    "Include newObject as one of the receiver's elements. ..."

    self subclassResponsibility
```

Thus, `add:` is another abstract method that all direct subclasses must override.

Another method in `Collection`, one that seems simple enough to be primitive but is actually a template method, is `remove:`.

```
Collection>>remove: oldObject
    "Remove oldObject as one of the receiver's elements. ..."

    ^self remove: oldObject ifAbsent: [self notFoundError]
```

The first primitive message is `remove:ifAbsent:`. Like `add:`, it is deferred to subclasses:

```
Collection>>remove: oldObject ifAbsent: anExceptionBlock
    "Remove oldObject as one of the receiver's elements. ..."

    self subclassResponsibility
```

Thus `remove:ifAbsent:` is an abstract method. The important insight is that `remove:` doesn't remove anything; it gets `remove:ifAbsent:` to do all of the work. Thus, `remove:` isn't really a primitive method, it's a Template Method.

The other primitive message that `remove:` sends is `notFoundError:`

```
Collection>>notFoundError
    "Raise a signal indicating that an object is not
     in the collection."

    ^self class notFoundSignal raise
```

This works for all of the `Collection` classes, so none of them overrides it. Thus, it is a concrete method because it implements real behavior, and the subclasses don't change that behavior. If any subclasses did change the behavior, `notFoundError` would become a hook method.

Magnitude Examples

Another excellent place to look for template methods is in the `Magnitude` hierarchy. For instance, consider the abstract class `Magnitude` in IBM Smalltalk. Its Common Language Definition API protocol supplies the messages `>`, `<=`, `>=`, `between:and:`, `max:`, and `min:`. The first method, `>`, is an abstract method that all subclasses must implement. The other methods are template methods that are defined in terms of `>`, so any new subclass that implements `>` inherits the others for free. For example, if you implement `DollarAmount` as a new subclass of `Magnitude`, you would only need to override `>` to gain the rest of the `Magnitude` behavior.

Similarly, in VisualWorks, different `Magnitude` subclasses may implement local versions of the `<` or `>` methods. Other `Magnitude` methods invoke these methods by sending "`self >`" or "`self <`". For example, the `>=` method is defined to use `<` as follows:

```
Magnitude>>>= aMagnitude
    "Answer whether the receiver is greater than or
     equal to the argument."

    ^(self < aMagnitude) not
```

The beauty of this approach is that subclasses may redefine `<` and then need not redefine `>=`.

Object>>printString

An excellent example of a hook method providing a reasonable default is `Object>>printOn:`. The template method `printString` defined in `Object` operates by using the local implementation of `printOn:` as shown on the next page:

```
Object>>printString
    "Answer a String that is an ASCII representation
    of the receiver."

    | aStream aString |
    aString := String new: 20.
    self printOn: (aStream := WriteStream on: aString).
    ^aStream contents
```

The definition of printOn: in Object, shown below, conveys only a minimum of information about the object receiving the message:

```
Object>>printOn: aStream
    "Append the ASCII representation of the receiver
    to aStream. This is the default implementation which
    prints 'a' ('an') followed by the receiver class name."

    | aString |
    aString := self class name.
    (aString at: 1) isVowel
        ifTrue: [aStream nextPutAll: 'an ']
        ifFalse: [aStream nextPutAll: 'a '].
    aStream nextPutAll: aString
```

However, in many subclasses, more information is useful. For instance, in String, the actual characters are shown as a quoted string. To achieve this, String overrides the default implementation of printOn:.

```
String>>printOn: aStream
    "Append the receiver as a quoted string
    to aStream doubling all internal single
    quote characters."

    aStream nextPut: $'.
    self do:
        [ :character |
        aStream nextPut: character.
        character = $'
            ifTrue: [aStream nextPut: character]].
    aStream nextPut: $'
```

In this way, printString can remain unchanged while its behavior for individual classes can vary. Those classes need only override the hook method, printOn:.

VISITOR (DP 331)   Object Behavioral

Intent

Represent an operation to be performed on the elements of an object structure in a class separate from the elements themselves. Visitor lets you define a new operation without changing the classes of the elements on which it operates.

Structure

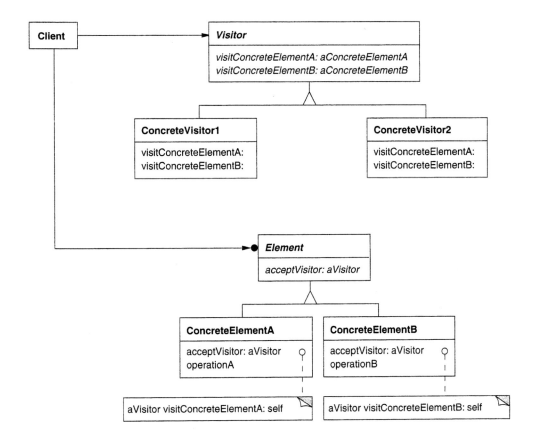

Discussion

Is This Object-Oriented Design?

At first glance, the Visitor pattern seems contrary to classic object-oriented design. Most, if not all, of us who program in Smalltalk or other object-oriented languages have previously worked with procedural languages. When we were learning the object-oriented way of doing things, we learned that the procedural style of code operating on inert data is "wrong," or, at the least, the wrong way to think about object-oriented design. The issue is basically assigning responsibility for behaviors to the appropriate place (read, *object*). After internalizing the classic writings and concepts of object-oriented design, it seems natural for a service that involves an object to be included among *that* object's repertoire of behaviors rather than in some external code that acts on the object as a passive entity. This implies that an associated message ought to be included in the definition of that object's class and the object should be an active participant in the process. As Wirfs-Brock, Wilkerson, and Wiener (1990) assert, "If an object is responsible for maintaining certain information, it is logical also to assign it the responsibility of performing any operations necessary upon that information" (p. 65).

In his seminal book, Brad Cox (1986) describes why including operations *in* the object is preferable to having an external, active procedure act *on* the object as a passive commodity, especially when the procedure must act *on* multiple objects of differing types. The essential point is that by polymorphically defining the operation in the relevant yet disparate classes, we can avoid case statements or other conditionals that test the objects' types and perform different code accordingly. Let's look at a concrete example.

Suppose we have a drawing editor in which different types of graphical objects are drawn; there may be rectangles, ellipses, polylines. When the drawing editor needs to redraw the objects, it might, in a procedural programming manner, do something like the following:

```
DrawingEditor>>refresh
    "Don't do it this way!"
    graphicElements do: [:anElement |
      (anElement isMemberOf: Rectangle)
        ifTrue: ["code to draw a rectangle"]
        ifFalse:
          [(anElement isMemberOf: Ellipse)
             ifTrue: ["code to draw an ellipse"]
             ifFalse:
               [(anElement isMemberOf: PolyLine)
                  ifTrue: ["code to draw a polyline"]
                  ...
```

If we later wish to add a new type of graphical object (say, a polygon), we have to find all such conditional code and splice in a new condition to test for the new type.

Alternatively, in a more object-oriented fashion, we may define a `draw` method in each of the classes representing our graphical objects. The `draw` method within each class knows exactly how to paint the objects of *that* class. So, we would define:

```
Rectangle>>draw
    "I'm a rectangle; here's the code to draw me."
    ...
```

We would code `Ellipse>>draw` and `PolyLine>>draw` similarly. Now the redraw code in the drawing editor looks like this:

```
DrawingEditor>>refresh
    graphicElements do: [:anElement | anElement draw]
```

If we ever add new graphical object classes, this redraw code need not change. Instead, each new graphical object class would merely need to support the `draw` message.

However, there are a couple of downsides to this approach. First, nobody wants to—or does—talk about this in the object-oriented literature, but dispersing the *draw* code all over the class hierarchy is problematic from a program understanding perspective. Watch a novice object-oriented programmer attempt to understand this code. She'll encounter quite a bit of difficulty in finding all the pieces and forming a coherent mental model of what's going on. It's easier when all the classes that implement `draw` are in a single hierarchy branch (e.g., abstract superclass Geometric with subclasses representing concrete geometrics like `Rectangle` and `Ellipse`) and worse when the classes are discontiguous. But it can be difficult.

Second, when we distribute the responsibility and implementation of an operation involving the graphic element classes to each class, it's harder to add a new operation. Doing so means adding a new method to every `Geometric` class. Hence, this solution is better when the set of operations is basically static.

The Visitor Solution

So far we have two possible solution approaches: a conditional in the drawing editor or a dispersion of responsibility to each graphical object class, with the `draw` operation intrinsic to the object being drawn. Visitor provides a third alternative. In the Visitor solution, all of the drawing code (the code required for drawing all types of graphical objects) resides in a single drawing Visitor class, separate from all the graphical object classes. When a graphical object must be drawn, the job is delegated to a drawing Visitor instance. The Visitor does all the real work, possibly asking the graphical object for information along the way.

Hence the pattern has external code operating on the objects as if they were passive entities, much as in the procedural programming world . . . but not quite: it is the graphical objects that invoke the appropriate code to operate on themselves. When the drawing editor has to draw a graphical object, the editor sends a message to the graphic, not to the Visitor. The graphical object in turn simply sends a message to the Visitor, and this message encodes the graphical object's class, in essence telling the Visitor what to do. Let's look at a concrete example on the next page:

```
DrawingEditor>>refresh
   "Redraw all the elements in the drawing"
   | visitor |
   visitor := DrawingVisitor for: self.
   graphicElements do: [:aGraphic |
      aGraphic acceptVisitor: visitor]

Rectangle>>acceptVisitor: aVisitor
   aVisitor visitRectangle: self

Ellipse>>acceptVisitor: aVisitor
   aVisitor visitEllipse: self
```

Notice that the message sent by each graphic object incorporates information about the class itself. In DrawingVisitor, we have one method for each possible class that can be visited: visitEllipse:, visitRectangle:, visit-Polyline:. Each of these methods knows how to draw a graphical object of a specific class.

So what have we gained? We avoid a case-like statement to choose among disparate drawing algorithms—the drawing editor still sends a single message to each graphical object. And we've modularized all drawing code into a single location rather than many separate locations (multiple draw methods in each graphical object class).

Furthermore, other operations involve graphical objects, not just drawing. When we want to add a new operation that acts on graphic elements, we can code another Visitor class that groups that operation into a single location. We can have a Visitor that knows how to save graphics to a database; we might have Visitors that perform transformation operations—flip horizontally or vertically, rotate, skew, snap to grid—on the set of selected graphical objects; in a computer-aided drawing (CAD) context, the graphical objects may have associated part numbers, and we could have Visitors that print a Bill of Materials, compute the cost of an assembled product, or send part information to a Purchase Order application and an Inventory system. The upshot is that we can add new operations on graphical objects without changing the graphical object classes in any way. Once each class implements acceptVisitor:, we can invoke any sort of Visitor in the same fashion:

```
CADEditor>>printBOM
   | visitor |
   visitor := BillOfMaterialsVisitor for: self.
   graphicElements do: [:aGraphic |
      aGraphic acceptVisitor: visitor]
```

There's further rationale for having operations that act on a class reside outside of that class (see also DP 333; Liu, 1996). If we implement application-specific methods for many different applications within the class itself, we run the risk of muddying the class definition. This is particularly true when the class defines a general-purpose (that is, not application- or domain-specific) object. Suppose we have a set of classes defining the nodes of a parse tree for Smalltalk language statements (thus, an `AssignmentNode` class, a `VariableNode` class, a `MessageNode` class, and so on, as in VisualWorks). Such classes are normally used for the compilation process. The Smalltalk compiler parses (decomposes) Smalltalk source statements into trees of nodes and then iterates over the parse tree to generate bytecodes for the Smalltalk virtual machine. But someone else might decide to use the tree of parse nodes for a Smalltalk-to-C++ translation program. And then later someone else may want to implement a Smalltalk-to-Java translator. The question to ask is, Do we really want application-specific code for all such applications to reside within the relatively simple node classes? Instead, we can have operations like these performed by a Smalltalk-to-C++ Visitor or a Smalltalk-to-Java Visitor which visit each node of the parse tree and perform their application-specific operations. (It turns out that VisualWorks does use a Visitor to operate on Smalltalk parse trees for yet another purpose; see the Known Smalltalk Uses section).

Double Dispatch

As pointed out in *Design Patterns,* Visitor implements a form of **double dispatch.** Before explaining how double dispatch operates, let's look at the problem it solves. In some situations, the behavior of a method depends not only on the class that implements the method but on the classes of the method's arguments as well. Let's look specifically at the case in which the method has a single argument. Here's the code from the Visual Smalltalk image for adding to a `Point`:

```
Point>>+ delta
    "delta can be a Number or a Point."
    ^delta isPoint
        ifTrue: [(x + delta x) @ (y + delta y)
        ifFalse: [(x + delta) @ (y + delta)]
```

Here we see that the algorithm does not depend on the + message receiver alone, but rather is a function of both the receiver (a `Point`) *and* the argument (a `Number` or a `Point`). Here the possible types of arguments include instances of only two classes (and, of course, their subclasses: `Number` is an abstract class and the argument may actually be an `Integer`, `Float`, etc.). Hence there's no real problem with having a conditional to test for the argument's class and performing different behaviors accordingly (notwithstanding those purists who believe we ought never perform such a test). But suppose we had many possible types of arguments. We might have an Adapter that wraps a `Number` or a `Point` (see the Adapter (105) pattern). Retrieving the embedded object from an Adapter requires sending the `value` message to it. So we'd need code like:

```
Point>>+ delta
    "delta can be a Number or a Point or an Adapter on a
    Number or a Point."
```

```
| addend |
addend := delta isAdapter
            ifTrue: [delta value]
            ifFalse: [delta].
^addend isPoint
   ifTrue: [(x + addend x) @ (y + addend y)
   ifFalse: [(x + addend) @ (y + addend)]
```

Of course, as we allow additional types of arguments, the + method gets increasingly messy. So, how do we make things better? The answer is by using the double dispatch idiom. We dispatch a second message back to the + method's argument, passing the original receiver as this second message's argument. The + method would now look like this:

```
Point>>+ delta
   "delta can be anything that understands 'addPoint:'."
   ^delta addPoint: self
```

We've now shifted responsibility back to all the classes whose instances may appear as an argument to Point>>+. Note how the redispatched message, as in the Visitor pattern, announces the class of its argument: in any addPoint: method implementation, we *know* the parameter is a Point and no further class tests are necessary. So coding this second method is simplified.

We would now require the following additional methods:

```
Number>>addPoint: aPoint
   ^(self + aPoint x) @ (self + aPoint y)

Point>>addPoint: aPoint
   ^(self x + aPoint x) @ (self y + aPoint y)

Adapter>>addPoint: aPoint
   ^self value addPoint: aPoint
```

To implement the double dispatch solution, we've written more methods, but we really haven't written any more code. Much more important, extending the system is now much easier. If we want to be able to add instances of class Zot to Points, we need not change the + method in the Point class at all. Instead, we just have to implement Zot>>addPoint:. The potential downside—and again this is particularly problematic for novice Smalltalk programmers—is that without double dispatch, all the code to add things to a Point resides in one location, Point>>+, whereas with the double dispatch implementation, the code is distributed to several classes; hence some users may find it harder to locate and understand this behavior completely.

Others have spoken of the double dispatch idiom using alternative terminology. Liu (1996) suggests the pattern may also be called Duet or Pas de Deux. Ingalls (1986) refers to the redispatched message as a "relay message." Ingalls also deals with the more general problem, which the Visitor pattern handles, wherein both the original message and the relayed message are implemented polymorphically by multiple classes. More on double dispatch may be found in Liu's excellent book, the Ingalls paper, Beck (1997), and *Design Patterns* (DP 338–339).

Collaborations

Following is the collaboration diagram portraying the interactions among the participant objects. Notice that a Visitor may or may not send messages to its Elements in the course of doing its job. In the following, aVisitor sends the message operationA when it is processing a ConcreteElementA object, but when working on a ConcreteElementB instance, the Visitor's algorithm is "self-contained" and does not require invoking behavior in the Element.

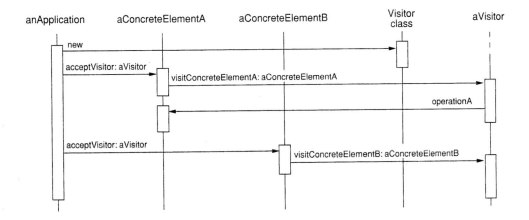

Applicability

Under what circumstances does the Visitor pattern apply? The answer turns out to be an interesting reflection on many design patterns. Sometimes a design is better without incorporating a particular design pattern, but as the application evolves that pattern first *becomes* applicable or beneficial. This is the case with Visitor. We'll take a look here at the issues involved in deciding whether to apply the Visitor pattern to a design.

When *Not* to Use the Visitor Pattern

Visitor should be used only when the set of classes being operated on (the Element classes) is stable; that is, there's little chance of adding new ones, although the set of operations may expand. Thus, the pattern allows for a sort of biased extensibility. It makes it easy to add new operations; when we add a new one, we do so in one place (a new class) rather than in many locations (methods spread throughout the classes being operated on). On the other hand, it's difficult to add new Element classes (in this example, new Geometric subclasses). Suppose

we add the Curve class. First, we need to be sure to have it include an accept-
Visitor: method, which looks like this:

```
Curve>>acceptVisitor: aVisitor
    aVisitor visitCurve: self
```

That's the easy part. But then we need to revisit (no pun intended) every existing
Visitor class to add a visitCurve: method. Each of these methods must implement the appropriate algorithm (depending on the Visitor type) for Curve
objects; for example, DrawingVisitor>>visitCurve: would implement the
code for drawing curves. This process—adding a bunch of methods in multiple
disparate locations—is one of the very things we're trying to *avoid* by using the
Visitor pattern. So, clearly, Visitor is applicable only when we may need to add
new operations but it is unlikely that we will need to add new Element classes.

When Do We Know If the Pattern Applies?

The previous point bears further consideration. We just asserted that Visitor is
the solution of choice when the set of Element classes is stable but we may want
to enhance the system with new operations on those Elements. Previously we
mentioned that the converse is true: distributing an operation to each of the Element classes is a more appropriate solution when the set of operations is basically
constant but we may need to add new Element subclasses later. The problem, of
course, is that we often don't know a priori, when an application or framework is
first being designed, which design problem we're going to be faced with down
the road. "Only after the system has been running and several extensions have
been made will it become apparent whether to use a Visitor or a distributed
algorithm" (Roberts, Brant, & Johnson, 1997a, p. 15).

This is the case in using many design patterns: you can't always make the decision to apply a particular pattern up front or you may have to retrofit design
patterns into an existing system to improve it. This is an important point for the
application of design patterns: design does not occur once and for all before a
system is built. It is often an ongoing process that takes place throughout the life
of the system: before it's implemented, as it's being implemented and we learn
more about its requirements, during maintenance, and when implementing
enhancements. All of these are opportunities for applying design patterns to the
problems at hand.

Avoiding Recompilation?

Another reason for using the Visitor pattern in C++ is that adding a new method
(for a new operation) to an Element class means we have to recompile the entire
class (DP 331). And if we require that same operation in all Element classes, we'll
have to recompile all of them. At the least, this is time-consuming; at its worst, it
is impossible when we do not possess the source code for the entire class.

In Smalltalk, this is a nonissue. The coding tools in Smalltalk's interactive development environment provide for incremental compilation. When we write and save a new method, it is compiled immediately without affecting other previously compiled methods in the same class. Thus, adding a method to a class implies no recompilation impact.

Implementation

In addition to the following subsection regarding alternative ways of invoking the Visitor, see the Enumerating ProgramNodes Again example in Known Smalltalk Uses for a discussion concerning whose responsibility it is to traverse the object structure in Visitor. The latter is an implementation issue but is presented in the context of an existing Visitor example.

Saving Steps

Another issue contrasting with C++ regards the runtime retrieval of class information. One reason the `acceptVisitor:` message is sent to each Element being iterated over (rather than sending a message directly to the Visitor telling it to operate on the Element) is so *the Element* can decide which Visitor method to invoke; this determination is based on the Element's class. That is, the choice of which method to invoke in the Visitor is delegated to the Element. So the client application does this:

```
graphicalElements do: [:anElement |
    anElement acceptVisitor: drawingVisitor]
```

instead of this:

```
graphicalElements do: [:anElement |
    drawingVisitor operateOn: anElement]
```

All the `acceptVisitor:` method in each Element class does is send a single message back to the Visitor, which encodes the Element's class in its name and basically tells the Visitor, "Use *this* method for me." Thus, `Rectangle>>acceptVisitor:` sends the `visitRectangle:` message to tell the Visitor to use its `Rectangle` method, `visitEllipse:` invokes the method for `Ellipses`, and so on. In Smalltalk, however, we can determine the Element's class at runtime, and so we can simplify the problem in one of two ways.

We can leave the rest of the pattern as is, letting the client (in our example, the `DrawingEditor`) iterate over the Elements and pass a Visitor object to each. However, we can make the `acceptVisitor:` code much easier. In what we've coded so far, the abstract Element superclass implements `acceptVisitor:` to signal an error (via `subclassResponsibility` or `implementedBySub-class`) or do nothing at all, and each concrete Element subclass hard-codes a specific callback message (e.g., visitRectangle:). Instead, we can code a single acceptVisitor: method, in the superclass:

```
Geometric >>acceptVisitor: aVisitor
    aVisitor
        perform: ('visit', self class symbol, ':') asSymbol
        with: self
```

With this code in the top-most class of the subhierarchy, subclasses of Geometric need not implement any specialized "accept visitor" methods. The callback method selector will be built generically and still encode the receiver's class and invoke the correct Visitor method.

The first downside consequence of this approach is that it is somewhat slower than a hard-coded message. It uses string concatenation, converts a String to a Symbol, and sends the resultant message using perform:with:, all of which are relatively slow operations. But it is more flexible and avoids having to (or possibly forgetting to) code the "accept visitor" method when new classes are added.

More important, code of this nature is difficult from a program understanding perspective. We've discussed this in other patterns, but to reiterate, you can't really see what messages are being sent by Geometric>>acceptVisitor: by reading the code, plus the normally extremely useful tools of the Smalltalk interactive development environment are abrogated. If you use the "messages" tool on the Geometric>>acceptVisitor: method, the resulting list will not include the actual visit . . . messages sent by the method; if you look at "senders" of, say, DrawingVisitor>>visitEllipse:, you won't find Geometric>>acceptVisitor: listed either.

If you do choose to use this general approach, a second alternative is to elide the acceptVisitor: method and the Element-Visitor handshake protocol altogether. Instead of the client iterating over Elements and sending them the acceptVisitor: message, we can have the Visitor make the method invocation decision on its own. First, the client code changes slightly:

```
DrawingEditor>>refresh
    | drawingVisitor |
    drawingVisitor := DrawingVisitor for: self.
    "Iterate over the graphics, passing each
     TO the drawing visitor:"
    graphicalElements do: [:anElement |
        drawingVisitor operateOn: anElement]
```

Then we need a single generic operateOn: method in the Visitor class (or, better still, in the abstract superclass of an entire Visitor hierarchy):

```
GeometricVisitor>>operateOn: anElement
    self
        perform: (visit, anElement class symbol, ':') asSymbol
        with: anElement
```

Sample Code

Returning to our `draw` example, we have two associated hierarchies. First is a set of graphical object classes, such as in the following diagram:

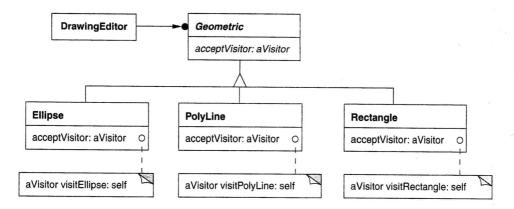

And to operate on these graphics classes, we have a set of Visitor classes:

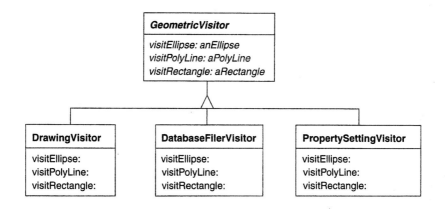

A sampling of the definitions for these classes follows:

```
Object subclass: #Geometric
    instanceVariableNames:
        'lineStyle lineWidth lineColor fillColor'
    classVariableNames: ''
    poolDictionaries: ''

Geometric subclass: #PolyLine
    instanceVariableNames: 'vertices'
    classVariableNames: ''
    poolDictionaries: ''
```

```
Geometric subclass: #Rectangle
   instanceVariableNames: 'leftTop rightBottom'
   classVariableNames: ''
   poolDictionaries: ''

Object subclass: #GeometricVisitor
   instanceVariableNames: ''
   classVariableNames: ''
   poolDictionaries: ''


GeometricVisitor subclass: #DrawingVisitor
   instanceVariableNames: 'pen'
   classVariableNames: ''
   poolDictionaries: ''


DrawingVisitor>>pen: aPen
   "Set up the pen I will use to do my drawing"
   pen := aPen
```

Note that a `DrawingVisitor` includes a pen instance variable. Its client passes it the actual `Pen` to use for drawing. Since (in Visual Smalltalk) both `Graphics-Mediums` and some panes (such as `GraphPanes`) incorporate drawing pens, a `DrawingVisitor` can be reused for painting on a `Bitmap`, a `Printer`, or any other concrete `GraphicsMedium` subclass, as well as instances of `GraphPane` and its subclasses. This demonstrates that the classes on which a single Visitor operates need not be in the same subhierarchy.

When the drawing editor needs to perform an operation on some or all of its graphical objects, the flow of control is as follows:

1. The drawing editor instantiates the appropriate Visitor class associated with the particular operation (e.g., for a drawing operation, a `DrawingVisitor` instance is created).

2. The drawing editor iterates over the relevant graphical elements and sends each the `acceptVisitor:` message, with the Visitor object as the argument.

   So far, we have:

```
Object subclass: #DrawingEditor
   instanceVariableNames: 'graphicalElements graphPane'
   classVariableNames: ''
   poolDictionaries: ''

DrawingEditor>>refresh
      | visitor |
      visitor:= DrawingVisitor new.
      visitor pen: self graphPane pen.
      graphicalElements do: [:anElement |
         anElement acceptVisitor: visitor]
```

3. Each graphical element's `acceptVisitor:` method does just one thing: it calls back to the Visitor object. The message sent to the Visitor encodes the exact class of the graphical object in the message name, thus invoking the correspondingly relevant method in the Visitor. The message's argument is the graphical object itself, so the two objects can be temporarily tightly coupled; thus, the Visitor can obtain any information about the graphical object required for the Visitor's operation by sending messages to it:

```
Geometric>>acceptVisitor: aVisitor
    self implementedBySubclass          "Visual Smalltalk"
    "self subclassResponsibility"       "VisualWorks, IBM"

Rectangle>>acceptVisitor: aVisitor
    aVisitor visitRectangle: self

Ellipse>>acceptVisitor: aVisitor
    aVisitor visitEllipse: self

PolyLine>>acceptVisitor: aVisitor
    aVisitor visitPolyLine: self
```

4. The Visitor performs the appropriate algorithm (here, drawing). This example uses existing Visual Smalltalk `Pen` messages:

```
DrawingVisitor>>visitRectangle: aRectangle
    "Use the Rectangle's properties to set properties
     of my drawing Pen; then, draw the rectangle."
    pen
      setPenStyle: aRectangle lineStyle  "dashed/solid/etc."
          color: aRectangle lineColor
          width: aRectangle lineWidth;
        setFillColor: aRectangle fillColor;
        place: aRectangle leftTop;
        rectangleFilled: aRectangle rightBottom
```

We similarly code `DrawingVisitor>>visitPolyLine:` and `Drawing-Visitor>>visitEllipse:`.

Known Smalltalk Uses

Generating Code

When a Smalltalk method is compiled in VisualWorks, it is first parsed into a tree of `ProgramNodes`. The root of the tree is a `MethodNode`. When the `Method-Node` is asked to emit code onto a `CodeStream`, it initiates a recursive traversal of its subcomponent nodes, resulting in the overall traversal of the entire parse tree. In the course of this iteration, each node is asked to emit its bytecodes onto the `CodeStream`. This request ultimately results in a message, which encodes the node type, that is sent by the node to the CodeStream. The invoked node-specific CodeStream method generates the actual code.

Enumerating ProgramNodes Again

Another example involving ProgramNodes: a ReadBeforeWrittenTester (a subclass of ProgramNodeEnumerator) iterates over ProgramNodes in a method's parse tree to determine if the method references a variable before its value is set. The ReadBeforeWrittenTester sends a generic message to each ProgramNode (node nodeDo: self), and each ProgramNode subclass implements this message to double-dispatch a message back to the ReadBefore-WrittenTester; this secondary message encodes the class of the ProgramNode object—for example,

```
AssignmentNode>>nodeDo: anEnumerator
    ^anEnumerator doAssignment: self ...

VariableNode>>nodeDo: anEnumerator
    ^anEnumerator doVariable: self ...
```

This example raises the question: Who is responsible for traversing the object structure? Here, it is the Visitor—the ReadBeforeWrittenTester—that iterates over the Elements structure, rather than a third party. In our drawing example, the drawing editor—the object structure's client—performed the iteration over the graphical elements, passing each a Visitor; in the ReadBeforeWrittenTester implementation, the ReadBeforeWrittenTester fulfills the role of Visitor *and* the task of traversing the object structure and sending the "accept visitor" message to each Element. Another possibility for the "traverser" role is the object structure itself; we saw this case in the Generating Code known use.

The Smalltalk Refactoring Browser

The Smalltalk Refactoring Browser (Roberts, Brant, & Johnson, 1997a, 1997b) partially or completely automates many of the program transformations (refactorings) that programmers perform as systems mature. Refactorings are changes to a class or classes intended to make them more reusable, extensible, or easier to understand. Refactorings do not involve the addition of new behavior but, rather, a transformation of the design or the relocation of existing behavior. For example, a common refactoring involves pushing code or entire methods duplicated in two or more sibling classes up to a common superclass. Interestingly, one of the transformations supported by the Refactoring Browser involves converting a distributed operation (an operation implemented in multiple Element classes) into a Visitor pattern implementation (see When Do We Know If the Pattern Applies? on page 378).

The Visitor pattern is used in several places in the Refactoring Browser's implementation. The Browser's refactorings result in modifying the source code of (perhaps multiple) methods. These changes are effected not by directly modifying the textual source of a method but by first modifying the parse tree produced by compiling that source and then decompiling the parse tree into text. This involves two Visitor objects. First, code transformations are often performed based on pattern matching. For example, for a rename-method refactoring—say, renaming method `length` to `size`—the transformation involves finding all existing methods that send length and changing them to send the `size` message instead. This entails scanning all methods looking for the `length` message-send—it is a Visitor that walks the methods' parse trees, asking each `Program-Node` if it matches this pattern. After methods are matched, their parse trees are modified, and a second Visitor traverses those trees to format the methods' textual source code.

(You can obtain the code for the Smalltalk Refactoring Browser at: `http://st-www.cs.uiuc.edu/users/brant/Refactory/`).

Displaying VisualComponents on a GraphicsContext

In VisualWorks, when instances of classes in the `VisualComponent` hierarchy (e.g., `PixelArray`, `Image`), the `Geometric` hierarchy (e.g., `Rectangle`, `Line-Segment`, `Polyline`, `Circle`), and other visual classes (e.g., `CharacterArray`, `Mask`) are asked to display themselves on a `GraphicsContext` (a screen or a printer), they ask the `GraphicsContext` to do the work. The actual work is dispatched back to the `GraphicsContext`, which is passed (as a message argument) to the visual object. The message sent to the `GraphicsContext` includes in its signature the class of the visual that wants to be drawn. Different classes in the `GraphicsContext` subhierarchy may respond with different behavior to these double-dispatched messages. Here are some concrete examples:

```
Image>>displayOn: aGraphicsContext at: aPoint
    aGraphicsContext displayImage: self at: aPoint

Mask>>displayOn: aGraphicsContext at: aPoint
    aGraphicsContext displayMask: self at: aPoint

PixelArray>>displayOn: aGraphicsContext at: aPoint
    aGraphicsContext displayPixelArray: self at: aPoint

Rectangle>>displayFilledOn: aGraphicsContext
    aGraphicsContext displayRectangle: self
```

Related Patterns

There are a few patterns that are obviously related to Visitor. A Visitor is invoked during the course of an iteration over a structure of Elements—hence the Iterator (273) pattern is typically used in coordination with Visitor. Also, the structure being iterated over is most likely a Composite (137), although sometimes it is the tree structure representing a linguistic parse—in the latter case, the Visitor is participating in an Interpreter (261) pattern implementation.

Chapter 6

Conclusion

We've discussed, analyzed, and implemented all 23 design patterns from the Gang of Four's *Design Patterns* book. Of course, 23 patterns do not make up the entire patterns universe. There are many already in the design patterns literature, many more known but yet to be written about, and still others yet to be pattern-mined from existing applications. But, in truth, design patterns are really just the application of good design techniques. The Gang of Four patterns make use of the basic ingredients of object-oriented programming and design to provide cleaner, more modular, more maintainable and extensible solutions. They incorporate polymorphism and late binding, modularization and separation of responsibilities, encapsulation and information- and implementation-hiding, abstraction and shared behaviors via inheritance where necessary. . . . Design patterns simply capture one piece of what expert designers have been doing all along, before there were design patterns books, articles, or a design patterns community. Erich Gamma (1991) just had the insight that these higher-level design concepts—these recurring, successful patterns of interacting objects—ought to be given a name and ought to be captured and articulated in a literature for others to share and learn from. (It would be difficult to assign to a single person the role of the "father" of design patterns, but Erich was the first to use the term "design patterns" in the context of software design.)

The core, overarching characteristics defining the Gang of Four patterns are abstraction, delegation, and extensibility. Many patterns involve abstracting specific behaviors and responsibilities out of a single object and into one or more separate helper objects. When we have multiple algorithmic strategies to choose from, for example, we don't incorporate all of them as methods *within* the primary application object, along with a case-like conditional to decide which one to invoke. Instead, we configure the application object with a separate Strategy helper object, instantiated from one of several Strategy classes, and have the application merely delegate the execution of the algorithm to that helper. With regard to extensibility, if the algorithm needs to change, we know where to go to make our modifications; if a new algorithm is added, we add a new Strategy class, but we need not change the client code in the application object.

Similarly, state-based implementation decisions can be delegated to a dynamically changing State object. Adding states when users or the domain demand it requires little or no modification to the application object that delegates these implementation details to its State object. Command allows a programmer to separate the request for an action from the implementation of the action. A client can know how to ask for an action to be performed, but the details of how the action is performed can be hidden from the client altogether.

Patterns like Facade and Bridge are about hiding complex implementation details behind an abstract interface provided by a separate object. In the case of Bridge, the hidden details involve yet another object, in Facade, an entire subsystem of objects. Similarly, Adapter is about making objects work together even if their interfaces are incompatible.

Abstract Factory and Builder let different sorts of things get constructed by the same application code. Clients control what categories of parts to include in the construction, but the part instantiation is delegated to an external factory or builder. The Client communicates with an abstract protocol to its factory or builder object, but doesn't know which classes its helper object instantiates. Thus, with regard to extensibility, new parts families may be added to the system as a whole by defining new factories or builders, but the client code remains the same.

In Smalltalk, Iterators offer an abstraction for iteration operations, allowing clients to traverse aggregate collections in a generic fashion even if those collections contain objects of disparate types. Smalltalk Iterators also support extensibility. Even if new types (classes) of objects are added to these collections, the Iterator clients need not change. Composite provides the same sort of abstraction for its elements.

Template Method lets us define complex algorithms in a generic way and lets individual classes implement portions of these algorithms to suit their own purposes. Adding new subclasses to the hierarchy allows them to participate in the generically defined algorithm with their own versions of implementing the algorithm. Again, the client code need not change; it merely sends the same message to initiate the algorithm's execution.

Visitor allows us to easily add new operations on objects or aggregates of objects—in fact, on aggregates containing very different component objects. Adding a new operation entails adding a new class with a Visitor-compliant interface, but the classes being operated on do not change.

When we modularize responsibilities by delegating them to multiple objects, we unclutter the design of individual object classes. When we abstract major responsibilities out of an application object and distribute knowledge and details into helpers, the application need only know the abstract messages to send to those assistants in order to effect a chunk of the application's overall functionality.

When we decompose problems into smaller, modular subproblems, we can represent those subcomponents with additional helper objects or even **helper patterns,** patterns that play a subordinate role to other patterns. Sometimes patterns are competitors for the same task; Abstract Factory and Builder compete for the same basic job. Yet, patterns may also be combined to solve problems: a UIBuilder object participates in the Builder pattern with its client but also invokes the Abstract Factory pattern to do its own work. By configuring the UIBuilder with a UILookPolicy, we can vary the Builder's behavior to create widgets from one of several possible platform-specific families of widgets.

The result is more maintainable, extensible programs. We must always keep in mind that initial designs depend on limited information. No matter how much knowledge we have at design time, we all know that by the time we're finished implementing the application, users or the domain will demand further extensions and enhancements. This is why the explicit goal of so many of our patterns is extensibility.

The intelligent use of patterns is one tool in ameliorating later maintenance and enhancement difficulties. For example, many patterns allow changes to be isolated to individual methods or classes. They thereby permit a style of maintenance wherein the addition of new classes necessitates only additions, not modifications in multiple locations (Pascoe, 1986). In general, virtually all of the Gang of Four patterns help to develop what Cox (1986) has labeled "malleable" software—software that supports and facilitates change, reusability, and enhancement rather than standing in their way.

Lastly, the opportunity to apply design patterns will occur more frequently if software developers are reflective in their work. We know that it is not until we are actually in the midst of implementation that many design challenges (*opportunities*) arise. Despite the plethora of design methodologies, despite design patterns, there is no way to understand and foresee all problems at design time; the notion of having "designers" simply hand a design over the wall to "implementers" has been shown to be erroneous. Design occurs not only up front, but during implementation and even during maintenance. It's important for software developers to step back from their work periodically and reflect on whether the current design is adequate or needs something "more," whether a new design opportunity—or necessity—has arisen, whether a new opening or requirement for a design pattern can be perceived.

Donald Schöen (1987) has extensively studied and written about reflection in professional practice. He asserts that obtaining successful solutions to difficult problems frequently requires the coordination of reflection and action, periodically stepping back from and analyzing the task at hand, while at the same time performing that task. He considers the ability and willingness to reflect in action a higher-order skill. So don't be afraid to *re*design during implementation. It may be that you see an opportunity for plugging in a design pattern where the original design had none. Anyone who has worked with design patterns has had this experience.

Pointers to the Patterns Community:
How Can I Learn More?

In the short time since the publication of *Design Patterns*, the patterns world has exploded. Patterns are now being applied in areas of computer science other than object-oriented design. They're even being applied to noncomputer domains, such as organizational dynamics. There now exist *lots* of resources made available by the patterns community. Here, we offer a small road map to some of these resources by highlighting some of the more interesting ones.

Patterns Web Sites

We can't list all of the World Wide Web pages dedicated to software patterns—there are just too many. Here's a small sampling of sites you'll want to visit:

- The Patterns Home Page (`http://hillside.net/patterns/patterns.html`). If you want to learn more about patterns, this is probably the best place to start. Ralph Johnson's group at the University of Illinois, Urbana-Champaign (UIUC) maintains this Web site, which contains a lot of information about patterns, including links to papers and articles available for download. Another feature of the Patterns Home Page is the PatternStoriesWeb (direct address: `http://st-www.cs.uiuc.edu/cgi-bin/wikic/wikic`). This is dedicated to discussing ways in which people have used the Gang of Four patterns. The known uses discussed here include many Smalltalk examples. It's a collaborative Web site, meaning you can both read about examples and add your own for others to see.

- The Portland Patterns Repository (`http://www.c2.com/ppr`). Ward Cunningham maintains this Web site, which contains a wealth of information about patterns, including examples, links to other patterns sites, and a list of people active in the patterns community. It also is a collaborative Web site.

- Dolphin Smalltalk (`http://www.object-arts.com/EducationCentre/Patterns/Patterns.htm`). The Dolphin Smalltalk Web site includes a page focused on Smalltalk patterns, many of a generally applicable nature, some relevant specifically to Dolphin Smalltalk. Their patterns include known uses from the Dolphin image. These patterns range from low-level idioms and conventions, such as method naming, to design patterns from the Gang of Four.

- AG Communications Systems Patterns page (`http://www.agcs.com/patterns/index.html`). Maintained by Linda Rising and David DeLano, this site contains a lot of information about patterns and the patterns activities at AG Communication Systems. It also has pointers to many other patterns-related Web sites (click the Other Resources button on the Patterns page).

- "Patterns and Software: Essential Concepts and Terminology" (`http://www.enteract.com/~bradapp/docs/patterns-intro.html`). Brad Appleton's patterns site has a bunch of useful information including a patterns glossary and pointers to other Web sites.

Patterns Conferences

A number of patterns workshops have been held within larger conferences; for example, OOPSLA '96[1] included a design patterns workshop. At least four conferences focused exclusively on patterns also exist:

- PLoP (Pattern Languages of Programs). This conference was the first of the patterns conferences and is still the largest. It is held every year at the Allerton Park conference center in Monticello, Illinois. The primary focus is the presentation of new patterns. Patterns and pattern languages are reviewed in a writers' workshop format, with the audience acting as reviewers and editors. For information on the current (as of this writing) PLoP, see `http://st-www.cs.uiuc.edu/~hanmer/PLoP-97.html`.

- EuroPLoP. This conference is held each year in Kloster Irsee, Germany. It also centers on presenting new patterns but includes special birds-of-a-feather sessions on other topics as well. See `http://www.cs.wustl.edu/~schmidt/EuroPLoP-97.html` and `http://www.sdm.de/europlop98/`.

- UP (Using Patterns). This conference was held for the first time in March 1997 at the Mohonk Mountain House in New Paltz, New York. UP focuses on helping people learn how to apply existing patterns, as well as sharing novel ways to use such patterns. See `http://www.panix.com/~k2/up.html`.

- ChiliPLoP. The first ChiliPLoP conference will be held in March 1998 in Phoenix, Arizona. It is the organizers' intention to provide a mix of workshopping new patterns and helping people to learn how to apply patterns to their work. See `http://www.agcs.com/patterns/chiliplop/index.html` for more information.

For a complete list of the conferences and workshops available each year, plus information on registration and paper submissions, see `http://hillside.net/patterns/conferences`.

---

[1] The Conference on Object-Oriented Programming Systems, Languages and Applications.

Patterns Discussion Groups

Another way to get involved more with patterns is in face-to-face and electronic patterns discussion groups. Quite a few discussion groups have sprung up in cities throughout the world. The best way to find what's available near you is to check the Pattern Discussion Groups' Web page at `http://hillside.net/patterns/Groups.html`.

There also are many e-mail distribution lists covering different topics related to patterns. Here's a sampling of non-language-specific groups:

- `business-patterns@cs.uiuc.edu` discusses business-oriented patterns.
- `dacm-patterns@cs.uiuc.edu` concerns decoupling and complexity management.
- `gang-of-4-patterns@cs.uiuc.edu` is about the patterns in *Design Patterns*.
- `ipc-patterns@cs.uiuc.edu` is about patterns concerning concurrency and distribution.
- `organization-patterns@cs.uiuc.edu` is for discussing organizational patterns.
- `patterns@cs.uiuc.edu` is a general software patterns list.
- `patterns-discussion@cs.uiuc.edu` discusses patterns in general (not just software!).
- `siemens-patterns@cs.uiuc.edu` focuses on the patterns described in *Pattern-Oriented Software Architectures* (Buschmann et al., 1996).

This list was derived from the Web page at `http://hillside.net/patterns/Lists.html`. Each of these distribution lists has a slightly different method for subscribing. For instructions, point your Web browser to the above site.

Patterns Books

Many books and numerous articles about patterns have appeared since the publication of *Design Patterns*. Here, we're just going to mention those patterns books with a direct link to Smalltalk:

- Beck, Kent, 1997, *Smalltalk Best Practices Patterns*, Upper Saddle River, NJ, Prentice Hall PTR.

  One of the best resources for learning how to make poor Smalltalk code better. Its patterns are largely what Buschmann et al. (1996) refer to as idioms, of a smaller-grain size than the Gang of Four design patterns. The book covers issues ranging from style (formatting and variable naming) through class factoring.

- Fowler, Martin, 1997, *Analysis Patterns: Reusable Object Models*, Reading, MA, Addison-Wesley.

    Considers analysis patterns rather than strictly implementation-oriented design patterns—that is, it covers patterns for modeling business processes and relationships. This results in patterns for specific application domains, as opposed to generically applicable software patterns like the Gang of Four's. Fowler is a Smalltalker and some of his patterns are illustrated with Smalltalk code.

- Liu, Chamond, 1996, *Smalltalk, Objects, and Design*, Greenwich, CT, Manning.

    An excellent broad-ranging book on Smalltalk programming and design with a chapter on Smalltalk patterns.

- Buschmann, Frank, Regine Meunier, Hans Rohnert, Peter Sommerlad, & Michael Stal, 1996, *Pattern-Oriented Software Architecture: A System of Patterns*, West Sussex, England, Wiley.

    Presents software patterns of a broad range of abstraction and grain-size, from idioms to design patterns to architectural patterns. Some patterns include Smalltalk-implemented known uses and there is a small amount of Smalltalk code sprinkled throughout the book.

- PLoP Proceedings

    A selection of the best new patterns presented at each PLoP conference. So far, these books have appeared for the 1994 through 1996 conferences. These collections include patterns for Smalltalk and patterns illustrated with Smalltalk code.

    - Coplien, James O. and Douglas C. Schmidt (Eds.), 1995, *Pattern Languages of Program Design*, Reading, MA, Addison-Wesley.

    - Vlissides, John M., James O. Coplien, and Norman L. Kerth (Eds.), 1996, *Pattern Languages of Program Design 2*, Reading, MA, Addison-Wesley.

    - Martin, Robert, Dirk Riehle, and Frank Buschmann (Eds.), 1998, *Pattern Languages of Program Design 3*, Reading, MA, Addison-Wesley.

New patterns publications are appearing even as we speak. The best way to keep current is to visit the Patterns Home Page periodically.

Closing Remarks from Us and Christopher Alexander

Design patterns are not so much hard-and-fast *rules* that must be followed without deviation as they are *rules of thumb,* as Christopher Alexander (1979) often calls them.

"Each pattern describes a problem which occurs over and over again in our environment, and then describes the *core* of the solution to that problem, in such a way that you can use this solution a million times over, without ever doing it the same way twice" (Alexander et al., 1977, p. x, *emphasis ours*). A pattern offers guidelines for solving a particular type of recurring problem, and using its essential ideas "you can solve the problem for yourself, in your own way, by adapting it to your preferences, and the local conditions" (Alexander et al., 1977, p. xiii). Our pattern implementations have shown one or more possible ways to solve a problem, but they can be adapted, molded and modified to suit your own aesthetics and your particular application context. "We hope, of course, that many of the people who read, and use [them], will try to improve these patterns—will put their energy to work, in [the] task of finding more true, more profound variants" (Alexander et al., 1979, p. xv).

Finally, we hope you've learned something of value and usefulness from our book, for "at the time of any act of design, all we can hope to do is use the rules of thumb we have collected, in the best way we know how" (Alexander, 1979, p. 205).

References

Abell, Steven T., 1996, "ValueInterface: The complete application framework in a can," *1996 ParcPlace-Digitalk International Users Conference*, San Jose, CA.

Alexander, Christopher, 1979, *The Timeless Way of Building*, New York, Oxford University Press.

Alexander, Christopher, Sara Ishikawa, Murray Silverstein, Max Jacobson, Ingrid Fiksdahl-King, & Shlomo Angel, 1977, *A Pattern Language: Towns, Buildings, Construction*, New York, Oxford University Press.

Alpert, Sherman R., 1993, "Graceful interaction with graphical constraints," *IEEE Computer Graphics and Applications*, 13:2, pp. 82–91.

Alpert, Sherman R., Mark R. Laff, W. Randy Koons, David A. Epstein, Dan Soroker, David C. Morrill, & Arthur J. Stein, 1995, "The EFX editing and effects environment," *IEEE MultiMedia*, 3:1, pp. 15–29.

Alpert, Sherman R. & Mary Beth Rosson, 1992, "ParCE: An object-oriented approach to context-free parsing," *Computer Systems Science and Engineering (Special Issue on Object-Oriented Systems)*, 7:2, pp. 136–144.

Anderson, John R., 1985, *Cognitive Psychology and Its Implications* (Second Edition), New York, W. H. Freeman.

Auer, Ken, 1995, "Reusability through self-encapsulation," in J. O. Coplien & D. C. Schmidt (Eds.), *Pattern Languages of Program Design*, pp. 505–516, Reading, MA, Addison-Wesley.

Beck, Kent, 1992, "Collection idioms," *Smalltalk Report*, 2:2, pp. 15–18, October.

Beck, Kent, 1996, "Patterns 101," *Object Magazine*, 5:8, pp. 24–30, January.

Beck, Kent, 1997, *Smalltalk Best Practices Patterns*, Upper Saddle River, NJ, Prentice Hall PTR.

Borning, Alan, 1981, "The programming language aspects of ThingLab, a constraint-oriented simulation laboratory," *ACM Transactions on Programming Languages*, 3:4, pp. 353–387, October.

Borning, Alan, 1986, "Defining constraints graphically," in *Human Factors in Computing Systems: CHI '86 Conference Proceedings*, pp. 137–143, New York, ACM.

Brown, Kyle, et al., 1994, "Hm3270: An evolving framework for client-server communication," in *Proceedings of the Fourteenth Annual Conference on Technology of Object Oriented Languages and Systems: TOOLS '94*.

Brown, Kyle, 1995a, "Remembrance of things past: Layered architectures for Smalltalk applications," *Smalltalk Report*, 4:9, pp. 4–7, July–August.

Brown, Kyle, 1995b, "Understanding inter-layer communication with the SASE pattern," *Smalltalk Report*, 5:3, pp. 4–8, November–December.

Brown, Kyle, 1996, "Experiencing patterns at the design level," *Object Magazine*, 5:8, pp. 40–48, January.

Brown, Kyle & Bruce Whitenack, 1996, "Pattern language for Smalltalk and RDB's," *Object Magazine*, 6:7, pp. 50–55, September.

Buschmann, Frank, Regine Meunier, Hans Rohnert, Peter Sommerlad, & Michael Stal, 1996, *Pattern-Oriented Software Architecture: A System of Patterns*, West Sussex, England, Wiley.

Carroll, John M., Sherman R. Alpert, John Karat, Mary van Deusen, & Mary Beth Rosson, 1994, "Raison d'Etre: Capturing design history and rationale in multimedia narratives," in *Human Factors in Computing Systems: Proceedings of CHI'94*, pp. 192–197, New York, ACM.

Carroll, John M., Janice A. Singer, Rachel K. E. Bellamy, & Sherman R. Alpert, 1990, "A View Matcher for learning Smalltalk," in J. C. Chew & J. Whiteside (Eds.), *Human Factors in Computing Systems: Proceedings of CHI'90*, pp. 431–437, New York, ACM.

Collins, Dave, 1995, *Designing Object-Oriented User Interfaces*, Redwood City, CA, Benjamin/Cummings.

Cornell, Gary & Cay S. Horstmann, 1996, *Core Java*, Mountain View, CA, SunSoft Press.

Cox, Brad J., 1984, "Message/object programming: An evolutionary change in programming technology," *IEEE Software*, 1, 50–61.

Cox, Brad J., 1986, *Object-Oriented Programming: An Evolutionary Approach*, Reading, MA, Addison-Wesley.

Curtis, Bill (Ed.), 1985, *Human Factors in Software Development* (Second Edition), Washington, DC, IEEE Computer Society Press.

Davidowitz, Paul, 1996, "Externalizing business-object behavior: A point-and-click rule editor," *Smalltalk Report*, 6:1, pp. 4–10, September.

Duego, Dwight & Allen Benson, 1996, "Patterns: Object-oriented wisdom," *Java Report*, 1:5, pp. 47–49, October.

Ewing, Juanita, 1994, "Pools: An attractive nuisance," *Smalltalk Report*, 3:6, pp. 1, 4–6, March–April.

Fowler, Martin, 1997, *Analysis Patterns: Reusable Object Models*, Reading, MA, Addison-Wesley.

Gamma, Erich, 1991, *Object-Oriented Software Development Based on ET++: Design Patterns, Class Library, Tools* (in German), Ph.D. thesis, University of Zurich Institut für Informatik. (Also published with same title, 1992, Berlin, Springer-Verlag).

Gamma, Erich, Richard Helm, Ralph Johnson, & John Vlissides, 1995, *Design Patterns: Elements of Reusable Object-Oriented Software*, Reading, MA, Addison-Wesley.

Goldberg, Adele & Alan Kay, 1977, "Methods for teaching the programming language Smalltalk," Report No. SSL 77–2, Palo Alto, CA, Xerox Palo Alto Research Center.

Goldberg, Adele & David Robson, 1983, *Smalltalk-80: The Language and Its Implementation*, Reading, MA, Addison-Wesley.

Goldberg, Adele & David Robson, 1989, *Smalltalk-80: The Language*, Reading, MA, Addison-Wesley.

Griffin, Susan, 1993, "What if? A protocol for object validation," *Smalltalk Report*, 3:3, pp. 4–6, November–December.

Hendley, Greg & Eric Smith, 1992, "Separating the GUI from the application," *Smalltalk Report*, 1:7, pp. 19–22, May.

Hopkins, Trevor & Bernard Horan, 1995, *Smalltalk: An Introduction to Application Development Using VisualWorks*, Hertfordshire, UK, Prentice Hall.

Howard, Tim, 1995, *The Smalltalk Developer's Guide to VisualWorks*, New York, SIGS.

Ingalls, Dan H. H., 1986, "A simple technique for multiple polymorphism," in N. Meyrowitz (Ed.), *Proceedings of the First Annual Conference on Object-Oriented Programming Systems, Languages, and Applications: OOPSLA '86*, pp. 347–349, New York, ACM.

Jacobson, Ivar, Magnus Christerson, Patrik Jonsson, & Gunnar Overgaard, 1992, *Object-Oriented Software Engineering: A Use Case Driven Approach*, Wokingham, UK, Addison-Wesley.

Johnson, Ralph & Brian Foote, 1988, "Designing reusable classes," *Journal of Object-Oriented Programming*, 1:2, pp. 22–35, June–July.

Johnson, Ralph & Bobby Woolf, 1998, "The Type Object Pattern," in Robert Martin, Dirk Riehle, & Frank Buschmann (Eds.), *Pattern Languages of Program Design 3*, Reading, MA, Addison-Wesley.

Krasner, Glen E. & Stephen T. Pope, 1988, "A cookbook for using the Model-View-Controller user interface paradigm in Smalltalk-80," *Journal of Object-Oriented Programming*, 1:3, pp. 26–49, August–September.

LaLonde, Wilf & John Pugh, 1994a, *Smalltalk/V: Practice and Experience*, Englewood Cliffs, NJ, Prentice Hall.

LaLonde, Wilf & John Pugh, 1994b, "Just cloning around," *Journal of Object-Oriented Programming*, 7:5, pp. 73–76, September.

LaLonde, Wilf & John Pugh, 1995, "Communicating reusable designs via design patterns," *Journal of Object-Oriented Programming*, 7:8, pp. 69–71, January.

Lewis, Simon, 1995, *The Art and Science of Smalltalk: An Introduction to Object-Oriented Programming Using VisualWorks*, Hertfordshire, UK, Prentice Hall.

Lewis, Ted, et al., 1995, *Object-Oriented Application Frameworks*, Greenwich, CT, Manning.

Liu, Chamond, 1996, *Smalltalk, Objects, and Design*, Greenwich, CT, Manning.

ParcPlace-Digitalk, 1996, "A very simple VSE SMTP client," *ParcTalk, The ObjectSupport Newsletter for ParcPlace-Digitalk Customers*, pp. 8–9, Summer–Fall.

Pascoe, Geoffrey A., 1986, "Encapsulators: A new software paradigm in Smalltalk-80," in *Proceedings of the First Annual Conference on Object-Oriented Programming Systems, Languages and Applications: OOPSLA '86*, pp. 341–346, New York, ACM.

Rivard, Fred, 1996, "Smalltalk: A reflective language," in G. Kiczales (Ed.), *Proceedings of Reflection '96*, pp. 21–38, http://www.emn.fr/dept_info/perso/ rivard/informatique/reflection96/reflection96.html.

Roberts, Don, John Brant, & Ralph Johnson, 1997a, "A refactoring tool for Smalltalk," http://st-www.cs.uiuc.edu/~droberts/tapos/TAPOS.htm.

Roberts, Don, John Brant, & Ralph Johnson, 1997b, "Why every Smalltalker should use the Refactoring Browser," *Smalltalk Report*, 6:10, pp. 4–11, 14, September.

Rosson, Mary Beth & Sherman R. Alpert, 1990, "The cognitive consequences of object-oriented design," *Human-Computer Interaction*, 5:4, pp. 345–379.

Rosson, Mary Beth & John M. Carroll, 1990, "Climbing the Smalltalk mountain," *SIG-CHI Bulletin*, 21, pp. 76–79.

Rubin, Kenneth & David Liebs, 1992, "Reimplementing Model-View-Controller," *Smalltalk Report*, 1:4, pp. 1–7, March–April.

Rumbaugh, James, Michael Blaha, William Premerlani, Frederick Eddy, & William Lorensen, 1991, *Object-Oriented Modeling and Design,* Englewood Cliffs, NJ, Prentice-Hall.

Schmucker, Kurt J., 1986, *Object-Oriented Programming for the Macintosh,* Hasbrouck Heights, NJ, Hayden.

Schöen, Donald, 1987, *Educating the Reflective Practitioner,* San Francisco, Jossey-Bass.

Sedgewick, Robert, 1988, *Algorithms* (Second Edition), Reading, MA, Addison-Wesley.

Shafer, Dan & Scott Herndon, 1995, *IBM Smalltalk Programming for Windows and OS/2,* Rocklin, CA, Prima.

Shafer, Dan, with Scott Herndon & Laurence Rozier, 1993, *Smalltalk Programming for Windows,* Rocklin, CA, Prima.

Singley, Mark K., John M. Carroll, & Sherman R. Alpert, 1991, "Psychological design rationale for an intelligent tutoring system for Smalltalk," in J. Koenemann-Belliveau, T. G. Moher, & S. P. Robertson (Eds.), *Empirical Studies of Programmers: Fourth Workshop,* pp. 196–209, Norwood, NJ, Ablex.

Skublics, Susan, Ed J. Klimas, & David A. Thomas, 1996, *Smalltalk with Style,* Englewood Cliffs, NJ, Prentice Hall.

Smith, David N., 1995, *IBM Smalltalk: The Language,* Redwood City, CA, Benjamin/Cummings.

Smith, David N., 1996a, *SmallFAQ: Smalltalk Frequently Asked Questions,* http://www.dnsmith.com/SmallFAQ/.

Smith, David N., 1996b, Posting on comp.lang.smalltalk, November 11.

Snyder, Alan, 1986, "Encapsulation and inheritance in object-oriented programming languages," in N. Meyrowitz (Ed.), *Proceedings of the First Annual Conference on Object-Oriented Programming Systems, Languages, and Applications: OOPSLA '86,* pp. 38–45, New York, ACM.

Soloway, Eliot, Jeffrey Bonar, & Kate Ehrlich, 1983, "Cognitive strategies and looping constructs: An empirical study," *Communications of the ACM,* 26:11, pp. 853–860.

Ungar, David & Robert B. Smith, 1987, "Self: The power of simplicity," in *Proceedings of the Second Annual Conference on Object-Oriented Programming Systems, Languages and Applications: OOPSLA '87,* pp. 227–242, New York, ACM.

Vlissides, John, 1997, "Patterns: The top ten misconceptions," *Object Magazine,* 71, pp. 31–33, March.

Whorf, Benjamin L., 1956, *Language, Thought, and Reality,* Cambridge, MA, MIT Press.

Wilson, Gregory V., 1997, "First-year C++ text outdated by Java" (book review), *IEEE Software,* 14:3, p. 122.

Wirfs-Brock, Rebecca, Brian Wilkerson, & Laura Wiener, 1990, *Designing Object-Oriented Software*, Englewood Cliffs, NJ, Prentice Hall.

Woolf, Bobby, 1994, "Improving dependency notification," *Smalltalk Report*, 4:3, pp. 4–11, November–December.

Woolf, Bobby, 1995a, "Making MVC more reusable," *Smalltalk Report*, 4:4, pp. 15–18, January.

Woolf, Bobby, 1995b, "Understanding and using the ValueModel framework in Visual-Works Smalltalk," in J. O. Coplien & D. C. Schmidt (Eds.), *Pattern Languages of Program Design*, pp. 467–494, Reading, MA, Addison-Wesley.

Woolf, Bobby, 1996, "Equality versus identity," *Smalltalk Report*, 5:7, pp. 10–13, May.

Woolf, Bobby, 1997, "The File Reader," *Smalltalk Report*, 6:6, pp. 3–12, March–April, http://www.ksccary.com/Reader/readme.com.

X3J20 Committee, 1996, *X3J20 Working Draft of ANSI Smalltalk Standard*, Washington, DC, American National Standards Institute.

Yelland, Phillip, 1996, "Creating host compliance in a portable framework: A study in the reuse of design patterns," in *Proceedings of the Eleventh Annual Conference on Object-Oriented Programming Systems, Languages and Applications: OOPSLA '96*, pp. 18–29, New York, ACM.

Index

A

Abell, Steven T.
 [Abell 1996], 395
  in Decorator, 171 (DE)
abstract
 classes, 356 (TM)
  as source of common behavior, 144 (CP)
  core functionality location in, 164 (DE)
  term description, 356 (TM)
 data types, reuse, 273 (IT)
 methods
  Collection (VisualWorks) example, 367
   (TM), 368 (TM)
  displayOn: as, 132 (BR)
  hook method comparison with, 358 (TM)
  term description, 357 (TM)
Abstract Factory pattern, 31-46 (AF)
 See also behavioral patterns; [DP 87]; structural
  patterns
 applications of. *See,* UIBuilder framework
  (VisualWorks)
 Builder
  compared with, 59 (BU)
  differences, 34 (AF)
  importance for understanding, 47 (BU)
  relationship with, 31 (AF), 45 (AF), 61 (BU)
  use of, 52 (BU)
 as creational pattern. *See* creational patterns
 Factory Method, relationship with, 76 (FM),
  45 (AF)
 intent, 61 (BU), 31 (AF), 388, 389
  Factory Method similarities, 76 (FM)
 known uses, 44 (AF)

metaclass model impact on, 79 (PR)
not used in Bridge, 126 (BR)
Strategy relationship with, 352 (SR)
variations. *See* Constant Method pattern
abstractions
 Abstraction class, as interface, 121 (BR)
 as good design technique, 387
 level, determining, 360 (TM)
 levels of, as Chain of Responsibility distin-
  guishing characteristic, 226 (CR)
 procedural
  iteration use, 284 (IT)
  term description, 180 (FA)
access
 class, providing a global point for, 91 (SI)
 control, 213 (PX)
  as basic intent of Proxy, 176 (DE)
  class method advantages, 95 (SI)
 internal state, implementation issues, 298
  (MM)
 methods
  in Sharable pattern class-side factory implementation, 207 (FL)
  naming conventions, 97 (SI)
  Sharable creation use, 202 (FL)
 new semantics issues, 96 (SI)
 sequential, preserving encapsulation during,
  273 (IT)
 subsystem, Facade use for unified, 179 (FA)
active variable
 term description, 311 (OB)
Adapter pattern, 105-120 (AD)
 See also behavioral patterns; creational patterns;
  [DP 139]

Page Suffix Legend: AD - Adapter; AF - Abstract Factory; BR - Bridge; BU - Builder; CM - Command;
CP - Composite; CR - Chain of Responsibility; DE -Decorator; FA - Facade; FL - Flyweight; FM - Factory
Method; IN - Interpreter; IT - Iterator; MD - Mediator; MM - Memento; OB - Observer; PR - Prototype;
PX - Proxy; SI - Singleton; SR - Strategy; ST - State; TM - Template Method; VI - Visitor; [DP nn] = *Design
Patterns* page number reference

COMMAND pattern, 245-260 (CM)
See also creational patterns; [DP 233]; structural
    patterns
ADAPTER relationship with, 119 (AD), 258 (CM)
as behavioral pattern. *See* behavioral patterns
implementation
    Hard-Coded Command pattern, 246 (CM)
    Pluggable Command pattern, 252 (CM)
intent, 245 (CM)
INTERPRETER vs, for macro handling, 262 (IN)
ITERATOR relationship with, 286 (IT)
known uses, 256 (CM)
macro recording use, 263 (IN)
MEMENTO relationship with, 303 (MM)
OBSERVER relationship with, 259 (CM)
sample code
    Hard-Coded Command pattern, 246 (CM)
    Pluggable Command pattern, 252 (CM)
SASE pattern, 313 (OB)
    letter object as, 313 (OB)
variations. *See*
    Hard-Coded Command pattern
    Pluggable Command pattern
"What If?" protocol MEMENTO use relationship
    to, 304 (MM)
commands
chain of, CHAIN OF RESPONSIBILITY as model of,
    227 (CR)
Hard-Coded Command pattern, 246 (CM)
Pluggable Command pattern implementation,
    252 (CM)
communications
MEDIATOR use, 296 (MD)
protocols, multiple facade handling of, 182 (FA)
comparison
complex query language handling, 269 (IN)
efficient, as FLYWEIGHT advantage, 195 (FL)
symbol, 195 (FL)
compilation
incremental, impact on ADAPTER, 110 (AD)
compiler
Compiler (VisualWorks), 188 (FA)
construction, value of training in, 262 (IN)
-type operations at runtime, 261 (IN)
complexity
as BRIDGE issue, 124 (BR)
as deep copy implementation problem, 86 (PR)
FACADE implementation issues, 185 (FA)
management, 179 (FA)
    as OO design advantage, 287 (MD)
    delegation as tool for, 180 (FA)
object interactions
    event handling in a system with, 288 (MD)
    MEDIATOR management of, 287 (MD)

components
building products from, 31 (AF)
class, DECORATOR class relationship with, 165
    (DE)
composite relationship with, 145 (CP)
window tree, term description, 139 (CP)
COMPOSITE pattern, 137-160 (CP)
See also behavioral patterns; creational patterns;
    [DP 163]
BRIDGE use of, 126 (BR)
CHAIN OF RESPONSIBILITY relationship with, 158
    (CP)
composite number representation of, 158 (CP)
DECORATOR relationship with, 158 (CP), 177
    (DE)
IBM Smalltalk classes, 140 (CP)
intent, 137 (CP), 388
iterating over trees produced by, 278 (IT)
ITERATOR relationship with, 158 (CP), 286 (IT)
known uses, 154 (CP)
object-oriented tree implementation, DECORA-
    TOR and OO Recursion pattern interaction
    with, 238 (CR)
OO Recursion pattern relationship with, 177
    (DE), 243 (CR)
sample code, 152 (CP)
as structural pattern. *See* structural patterns
VISITOR relationship with, 385 (VI)
Visual Smalltalk classes, 140 (CP)
VisualWorks classes, 140 (CP)
composites
COMPOSITE classes (VisualWorks), 140 (CP)
CompositeFont (ImplementationFont
    hierarchy) (VisualWorks), 157 (CP)
CompositePart (VisualWorks), 162 (DE), 140
    (CP)
    subclass of VisualPart (VisualWorks), 362
    (TM)
CompositeView (VisualWorks), subclass of
    VisualPart (VisualWorks), 362 (TM)
CsComposite (IBM Smalltalk), 140 (CP)
CwBasicWidget (IBM Smalltalk), 140 (CP)
CwPrimitive (IBM Smalltalk), 140 (CP)
GroupPane (Visual Smalltalk), 140 (CP)
composition
object
    inheritance compared with, 356 (TM)
    into compound documents, STRATEGY han-
    dling of, 340 (SR)
    into trees, as intent of COMPOSITE, 137 (CP)
streams use for, 284 (IT)
compression
algorithm tradeoffs, as motivation for STRAT-
    EGY, 339 (SR)

Woolf, Bobby (*cont.*)
  [Woolf 1997], 400
    in CHAIN OF RESPONSIBILITY, 235 (CR), 240
      (CR)
    in COMPOSITE, 154 (CP)
    in DECORATOR, 170 (DE)
wrappers
  ADAPTER vs DECORATOR, 176 (DE)
  DECORATOR compared with ADAPTER, 129 (BR)
  DECORATOR use as, 161 (DE)
  displaying implementation issues, 132 (BR)
  as forms of ADAPTER, 118 (AD)
  Geometric/GeometricWrapper (Visual-
    Works), 129 (BR)
  Wrapper (VisualWorks), 175 (DE), 162 (DE)
    behavior as top class DECORATOR hierarchy,
      163 (DE)
    common superclass value for, 166 (DE)
    DECORATOR use, 140 (CP)

subclass of VisualPart (VisualWorks), 362
  (TM)
VisualWorks window system containers as,
  234 (CR)

X

X3J20 Committee
  [X3J20 Committee 1996], 400
    in COMPOSITE, 146 (CP)
    in OBSERVER, 307 (OB)

Y

Yelland, Phillip
  [Yelland 1996], 400
    in BRIDGE, 125 (BR), 134 (BR)
    in FLYWEIGHT, 209 (FL)
    in INTERPRETER, 271 (IN)